D0269187

142 Strand

142 Strand

A Radical Address in Victorian London

Rosemary Ashton

Chatto & Windus
LONDON

Published by Chatto & Windus 2006

2 4 6 8 10 9 7 5 3 1

First published in Great Britain in 2006 by
Chatto & Windus
Random House, 20 Vauxhall Bridge Road,
London SW1V 2SA

Random House Australia (Pty) Limited
20 Alfred Street, Milsons Point, Sydney,
New South Wales 2061, Australia

Random House New Zealand Limited
18 Poland Road, Glenfield,
Auckland 10, New Zealand

Random House (Pty) Limited
Isle of Houghton, Corner of Boundary Road & Carse O'Gowrie,
Houghton 2198, South Africa

Random House Publishers India Private Limited
301 World Trade Tower, Hotel Intercontinental Grand Complex,
Barakhamba Lane, New Delhi 110 001, India

The Random House Group Limited Reg. No. 954009
www.randomhouse.co.uk

A CIP catalogue record for this book is available from the British Library

ISBN 0 7011 7370 X
ISBN 13 9780701173708 (from January 2007)

Papers used by Random House are natural,
recyclable products made from wood grown in sustainable forests;
the manufacturing processes conform to the environmental
regulations of the country of origin

Typeset in Goudy by Palimpsest Book Production Limited, Grangemouth, Stirlingshire

Printed and bound in Great Britain by William Clowes Ltd, Beccles, Suffolk

Contents

List of Illustrations

I

II

Illustration Acknowledgments

The author and publishers gratefully acknowledge permission to use the illustrations in this book as follows:

Kathleen Adams (George Eliot Fellowship), 1; Ina Taylor, 2; RIBA British Architectural Library, 3, 4; Guildhall Library, City of London, 5, 6; National Portrait Gallery, London, 7, 10 (on loan to National Portrait Gallery), 22; Trustees of Dr Williams's Library, London, 8, 9; Trustees of the British Museum, 11; Rare Book and Manuscript Library, Columbia University, New York, 12, 21; Henry Woudhuysen, 13; UCL Art Collections, University College London, 14; Carlyle's House, Chelsea (The National Trust), 15; Senate House Library, University of London, 16, 25, 27, 29; Wellcome Library, London, 17, 28; National Library of Scotland, 18, 19; Rare Book, Manuscript, & Special Collections Library, Duke University, Durham, North Carolina, 20; the Mistress and Fellows, Girton College, Cambridge, 23, 24; James and Susan Cash, 26.

Preface and Acknowledgments

John Chapman (1821–94) played an important part in the drama of Victorian intellectual and cultural life. As a publisher and owner-editor of the radical quarterly journal, the *Westminster Review*, from 1851, he was an invaluable enabler, the man who gave a start to the careers of writers later to become as famous and significant as George Eliot, Thomas Henry Huxley, Carlyle's biographer James Anthony Froude, and the American historian of the Netherlands, John Lothrop Motley.

Writers, both beginners and established authors, sought out Chapman when they had a book to publish which was too radical or unorthodox – in religion, philosophy, politics, or science – for other publishers to risk, or when they were looking for a periodical to print their articles or give them a favourable review. Among these were John Stuart Mill, Harriet Martineau, Herbert Spencer, George Henry Lewes, Francis William Newman (brother of John Henry Newman), the poet Arthur Hugh Clough, the Oxford scholar Mark Pattison, and Ralph Waldo Emerson, whose work Chapman first introduced to British readers.

Men like Dickens, Carlyle, Gladstone, Mill, and Darwin joined Chapman in various causes he espoused, from free trade in publishing to reform of the copyright laws and reform in the fields of medical education, public health, divorce, married women's property, and legislation on prostitution and contagious diseases. Women with a wish to have careers of their own or to agitate for equality found Chapman a sympathetic friend, employer, and supporter. In this category were Harriet Martineau; George Eliot, or Marian Evans, as she was when she first settled in London in 1851 to pursue a career in journalism; her feminist friends Bessie Rayner Parkes and Barbara Leigh Smith (later, as Barbara Bodichon, co-founder of Girton College, Cambridge), whose

ix

campaigning pamphlets Chapman published; and Mill's wife Harriet and stepdaughter Helen Taylor, who argued with Mill for equal property and voting rights for women in articles written for Chapman's *Westminster Review*. Another group, one which found itself effectively 'disenfranchised', was a set of Oxford-educated young men who became unsettled in their religious beliefs and so abandoned prospective careers in the Church or as fellows of Oxford colleges – such were Froude, Clough, F. W. Newman, and W. M. W. Call. All of them found an alternative career, whether temporary or permanent, through Chapman. So also did William Hale White, author of *The Autobiography of Mark Rutherford* (1881), who was expelled from his dissenting theological college in 1852 and knocked on Chapman's door to ask for a job.

The works of European authors in the vanguard of progressive thought were introduced to English readers when Chapman commissioned and published translations of their works. Marian Evans translated the controversial works of German historical criticism of Christianity and the Bible by David Friedrich Strauss (*The Life of Jesus*) in 1846 and Ludwig Feuerbach (*The Essence of Christianity*) in 1854. Chapman published Harriet Martineau's abridged English version of Auguste Comte's positivist philosophy in 1853. Exiles from the failed 1848 revolutions in Europe who fled to Britain found a welcome for their essays in the pages of the *Westminster Review* and a welcome for themselves at the weekly soirées Chapman held in his large house at 142 Strand. Two of the most famous refugees, Giuseppe Mazzini and Karl Marx, had dealings with Chapman, as did several others, French, Italian, German, and Hungarian.

The mid-nineteenth century was also a time of rapid change in matters other than religious or political; thanks to industrial and technological advances the face of Britain was changing fast. Communications were revolutionised by the expansion of the railway and the telegraph. London was a vast building site, with railway lines being laid and stations being built, as well as new housing in suburbs which had recently been outlying villages but now became absorbed into the expanding capital. The Great Exhibition of 1851 in the specially built Crystal Palace in Hyde Park – itself a wonder of modern construction – was the perfect emblem of a metropolis, and a country, which was thriving and full of initiative, leading the world in invention, manufacture, and design.

Chapman's establishment at 142 Strand, where he lived and carried on his publishing business between 1847 and 1854, was at the heart of this ever-changing city. The address came to symbolise the forces of non-physical change, a process inevitably less graspable, and more stubbornly resisted, than the outwardly visible ones of building and transport. The changes with which Chapman was associated were those in knowledge and belief which resulted from discoveries and interpretations in evolutionary science, comparative history and theology, and medicine. Radicalism in politics, religion, science, and the relations between the sexes characterised Chapman's attitudes and actions; his profession made him the conduit for reformers in every category. His position was often a difficult one, since many who wished for change in one field abhorred the agitation going forward in another. Religious dissenters who published with Chapman, like the Unitarian minister James Martineau, were horrified by the atheism of others of his writers, such as Martineau's own sister Harriet. Harriet Martineau herself, though uncompromisingly against religion, had no desire to be associated with those, like Marian Evans and G. H. Lewes, who lived together in a 'marriage' not sanctioned by law. The group which clustered round Chapman was thus far from homogeneous or harmonious; dramas, fallings-out, and splits characterised Chapman's associates even while unorthodoxy brought them together.

Chapman's unenviable task was to try to hold such disparate individuals and groups together, not least because he needed financial backing for his publishing ventures, since radicalism, by nature a minority activity, did not pay. The *Westminster Review* never covered its costs, and the publishing business was constantly near bankruptcy. Luckily, the combination of Chapman's energy, persistence, and charm with the desire of certain wealthy individuals for an outlet for their projects, ideals, and radical bees in their bonnets kept his enterprise going – just – for more than forty years. Among these individuals were an eccentric atheist landowner living in Florence, Edward Lombe; the leading British phrenologist, George Combe of Edinburgh; the philanthropic businessmen Samuel Courtauld and Octavius Smith; and, most surprisingly, the Tory MP and Cabinet member Lord Stanley, later fifteenth Earl of Derby. Without these and other benefactors, who included at different times Harriet Martineau and J. S. Mill, Chapman would have sunk, and radical publishing and the *Westminster Review* with him.

The present book is an account of Chapman's career, his dealings with his authors and theirs with him, and the contribution which between them they made to Victorian intellectual and cultural life. It is also the story of a building, 142 Strand, which he inhabited for seven years. The house's central position in London's leading street, its imposing size, its use as home to Chapman's unorthodox family household, his business, his helpers, including for a time Marian Evans, and visitors from outside London who lodged there, particularly Americans like Emerson, made 142 Strand a striking address. It was a handsome physical location of bricks and mortar which became famous for the people who inhabited it and who came and went on business, and for the ideas those people espoused and propounded. After Chapman left number 142, in the summer of 1854, he and his authors and acquaintances continued the activities they had begun there. 142 Strand becomes in the later chapters of this book a metaphor for those activities for which, in the earlier chapters, it is the physical setting. The building itself no longer stands; with its neighbours 138–41 it was extensively redeveloped in 1986–9. Three photographic images of number 142 before reconstruction exist, a coloured postcard of the Strand in the Guildhall Library collection, dated c. 1910, a photograph taken for the George Eliot Fellowship, probably in the 1970s, and a copy of a photograph taken by the architectural firm Rolfe Judd in about 1985. Earlier images of the house as it was when Chapman lived there are to be found in detailed contemporary line drawings commissioned by the printer John Tallis in 1838 and again in 1847, soon after Chapman and his family moved in. The RIBA British Architectural Library has a set of architectural drawings done in 1832 by John Buonarotti Papworth, who substantially redesigned the original late seventeenth-century building for Chapman's predecessor at number 142, the wine merchant and tavern keeper John Wright.

Chapman has had one chronicler. Gordon S. Haight, the biographer of George Eliot and editor of the nine volumes of her letters, published in 1940 his *George Eliot and John Chapman, with Chapman's Diaries*, which was reprinted with additions in 1969. As Haight pointed out in his preface, Chapman had been written out of the biography of George Eliot by John Cross, her husband of seven months, though he had enjoyed an interesting, fruitful, and close relationship with her in the years before she wrote her novels. Haight had access to two of Chapman's diaries, for 1851 and 1860, which had turned up on a second-hand bookstall in Nottingham in 1913 and found their way to the library at Yale University. He published these diaries in his book, with extensive comment and quotation from Marian Evans's letters during the early 1850s, when she lodged at 142 Strand and helped Chapman edit the *Westminster Review*. The notes and appendices to Haight's book include brief references to manuscript letters (also at Yale) from Chapman to one of his mistresses, Johanna von Heyligenstaedt, between 1859 and 1863, and to his second 'wife', Hannah Macdonald, in 1880. The chief focus of Haight's book is George Eliot, not Chapman, and he is sometimes less than fair to Chapman's talents and achievements. Some manuscript collections, including the large body of Chapman's letters to Harriet Martineau now in Birmingham University Library and the diaries and correspondence of Lord Stanley, in the Liverpool Record Office, were unknown to him.

Chapman's daughter Beatrice recounted her memories to her own daughter Annie; these were copied in typescript by the late John Wallis Chapman, Chapman's great-grandson, who drew on the material in his short article, 'John Chapman's Children', published in 1979, and who lent the typescript to Ina Taylor for her 1989 biography of George Eliot. I have been able to refer extensively to such unpublished as well as published material, though there are still periods in Chapman's life – his childhood, for example – about which relatively little is known. Nonetheless, substantial numbers of hitherto unpublished letters by him or to him survive, notably both sides of his correspondence with Harriet Martineau, George Combe, and Lord Stanley, letters from J. L. Motley to Chapman, and from Chapman to Barbara Leigh Smith and Johanna von Heyligenstaedt, as well as small numbers of letters to or from Froude, Huxley, Darwin, Gladstone, Carlyle, Lombe, James Martineau, F. W. Newman, and others. Chapman is also well represented in the published letters, memoirs, and biographies of many of his colleagues and acquaintances. It has therefore been possible to follow his career closely for much of its duration.

My aim is to put Chapman, the enabler of others, at the heart of his own story, while giving a detailed picture of those aspects of the intellectual and cultural life of London in the mid-nineteenth century with which he was closely associated. Chapman's story is the story of an unorthodox Victorian not only living and working in London at a time of unprecedented change, but also – by the causes he took up, the books he published, the authors he enabled – *making* changes happen in the intellectual life of Britain.

My thanks go to the librarians, curators, and trustees of manuscripts at the following institutions for permission to quote from unpublished material in their collections: the Bishopsgate Institute and Foundation; the British Library; Dr Williams's Library; Guildhall Library, City of London; Imperial

College London; the Institute of Historical Research; the Family Records
Centre; the London Metropolitan Archives; the Natural History Museum;
the RIBA British Architectural Library at the Victoria and Albert Museum;
Senate House Library, University of London; University College London
Library; the Westminster Archives Centre and the Planning Department of
Westminster City Council. Outside London, I have consulted material in
the Bodleian Library and Harris Manchester College in Oxford; Girton
College, Cambridge; Birmingham University Library; the Liverpool Record
Office; the Devon Record Office, Exeter; the National Co-operative Archive,
Manchester; the National Library of Scotland, Edinburgh; Columbia
University Library, New York; Duke University Library, Durham, North
Carolina; Yale University Library, New Haven, Connecticut.

Individuals who have helped me with information and encouragement,
and to whom I express my gratitude, are: Kathleen and Bill Adams, Iain G.
Brown, John Burton, James and Susan Cash, Kiera Chapman, Berry Chevasco,
Jim Cox and Simon Young of Rolfe Judd Architects, Mark Crees, Vincent
Giroud, Roderick Gordon, Oliver Herford, Charles Hind, Nicholas Jacobs,
Dan Jacobson, Scott Lewis, Philip Little of ESA Architecture, Charlotte
Mitchell, Sarah Millard, Richard North, Charlotte Podrow, Fred Schwarzbach,
Guilland Sutherland, Ina Taylor, Claire Tomalin, David Trotter, René Weis,
and especially Henry Woudhuysen. My warmest thanks go also to my editor
Jenny Uglow and my literary agent Victoria Hobbs.

Introduction

John Chapman and the Strand in 1847

On 24 July 1847 the following advertisement appeared in the weekly periodical, the *Athenaeum*:

> MR CHAPMAN, Bookseller and Publisher, begs to announce that he has REMOVED his Business from 121 Newgate Street, to more spacious premises on the South side of the STRAND, No 142, a few doors West of Somerset House; and requests, therefore, that all communications may be forwarded to the latter address.

For the next seven years John Chapman's 'spacious premises' – consisting of the bookselling business and publishing house, his family home, and rooms for literary lodgers – was the chief place of resort for writers with a book to publish which was in any way radical or unorthodox.

The move to the Strand was significant, signalling Chapman's arrival in the heart of London to take up residence in a handsome house on the city's most famous street. Just after Chapman moved in, John Tallis, a bookseller and publisher of St John's Lane, near Smithfield, published a second edition of his *London Street Views*, a set of cheap, handy booklets, each containing detailed drawings of the buildings in a particular area of London. He had first issued eighty-eight of these booklets in 1838–40; they measured approximately nine inches by five, had a pale green paper cover, and showed the engraved elevation, beautifully line-drawn, of London's buildings. The *Street Views* cost 1½d each.[1]

Tallis's revised and enlarged edition of 1847 included five separate plans covering the Strand, the longest street in London and the city's main east-west thoroughfare. The recently completed Trafalgar Square marked the beginning of the Strand at its western end, while Temple Bar formed the eastern boundary with Fleet Street. 142 Strand features in the section which includes Somerset House, nine houses east of number 142 on the south side near Temple Bar.

The Strand had long been one of the most important of London's streets. It runs north of, and parallel to, the Thames. From the Middle Ages until the later seventeenth century its south side was lined with mansions built for lords and bishops who found its easy access to the Thames invaluable when they visited London from their country estates in order to attend Court or Parliament. Their gardens ran down to the river, where boats were moored ready to take them to Westminster. Britain's kings and queens progressed not only up the river but also up and down the Strand. John Evelyn noted one momentous procession in his diary on 29 May 1660, when Charles II returned from exile in Flanders to be restored to the throne. His way to Westminster lay through the City of London, where he was greeted by 'the mayor, aldermen, and all the companies in their liveries, chains of gold, and banners', and 'lords and nobles clad in cloth of silver, gold, and velvet', the whole procession lasting eight hours, according to Evelyn, who 'stood in the Strand, and beheld it, and blessed God'.[2]

In the nineteenth century the Strand retained its importance as the geographical link between Court, Parliament, and Westminster Abbey in the west and financial centre, heart of the legal establishment, and St Paul's Cathedral in the east. Queen Victoria had to do as her predecessors had done when seeking to enter the City of London, namely stop at Temple Bar (built in 1672 by Sir Christopher Wren to mark the point where Westminster ends and the City begins) to ask permission of the Lord Mayor to enter his territory. But the character of the street had changed. The grand mansions along the south side decayed and were demolished, as courtiers chose from the later seventeenth century to build their London homes in Whitehall and St James's, close to Parliament and the Court. By the mid-nineteenth century only two great houses remained on the Strand, Northumberland House near Trafalgar Square and Somerset House. Of these two, only Somerset House still stands.

By 1847 the Strand had become, in the words of an article in the *Strand Magazine* in 1891, 'in many regards, the most interesting street in the world'.[3] It was London's foremost shopping street. Tallis's plans give a sense of its variety; here are shoemakers, watchmakers, tailors, wax chandlers, tobacconists, umbrella makers, cutlers, linen drapers, pianoforte makers, hatmakers, wigmakers, shirtmakers, mapmakers, lozenge manufacturers, and sellers of food of all sorts, including shellfish, Italian oil, and Twining's famous tea, sold at number 216, near Temple Bar. Warren's Blacking Manufactory was at number 30, on the south side. The name struck lifelong horror into Dickens, who in 1823 was sent, aged eleven, to work in its shabby namesake round the corner near the river for six shillings a week when his father got into debt. He never forgot the humiliation of his four months at Warren's, and reproduced it feelingly in *David Copperfield* (1849–50), in which young David endures a similar experience at Murdstone and Grinby's wine warehouse.

Further east, at numbers 101–2, was Ries's Grand Cigar Divan, a resort for gentlemen both respectable and bohemian who wanted a quiet place to smoke or play chess. Dickens's rival Thackeray, who was both respectable, by virtue of his family and education, and bohemian, by inclination and habit, frequented a number of such all-male establishments on or near the Strand. It was he who popularised, in *Vanity Fair* (1847–8), the term 'bohemian' to mean, in the words of the *Oxford English Dictionary*:

a gipsy of society; one who either cuts himself off, or is by his habits cut off, from society for which he is otherwise fitted; especially an artist, literary man, or actor, who leads a free, vagabond, or irregular life, not being particular as to the society he frequents, and despising conventionalities generally.[4]

Thackeray's chief fictional alter ego Pendennis in the novel of the same name, published in 1850, is a regular at 'the Back Kitchen', an amalgam of several clubs and 'dives' on or near the Strand at which Thackeray was a frequent visitor along with his colleagues on *Punch* magazine. All these establishments offered entertainment of a risqué kind. The Cider Cellars on Maiden Lane, described by another contemporary, the journalist and theatrical man-about-town John Hollingshead, as a 'harmonious sewer', specialised in 'flash' or bawdy songs and ballet girls. Evans's supper rooms in Covent Garden, or 'the Cave of Harmony', as Thackeray renames the establishment in *The*

Newcomes (1853–5), were famous for the piquant contrast between the raucous singing of the post-theatre clientele and the angelic voices of choirboys hired to entertain them. And the Coal Hole, on the Strand itself, positioned exactly opposite Exeter Hall, famous for its huge meetings of reforming and evangelical groups, including the Temperance League, had as its main attraction naked or near-naked women arranged in 'poses plastiques' or 'tableaux vivants'. Here also the disreputable 'Baron' Renton Nicholson held some of his 'Judge and Jury' shows, in which, with participation from the audience, he acted out versions of real criminal trials currently preoccupying Londoners.[5]

The 'bohemian' set, of which Thackeray and his *Punch* colleague Douglas Jerrold were perhaps the most famous members, consisted of young (or youngish) men of varied backgrounds and education set loose in London to pursue a career. They gathered mainly in the Strand because many were journalists, working for some of the thirty or so newspapers and magazines which had their offices on the Strand or one of the roads leading off it;[6] others were fledgling lawyers who lodged in bachelor chambers in the Inns of Court, just off Fleet Street. A number of theatres were situated in the Strand-Covent Garden area; attendance at a play, opera, or concert could be followed by a visit to one of those late-night entertainments at the restaurants, pubs, and supper rooms close by.

Some of these men were radical in their social and political views; Jerrold, for instance, was an active campaigner against the death penalty.[7] Thackeray himself was equivocal in these matters, never campaigning overtly for political reform and keeping his religious scepticism to himself. In June 1851 he confided to Chapman on a visit to 142 Strand that though his religious views were 'perfectly *free*', he did not 'mean to lessen his popularity by fully avowing them', as Chapman puts it in his diary for 14 June.[8] Of Chapman's other regular visitors, most were radicals but hardly any could be described as bohemian. Even Chapman himself, who kept a lover at 142 Strand in addition to his wife and children, was no urban gipsy or vagabond, but a man who worked hard, loved his children (if not his wife), and took himself seriously as a radical thinker.

The people among whom Chapman moved, or rather – since he was the publisher and they the authors with manuscripts unlikely to be accepted by more orthodox publishers – the people who surrounded him, had a number of attributes in common with Thackeray's bohemians. Chapman's friends were writers, many of them journalists; they were mainly young and mainly poor. Unlike the bohemians, however, some of them were women, and none of them – ranging from Marian Evans, before she became famous as George Eliot, to Unitarian leaders like James Martineau and his redoubtable sister Harriet, American authors and visitors including Ralph Waldo Emerson, the as yet unknown social philosopher Herbert Spencer, and the young scientist Thomas Henry Huxley, later to be Darwin's colleague and supporter – could possibly be described as idle saunterers or frequenters of taverns in the small hours. G. H. Lewes, whom Chapman introduced to Marian Evans in 1851, was the nearest to a bohemian among Chapman's friends and colleagues. He consorted with the *Punch* writers and was well known in London's literary circles for his 'open' marriage. His miscellaneous journalism included many light-hearted sketches and dashed-off articles, but he also wrote serious books and essays on English and European literature, philosophy, history, and science; in 1854 he settled into a happy, monogamous, and lifelong relationship with Marian Evans.[9]

In the 1840s, the Strand was the heart of the newspaper publishing business, though its neighbour Fleet Street began to take over soon after that.[10] In *Pendennis* Thackeray describes his young wastrel-hero walking home along the Strand at dawn to his chambers in the Inns of Court after a typical night out in the Back Kitchen. Pendennis and his friend Warrington pass a newspaper office, 'which was all lighted up and bright'. A vignette of Strand life follows, with sly references to naughty nights out, but also a semi-serious, rather awestruck account of the national and public importance of some of the activities taking place along this street, which here represents London itself in its capacity as great metropolis and capital of the most powerful country in the world:

> Reporters were coming out of the place, or rushing up to it in cabs; there were lamps burning in the editors' rooms, and above where the compositors were at work: the windows of the building were in a blaze of gas.
>
> 'Look at that, Pen,' Warrington said. 'There she is – the great engine – she never sleeps. She has her ambassadors in every quarter of the world – her couriers upon every road. Her officers march along with armies, and her envoys walk into statesmen's cabinets. They are ubiquitous. Yonder journal has an agent, at this minute, giving bribes at

5

Madrid; and another inspecting the price of potatoes in Covent Garden. Look! Here comes the Foreign Express galloping in. They will be able to give news to Downing Street to-morrow: funds will rise or fall, fortunes be made or lost; Lord B. will get up, and, holding the paper in his hand, and seeing the noble marquis in his place, will make a great speech; and – and Mr Doolan will be called away from his supper at the Back Kitchen; for he is foreign sub-editor, and sees the mail on the newspaper sheet before he goes to his own.'[11]

More than twenty newspapers and magazines had their offices in the Strand. Dickens's early journalism in the 1830s was done for the *Morning Chronicle*, which published some of his 'Sketches by Boz' from its offices at number 332, opposite Somerset House.[12] On the south side, at number 198, was the *Illustrated London News*, the weekly paper founded in 1842 to record in words and lavishly engraved illustrations the daily life and culture of London. Almost exactly opposite Chapman's establishment was the office of *The Economist* newspaper, which shared its premises at number 340 with the *Railway Monitor*. Here Herbert Spencer, who had trained as a railway engineer in the Midlands, worked and lived on first coming to London in the mid-1840s; he recalled sixty years later in his autobiography that 'the eternal rattle of the Strand', 'the close atmosphere', and the offensive smell of the drains eventually drove him to seek lodgings elsewhere. Spencer had got to know Chapman in 1846; after Chapman's move to the Strand the two men met often, Spencer regularly crossing the road to attend evening parties at number 142, where he met, among others, Lewes, Marian Evans, and the Americans Emerson and Horace Greeley, editor of the *New York Daily Tribune*, who lodged with Chapman on their visits to London.[13]

Printers, publishers, and booksellers abounded. When Chapman moved his bookselling and publishing business from Newgate Street to the Strand in July 1847, he had for his immediate neighbours Thomas Cadell, bookseller, at number 141, and John Limbird, stationer, printer, and publisher at number 143.[14] Dickens's publishers, the unrelated Chapman & Hall, were to be found not far from John Chapman, at 186 Strand. At number 147, between Chapman's and Somerset House, was William S. Orr & Co., publisher of encyclopædias and illustrated books and until 1852 the London agent for the remarkably successful Edinburgh firm of W. & R. Chambers. At the other end, near Trafalgar Square, was the firm of John W. Parker & Son, printer to Cambridge University and from June 1847 owner and publisher of *Fraser's Magazine*. The younger Parker edited the magazine and began holding literary parties for his authors and contributors, some of whom also wrote for Chapman and attended *his* soirées at number 142.[15]

Chapman was the most radical of the 'respectable' publishers to settle in the Strand. He had for very close neighbours some rather less reputable ones, purveyors of pornography to the bohemian men about town. The publishers of pornography, chief among them William Dugdale, sold their wares on Holywell Street, a narrow alley running parallel to the Strand just north and east of Chapman's house. It was picturesque with its cobbles and houses dating from the sixteenth century, but squalid too, since its inhabitants were squeezed into packed, insanitary accommodation. Indeed, Holywell Street by the mid-nineteenth century had become a byword for dirt both literal and metaphorical. The Irish MP Justin McCarthy recalled his first sight of it in 1852 and the 'abominations' on display in broad daylight. When in 1861 Dante Gabriel Rossetti saw the sexual puns in a manuscript poem by William Blake which his friend Alexander Gilchrist was considering printing in his forthcoming biography of the poet, he advised against, noting with amusement that the publisher, Alexander Macmillan, known for his prud- ishness, had no 'branch office in Holywell Street'.[16] In May 1857 William Dugdale was prosecuted and convicted under the newly framed Obscene Publications Act. He was no stranger to prosecution, having led an earlier existence, also in Holywell Street, as a publisher in the 1820s of politically radical pamphlets influenced by the works of Tom Paine.[17]

In Dugdale's case, radical politics had given way by the middle of the century to pornography. Others, like his fellow radicals Richard Carlile and Henry Hetherington, kept clear of the trade, disapproving of those who gave all political and religious radicals a bad name by their underworld activities. These men, like their younger colleague Chapman, were intent on promoting freedom of speech, extension of the franchise, and a liberal education which was to include information about birth control. In the 1820s Richard Carlile sold freethinking books written by himself and others from a shop at 201 Strand, an activity for which he, his wife, and his shopmen were imprisoned more than once on grounds of blasphemy. Carlile was also the first Englishman to write directly and without anonymity about birth control. His pamphlet was published in 1826 with the cumbersome but unambiguous title *Every*

Woman's Book; or, What is Love? Containing Most Important Instructions for the Prudent Regulation of the Principle of Love and the Number of the Family.[18]

As the century progressed, more works were published on the subject, discussion of which was increasingly included in serious medical books intended for the general reader. Because of continuing opposition from orthodox politicians and religious authorities, however, such books were often issued anonymously. The most famous – and successful – of these was by a thirty-year-old Scottish doctor, George Drysdale. *Physical, Sexual, and Natural Religion* was published in 1855 by Edward Truelove of 240 Strand. Its title-page describes the author as 'a Student of Medicine', and declares that the book is 'dedicated to the poor and suffering'. Drysdale discusses frankly but unsensationally the various methods of contraception known to British and European doctors, harnessing his account of the state of medical knowledge on the subject to the social imperative for the poor to be taught how to limit their families. His genuinely philanthropic book clearly met a widely felt need, for by 1905 it had gone through thirty-five editions and sold 80,000 copies.[19] That it remained just the other side of complete respectability may perhaps be inferred from the fact that the British Library's copies of the editions of 1872, 1875, and 1886 are described in the catalogue as 'destroyed', and that of 1867 as 'missing'. During the 1850s Chapman read books by such pioneers as Carlile and Drysdale and their followers when he was preparing for a medical career; as editor of the *Westminster Review* from 1852, he encouraged discussion of the subject in its pages.

Two of Carlile's freethinking colleagues and followers, James Watson and Henry Hetherington, carried on publishing radical works into the 1850s. Hetherington published a translation of David Friedrich Strauss's *Life of Jesus* (*Das Leben Jesu*), which he issued in cheap parts in 1846, the year in which Chapman brought out a three-volume translation of the same work by Mary Ann Evans. Watson was the printer in 1850 of *The History of the Last Trial by Jury for Atheism in England* by George Jacob Holyoake, a self-taught man of great energy and talent, who dedicated his long life (1817–1906) to agitating in lectures, speeches, and printed works for the right to express freethinking opinions. His *History* was the story of his own trial and sentence to six months in Gloucester gaol in 1842 for answering a question at the end of a lecture he had given in Cheltenham on socialism; the question was about the place of religion in society, and the answer was that it had none.[20] Though Holyoake was a man without social or educational advantages and an uncompromising radical in all things, he was able, by dint of natural intelligence, assiduousness, and transparent honesty, to make friends of several members of the wider, and generally more educated, Chapman circle. These included Lewes, Marian Evans, Harriet Martineau, the Italian exile Mazzini and his English supporters, and – surprisingly, perhaps – the Oxford-educated Francis William Newman, brother of the future cardinal and a Professor of Latin at University College London. Newman's particular brand of radicalism was an idiosyncratic form of religion, shorn of Church of England doctrine but stopping short of agnosticism, which he expounded in a series of works published by Chapman, including *The Soul* (1849) and *Phases of Faith* (1850).

In short, radicalism came in a variety of forms, was embraced by people from all social classes, and by the middle of the century was in general no longer liable to prosecution. Representing the respectable face of radicalism was the *Westminster Review*, established in 1824 by Jeremy Bentham and James Mill (father of John Stuart Mill) to argue for social and political reform, a measure of which was granted by the Reform Act of 1832. Since then radicals had been elected to Parliament and agitation had continued, among both parliamentary radicals and extra-parliamentary Chartists, for further extension of the franchise, which was eventually achieved in the second great Reform Act of 1867. Bentham had also been prominent in the founding of University College London in 1826 to allow the sons (though not yet the daughters) of dissenters, Jews, Catholics, atheists, and other non-Anglicans to benefit from a university education. University College became a refuge not only for those who were born into Nonconformity, but also for a number of talented 'refugees' from the established universities, especially Oxford. These were young men, many of them destined for the Church, who found themselves unable to sign the Thirty-Nine Articles of the Church of England, an act required not only in order to be ordained, but also in order to graduate or take a fellowship. The poet Arthur Hugh Clough, the historian and biographer James Anthony Froude, and Francis Newman were three such Oxford exiles; all of them came into close connection with University College London and all of them found in John Chapman a willing publisher of their books and articles.

Social reform, including improved sanitation and the extension of education to the working class, became an urgent need as industrialisation put unprecedented pressure on cities, and outbreaks of cholera proved rather drastically the inadequacy of housing and sanitation arrangements. In the

1840s Thomas Carlyle, Dickens, Elizabeth Gaskell, and Charles Kingsley – writers not radical in the party-political sense – drew graphic pictures of urban despair and disease in their essays and novels with the intention of shaming Parliament and public bodies into taking remedial action. The *Westminster Review* under its current editor W. E. Hickson carried a number of articles urging progress in electoral reform, land reform for Ireland, and national secular education. Hickson, who did good solid work on the *Westminster* during the decade in which he owned and edited it, sold it in 1851 to Chapman, who was to preside over the periodical's best years in terms of the talent of its authors and the influence of its articles. Chapman's obituarist in the *Westminster* itself in January 1895 hardly exaggerated when he said that under Chapman the *Review* 'became the mouthpiece of the most advanced and the most respected thinkers of the day'.[21] By the time he took over in 1851, 'advanced' and 'respected', though terms still often in tension, were not mutually exclusive.

The Strand had always been a street where reformers and revolutionaries gathered. From the 1790s the Crown and Anchor Tavern, on the south side, east of number 142, had been a favoured venue for meetings of protest, agitation, or celebration of political successes. On 14 July 1790 Richard Brinsley Sheridan had proposed a toast there to the French Revolution on the first anniversary of its outbreak. The Whittington Club, begun in 1846 by Douglas Jerrold, met at the Crown and Anchor, as did the founding members of Mazzini's People's International League, intent on promoting freedom in the countries of continental Europe. Jerrold was among those who gathered here in April 1847, as were James Watson, Holyoake, the printer W. J. Linton, and a number of liberal MPs and lawyers dedicated to encouraging Italy's attempts at liberation from Austria.[22] The activities of European refugees of many nationalities were to increase as they fled to London a year later in the wake of the failed uprisings in European capitals from Paris to Vienna in the spring of 1848. A number of them, including Mazzini and Marx, became acquainted with Chapman, attending his soirées at number 142 and in some cases publishing their books and articles with him.

Number 142 itself, built about 1690, had been a tavern and coffee house, the Turk's Head, since at least 1815. The building was good-looking and imposing, being one storey higher than its immediate neighbours. It was taken over in 1832 by John Wright, a wine and spirit merchant, who extended it even further. In May 1832 Wright advertised in *The Times* the sale of the

wine stock and furniture of the Turk's Head 'in consequence of very extensive improvements being contemplated in the premises'.[23] He commissioned
the well-known architect John Buonarotti Papworth to rebuild the house on
a grand scale. Papworth's drawings of 1832 show that he retained the neo-
classical style of the front elevation, while altering the rest of the building,
which led back some distance from the Strand to look over the terrace of
Somerset House at the back – the inner buildings of Somerset House stretching
westward behind its Strand neighbours, then as now, as far as Waterloo
Bridge. The ground-floor plans show Wright's wine shop at the front, a wine
bar in the middle, and a large parlour at the back. In the basement, which
extends under the pavement at the front, is the wine cellar, together with
kitchen, scullery, larder, and 'maids' WC'. The upper floors – three of which
are outlined in Papworth's design, though four were eventually built – are
three rooms deep. With three windows across the front, the building is wider
than its immediate neighbours, as well as taller, and while it has a long dark
corridor along the side adjoining number 141, the plans show three side
windows towards the back of the building on its eastern side, where the
house extends further back than its other neighbour, number 143.[24] Chapman's
daughter Beatrice later remembered that the middle room on each floor,
between the back and front, was lit by a glass skylight at the top, with glass
panels in the ceilings of each of the middle rooms passing the light down
to the lower floors.[25]

The complete reconstruction of this large building was so ambitious that
it took several years to complete. It was not until May 1838 that Wright
could announce in the newspapers that the Turk's Head Coffee House and
Hotel had reopened for business, 'rebuilt and furnished at a very considerable
expense, with a view of affording superior accommodation' including a coffee
room, private sitting rooms and bedrooms. That summer Wright placed advertisements in *The Times* for venison suppers, turtle soup, and 'the finest Rhenish'
wines.[26] But Wright, like Chapman after him, overstretched himself financially. According to John Timbs, describing club life in London in 1866, the
'very lofty handsome house' had cost £8,000 to rebuild; 'it was opened as a
tavern and hotel, but did not long continue'.[27] In 1845 Wright was named
as a bad debtor in the celebrated bankruptcy case of the wine merchants Reay
& Reay; he owed the Reays £31,000 for the fine wines he stocked in his
cellar. Wright struggled on at 142 Strand, paying an annual rent of £230 and
rates at a rateable value of £195 – nearly twice as much as his neighbours –

until his death in January 1847.[28] (According to a Chapman family tradition, probably fanciful, Wright hanged himself in his despair.[29])

Chapman took over the house in July 1847. He was expanding his business, and was sufficiently optimistic about his prospects to place his large advertisement in the *Athenaeum* in July 1847, with another in *The Times*,[30] and also to pay whatever Tallis charged to include the proprietor's name in his enlarged edition of *London Street Views*, issued in the second half of 1847. 142 Strand appears there with 'JOHN CHAPMAN, BOOKSELLER AND PUBLISHER' printed above the line drawing of the front of the building.

In 1847 the twenty-six-year-old Chapman was keen to play a part in the reforming of British society and institutions. The move to the Strand was an inspired one, though it involved him in expenses he could never quite afford. Now he was at the heart of progressive London, as befitted a man known to Horace Greeley as 'the American bookseller' because he enterprisingly reprinted books published in the United States and acted as London agent for American firms, to the American Unitarian minister Theodore Parker as a 'transcendental bookseller' because he published and sold books by Emerson and his followers (of whom Parker was one), and to another American, R. W. Griswold, as the 'infidel publisher' because he issued works critical of Christianity.[31] The distinguished English Unitarian lawyer Henry Crabb Robinson described Chapman in 1849 as 'the U [i.e. Unitarian] – & worse publisher', thus suggesting the two sorts of books for which Chapman was known, those which were unorthodox because Unitarian in opposition to the Trinitarianism of the Church of England, and those which were unorthodox because unbelieving. With Mary Ann Evans's (anonymous) Strauss translation chiefly in mind, a writer in the *Critic* in 1852 referred to Chapman as the chief publisher in England of 'German rationalism'; Carlyle summed him up perhaps best of all when he called him, in a letter to Robert Browning in October 1851, a 'Publisher of Liberalisms, "Extinct-Socinianisms" [i.e. Unitarianism], and notable ware of that kind, in the Strand'.[32]

The novelist and critic Eliza Lynn (later Linton), who lodged with Chapman and his wife before their removal to the Strand, referred to him in her autobiography as 'the Raffaelle bookseller' on account of his striking good looks, which often drew comparisons with Byron.[33] Carlyle, having visited Chapman in August 1847, soon after the move to the Strand, described him in a letter to Emerson, in which he neatly alluded both to his appearance and to the 'infidel' side of his reputation. Chapman had called on

12

Carlyle in Chelsea with the considerably shorter Frederick Henry Hedge, an American Unitarian minister and friend of Emerson's. They looked, wrote Carlyle, 'like a circle and tangent – in more senses than one.'[34]

Chapman did indeed occupy a position at an angle from orthodoxy and tradition, as Carlyle hints. The activities he pursued during the best part of a decade at 142 Strand represented a challenge to conservatism in all its forms. His intelligent curiosity, his energy, and the usefulness to others of his chosen profession ensured that he was at the centre of Victorian radicalism in its many manifestations. Through him a number of important writers and thinkers from different backgrounds came together; there were disaffected Oxford men, earnest dissenters with an interest in education, philanthropists with a reforming streak, people from the provinces who came to London to make their mark (including clever women like Harriet Martineau, Eliza Lynn, and Marian Evans), scientists with stories to tell about natural history which did not fit well with a literal reading of the Old Testament, and exiled foreigners drawn to London as a haven of free speech and to Chapman's circle as the natural home of people who took full advantage of that freedom. Nowhere was the speech freer and the speculation more serious and intelligent than among the authors who gathered round Chapman in his headquarters at 142 Strand.

1

Adventurous Publishing: Emerson, Strauss, Newman (1844–8)

Chapman had tried more than one career before he took up bookselling and publishing in 1844. He was born in Nottingham on 16 June 1821, the third of four sons of William Chapman, who kept a chemist's shop, and a mother about whom little is known except that she died at the age of thirty-five in October 1824, when he was three years old.[1] After a brief apprenticeship to a watchmaker, Chapman appears to have stayed for a while with his older brother Thomas, who was studying medicine in Edinburgh. In September 1839 the eighteen-year-old had found his way to Australia, where he made and sold watches and chronometers in Adelaide. Three years later he was back in Europe, attending medical lectures in London and Paris, but not completing his course of study, presumably because of lack of funds. He married Susanna Brewitt in St Leodegarius Church, Basford, Nottingham, on 27 June 1843; he was just twenty-two and she nearly thirty-six.[2] Susanna had inherited some money from her father, a lace manufacturer. With this the couple moved to London and, according to his Edinburgh acquaintance George Combe, Chapman used '£4,600 of capital belonging to his wife and her aunt' to buy a bookselling business at 121 Newgate Street, near St Paul's Cathedral.[3]

The man from whom Chapman bought the business was John Green, 'the Unitarian & Transcendental Bibliopole for all England hitherto', as Theodore Parker described him in a letter to Emerson in August 1844 announcing that Chapman had taken over Green's role as chief London distributor of American books on philosophy and theology.[4] It was not entirely by chance that Chapman now became a specialist in works by Unitarians. Though nothing is known of his own religious background, he was evidently attracted to the minimalist doctrine and dogma of Unitarianism, with its emphasis on the humanity, not divinity, of Christ. This can be deduced from the lengthy title of a short work he had written which was the occasion of his taking over Green's business. He had visited Green's shop to ask if he would publish *Human Nature: A Philosophical Exposition of the Divine Institution of Reward and Punishment, which obtains in the physical, intellectual, and moral constitution of Man; with an introductory essay. To which is added, a series of ethical observations, written during the perusal of the Rev. James Martineau's recent work, entitled 'Endeavours after the Christian Life'.* Green replied that he was giving up the publishing business; Chapman bought it, and *Human Nature* was among the first works to be issued, anonymously, with the new imprint, 'John Chapman, 121 Newgate Street (late John Green)', in February 1844.

James Martineau, alluded to in the title, was one of the leading British Unitarians. He was minister of a chapel in Liverpool and taught moral philosophy and political economy at Manchester New College, the Nonconformist divinity college he had attended as a student. Martineau was also a chief contributor to the Unitarian periodical, the *Christian Teacher*, which Chapman took into his publishing portfolio with the rest of Green's titles, changing its name in 1845 to the *Prospective Review*.[5] Martineau was an influential thinker in dissenting circles, a reformer who was able to adapt his faith without losing it in the face of scientific and historical discoveries which tended to undermine a literal belief in the Bible. He was an energetic friend, but also a formidable opponent, as Chapman was to find after he had bought the *Westminster Review* in 1851 with Martineau's support.

Chapman's little book contains ninety-one pages of earnest, if rather vapid, discussion of 'religion, or the science of human Culture and development', put together by means of quoting passages from Martineau on the progress of mankind and the enlightened benevolence of God, along with a number of extracts from Emerson on 'Being' as affirmative, not negative.[6] It is hard not to sympathise with Henry Crabb Robinson, who, the following year, 'looked into, but could make nothing of, Chapman's little tract called *Human Nature*'.[7] Chapman took the opportunity of announcing at the back of his pamphlet – to whatever readers he managed to attract by the inclusion of Martineau's name in his title – some of the other books and periodicals he was now publishing. These included more American Unitarianism, including the *Complete Works* of William Ellery Channing, books and sermons by Theodore Parker, and Emerson's quarterly journal, the *Dial*, though this was taken on just as the last number was due to be published in 1844.

Chapman's modest publishing list for the year was made up mainly of dissenting works, many of them short pamphlets or reprints of sermons, by Unitarians and other Nonconformists on both sides of the Atlantic. The 'infidel' position was represented too, in one work, a forty-page lecture, *The Individuality of the Individual*, by William Maccall, a former Unitarian minister, now an earnest freethinker, one of a number, including Holyoake, who gave lectures on Sundays as an alternative attraction to church sermons but who, on his own admission, was too abstruse in his arguments to fill even the smallest lecture room.[8] William Hale White, a boarder at 142 who helped Chapman run the *Westminster Review* in 1852–3, remembered Maccall as a poor man's Carlyle, proud, uncompromising, and as eccentric and old-fashioned in his dress of black frock coat and wide-awake hat as his famous mentor. Carlyle himself, after meeting Maccall at a party in Chapman's house in 1848, tried to help him find a publisher who would pay him enough to live on, Chapman being willing to print his lectures but unable to pay anything in advance. Carlyle's wife Jane noted at this time that Maccall was 'within sight of starvation'.[9] He was the first of many ex-ministers of religion to seek out Chapman as his publisher.

Of the Americans on the list, Emerson was the most distinguished. Also a former Unitarian minister, now the leader of the Platonic-Kantian-Coleridgean religious philosophy known as Transcendentalism, Emerson was set to become the most famous American thinker of the nineteenth century, though his work was as yet little known in Britain. He was, nonetheless, a potential asset to Chapman, who took him over along with John Green's other Americans. Chapman opened his correspondence with Emerson in early August 1844, asking if he might publish, on a system of half-profits, a second series of Emerson's *Essays*, the first having been issued by James Munroe & Co. of Boston in 1841 with an influential preface by Carlyle. He received a cordial and encouraging reply. Emerson thanked him for 'the friendly gift of your little book on Human Nature', and promptly arranged for Chapman to co-publish the new series of essays with Munroe, whom he instructed in October to send copies to Chapman for reprinting. Because books on both sides of the Atlantic were inadequately protected by the copyright law and were therefore vulnerable to piracy, Emerson told Chapman that the Boston publisher would hold back publication until Chapman was ready. It must have been gratifying to Chapman, a very young man and a complete newcomer to publishing, to be told by Emerson that he would 'very cheerfully & thankfully confide the whole presentation of me to your countrymen to your kind charge'.[10]

Carlyle took an interest in the publication of the essays, not only because they contained his preface, but also because he felt he owed Emerson a return favour, since his own early books, in particular *Sartor Resartus* (1836), had been published first in America, the process being overseen by Emerson, who made strenuous efforts to get proper payment for Carlyle and prevent his work from being rushed out by American pirate publishers, who paid nothing.[11] Carlyle reported in lively fashion to Emerson on 29 September 1844:

> I have visited your Bookseller Chapman; seen the Proofsheets lying on his table; taken order that the reprint shall be well corrected, – indeed I am to read every sheet myself, and in that way get acquainted with it, before it go into stereotype. Chapman is a tall lank youth of five-and-twenty [actually twenty-three]; full of goodwill, but of what other equipment time must yet try. By a little Book of his, which I looked at some months ago, he seemed to me sunk very deep in the dust-hole of extinct Socinianism; a painful predicament for a man! He is not sure of saving much copyright for you; but he will do honestly what in that respect is doable; and he will print the Book correctly, and publish it decently, I saying *imprimatur* [let it be printed] if occasion be, – and your ever-increasing little congregation here will do with the new word what they can.

(Carlyle had naturally been rather more complimentary about *Human Nature* when thanking Chapman for sending it earlier in the year, saying tactfully that it showed 'the features of an earnest and piously meditative mind'.[12])

On the subject of piracy, Chapman was keen to add his voice to the protests already being made quite forcefully by Carlyle himself and by Dickens, who delivered several strong speeches on the subject, using Carlyle's authority, during his visit to the United States in 1842.[13] Dickens's main concern, understandably, was with the fate of British books in the free-for-all conditions of American publishing. Chapman, as the British co-publisher of

Emerson, was more worried about the increasing incidence of piracy in Britain of American books. Carlyle wrote in October 1844 to his friend John Forster, a lawyer who acted as unofficial literary agent for himself and Dickens, asking for help on behalf of Chapman and Emerson:

> A certain Bookseller, one Chapman in Newgate Street, is reprinting with authority from Emerson himself a new Book of Emerson's; in which operation I am of course bound to be in all ways helpful. Chapman hopes and believes that by making some kind of application to some kind of Privy Council by virtue of some kind of Act about International Copyright, he can secure the property of this British edition for Emerson and himself; – but the poor man does not know how to proceed; and the Attornies whom he consults shed on the operation only darkness visible. He has heard that Serg*t* Talfourd is the oracle on all such matters; and in his despair this poor Chapman wishes me to go and ask the learned Serg*t* direct. For Emerson's sake I will cheerfully do it, if it be feasible; – and it is upon this latter point that I now write to consult you.[14]

Carlyle reported to Emerson in November that Chapman had now advertised the *Essays*; on the copyright question he was, with reason, desponding, while Chapman, in an early demonstration of the attractive but often unrealistic optimism which was to survive many decades of disappointments, was hopeful. Carlyle announced:

> There proves, I believe, no visible real vestige of a Copyright obtainable here; only Chapman asserts that he *has* obtained one, and that he will take all contraveners into Chancery, – which has a terrible sound; and indeed the Act he founds on is of so distracted inextricable a character, it may mean anything and all things, and no Serj*t* Talfourd whom we could consult durst take upon him to say that it meant almost anything whatever. The sound of 'Chancery', the stereotype character of this volume [a printing method of relatively recent date], and its cheap price, may perhaps deter pirates, – who are but a weak body in this country as yet. I judged it right to help in that; and impertinent, at this stage of affairs, to go any further.

The Act referred to here was passed in 1842 after Thomas Noon Talfourd, a lawyer and MP, had agitated in Parliament, but, as Carlyle rightly pointed out, it only succeeded in making an already complicated situation even more convoluted and contradictory. The result was that solicitors and judges came to different conclusions about its provisions, and some publishers intent on piracy calculated that it was worth risking prosecution.[15] Chapman may have thought he could make further advances with the support of Carlyle, at this time the most influential writer in Britain, but Carlyle was not at all canny in financial matters; he and Emerson floundered mightily in the murky waters of international publishing.[16]

Another idea of Chapman's was to publish a new periodical to replace the *Dial*. Carlyle gave him encouragement, and he spoke to Theodore Parker, who was visiting London in the summer of 1844 and who passed on the news to Emerson that Chapman wanted to found a monthly magazine, to be published in London but have contributors (and, it was hoped, readers) in America too. Chapman had told Parker that Carlyle might contribute, also James Martineau and his fellow Unitarian John Hamilton Thom, as well as Tennyson and – if they were willing – Parker and Emerson. 'He is sanguine of writers – & readers none the less', wrote Parker; 'I am sanguine of neither, & think the thing will never go.'[17] Emerson was no more keen than Parker, and the plan went no further.

In spite of Carlyle's well-meaning efforts to proofread the *Essays* as they went through the press in London, Emerson was disappointed when he saw the edition, which was published early in 1845 with a number of errors introduced at the London end of the printing process. He protested mildly to Chapman in March, asking for a list of errata to be inserted in future copies, but assuring Chapman that on the whole 'I find your copy very faithful; and if we shall have occasion to print again hereafter, I will try to give you more time'.[18] Emerson's patience wore rather thin the following year, when Chapman's edition of his *Poems*, published at the end of 1846 by the same arrangement with Munroe, was disfigured by so many typographical errors that it was 'a magazine of vexations', as Emerson told his erstwhile co-editor of the *Dial*, Margaret Fuller, who was visiting England. 'The book, too, seems still-born in London', he added, 'for any sign I can find in the Journals.'[19]

The fact was that Chapman, with no experience, no training in business, no spare cash, and no contacts in the publishing world, was struggling to make ends meet. He could not afford to advertise his books regularly, and most items on his list were in any case unlikely to cover the costs of printing. Unitarian books appealed, after all, to a limited, if literate and supportive, readership; 'infidel' works by unknown writers like Maccall had little chance of selling; and even Emerson's books seem not to have made a profit, judging from his polite reply in May 1847 to a lament from Chapman: 'I am very much concerned to learn that my book of Poems is to be the occasion of loss to you, which I had ventured to hope might be a benefit.'[20] Emerson's success in Britain really began later in 1847, when he crossed the Atlantic to spend several months lecturing and socialising, using 142 Strand, to which Chapman had by then moved, as his base.

Meanwhile, Chapman struggled on with his venture. 1845 saw him publish fewer than twenty titles, most of them dissenting works, with a further four being on German subjects. One of these was a short pamphlet describing the liberal Catholic Johannes Ronge (later a refugee in London and intro-ducer of the kindergarten system to Britain) as 'Luther revived'.[21] Carlyle induced Chapman to reprint the autobiography of one of his favourite authors, Jean Paul Friedrich Richter, in a translation by the American Eliza Lee.[22] The third German work was an English version of the philosopher Friedrich Wilhelm Joseph von Schelling's lecture on the philosophy of art.[23] Chapman himself wrote the preface to J. Weiss's translation of Schiller's *Philosophical and Aesthetic Letters*, which he published in his 'Catholic Series', begun in 1844 and continued until 1854, by which time thirty-seven titles had been issued in the series. His choice of the word 'Catholic' was unfortunate, particu-larly after John Henry Newman's defection from Anglicanism to Roman Catholicism in 1845. Chapman intended the more general meaning: open-minded, tolerant, universal.

He expressed his own personal and professional creed in a pamphlet of 1847 called *Brief Outlines and Review of a Work entitled 'The Principles of Nature, her Divine Revelations, and a Voice to Mankind. By and through Andrew Jackson Davis, the "Poughkeepsie Seer" and "Clairvoyant"': being the Substance of a Preface to that Work.* As Chapman explains in this thirty-page booklet, he is publishing his preface separately from Davis's work itself – also in his 1847 list – 'in order to stimulate curiosity and call attention to its extraor-dinary merits and pretensions'. Most respectable publishers, he says, would 'shrink' from printing such a work, but he feels it the duty of a publisher 'to endeavour to afford every facility in his power for the dissemination of truly earnest and thoughtful books', whether 'orthodox or heterodox, conservative or radical'. Though Chapman does not identify himself completely with the visions of the American, he thinks there may be such a phenomenon as 'magnetic fluid', a 'mysterious and mediatorial element between mind and mind'. His willingness to publish Davis's book shows astuteness, for there was widespread speculation in the 1840s about the power, medicinal and other, of mesmerism.[24]

Though mesmerism had been known in Britain since its discovery in the late eighteenth century by Franz Anton Mesmer, who called it 'animal magnetism', it became a fashion, even a rage, in the 1840s. People held private parties and invited practitioners to exhibit their skills, which included rendering the subject immune to tickling or pinpricks, as Jane Carlyle reported half-sceptically of one such party in December 1844, by which time true mesmerism mania was sweeping the country.[25]

Its prominence was not entirely due to social fashion. John Elliotson, first Professor of Medicine at University College London, had experimented with mesmerism when treating patients with epilepsy and other ailments during the 1830s. His demonstrations began to be attended not just by medical students and colleagues, but also by MPs, peers, and other interested observers. The University College Hospital authorities became anxious about the unwanted notoriety of his activities; the 'godless institution of Gower Street', as the College was known in some quarters on account of its founding principles, was struggling against Church of England and Oxbridge prejudice in these early years, and did not welcome the controversy that Elliotson attracted.[26] After some damning articles in the *Lancet* in 1838, and alarming reports of Elliotson allowing a female patient into a men's ward to predict the outcome of their cases, Elliotson was forced, despite vigorous support from many of his students, to resign from University College. He went on to open the London Mesmeric Infirmary in 1849, but by then mesmerism had given way to chloroform as an anaesthetic in surgery and to hypnotism as a therapy – that being the term introduced by James Braid, a Scottish doctor practising in Manchester, whose method replaced the idea of magnetic fluids and 'emanations' with that of psychological suggestion.[27]

In spite of the scandal associated with him, Elliotson continued to be widely admired. Dickens, having observed his demonstrations in 1838, employed him as his family doctor, and even practised mesmerism himself, notably on the wife of his Swiss friend Emile de la Rue in December 1844, when he successfully relieved her *tic douloureux*.[28] Thackeray, who nearly died of a fever diagnosed as cholera in the autumn of 1849, dedicated *Pendennis* to Elliotson, expressing his gratitude for his 'constant watchfulness and skill' (though it is unlikely that mesmerism was part of the treatment in Thackeray's case).[29] The celebrity of the method reached its height in December 1844, when Harriet Martineau, the extraordinarily successful author of a series of short stories illustrating contemporary issues such as taxation, education, political economy, and the Poor Laws, wrote her 'Letters on Mesmerism' in the *Athenaeum*. This tough-minded, freethinking woman was convinced that mesmerism had cured her of a fatal tumour, and she wanted to tell the world about it. She was soon to become one of Chapman's authors and his staunchest supporter, for a time, in the financial management of the *Westminster Review*.

From the end of 1845 to the end of 1846 or beginning of 1847, Chapman published under the imprint 'Chapman Brothers'. He had brought his older brother Thomas, now a chemist and cutler in Glasgow, into the business, though it seems that Thomas remained in Glasgow and did not become an active partner.[30] By 1847 the name on the title-pages had reverted to 'John Chapman', and from then on Chapman managed the business alone, though there was talk of Thomas becoming his partner again in 1857, when Chapman's financial position was particularly precarious. Nothing came of it.[31]

What Chapman needed was a book which would attract attention beyond the tight-knit, if often squabbling, group of Unitarians who wrote for him and bought books from him. This he found in the form of the translation from German of a genuinely innovative and controversial work, Strauss's *Life of Jesus*, done by the formidably intelligent young woman who in later years would become one of the greatest of English novelists. As is the way of things, the book made neither money nor fame for translator and publisher – being issued anonymously in three solid volumes of solid intellectual matter – but it put an important work of scholarship into the public domain, and was the means of bringing Chapman and Marian Evans together in a partnership which offered her the opportunity to write forcefully, wittily, and anonymously in the *Westminster Review*, thereby gaining the confidence to try her hand at fiction. Her personal life, as well as her professional career, owed Chapman the greatest debt, since it was he who introduced her, in October 1851, to her future life's partner, G. H. Lewes. Chapman did well out of the connection too, for Marian Evans was acknowledged by the contributors and supporters of the *Westminster Review* to be an excellent reviewer and editorial adviser.

Though *The Life of Jesus* produced no financial reward for Chapman and Marian, it did attract a large amount of attention because of its thoughtful, scholarly assault on the authority of the Bible, not merely with regard to the Old Testament, which had long been considered by many as full of myth- ical elements, but also with reference to the New Testament, in particular the Gospels. Strauss painstakingly goes through these, identifying in the narratives of Christ's life the fulfilment of Old Testament prophecies, and concluding that such events are largely mythical, having been invented to fit the requirement raised by the Old Testament stories.[32] Marian Evans came to translate the work by accident. The task had been started by Rufa Brabant, who belonged in the circle of Charles Bray, a philanthropic and freethinking ribbon manufacturer of Coventry. In November 1843 Rufa married Charles Hennell, Bray's brother-in-law and author in 1838 of *An Inquiry Concerning the Origin of Christianity*, which had been written independently of Strauss but reached similar conclusions. On her marriage, Rufa gave up the trans- lation. The obvious person to take over was the twenty-four-year-old Mary Ann Evans, as she was then known, a neighbour of Bray and close friend of his wife Cara and her sister, Sara Hennell. Miss Evans knew German – and Latin, Greek, and Hebrew, which were also required. She had exchanged the evangelical piety of her teens for a sceptical, humanist position on reli- gious questions, and was therefore not at all shocked or troubled by Strauss's work. The translating task was taken on in January 1844, and finished just over two years later. For this work the anonymous translator received £20. Chapman Brothers published it, priced 1/6, on 15 June 1846 as *The Life of Jesus, critically examined, by Dr David Friedrich Strauss. Translated from the Fourth German Edition. In three volumes.*[33]

It had never been considered likely that the book's sales would cover the cost of printing. A radical lawyer and Birmingham MP, Joseph Parkes, put up £150, and there were probably one or two other willing subscribers. Charles Hennell negotiated with Chapman on behalf of the new translator, noting in April 1844: 'Mr Chapman agrees to my terms – ¹/₂ expense and ¹/₂ profit.'[34] There was to be no profit. A few months after publication, in February 1847, Mary Ann asked Sara Hennell to remind her what the print run had been and who was to be paid what when the money from sales came in. 'My strong impression was, that the first 250 copies were to be Mr C[hapman]'s', she wrote, while profits from the second 250 were to go to the subscribers. She added: 'We have a dispute here [in Coventry] as to the number of copies printed. Was it 1,000 or 2,000?' Sara did not know. Whatever the number, nearly six years after publication 350 copies of Strauss remained unsold.[35]

Mary Ann added a light-hearted remark in the same letter to Sara which suggests that, after only a brief acquaintance with Chapman, she was already aware of both his inexperience and possible unreliability as a publisher and his attractions as a man. 'I hope Mr Chapman will not misbehave', she wrote, meaning with regard to the fair distribution of profits, 'but he was always too much of the *interesting* gentleman to please me.' This last sentence, she indicated, was not for reading out to others.[36]

At this time the Chapmans were no longer living above the shop in Newgate Street, but further east, in Clapton. They had two young children, Beatrice, born in December 1844, and Ernest, born in March 1846; Susanna was expecting another, Walter, who was born in April 1847, shortly before the family moved to the Strand.[37] Sara Hennell, who visited the Brays in Coventry for long periods, lived most of the year in Clapton with her mother. She acted as go-between during the Strauss translation, proofreading the parcels of manuscript as Mary Ann sent them and taking them to Chapman for printing. Sara was invited to Chapman's literary parties, along with Herbert Spencer and other aspiring writers, many of them newly arrived in London. Among these was Eliza Lynn, who lodged with the Chapmans in 1846, the year in which the first of her learned and unsuccessful novels, *Azeth the Egyptian*, was published (not by Chapman). 'Very peculiar of Miss Sennacherib to take lodgings at Mr Chapman's', Cara Bray remarked to Sara in a letter of November 1846, adding, 'how many more young ladies is he going to have?'[38]

The question hangs in the air. Had Chapman begun to make a habit of offering lodgings – as a necessary supplement to the family income – to young women in particular? Was he, a man of twenty-five with a pregnant wife of thirty-nine, already inclined to look outside his marriage for emotional and sexual satisfaction? Cara Bray cannot have suspected quite as much, or she would not have accepted with equanimity her friend Mary Ann's becoming a lodger at 142 Strand a few years later, but she may have noticed, as others did, Chapman's attractiveness to women and possibly also the lack of sympathy between him and Susanna. Elizabeth Malleson (née Whitehead), a schoolgirl in Clapton in the early 1840s, met the Chapmans socially among her family's Unitarian circle. In autobiographical notes written some fifty years later, she recalled the 'strange contrast' between Chapman and Susanna:

He, tall with a fine expressive face, full of alert intellectual power, and absorbed in ideas; she, short, stout and unattractive. In after years I got to know both husband and wife well when he was the publisher of advanced Liberal literature. They were very good to me, for I had invitations to their wonderful parties of literary people. I remember the painful division in the household – the poor wife entirely devoid of tact, the husband with separate interests, the children victims of such divisions. I remember my first conviction of the wrong of such imperfect unions, and the odd sympathy claimed by both husband and wife.[39]

The Strauss translation was noticed by orthodox critics who distrusted 'German rationalism', but also by more friendly observers. Two of Chapman's Unitarians wrote reviews, James Martineau in Hickson's *Westminster Review*, and his fellow Unitarian minister Charles Wicksteed in Chapman's own *Prospective Review*. Both were respectful towards Strauss, though Martineau makes it clear that he dissents from Strauss's mythological conclusion. 'Strauss weighs evidence', he writes, 'as some homoeopathic chemist his medicines, in minutest scruples, and with balance trembling on the finest knife-edge that logical cutlery can produce.'[40] It is a neat example of Martineau's method of appearing widely neutral and utterly fair while suggesting disapproval, in this case of Strauss's attempt to measure scriptural texts with dissecting tools not appropriate for the task. Wicksteed's praise of the anonymous translator's thorough knowledge of the subject and the tact and accuracy of the translation pleased Mary Ann Evans, though she thought some of his remarks about the argument rather shallow.[41]

Young men like Clough and Froude, already grappling with doctrinal difficulties at Oxford, were affected by reading Strauss. Clough told the Provost of Oriel College in March 1849 that Froude's novel, *The Nemesis of Faith*, just published by Chapman, 'contains a good deal of what I imagine pervades the young world in general', namely doubts about 'the historical foundations of Christianity' as expressed most forcefully by Strauss.[42] In 1852 Charles Kingsley spoke with a Churchman's distress about the latest signs of the times, identifying 'Strauss, *Transcendentalism* – and Mr John Chapman's *Catholic Series*' as 'the appointed path' to scepticism and despair.[43] Others, like Herbert Spencer, of a Nonconformist family but now agnostic, recommended friends to read *The Life of Jesus*; and the eccentric Francis Newman, rumoured to be the translator, authorised Henry Crabb Robinson in July 1846 to deny the attribution, but with the assurance that he 'should not have thought it any imputation to be regarded that he is the translator'.[44]

Newman had just moved from Manchester New College to become Professor of Latin at University College London. Robinson, a member of Senate, was on the appointing committee and was pleased that this man with the brilliant double first in classics and mathematics from Oxford was joining the College. He had heard that Newman wanted to leave Manchester because his wife was a member of the Plymouth Brethren and had been 'uncomfortable' there.[45] Newman immediately became one of Chapman's authors, his works, *History of the Hebrew Monarchy* (1847), *The Soul, her Sorrows and Aspirations* (1849), and *Phases of Faith* (1850), going through several editions. Newman's books caused almost as much controversy as Strauss's, though he stopped some way short of agnosticism. There were several reasons for his celebrity. Firstly, his academic reputation ensured that his opinions were taken seriously. Secondly, the notoriety of John Henry Newman, who had gone over to Rome taking a number of Oxford disciples with him and leaving others, like Froude, unsettled and rudderless, rubbed off on the reluctant younger brother, giving him a kind of notoriety by proxy. Finally, there was an openness and honesty about his expressions of the shifting state of his religious opinions in his books, especially *Phases of Faith*, which impressed readers. At a time when many thoughtful people were troubled by the consequences for religion of advances in science and historical scholarship, Newman's appearance as an author on Chapman's list made him a representative figure, for all his idiosyncrasies.

Newman ploughed his lonely furrow, the cause of, or focus for, discord at University College and at University Hall, built in 1848–9 by the Unitarian supporters of the College as a hall of residence on the Oxbridge model. The implacable unbeliever Holyoake admired him, regularly praising his works – and Chapman as the publisher of them – in his secular journal, the *Reasoner*, and beginning a friendly correspondence in 1850 which lasted until Newman's death in 1897.[46] Henry Crabb Robinson, who saw him contributing to problems at University College London and University Hall, and observed him moving further and further from even Nonconformist 'orthodoxy', could not help thinking him nevertheless 'a delightful man'.[47]

Like his older brother, Frank Newman seems to have been unable to avoid causing splits and antagonisms as he went through his intellectual and spiritual 'phases'. When Elisabeth Reid, a wealthy Unitarian philanthropist, pioneered higher education for women by founding the Ladies' College in Bedford Square in 1849 (later to be renamed Bedford College and to join the University of London), she looked to the professors at University College to form a cadre of teachers. The only other such establishment was Queen's College, begun by Church of England clergymen in 1848 for the education of governesses. Mrs Reid's idea was to build a female equivalent of University College, free from Anglican influence and open to dissenters and others. However, her own ardent Unitarianism predisposed her towards appointing dissenters rather than unbelievers. Among the University College teachers she recruited, accordingly, were the Unitarian minister and professor of English Alexander Scott, the professor of physiology W. B. Carpenter, and the mathematician Augustus De Morgan.[48]

Newman was appointed to teach ancient history; he gave lectures in mathematics as well. Henry Crabb Robinson, a close friend of Mrs Reid, noted in his diary both his own admiration for Newman and his sense that Newman's unorthodoxy was too strong for some dissenting stomachs. He read *The Soul* as soon as Chapman brought it out in May 1849, finding the author's 'natural piety' 'beautifully combined with the freest speculation'.[49] He discussed the book with fellow Unitarians, who did not, on the whole, share his tolerance and enthusiasm for Newman, one objecting to his obscurity and 'German mysticism', another expressing annoyance at his disbelief in 'the ordinary grounds of historic testimony'.[50]

Robinson, who visited Chapman's shop regularly, first in Newgate Street and now in the Strand, to buy books and Unitarian journals, often stopped to talk to Chapman. They discussed the furore in dissenting circles over *The Soul*. The seventy-four-year-old Robinson attended some of Chapman's soirées at this time, where he met people of freer opinions than his own, liberal Unitarian though he was. His diary records for the evening of 20 June 1849 attendance at two evening parties, one a grand dinner among people 'all of the orthodox stamp', after which he 'stole out' to Chapman's, 'where was a very different party indeed with whom I was glad to talk'. Among the guests here were Rufa Hennell and her father Dr Brabant, Eliza Lynn, and Newman himself.[51]

The Soul, which Newman described as 'the work of my life' in a letter to James Martineau in February 1849, sold enough for Chapman to print a second edition at the end of the year. According to Newman the original print run was a thousand copies, of which two hundred and fifty had been sold to an American bookseller, fifty or so given away, and the remaining seven hundred sold in Britain within three months of publication. The book found admirers as well as critics. In 1851 Newman told Martineau that he had recently got to know Holyoake, who had written enthusiastically about *The Soul* and with whom Newman was now engaged in an earnest correspondence about theism and atheism. Newman was not alarmed by Holyoake's position; when 'spread by such agencies', he thought, atheism could 'surely only be a transition towards a new & better religion', since Holyoake was such a 'candid kind simpleminded man', full of 'moral power' and true enthusiasm.[52]

At the other end of the scale from Holyoake, Newman had a champion in Elizabeth Gaskell, wife of a Unitarian minister in Manchester. When asked by a friend if she knew the author of *The Soul*, she replied, 'Yes, I *do* know my dear Mr Newman'. She added that his face and voice at first sight told her 'he had been with Christ', and that his book was 'absolutely simply the utterance of the man'. To the same friend she gave in November 1849 a pen portrait of this intellectual man of the moment as she had known him in Manchester:

> His voice and pronunciation are perfect; I do like that rich melodious accent which Oxford men have, though it is called 'bumptious', but Mr Newman's self is not bumptious. He dresses so shabbily you would not see his full beauty, – he used to wear detestable bottle green coats, wh. never show off a man. Mrs Newman is a Plymouth Brother which is a sort of community-of-goods-and-equality-of-rank-on-religious-principles association and very calvinistic.[53]

If *The Soul* caused controversy, with its conclusion that a wavering religious belief can only be restored by direct communion with God, rather than through Church doctrine, Newman's next work, *Phases of Faith*, published by Chapman in May 1850, gladdened the heart of radicals like Holyoake and put the author beyond the pale in the minds of people with conservative religious opinions. It tells the story of Newman's progress from extreme Calvinism in his youth – already a source of disagreement with his brother – towards the stripped-down belief he now held. The process had begun with doubts at Oxford about the Thirty-Nine Articles of the Church of England. He never took his MA or became ordained, and resigned his Balliol fellowship in 1830. He then became caught up in a missionary enterprise to Baghdad with an assorted group of evangelicals and Plymouth Brethren. Before the party reached its destination the three women in the party died of fever and exhaustion; once there, the remaining members of the group made no headway in converting Muslims to Christianity. As Newman relates, he saw the pointlessness of the venture and realised that the *fact* of faith was more important than its specific content when he had a revelatory conversation with a carpenter at Aleppo who replied to his proselytising as follows:

> I will tell you, Sir, how the case stands. God has given to you English a great many good gifts. You make fine ships, and sharp penknives, and good cloth and cottons; and you have rich nobles and brave soldiers; and you write and print many learned books . . . all this is of God. But there is one thing that God has withheld from you, and has revealed to us; and that is, the knowledge of the true religion, by which one may be saved.[54]

Having given up the Church of England, Newman had been unable to pursue at Oxford the academic career for which he was so obviously suited; Manchester New College took him on in 1840. His reputation there and at University College London from 1846 was for extraordinary cleverness and learning, knowledge of several languages, and, over the years, a number of seriously held enthusiasms, including dedication to the cause of Hungarian unity and freedom, expressed through his support for the exiled Kossuth, a similar enthusiasm for Mazzini and the cause of Italian nationalism, and an embracing of teetotalism and vegetarianism.[55] His students corroborated Elizabeth Gaskell's description of his eccentricity of dress, telling of his wearing three coats and a rug with a hole cut for the head when lecturing in winter. Walter Bagehot, set to become the most distinguished of University College alumni, told his mother of a 'queer party' at Newman's house in December 1847 at which the men and women gathered in separate rooms, with Newman 'peering through the folding doors at the ladies'.[56]

Such eccentricities, when added to Newman's unorthodox religious beliefs, made him enemies at University College and the Ladies' College. He resigned from the latter in June 1851, having caused a storm with *Phases of Faith* and split the College Council by arguing vigorously against the opinion that teaching appointments should be made with a view to balancing creeds. It was a dilemma faced already by the sister institution University College: founded by sincere believers in freedom of worship, the College ran into constant difficulties between those members who took this to mean that there should be no appointments of ministers of religion, and those – Unitarians and other Nonconformists – who feared the 'godless' tag and favoured employing ministers or at least worshippers belonging to their own non-Anglican denominations. The proposal at the Ladies' College was to spread appointments across the different beliefs, to which Newman, whose view was that academic merit should be the sole criterion, responded by inventing an advertisement to expose the absurdity of the committee's position:

> Wanted, a Professor of Physical Geography . . . who must not be a Deist, nor a Puseyite [a High Church Anglican], nor a Unitarian, nor a Roman Catholic. A liberal Churchman or a Quaker will be acceptable, if not too deep in Rationalism.[57]

Henry Crabb Robinson shook his head in sorrow and recorded, 'It is a sad fact that Newman has been the ruin of the Ladies' College', adding that he was also 'the main occasion of the bad success of our University Hall'.[58]

The Hall, which opened in 1849, was located in Gordon Square, just round the corner from Gower Street. From the start there were difficulties: it was agreed that there should be prayers, but of what denomination? The majority on the board naturally wished them to be Unitarian in form. Robinson, though sharing the creed, considered this arrangement unfair on students of other denominations and none, and foresaw, as his diaries for 1848 show, a long series of arguments and complications.[59] Sure enough, at every stage opinion was divided. On financial grounds it was hoped that Manchester New College, which now had almost more professors than it had students, would move to London to share the building and the costs (and some of the teaching staff). This plan was greeted with suspicion by the Manchester men, who feared for their positions, but it was finally adopted, after much wrangling, in 1854.[60]

The pressing need in the summer of 1848, when building was about to begin, was to appoint a Principal of the Hall. The choice fell on Newman, who duly made a speech at the foundation ceremony on 20 July, when the first stone was laid. Henry Crabb Robinson admired the skill with which Newman 'asserted, without offence, the power of forming an institution open to all opinions whatever, even Jew and Mahometan'.[61] Walter Bagehot, who had graduated from University College in 1846, took a liberal Unitarian's interest in the speech, responding wryly to his old tutor's appointment:

> The only objection that any one could have to Newman as the head of a religious institution is that his own religion is such a thoroughly bad one. What he says about the magnanimity of founding an institution independent of opinions is marred to me by my being convinced that if the Council *had* known his creed they would never have appointed him.[62]

It was not long before Newman resigned, though not entirely because of Unitarian suspicion; he and his wife were unhappy with the architectural plans which would require them to live at closer quarters to the students than they liked. Bagehot guessed that the chief objection came from Maria Newman: 'She did not like housekeeping on a large scale I suppose and the commisariat is not exactly her line.'[63] Newman's resignation came in November 1848, several months before the Hall was due to open. The Council leapt from one unfortunate appointment to another, next choosing Clough, a bruised and semi-reluctant escapee from Oxford with no Unitarian background and no desire to take prayers of any kind. Clough lasted from the opening in October 1849 to the end of 1851, when the Unitarian scholar Richard Holt Hutton, another brilliant alumnus of University College and a close friend of Bagehot, replaced him. Hutton was forced to resign for health reasons after six months, and was followed in August 1852 by the University College scientist W. B. Carpenter, when at last some stability was achieved, though the Hall never attracted many students. Poor Henry Crabb Robinson, who had invested both money and time in the project, gloomily summed up its early history in June 1852, on hearing that Hutton had been obliged to give up:

> Another blow to this ill-fated institution, w[hi]ch cannot prosper except as a College for U[nitarian] ministers. Newman an avowed unbeliever, Clough of doubtful faith, bro[ugh]t with great personal attractions only harm to the Hall, and now Hutton retires from ill health.[64]

Newman was not quite the unbeliever asserted by Robinson; his travails, with all their quirks, were in many ways characteristic of his times. He was for that reason widely noticed in his own day, though utterly unread since. In 1874 George Eliot could look back on her early days at 142 Strand, when she attended some of his lectures on geometry at the Ladies' College in 1851, and smile at how far she and the world in general had come since then:

> I have a sort of affectionate sadness in thinking of the interest which in far-off days I felt in his 'Soul' and Phases of Faith, and of the awe I had of him as a lecturer on mathematics at the Ladies' College. How much work he has done in the world, which has left no deep, conspicuous mark, but has probably entered beneficently into many lives![65]

In Chapman's early days as a publisher, Newman was one of his star authors. Like so many writers whose subject was religion but who had travelled away from orthodoxy, he turned to Chapman as the only outlet – and a willing and encouraging one – for his opinions. Though more than fifteen years older than his publisher and a man of much greater intellect and attainment, Newman needed Chapman for the dissemination of his ideas. He was to write a large number of articles for the *Westminster Review*, many of them for no payment, as Chapman was frequently on the verge of bankruptcy. Theirs was one of several writer-publisher relationships involving Chapman which demonstrated a genuine mutuality. It was a case of books – sometimes of far-reaching influence – finding a public only because Chapman was prepared to publish them.

Chapman's recently formed relationship with Emerson was also of importance to both author and publisher, though Emerson had already established connections with Britain during his first visit as a young man in 1833, when he sought out admired writers like Wordsworth and Coleridge and made a pilgrimage to the then little known Carlyle at Craigenputtoch, his remote Dumfriesshire farmhouse, on the strength of having read Carlyle's trenchant essays on English and German culture in the *Edinburgh Review*.[66] The two men had corresponded over the years; Emerson had overseen the publication in America of *Sartor Resartus* and *The French Revolution* (1837), which made Carlyle famous, and now Carlyle had helped see the new edition of Emerson's *Essays* through the press with Chapman. In 1847 Emerson was persuaded by Alexander Ireland, editor of the *Manchester Examiner and Times*, to undertake a lecture tour of Britain, for which Ireland would make the arrangements. Emerson left Boston on 5 October 1847, arriving in Liverpool on the 22nd. Manchester was to be his base for the first few months of his stay; he lectured there and in Liverpool for several weeks, after which he travelled to a number of towns in England and Scotland, the guest of prominent writers, academics, journalists, and Unitarians wherever he went. Early in March 1848 he swapped Manchester for London, where he took lodgings at 142 Strand until making his way home again in July.

Carlyle had sent a note via Alexander Ireland and a young acquaintance, Francis Espinasse, urging his American friend to come straight to London on his arrival in England to spend a few days with him. This Emerson did, turning up on the Carlyles' Chelsea doorstep at ten p.m. on 25 October 1847, much as he had arrived out of the blue in Craigenputtoch fourteen years earlier. After staying up half the night talking, he and Carlyle went out the next day 'to Hyde Park and the palaces', to the National Gallery 'and into the "Strand" to Chapman's shop', with Carlyle 'melting all Westminster & London down into his talk & laughter as we walked'.[67] Thus the handsome, sanguine young publisher was introduced by the Sage of Chelsea to cool, detached, benign Emerson, christened the 'Yankee-Seraph' by Jane Carlyle, who told friends he was inclined to 'slip thro' your fingers' like water – 'fine pure spring water, but water all the same'.[68]

During this fleeting visit to London, Emerson ran into the wife of George Bancroft, the American ambassador, while looking round the National Gallery. Elizabeth Bancroft introduced him to the octogenarian banker-poet Samuel Rogers, who promptly invited Emerson to one of his famous breakfast parties. Here he was shown Rogers's treasures, which included a marble head by Canova, a mantelpiece by Flaxman, a bust of Alexander Pope, and autograph letters of Milton, Mozart, Burke, Samuel Johnson, and Emerson's compatriots George

Washington and Benjamin Franklin.[69] On his return to London the following spring Emerson was introduced – through the Bancrofts, through Carlyle, whom everyone knew and everyone courted, and also through Chapman, who organised the six lectures he gave in the capital in June 1848 and held parties in his honour at 142 Strand – to the widest possible spectrum of literate Londoners, from the fabulously rich Duchess of Sutherland and Lord and Lady Palmerston to the starving, freethinking ex-Unitarian Maccall.

Back in the North-West by the end of October 1847 after his quick dash to see Carlyle, Emerson settled into giving lectures on 'Representative Men' (among them Shakespeare, Montaigne, and Napoleon), and topics such as eloquence, domestic life, and reading, at literary societies and Mechanics' Institutes.[70] He had tea with James Martineau in Liverpool, and heard him preach. Most of his hosts there and in Manchester were 'adorers' of Carlyle, he reported to friends and family back home. 'They keep Carlyle as a cathedral-bell here', he told his wife Lidian on 13 November, 'which they like to produce in companies where he is unknown & set a-swinging to the surprise & consternation of all persons.'[71] To Carlyle himself he wrote that he met nothing but friends and disciples – Ireland, Espinasse, Jane Carlyle's friend Geraldine Jewsbury, W. B. Hodgson, headmaster of a Manchester school and friend of Martineau – all of whom were being kind to him for Carlyle's sake.[72] Others from whom he accepted hospitality as he travelled the country during December and January included the Unitarian minister Charles Wicksteed (reviewer of the Strauss translation) in Leeds, and a scholarly German businessman, Joseph Neuberg, in Nottingham.[73]

As a kind of modern mystic, a worshipper of God in nature, an ex-Unitarian with a leaning towards Platonic idealism transported into modern culture and an interest in social problems, Emerson went down well with the intellectuals of Manchester and Liverpool. These towns were strongholds of Nonconformism and the ideals of secular education, free trade, and the alleviation of mass poverty. The years of potato failure in Ireland in the mid-1840s had sent thousands of emigrants to Liverpool, some of whom settled in Lancashire, working for starvation wages, while others took ship again for America and a new life. Friedrich Engels had written about the gulf between rich and poor, master and man, in Manchester in his *Condition of the Working Class in England* (published in German in 1845), and Elizabeth Gaskell was soon to have her first novelistic success with *Mary Barton: A Tale of Manchester Life*, published in October 1848.

Even Manchester and Liverpool, however, had their share of orthodox believers who observed Emerson's successes with suspicion. 'I am preached against every Sunday by the Church of England', he told his wife in December 1847. In the same letter he mentioned that the distinctly unorthodox Harriet Martineau 'pursues me with kind letters and introductions of friends'.[74] He was to spend a few days at the end of February 1848 as her guest at Ambleside in the Lake District and to be taken to renew his acquaintance with the now elderly Wordsworth at nearby Rydal Mount.[75]

Writing to his friend Thoreau on 2 December, Emerson announced an important change which had taken place the previous day as proof that England, already 'manufacturer for the world', was becoming 'one complete tool or engine in herself':

> Yesterday the time all over the kingdom was reduced to Greenwich time. At Liverpool, where I was, the clocks were put forward 12 minutes. This had become quite necessary on account of the railroads which bind the whole country into swiftest connexion, and require so much accurate interlocking, intersection, & simultaneous arrival, that the difference of time produced confusion. Every man in England carries a little book in his pocket called 'Bradshaws Guide', which contains time tables of every arrival & departure at every station on all the railroads of the kingdom. It is published anew on the first day of every month & costs sixpence. The proceeding effects of the Electric telegraph will give a new importance to such arrangements.[76]

(The electric telegraph, invented in the 1830s by the American Samuel Morse, had been quickly adopted in Britain; when Tallis compiled his street directory in 1847, he noted that the Electric Telegraph Company had an office at none other than Chapman's 142 Strand.)

Emerson was impressed by the advanced state of British train travel as he shuttled between Manchester and Liverpool and made forays into towns in Yorkshire and the Midlands. His letters and journals, on which he based his book *English Traits* (1856), frequently note its wonders. 'I ride everywhere as on a cannnonball (though cushioned & comforted in every manner)', he wrote from another modern town, Birmingham, 'high & low over rivers & towns', through mountains in tunnels three miles long at 'twice the speed & with half the motion' of carriages in America, all the while reading *The Times*, 'which seems to have machinized the world, for my occasion'.[77]

On 11 February 1848 Emerson arrived in Edinburgh, where, thanks to arrangements made by Alexander Ireland, a native of the city, he was introduced to all the literati and professors. He stayed for two weeks as the guest of Dr Samuel Brown, an experimental chemist, delivering lectures to 'brilliant assemblies' and meeting all the famous residents. There was De Quincey, 'a small old man of 70 years, with a very handsome face', living among friends who protected him from the worst effects of his opium addiction, and the great Whig lawyer and erstwhile editor of the *Edinburgh Review*, Francis – now Lord – Jeffrey, and George Combe, Britain's foremost exponent of phrenology. Most interesting of all was Ireland's close friend Robert Chambers, younger half of the publishing firm of W. & R. Chambers and the anonymous author of a book which had rivalled Strauss's *Life of Jesus* as the most unsettling work of the decade. This was *Vestiges of the Natural History of Creation*, published in 1844 with the utmost secrecy because the respectable publisher of encyclopædias and writer of books on Scottish literature and history could not be seen to have written this account of evolution of species over millions of years according to a nebular theory of the origin of the universe which left God out of the picture.

The work, appearing fifteen years before Darwin found the courage and opportunity to publish his own account in *The Origin of Species*, became an overnight sensation. Written in an accessible style by an intelligent layman, it was devoured in fashionable parlours and Working Men's Clubs alike. Its publisher John Churchill of Soho, the chief London publisher of medical and scientific literature, issued four editions in seven months; in May 1847 the seventh edition appeared, the first cheap 'people's edition' at 2/6, with a print run of 5,000 to add to nearly 8,000 copies already sold at the original price of 7/6. Chambers went to elaborate lengths to hide his authorship, getting his wife to copy out the manuscript, which was sent to Alexander Ireland in Manchester, who in turn sent it to London to be printed, without ever telling Churchill who the author was.[78] Chambers and Ireland enjoyed their secret, writing to one another as 'Alexius' (Ireland) and 'Ignotus' (Chambers) and punning on their joint enterprise. Ignotus writes to Alexius, for example, in April 1845 asking his friend to 'excuse a *vestige* of paper to apprize you that I leave London for the North'.[79]

Chambers's authorship was not made public until 1884, thirteen years after his death; it was not even hinted at by his straitlaced brother William in his *Memoir of Robert Chambers* of 1872. Speculation about the author on the book's first appearance was unbridled. Thackeray's name was suggested, as were those of Lord Brougham (one of the founders of University College London), Harriet Martineau, Byron's mathematical daughter Ada, Countess of Lovelace, and her collaborator on the 'calculating engine' – a prototype of the modern computer – Charles Babbage. Some suspected Darwin, and some the celebrated geologist Charles Lyell. Even Prince Albert was a candidate.[80] Suspicion fell on both Chambers and his friend George Combe, as *Vestiges* contained some discussion of phrenology, the 'science' of reading character through measuring the contours of the head. But Chambers kept silent in Edinburgh, where he apparently allayed suspicion about his religious views by keeping a pew in two churches, so that if he was found to be missing from one, 'it will always be concluded by the charitable that I am in the other'.[81]

If he was thus more or less successful in keeping his secret from the good burghers of Edinburgh, it was common knowledge in radical circles. Though not told directly, Combe guessed; Holyoake, always eager for such information, heard from a Bristol friend: 'It leaked out, I believe, through one of the printers'. In January 1848 Chapman was showing how up to date he was in these matters by assuring Richard Owen, Professor of Comparative Anatomy at the Royal College of Surgeons, that 'there is now pretty strong evidence to fix the paternity' on Chambers.[82] Emerson himself had been told, no doubt by Ireland, and lost no time in passing the news on to his wife in the course of a long letter detailing his Edinburgh doings, which included a dinner at Chambers's house with 'my London friend John Chapman the bookseller', who was making a brief visit to the city.[83]

On 2 March Emerson, back in Manchester, alerted Carlyle to his imminent removal to London. 'I hope to set forward today for London', he wrote; 'I am to go first to Chapman's house, where I shall lodge for a time. If it is too noisy, I shall move westward.'[84] He had no need to move. The Strand proved the perfect billet for the next few months. Emerson's lectures in the provinces had been noticed in the national press, so he was assured of attention in the capital. The Bancrofts would bring him into aristocratic and political circles, while Carlyle could command the society of literary figures like Tennyson and Thackeray, as well as members of the liberal, cultured aristocracy in the shape of the Barings and Ashburtons, and Chapman was the conduit for writers of all kinds of unorthodoxy who came to his publishing office downstairs and his evening parties upstairs at number 142.

The Chapman family were by now well settled in. The imposing house led back from the Strand to overlook the riverside terrace of Somerset House and the Thames itself. Though the lower floors were dark, from the upper floors the view at the back stretched across the river to the Norwood hills, as William Hale White, who lodged here in 1852–3, remembered in newspaper articles written more than thirty years later. Emerson was anxious that he might find his rooms there too noisy, but Hale White recalled that his own life was 'never quieter' than when he lived at the top of number 142, with the traffic's roar 'subdued to a kind of hum' far below.[85] Chapman advertised space for up to twelve paying guests in addition to the rooms used by the family and by the publishing business, not to mention the space let to the Electric Telegraph Company. He had to take in lodgers to help defray the high cost of the rent, £400 a year, with rates, water, and gas costing a further £100, as Susanna Chapman explained in a letter of July 1852 to George Combe, adding that the income from the house never quite equalled the outlay.[86]

Chapman must have thought it worth the risk to procure such handsome premises in the best location in London for the work he wanted to do. There was undoubtedly some grandiose folly in his choice: he wished to make his mark. But the risk was reduced by the fact of his ready-made American publishing connections, which ensured that he could find amenable lodgers for short periods when Americans visited London. The publishing business and the boarding-house business would thus complement and perhaps even augment one another. In such a large house he could hold literary parties and bring people together. On taking over the former Turk's Head, he produced a card advertising its attractions, particularly to Americans:

Visitors to London are respectfully informed that the House occupied by Mr John Chapman, Publisher, being a very large and superior one, and having been recently built for a First Class Hotel, has been furnished and the requisite arrangements effected with a view of affording to Ladies and Gentlemen either for a few days or a longer period, the advantages of an Hotel, combined with the quiet and comfort of a Private Residence. The number of Visitors is limited to ten or twelve persons, and the Sleeping Rooms are all quite free from noise.

The central position of the House (midway between the City and West End, near the Theatres and Houses of Parliament, and within reach of the Thames Steamers and of Omnibuses to all parts of the Metropolis) affords peculiar facilities to Strangers and to all who wish to economise their time. For terms and address see the other side. Reference is permitted to be made in America to Messrs Little and Brown, Booksellers, Boston, and will be given in England if required.

To American Gentlemen desirous of adding to their Libraries while in London, Mr Chapman is prepared to render every aid they may require, being from his long experience as an extensive publisher of all kinds of Old and New Books for Exportation, enabled to do so on the most advantageous terms.[87]

While the husband thus offered his bookselling services to visitors, the wife ran the boarding house. The reverse side of the card reads:

MRS CHAPMAN'S TERMS.
Board and Residence at 142, Strand.
10 doors west of Somerset House.

	per wk.
Visitors occupying First class Bed rooms	2 10 0
" " Second " " "	2 5 0
For a Second Person in any of the Rooms	1 10 0
Fires in Bed Rooms	3 6
Boot Cleaning and Attendance	3 6

Exclusive of Wines, Spirits and Malt Liquors.

Friends introduced to dinner at 3/-.
Breakfast hour ½ past 8 o'clock.
Luncheon 1 o'clock. Dinner at 6 o'clock.
Tea ½ past 8 o'clock.[88]

Emerson settled in well, and brought the Chapmans extra custom by inviting friends to dine with him and renting extra rooms occasionally for his own guests. In return for Ireland's kindness and management of his lecture courses in the North, for example, Emerson invited him to stay in the Strand in June 1848 to hear him lecture at Portman Square.[89] The London lectures were arranged by Chapman, who also sold the tickets. First, though, Emerson surrendered himself to two months of socialising.

A letter to his wife on 8 March summarises his first week's activities in a London even more buzzing than usual because of the February revolution in Paris and the subsequent flight of Louis Philippe to England on 3 March. British radicals and non-radicals rejoiced at the fall of the French king. Dickens signed his letters 'Citoyen' and Carlyle was gleeful: 'There is one *phantasm* less in our poor distracted world.'[90] Emerson heard such talk at first hand, as he was a frequent guest in Chelsea. Acting on Carlyle's advice, he attended a Chartist meeting, at which 'La Marseillaise' was sung. On Sunday 12 March Carlyle took him to meet Lady Harriet Baring, soon to become Lady Ashburton on the death in May of her father-in-law. The best-known intellectual hostess in London, she collected great men to invite to her parties, exercising a strong fascination on them all, from Carlyle to Thackeray and Tennyson, and even the ascetic John Stuart Mill.[91] Emerson reported to an American friend that he had seen Lady Harriet, 'esteemed the wittiest woman in London'; he was to dine with her and her unwitty husband on 23 March.[92]

And so it went on. Tuesday 14 March saw him and a reluctant Carlyle attending a soirée in Emerson's honour at the Bancrofts' house, where Macaulay, Richard Monckton Milnes, Charles Lyell and his wife, and the Prussian ambassador and scholar Chevalier Bunsen were among the other guests. By contrast, Chapman invited the shabby scholar Frank Newman to a small evening party for Emerson on the following Thursday.[93] Carlyle described the great dinner at the Barings' on 23 March with a touch of contempt for the whole Emersonian roadshow (though it was not of Emerson's seeking, as Carlyle saw):

> On Thursday I had again an eight-o'-clock *dinner* to execute at the Barings's, on occasion of Emerson, – or rather Emerson was but the *excuse* of it, for he kept very quiet; mild modest eyes, lips sealed together like a pair of pincers, and nobody minded him much: we had quantities of Lords, Town-wits (Thackeray &c), beautiful Ladies . . .[94]

At the end of March Emerson took up a long-standing invitation from Clough to visit Oxford. Here he met some of the young men for whom reading Strauss's *Life of Jesus* had been an unnerving experience. They had looked

for a kind of salvation to the stirring spiritual but non-denominational rhetoric of Carlyle, especially his espousal in *Sartor Resartus* of 'natural supernaturalism', a spirit of religion freed from the 'old clothes' of dogma and
tradition and affirming God's presence in nature.[95] Emerson's Carlyle-
influenced essays were known to them too. When Clough first wrote his
invitation in November 1847, he gave a hint of the divided nature of Oxford
academic life with its strong Church of England and establishment tradi-
tions on the one hand, and the spiritual and intellectual upheaval among
the younger fellows on the other. Men like Clough and Froude, and the
brothers Tom and Matthew Arnold, sat uneasily in their tutorships and
fellowships, disinclined to embrace the Thirty-Nine Articles but reluctant
either to follow the older Newman to Rome or to give up their faith altogether. Carlyle and Emerson seemed to offer them a safe landing place some-
where between Church dogma and atheism. Clough was eager to attract
Emerson to Oxford, but frank about the reception he might expect:

> Your name is not a thing unknown to us – I do not say it would be a
> passport in a society fenced about by Church Articles. But amongst
> the juniors there are many that have read and studied your books, and
> not a few that have largely learnt from them, and would gladly welcome
> their author.[96]

Emerson's report to his wife of his two days in Oxford was brief. He had
been introduced to a few professors and 'some Deans and Doctors', as well
as to Froude of Exeter College, whom Emerson described as 'a noble youth,
to whom my heart warms'.[97] For his part, Froude later recalled confessing his
doctrinal difficulties to Emerson:

> I told him that he was in part responsible for my present state of mind,
> that I thought of giving up my profession and my fellowship. He did
> not advise. He did not dissuade, but characteristically he urged the
> propriety of doing nothing in a hurry. He had himself the calmness, I
> could almost say, of a rock.[98]

By the beginning of April Emerson was back at 142 Strand, where on 8
April Clough breakfasted with him and Chapman.[99] The social whirl was
renewed. Milnes got him an invitation to a party given by Lady Palmerston,

where he saw 'a quite illustrious collection, such as only London & Lord Palmerston could collect'. Here were the Crown Prince of Prussia, the Prince of Syracuse, the Turkish ambassador 'in costume', Bunsen, Lord and Lady Rothschild, Disraeli, and the celebrated historian Macaulay. There was another soirée at the Marquis of Northampton's, where various scientists were gathered around Prince Albert, 'to whom Dr Buckland was showing some microscopic phenomena'. Henry Crabb Robinson was there too, a man who 'knew all men, Lamb, Southey, Wordsworth, Madame de Stael & Goethe', as Emerson told his wife.[100]

Robinson attended this party with a predetermined dislike of Emerson, having read the *Essays* and found the writer to be 'a bad imitation of Carlyle who himself imitates Coleridge ill, who is a general imitator of the Germans'.[101] His opinion, as it happens, was remarkably similar to Jane Carlyle's; her sharp comment about the *Essays* on their first appearance in 1841 had been that they were 'a bad imitation of Carlyle's most Carlylish *translations* of Goethe's most Goetheish passages'.[102] Unlike Jane Carlyle, Robinson was won over by Emerson the man. 'He has one of the most interesting countenances I ever beheld', he told his brother Thomas, 'a combination of intelligence & sweetness that quite disarmed me.' The two men met at other parties, for Robinson's circle was a wide one. At a gathering on 16 April Robinson saw Chapman, who 'hinted at a scheme to have a couple of lectures by the American and I said I would attend'.[103]

A discussion of male and female chastity in Britain and America took place on 25 April when John Forster invited Emerson to meet Dickens at dinner. Carlyle was also there. Emerson noted in his journal:

> There were only gentlemen present, & the conversation turned on the shameful lewdness of the London streets at night . . . I said, that, when I came to Liverpool, I inquired whether the prostitution was always as gross in that city as it then appeared? for, to me, it seemed to betoken a fatal rottenness in the state, & I saw not how any boy could grow up safe . . . C & D replied, that chastity in the male sex was as good as gone in our times . . . Carlyle evidently believed that the same things were true in America. – He had heard this & that, of New York, &c. I assured them that it was not so with us . . . Dickens told me, that Miss Coutts had undertaken to establish an asylum [Urania Cottage] for vicious girls taken out of the street. She had bed, clothed, schooled

them, & had them taught to sew, & knit, & bake, that they might be wives for the Australians. Then she proposed to send them out, at her charge, & have them provided for until they married. They liked all this, very well, until it came to sailing for Australia. Then, they preferred going back to the Strand.[104]

Emerson was not enthusiastic about giving lectures in London, but Chapman was 'very busy about it', as he told his wife on 20 April; by 6 May it had been fixed that he would give six lectures on 'The Mind and Manners of the Nineteenth Century' at the Marylebone Literary and Scientific Institution in Portman Square the following month. Meanwhile he was off to Paris for three weeks to see the sights and observe the post-revolutionary National Assembly at work. He found there a number of acquaintances who had gone for the same purpose, among them Milnes, Clough, and Geraldine Jewsbury.[105]

Chapman and Emerson were once more mulling over the idea of founding a 'journal for New & Old England', to be published simultaneously in London and Boston. Emerson had mentioned the plan to the young men of Oxford, who were enthusiastic, 'Froude & Clough, particularly'. Though Emerson was doubtful whether such a journal would cover its costs, he was impressed by Chapman's enterprising attitude, telling an American friend that 'in Chapman's plan of a common Journal, we should really secure a phoenix of a publisher', a man 'of integrity & of talent in his trade with the liveliest interest in the project itself'.[106] Chapman's dream was not realised this time, but his ambition to become the proprietor and editor of a radical periodical remained strong, and eventually he succeeded with the *Westminster Review*, though Emerson's fears about the finances of such a journal were unfortunately proved prescient.

The lectures began on 6 June. Emerson himself thought they met with only moderate success, though Clough enjoyed them. Cobwebs and moonshine was Carlyle's verdict, while Jane Carlyle found her attention wandering away from the vague beauty of the rhetoric towards the audience at the lecture on 13 June. While Emerson was talking about 'Poetry and Eloquence', the Duchess of Sutherland sat in a prominent position with her arms all but bare, wearing a gown on which white lace 'wandered' over grey silk and a cloak and bonnet which defied even Jane's powers of description.[107] Emerson soon received an invitation to lunch with the Duchess at Stafford House, 'the best house in the kingdom, the Queen's not excepted', as he told friends.[108]

He did not enjoy lecturing, nor did he do well financially. His friends, no doubt Chapman chief among them, had urged him to undertake the course in the hope of earning about £200, but in fact he was paid £80.[109] He was not a lively speaker, and he read from a script, but his name had become so well known by now that he was asked to give an extra three lectures priced at a shilling each to attract a wider audience than his 'aristocratic Lecturing' at Portman Square had done. He agreed to give three of his old lectures, on Napoleon, Domestic Life, and Shakespeare, in nearby Exeter Hall. Emerson wrote apprehensively to his wife on 23 June:

> Tonight I am to cry aloud in the Cave of the Winds at Exeter Hall. Ah could you see the advertising Vans that go up & down the Strand announcing to all millions in huge red letters that RWE is to speak, you would pity me & believe that we must pay the full price of all we get.[110]

After all the successful socialising and the not quite so successful lecturing, Emerson was preparing to return to America. Chapman threw a farewell party for him on 1 July. A visit to Eton and Windsor, another to Cambridge, and a three-day trip to Stonehenge with Carlyle followed, then Emerson made his way back to Manchester and Liverpool and his ship. Chapman made all the travel arrangements for him, including a stopover in Coventry, where Charles Bray was to be his host and show him nearby Stratford-on-Avon. Mary Ann Evans was with her friends when Emerson arrived; according to Bray's wife Cara, he was 'much struck' with her.[111] Farewells were said to Ireland and other Manchester friends. Clough saw Emerson to his ship, and he sailed on 15 July, pleased with the warm reception he had enjoyed in Britain.

Clough looked back on Emerson's visit, summing it up for his friend Tom Arnold the following day. At Oxford, Clough wrote, 'everyone liked him, and as the orthodox mostly had never heard of him, they did not suspect him' (of heresy). In the next breath Clough tells Arnold that he has given up his tutorship at Oriel and is planning to 'send the Fellowship after it' in October.[112] The presence of Emerson with his simple, unobtrusive manner and his cool 'paganism' may have been the catalyst which took the long-wavering Clough past this point of no return in terms of his Oxford career. In October he resigned, taking up the post of Principal of University Hall in London soon after that.

Chapman had served Emerson well during his London visit, and they ought both to have benefited from Emerson's enhanced reputation in Britain when Chapman issued reprints of his essays and poems and published his next new work in London. This did not happen, however, because of Chapman's continuing misfortunes with copyright. In February 1848, while Emerson was in England, he complained that he had not received a penny for the English editions of *Essays* and *Poems*. Chapman, he knew, was not to blame; two pirated editions of the essays had been issued in London, by William Tegg & Co. and William S. Orr & Co., Chapman's near neighbour at 147 Strand.[113] Poor Chapman was forced to reduce his price to four shillings in March. Much the same thing happened with *Poems*, reduced to four shillings in January 1850, and *Representative Men*, Emerson's next book, which was based on the lectures on Napoleon, Shakespeare, and others, and which Chapman published at the end of 1849.[114]

Emerson's much increased fame should have guaranteed a healthy sale for the new work. Unfortunately, other publishers thought so too, and in 1850 Bohn and Routledge took advantage of the confusion which followed a ruling the previous year withdrawing all rights to copyright; each brought out cheap copies, Bohn in his shilling series. In July 1852 Susanna Chapman, writing to George Combe to defend her husband from accusations of bad management, described his skirmishes with the copyright law:

> He has been very unfortunate; he published the life of Channing and under the existing law procured a copyright for it in this country. When the edition was about half sold the decision was given against the legality of the copyright, and the book was republished for 7/- and an abridgement for five. He was obliged to reduce the price to 10/6; the same thing happened with Emerson's Representative Men, from which he might have been expected to reap some profit to compensate for the loss on the second series of Emerson's Essays and the Poems.[115]

As Susanna's explanation suggests, according to some interpretations of copyright law Routledge and Bohn were not technically committing piracy when they reproduced their cheap editions of Emerson's works. The two most prestigious publishers in England, John Murray and Thomas Longman, launched an action against these same reprinters in 1850 for undercutting their copyrighted editions of works by Washington Irving and Herman Melville. The case lasted four years, cost a fortune, and ended in a victory for the purveyors of cheap reprints. The net result for Chapman, who could not afford to take Routledge and Bohn to court, was also a financial loss, though a less severe one than if he had been foolhardy enough to try legal action.[116]

Back in America, Emerson continued to write friendly letters to his London publisher, offering *Representative Men* on the half-profits system in May 1849 and telling Chapman that he had changed his American publishers to Phillips & Sampson, who would send copy to Chapman for printing towards the end of the year.[117] Never astute in his dealings with publishers, he was himself at least partly responsible for getting Chapman into a mess over *Representative Men*. On 28 August 1849 he had to confess that, 'wholly unauthorised by me', his new American publisher had promised Bohn that he could co-publish the work. Because of the recent English legal decision against copyright held by Americans, there was nothing he or Chapman could do to prevent Bohn. A further complication was added by Chapman's new colleague Thomas Delf, an American agent who had joined the Putnam half of the former American firm of Wiley & Putnam, or '*Wily and Put-on-him*', as Carlyle had called them when frustrated over his own dealings with them in 1846. Delf split from Chapman at the end of June 1849, setting up his own office in Cheapside and offering Emerson full profits if *he* were permitted to publish *Representative Men* in England.[118]

Delf's associate, George Putnam, was an ambitious young man who had dissolved his partnership with Wiley in March 1848 and started his own London office in Paternoster Row. He was keen to expand his interests in England, and joined with Delf to do so. Since Chapman already had transatlantic connections with Emerson and the Boston Unitarians, it made sense for him and Putnam to enter into a mutually agreeable arrangement. In July 1848 Chapman therefore became Putnam's official London agent.[119] On 15 December he took out a full-page advertisement in the *Publishers' Circular* (having scarcely advertised at all between 1845 and 1848), announcing the new connection and a vastly increased publishing list, largely made up of American books for which he was the London agent. He took advantage of the unwonted advertising opportunity to make mention of his own English publications as well:

MR JOHN CHAPMAN begs to announce that he has made an arrange-ment with MR G. P. PUTNAM, (of the late firm of WILEY and PUTNAM, American Booksellers), to continue the business of supplying American Publications of every description, both for the trade in quantities, and for special orders, whereby he has secured the valuable co-operation of MR PUTNAM, who, in consequence of his residence in New York, his long-established business, and extensive experience, possesses every facility for selecting and sending full supplies by each steamer of all new and desirable books published in every part of the United States, immediately after publication.

The above arrangement, in addition to MR CHAPMAN's already exten-sively established connection in various parts of America, places him in the most advantageous position to execute orders in every depart-ment of American Literature with the greatest promptitude, and on the most favourable terms.

Libraries and Public Institutions in England, or on the Continent, requiring American Works, carefully supplied; and if desirable, when books are ordered in quantities, shipments can be made direct from the United States to their appointed destination.

American Periodicals punctually furnished to subscribers, and those not generally imported, *as well as all works not in stock*, may be obtained in about five or six weeks after the date of the order.

Catalogues and Lists of American Books, *as well as of Mr Chapman's English Publications*, will be sent *gratis* on application. Persons ordering from them, direct or through other Booksellers, will please to state if such works shall be obtained from America should they not be in stock.

Parcels and Cases are made up and forwarded by each Steamer and regular sailing Packet to New York, Boston, and Philadelphia, in which works for Review may be inclosed.

MR CHAPMAN invites the attention of the Literary Public to the extensive Stock in his American Department, which is conveniently displayed for inspection in a spacious room, affording the desirable facility of leisurely examining such books as visitors may wish to see before giving their orders.

LONDON, 142, STRAND.

December 10, 1848.[120]

This lengthy passage is perhaps especially notable for two things: Chapman's serious determination to play a significant role in publishing connections between Britain and America, and an unfortunate verbosity of style.

Chapman's list was thus boosted; from an average of about twenty books a year, he now claimed over ninety in 1848 and 140 in 1849, though of course for most of these he was merely the distributor, not the publisher. In any case, the partnership with Putnam proved shortlived. On 1 September 1849, Thomas Delf advertised American books in the *Publishers' Circular*, giving his address as 49 Bow Lane, Cheapside and adding in brackets 'Putnam's American Agency, removed from 142 Strand'.[121] Delf seems to have indulged in some sharp practice over this, or at least Chapman thought so, for Emerson wrote to the latter on 10 October expressing his regret that Delf had 'given you any ground to distrust his honesty', and assuring Chapman that he would personally send him the manuscript copy of *Representative Men* before printing began in America, to prevent Delf's rushing it out. Chapman did manage to publish the book first, but could not stop other publishers from reissuing their cheaper editions.[122]

The book made only a little money for author and publisher; Emerson received £10 from Chapman in November 1850. In October 1851 he offered Chapman a memoir of Margaret Fuller, to be compiled by W. H. Channing, J. F. Clarke, and himself. Chapman seems to have refused, perhaps because of his precarious financial situation, perhaps because his energies were just then being invested in his takeover of the *Westminster Review*. Relations continued to be cordial, however. Chapman sent Emerson copies of the first two numbers of the *Review* under his ownership and his and Marian Evans's joint editorship – those for January and April 1852 – and received Emerson's thanks and wishes for the *Westminster*'s 'best success'.[123] Chapman published no more of Emerson's works; it was Routledge who issued *English Traits* in 1856. Nevertheless, Emerson continued to use Chapman as a supplier of books, and he took an interest in his fortunes, expressing himself 'grieved' to hear of Chapman's near-bankruptcy in August 1854, and advising one of his correspondents, an American visiting London, to call on Chapman, 'for he knows all the details you will wish to possess of the city'.[124]

The relationship between Emerson and Chapman was not in the end as fruitful for either of them as it might have been, though they were not to blame for this. A veritable battle of the publishers erupted in 1849, with John Wiley taking out large advertisements for American books in the

Publishers' Circular in February in direct competition with his erstwhile partner Putnam and *his* new partner Chapman.[125] The free-for-all that now obtained in the field of British reissuing of American books matched the long-standing scandal of American piracy of British books. In 1851 new editions of works by Washington Irving and Nathaniel Hawthorne were printed by Bohn and Routledge in their cheap series; in 1852 Sampson & Low started an American series, and Delf, now partnering Trübner, was still offering American books for sale.[126]

Carlyle and Emerson continued to send books and manuscripts to one another via Chapman, who dispatched regular parcels across the Atlantic as a matter of business and was glad to include theirs. He was rewarded, if that is the right word, by Carlyle's accepting with alacrity his offer to print off copies of Carlyle's vituperative *Latter-Day Pamphlets* as they came out monthly during 1850 – Chapman's copies being sent to an American publisher for distribution in the United States. As the English publisher of the *Pamphlets* was Chapman & Hall, Carlyle found himself explaining cheerfully to his mother on 29 March how 'a certain *second* Chapman' had called the other morning with an offer of £4.10.0 'for a copy of each No "*one steamer* before it was published". I instantly said, "Done!"'[127]

The *Pamphlets*, widely read and discussed in both Britain and America, turned Carlyle's celebrity into notoriety in many quarters, so intemperate were they on subjects such as the prison system and slavery. Carlyle's friends and admirers could agree heartily with him as he lambasted Parliament for its uselessness and exposed hypocrisies in the world of politics and finance. But few enjoyed his support of slavery or his exhortation to bring back the whip in prisons at home. In the first pamphlet, 'The Present Time', he indulged in some comic exaggeration at the expense of American democracy. What use are these people sitting around 'idly *caucasing* and ballot-boxing'? What has America achieved, after all, except the production of 'Eighteen Million of the greatest *bores* ever seen in this world before?'[128] Chapman was the means by which this pamphlet reached Americans, and he was also the conduit through which a rapid rebuttal was sent from Elizur Wright, an anti-slavery campaigner in Boston. In September 1850 Jane Carlyle reported to her husband, who was away from home, that something had come for Carlyle via Emerson, namely a pamphlet entitled *Perforations in the "Latter-Day Pamphlets", By One of the "Eighteen Millions of Bores"*. Should she send it on to Carlyle, she asked, or put it on the fire?[129]

Chapman had been one of Emerson's earliest admirers in England; his first publication in 1844, his own booklet *Human Nature*, quotes and praises Emerson liberally. In 1854 he was described by one of his *Westminster* reviewers, James Hannay, as 'the most spiritualistic-romantic of publishers', 'an Inspired Bagman; or Emersonian Policeman in plain clothes'.[130] By that time, Chapman was really more freethinking than Emersonian, though he always retained some of the sentiment of religious belief. Publishing free-thinking books had become his trademark. If Strauss, Newman, and Emerson were the most important, or striking, writers to be published by him in his first five years in the profession, the next was to be another man of troubled faith, one of Emerson's greatest English admirers, J. A. Froude. Chapman published his novel, *The Nemesis of Faith*, in 1849 to a storm of protest.

2

Publishing Sensation: The Nemesis of Faith *(1849)*

Like Frank Newman, J. A. Froude, known as Anthony, was the brilliant and troubled younger brother of an even more brilliant scholar, Richard Hurrell Froude, his senior by nearly fifteen years and a close friend and follower of John Henry Newman at Oxford.[1] Hurrell wrote some of the *Tracts for the Times*, published by Oxford dons and fellows during the 1830s and culminating in Newman's *Tract* XC (1841), which achieved notoriety by claiming that the similarities between Anglican and Roman Catholic doctrine are greater than the differences. Tractarianism was a response to a number of intellectual currents which seemed to the set of pious young Oxford scholars surrounding Newman at Oriel College – among them John Keble and Edward Pusey, who stopped short of following him into Catholicism in 1845, remaining High Anglican instead – to threaten the true belief and doctrine. These currents included evangelicalism and various kinds of Nonconformism which had flourished since taking hold, particularly in northern and Midland manufacturing districts, in the period of industrialisation in the late eighteenth century. More recently, advances in geological and evolutionary science and German historical studies of the Bible, particularly the work of Strauss, had undermined literal belief in scripture and led to intense questioning of doctrinal issues.

During the 1830s and 1840s there was also Arnoldianism, an intellectual position of great influence at Oxford. Dr Thomas Arnold, headmaster of Rugby School until his sudden death in 1842, had been important not only as a reformer of the cruel and chaotic public school system, but also as a religious thinker who embraced a tolerant Anglicanism, the idea of a 'Broad Church' advocated by Coleridge in his late work, *On the Constitution of Church and State* (1830). Arnold was attracted by Coleridge's coinage of the term 'clerisy' to describe a body of scholars, including clergymen and teachers, who were to contribute to the intellectual, cultural, and religious life of the nation, accepting Anglicanism because of its historical roots, its embeddedness in English national life, and its disinclination to extremes of doctrine or ritual, but recognising the need for gradual reform from within.[2] Arnold sent a generation of Arnoldians, a set of clever Rugby boys, to Oxford, including his star pupil Clough and his own sons, Matthew and Tom Arnold, who were all students at the same time as Anthony Froude.

The Tractarians moved, in reaction against these opposing forces, on to the high ground of tradition and ritual in order to escape the shifting sands; others, Clough and the younger Froude among them, followed Carlyle and Emerson to the dry land of a de-ritualised religion-without-a-church, though Clough is said to have complained to Emerson when seeing him off at Liverpool docks in July 1848 that Carlyle had merely led all the young men out into the desert and left them there.[3] The protagonist of Froude's *Nemesis of Faith*, the young clergyman Markham Sutherland, says much the same thing when grappling with doctrinal problems: 'Carlyle! Carlyle only raises questions he cannot answer, and seems best contented if he can make the rest of us as discontented as himself.'[4] Nevertheless, Carlyle is pitted favourably against Newman in Froude's novel; these are the two most influential thinkers of the time, the one calling strongly with a voice 'like the sound of "ten thousand trumpets"', as Froude later wrote in his biography of Carlyle, the other – in his fictional incarnation in the novel, Frederick Mornington – possessing a voice described as 'preternaturally sweet' and a 'gentleness and fascination' that acts on Sutherland 'like a magnetic stream'.[5] Though Sutherland is crushed between the two forces, his creator survived to take the Carlylean side of the question, becoming one of the most devoted disciples of the Sage of Chelsea and his author-ised biographer.

Froude had come under Newman's mesmeric influence at Oxford, but had steered away, partly, as he revealed in an autobiographical fragment written late in life, in rebellion against his hated and admired brother

Hurrell, who, if he had lived, would have converted to Rome with Newman.
'The Pope would have found him an unmanageable subject', Froude adds
sharply.[6] Hurrell died in 1836, aged thirty-three, just as his eighteen-year-
old brother was about to join him at Oriel. Anthony's novel, written in
1847–8 and published by Chapman in February 1849 as he was on the
brink of resigning his fellowship at Exeter College, is a confused and
confusing, but compellingly raw account of the travails of a young man
unable to continue preaching in the Church of England. Markham
Sutherland comes to this realisation somewhat later in his career than his
author, who left Oxford immediately after publication without taking full
orders. Froude compounds his protagonist's troubles (and his own, as the
author) by adding a would-be adulterous relationship borrowed from
Goethe's novel *Elective Affinities* (*Die Wahlverwandtschaften*, 1809); in most
other respects the novel is plainly autobiographical.

As in Frank Newman's case, Froude and his work are representative of
the woes of a generation, while exhibiting features peculiar to himself and
his extraordinary family history. Since no correspondence between Froude
and Chapman survives from this time, we do not know details of the
arrangements for publication. Chapman was the obvious publisher to
approach. Froude had read Mary Ann Evans's anonymous translation of
Strauss's *Life of Jesus*, and no doubt chose to approach Chapman on the
strength of that and his other freethinking publications. Chapman, for his
part, though not known as a publisher of novels, must have recognised the
topical nature of this one and appreciated, as sympathetic readers and
reviewers like Mary Ann Evans also did, the thinly veiled cry of distress
from a tormented soul. The novel catches the intellectual atmosphere of
the mid-century at a particularly sensitive moment, at the same time landing
some blows, half-reluctantly, against religious orthodoxy. Though a product
of the hothouse environment of Oxford, its interest extends – as the influence of the Oxford Movement and Arnoldianism also did – far beyond
the dreaming spires into the intellectual, cultural, and spiritual life of
thinking men and women in London and the provinces, in Great Britain
as a whole, and in the United States too. The excited response to *The
Nemesis of Faith* made it one of the publishing sensations of the century.

Froude was born in Devon in April 1818, the eighth and last child of
a forbidding clergyman who became Archdeacon of Totnes in 1820 and a
mother who died two months before his third birthday. Family life was a

series of horrors for Anthony; his father 'never spoke even in private of feeling or sentiment, and never showed any in word or action', not once mentioning his late wife and keeping no portrait of her, as the son recalled. 'Whipping', he added, 'was always resorted to as the prompt consequence of naughtiness.'[7] The eldest son, Hurrell, was considered a genius by all the family, but he had a sinister, even sadistic side. Anthony remembered being turned upside down as a very small child by his brother, who proceeded to stir the bottom of the garden stream 'with my head'. Their mother expressed her anxiety about Hurrell in a letter written shortly before her death, when he was seventeen. She wrote of his having a 'peculiar' temper, being charming and pleasant but finding his amusement in 'teasing and vexing others', particularly his baby brother. He was, she thought, 'almost entirely incorrigible'.[8]

Bullied, beaten, and emotionally deprived at home, Anthony was sent at eleven – 'two years below the proper age and small and feeble for my own' – to Westminster School, where he was bullied, beaten, and burnt by the older boys, half starved and frozen in the spartan conditions, and generally made to endure treatment 'as barbarous as that of the negroes in Virginia'.[9] The latter phrase comes from Froude's first attempt at fiction, a story called 'The Spirit's Trials' published in a small volume entitled *Shadows of the Clouds*. This work appeared in 1847 under the pseudonym 'Zeta' with a publishing house, John Ollivier of Pall Mall, which was known chiefly for printing pamphlets and parliamentary speeches. Edward Fowler, the 'spirit' of the title, suffers everything his author did. Both Froude and his fictional counterpart become physical and emotional wrecks at school. Each is sent home in disgrace after three years during which he is rendered incapable, through fear, of learning anything. At home Froude was beaten by his father, with Hurrell, on vacation from Oxford, 'standing by and approving'.[10] Relief came in 1836 with the death of Hurrell from consumption – two sisters and another brother also succumbed to the disease at this time – and Anthony's escape from his father's sullenness and sarcasm when he went up to Oriel College later that year.

Newman was kind to Froude for Hurrell's sake, and Froude came under the influence of his personality along with the rest. His vengeful feelings towards Hurrell, however, made him less susceptible to the lure of Tractarianism than some of his fellow students; moreover, as he remembered, 'another influence of a wholly novel kind' began to pull him in the opposite direction. In 1842 he read Carlyle's books, which 'passed across' his 'perplexities' like a 'flash of lightning', offering relief from doctrinal controversies because they discarded doctrine and described a world full of wonders created by God but not requiring to be understood in terms of any church. Less scrupulous than Clough, whom he now befriended, and still half clinging to the old belief, Froude nervously took the first step towards becoming a clergyman by being ordained deacon in 1845, a move which he immediately regretted. He had already accepted a fellowship at Exeter College, and for the next few years he struggled on, reading 'commentators English and German, orthodox and unorthodox', and arriving only at uncertainty.[11]

Newman's admission to the Roman Catholic church in October 1845 shook Froude. Could Newman be right when he suggested that there were only two possible positions, Catholicism or unbelief? How could Froude take the next step towards becoming a clergyman? He and Clough talked of emigrating to New Zealand to try farming, as their friend Tom Arnold did (unsuccessfully) in November 1847. Though to some extent cocooned in the privileged world of Oxford, they also took note of social and political inequalities, partly through reading Carlyle's analyses of mass poverty and parliamentary donothingism in *Past and Present* (1843) and other works. Chartism and the bids for freedom in European cities in 1848 made their impression too, as did Emerson's presence in Oxford that spring. All these factors contributed to the inevitable loosening of Oxford's grip on Froude, as well as on Clough. The latter went off to Paris with Emerson in May 1848, and Froude spent his long vacation in Ireland, where he wrote most of *The Nemesis of Faith.* When he returned to Oxford in the autumn he had made up his mind that 'Oxford was no longer the place for me', though it was a few more months before he took the double plunge of publishing his novel and resigning his fellowship.[12]

Froude's resolve may have been strengthened by Clough's actions at this time. He, too, had spent the summer writing. His poem, *The Bothie of Toper-na-Fuosich: A Long-Vacation Pastoral,* was published early in November 1848 by the Oxford publisher Francis Macpherson and by Chapman & Hall in London. Written in rolling hexameters, this narrative of an Oxford reading party in the Scottish Highlands, though keeping off the controversial subject of religious doubt, lays claim to topicality by having its protagonist, a student named Philip, talk Chartism and go off to New Zealand with his bride, the daughter of the farmer who inhabits the bothie of the title, under whom Philip first studies 'the handling of hoe and of hatchet'. There is much talk in the poem of Philip's boldness in turning his back on Oxford and the life of an English gentleman, though Clough makes his alter ego prudently return to Oxford to take his degree – 'Got a first, 'tis said' – and notes that he has 'five hundred pounds in pocket' when he subsequently leaves these shores.[13]

It is a cautious act of rebellion, partly based on Tom Arnold's departure for New Zealand exactly a year previously; Tom also had money in his pocket – though no Highland lass on his arm – and was heading for land which his father had bought as an investment.[14] For the oversensitive, guilt-ridden Arnoldian scholar who wrote it, however, the poem represented a tremendous release of pent-up feelings and anxieties. The hexameters, always hinting at movement and irony and fun, allow him to describe the peasant heroine Elspie in frankly sensuous terms. Clough gazes with his hero:

> How could he help but love her? nor lacked there perhaps the
>   attraction
> That, in a blue cotton print tucked up over striped linsey-wolsey,
> Barefoot, barelegged, he beheld her, with arms bare up to the
>   elbows,
> Bending with fork in her hand in a garden uprooting potatoes.[15]

Thackeray, for one, recognised the expression of a young man's longing for a love affair, writing to Clough in friendly terms on 26 November after receiving a complimentary copy:

My dear Mr Clough
    I have been reading the Bothy all morning and am charmed with it. I have never been there but I think it must be like Scotland – Scotland hexametrically laid out that is . . . and it seems to me to give one the proper Idyllic feeling wh[ich] is ½ sensual & ½ spiritual I take it – serene beauty awakening pleasant meditation . . . I can imagine to myself the Goddess of bathing in a sort of shimmer under the water . . . I have been going over some of the same ground (of youth) in this present number of Pendennis, wh[ich] I fear will be considered rather warm by the puritans: but I think you'll understand it

– that is if you care for such trivialities, or take the trouble to look under the stream of the story.

I must tell you that I was very much pleased indeed by your sending me the book, and don't mind owning that I took a great liking to you. When you come to London I hope you will come and see me.[16]

One wonders what Clough made of this comparison between *Pendennis* and his poem. Thackeray is referring to the opening chapters of his novel, in which the seventeen-year-old Pen falls in love with an actress twelve years his senior, announcing his intention of marrying her, much to the horror of his family. It is, in truth, a knowing, metropolitan version of young love, not much like the wholesome rural idyll of Clough's Philip and Elspie, though sexual awakening is at the heart of both episodes.

By this time Clough had left Oxford for London. He had resigned his Fellowship, writing to the Provost of Oriel, Edward Hawkins, on 8 October, to declare that he could have 'nothing whatever to do with a subscription to the xxxix articles – and deeply repent of having ever submitted to one'.[17] He tried for a chair in English at University College London, but came second to Alexander Scott. However, Henry Crabb Robinson and other University College grandees now took an interest in him; they invited him to apply for the post of Principal of University Hall on Frank Newman's relinquishing it towards the end of the year. Characteristically for the poet who would call himself 'Dipsychus' (double-souled) in the poem of that title in 1849, Clough confessed to Tom Arnold on 27 November that he could not make up his mind whether to take the post if offered it. On 17 January 1849 Frank Newman told James Martineau that Clough was in London waiting to hear if the appointment would be approved.[18] The delay in confirming it was due to the doubts of several members of the committee who wanted an 'out-and-out' Unitarian, as Crabb Robinson, a warm supporter of Clough, noted.[19] Clough attempted to clarify his position in a letter to one committee member explaining that he was not against prayers being said at University Hall; he just did not want to superintend them himself. On questions of doctrine he had, he said, not made up his own mind, except for his rejection of the Thirty-Nine Articles; he therefore felt 'shy of meddling' with the beliefs of his students.[20] With this explanation he reluctantly accepted the post thus reluctantly offered to him.

*

Meanwhile, Froude had realised that he could not become a clergyman. He too would have to resign. He would also have to find a job, as his father was sure to stop supporting him financially. Froude asked a friend in the autumn of 1848 to look out for a position of agent in 'some established mercantile house, either in a foreign port, or in one of our own colonies'.[21] Nothing came of this plan, but another colonial appointment seemed likely at the end of the year. Froude reported to his friend William Long on 29 December that his name had gone forward for a schoolmaster's job in Hobart Town, Van Diemen's Land, later known as Tasmania. His father, seeing that 'there is nothing left for me to do in England', was encouraging this idea.[22]

The New Year was spent at the family home in Devon. From there Froude wrote miserably to Clough on 31 December:

> I must do ten days more duty here at least. It is *duty* & I haven't learnt to find it pleasant. I can't say what I like & I hear what I don't like . . . and I get asked to help in Church & have to say I can't, which in the home idea means only an ungracious I *won't*. On the whole I shall be very glad if I do get this School affair . . . It is not the very delightfullest of employments, but one would be doing something in one's generation & besides as the poor Frenchman said il faut vivre, a process if I give up my Fellowship I may not find easy as I shall incur infinite anger in the quarters here.
>
> So if you will say to Newman what you can in conscience you will do me much service. From what Mr Atkinson wrote to me I conclude the thing will *soon be settled*.[23]

Henry Atkinson was Secretary of University College, the institution responsible for recommending appointment to the Hobart post. Frank Newman was on the committee, as was Henry Crabb Robinson. Both men set about reading Froude's story 'The Spirit's Trials' to find out what kind of man he was. Newman had heard that the work was 'of *morally sceptical* tendency' and that a '*liberal* clergyman' had written the word 'Poison' on its cover. 'I got it', he told James Martineau on 17 January 1849, '& was *delighted* with it; & felt that I quite loved the writer, both for his own sake, & for the illiberality and misrepresentation he endured.' He introduced himself to Froude (probably at Chapman's house), and invited him to stay.[24] Robinson was also won over by reading 'The Spirit's Trials' in preparation for the meeting of University College Council on 3 February to decide on the Hobart recommendation. The committee was split on the issue of whether the story – in which Edward Fowler has doubts about immortality and questions the Anglican belief in eternal punishment for those who do not believe in Christianity – tended to undermine religion. Newman and Robinson spoke up for Froude, and his appointment was recommended.[25]

Froude wrote to another friend, Charles Kingsley, on New Year's Day, telling him about his candidacy for the Hobart post and confiding his intention of resigning his fellowship. 'I hate the Articles', he wrote bluntly, following this with news of the forthcoming *Nemesis*:

I have a book advertised – you may have seen it. It is too utterly subjective to please you. I can't help it. If the creatures breed, they must come to the birth. There is something in the thing, I know, for I cut a hole in my heart and wrote with the blood.[26]

On 29 January Froude, back in Oxford, told Clough, 'My printing proceeds.' Chapman showed off his new author at one of his evening parties on 14 February; Crabb Robinson was invited and regretted that he could not attend and get to know this young man who had aroused his curiosity and sympathy.[27] On Sunday 25 February Froude reported to Clough that his book was now out. 'If the Rector will permit me, tomorrow I cease to be a Fellow of the College', he added. 'But there is a doubt if he will permit it – and will not try rather to send me out in true heretic style.'[28]

Things moved rapidly after that. On Tuesday 27 February William Sewell, Sub-Rector of Exeter College, burnt a copy of the novel in front of the undergraduates. A student called Arthur Blomfield owned the copy in question, as he recalled in a letter to the *Daily News* in 1892:

The burnt book was mine. I had just bought *The Nemesis of Faith* . . . when on Tuesday morning, 27 Feb. 1849, I, an undergraduate of Exeter College, attended a lecture in hall. The Rev. William Sewell . . . was lecturer. He declaimed loudly against 'Froude's *Nemesis of Faith*'. Hearing, on my own confession, that I possessed it, he requested me to bring 'that book' to him . . . No sooner had I complied with his request (Sewell was my college tutor) than he snatched the book from my hands and thrust it into the blazing fire of the college hall . . . I see him now, with hall poker in hand, in delightful indignation, poking at this, to him, obnoxious book. In a few hours this 'burning of the book' was known all over Oxford.[29]

Froude resigned the same day. The following day he told Clough he was coming to London. 'Oxford grows rapidly too hot for me. I have *resigned*. I was *preached* against Sunday in Chapel, denounced in Hall, and yesterday *burnt* publicly (by Sewell) before two Lectures.'[30] He foresaw that the Hobart school would take fright, which it duly did. Froude fled to the country, taking up an invitation to join Kingsley and his wife in Devon until the controversy died down and his future was decided. The talk in Oxford was all of the burning of the book. For its part University College came under criticism in the newspapers for recommending the 'infidel' author for a teaching post. The College Council met on 17 March and decided not to interfere, but to leave Froude to correspond directly with the agents for the Hobart school.[31]

When Robinson called on Chapman on 13 March, the chief topic of conversation was Froude, whom Chapman described as 'needy'.[32] Froude had to resign from the Hobart post to avoid having the offer rescinded, whereupon Frank Newman wrote to Robinson on 4 April, anxious that the young man, being 'refused all aid from his natural relations', was now nearly destitute.[33] Carlyle was told by Clough that Froude had only £100 a year to live on, though his father was extremely wealthy. Everyone was talking about the book and its author, and taking sides, though Matthew Arnold, secure in his job as private secretary to the Marquis of Lansdowne and now relatively untroubled by doctrinal doubts, wrote calmly to his mother that while he thought the book 'unpleasant', he had nothing but contempt for 'all this shrieking and cursing' at Froude.[34]

The work which caused the burning and the shrieking and the cursing was a modest book of 227 pages bound in dark brown leather with a title-page which read 'The Nemesis of Faith. By J. A. Froude, MA, Fellow of Exeter College, Oxford'. It was printed by George Woodfall & Son, of Angel Court, Skinner Street, and published by 'John Chapman of 142 Strand', priced six shillings. It is a puzzling book in several ways. What, asked readers at the time, does the title mean? Does 'faith' take revenge on Markham Sutherland, or is faith itself the recipient of a 'nemesis'? Froude seems to have discussed the title with friends; he saw that it was problematic and told Chapman so. The latter, perhaps relishing the ambiguity as a possible attraction, favoured it, according to a letter from Froude to Clough on 21 January 1849:

> You may have seen me advertised. I doubt my title. I told Chapman opinions were divided about it. It was thought absolutely good and absolutely beastly. He took the first view, and without another word put it in the *Spectator*. So now I must hold on, I suppose.[35]

The title is at least appropriate in that, in pulling two ways, it reflects the ambiguity of the novel's 'tendency', which in turn represents accurately enough the turmoil Froude himself had experienced in the years leading up to its writing. Like Froude, Sutherland reads Strauss and doubts the authority of the Bible. In signing the Thirty-Nine Articles he is subscribing to certain beliefs he cannot truthfully hold. Article VI requires him to avow the canonicity of the Old Testament; how can he do so since German historical criticism and geological studies have shown the mythological nature of so many of its elements? How could one square the story of the creation or the flood with the gradualist theory of Lyell's *Principles of Geology*, which explained the state of the earth's crust in terms of progressive erosion over millions of years? What was one to make of the angry, vengeful God of so many Old Testament stories? As for Article XVIII, which stated that only those believing in 'the Name of Jesus Christ' will be saved, was one really to subscribe to such a cruel, arbitrary law with its disregard for all those good men and women who were born in pagan times or under other belief systems? Sutherland expresses his disillusionment with the same irony and vehemence which characterised his author:

> What, gentlemen, do you suppose that I am to make friends with Socrates and Phocion, and believe that human nature is full of the devil, and that only baptism can give a chance of a holy life? That I will hand Plato into destruction; that Sophocles, and Phidias, and Pindar, and Germanicus, and Tacitus, and Aurelius, and Trajan were

61

no better than poor unenlightened Pagans, and that, where you not only permit me to make acquaintance with them, but compel me to it as a condition, forsooth, under which I may become a minister of the Christian faith![36]

This outcry occurs in the middle section of the novel, entitled 'Confessions of a Sceptic' in imitation of Goethe's interpolation in *Wilhelm Meister's Apprenticeship* (*Wilhelm Meisters Lehrjahre*) of 'Confessions of a Beautiful Soul' and Carlyle's Goethe-inspired 'thoughts' of Diogenes Teufelsdröckh in *Sartor Resartus*.[37] Froude follows in part the loose structure of Goethe's novel and Carlyle's satirical extravaganza. The first section of *Nemesis* is composed of Sutherland's increasingly desperate letters to a friend, Arthur, about his shifting beliefs and stumbling career. The letters give way after his abandonment of the Church to aphorism and stray fragments of his thoughts, lightly annotated by his friend. This is where the confessions of a sceptic appear, rehearsing Froude's experience of Tractarianism, which he accuses, through Markham, of undermining his belief until it seemed that there were only two options, Catholicism (whether Roman or High Anglican) or atheism.

But Froude does not stop there. He told a friend in 1851 that 'we Froudes have a way of our own of laying hold of the burnt end of the stick, and making the worst rather than the best of everything'. He had used the same phrase to describe Edward Fowler in 'The Spirit's Trials', and it is equally true of his new alter ego, Sutherland.[38] Froude lets him take his sceptical thoughts a step further: when Sutherland's belief in religion crumbles, so also does his belief in sin. This alleged consequence of honest doubt, which was to alienate a number of honest doubters among his readers who did not accept that religious scepticism leads of necessity to immoral or amoral behaviour, prepares the reader for the otherwise unconnected last section of the novel. Here Sutherland, recovering on the shores of Lake Como from the trauma of leaving his ministry, falls in love with a married woman, with whom he is only prevented from committing adultery by the intervention of a tragic accident.

The narrator – Froude himself, we suppose, as Arthur can hardly be believed to be inward with the details of Sutherland's motives and actions, even allowing for the now largely abandoned device of letters and autobiographical scraps – seems to endorse the narrow conservative view that religion alone acts as a guarantee of morality. Remarking that Sutherland knew he ought to remove himself from Helen Leonard's company in the absence of her husband, the narrator declares firmly:

> Markham did not go. He never thought of going now. His conscience was satisfied with what he had done. Unsteady as it was, and without the support which a strongly believed religious faith had once provided for it, he experienced at last what so long he had denied, that to attempt to separate morality from religion is madness; that religion, reduced to a sentiment resting only on internal emotion, is like a dissolving view, which will change its image as the passions shift their focal distances; that, unrealized in some constant eternal form, obeying inclination, not controlling it, it is but a dreamy phantom of painted shadow, and vanishes before temptation as the bright colours fade from off the earth when a storm covers the sun.[39]

So Sutherland becomes a moral nonentity as a result of having abandoned his faith. Yet here the complexity of the subject and the confusion inherent in the title come into play, for it might be truer to say that Markham has been abandoned by a Church inadequate to the demands of modern knowledge and inclined to stick its head in the sand while its clergymen and bishops simply say to waverers like Markham, 'Sign the Articles!' His account to Arthur of his sudden and rapid ordination despite his doubts is full of satirical bitterness:

> I was ordained deacon privately a fortnight before Christmas, and priest yesterday – the Sunday after it. Exquisite satire on my state of mind! – I was complimented publicly on my examination, as having shown myself possessed of so much well-digested information, and on being so prudent in avoiding extremes . . . I was told privately that I only had to persist in such sensible moderation, and that with my talents, in these trying times, I should be an ornament to the Church, and that its highest places might be open to me. But, above all, my admonition concluded – 'Be extreme in nothing . . . Puseyism is the error on one side, German rationalism on the other. Walk steadily in the position which our own admirable Church has so wisely chosen, equidistant between these two. Throw yourself into her spirit, and,

with God's grace, you may rise hereafter to be one of those strong lights which it is her highest honour and her highest witness to have nurtured.' I felt so sick, Arthur.[40]

There is a sense, therefore, in which Markham's faith becomes his ruin, since the particular form it takes, that of an Anglican clergyman, does not sustain him. Froude said as much in the preface he wrote for the second edition, published by Chapman early in July 1849. Defending himself against attacks by critics, he writes bullishly, 'Faith ought to have been Sutherland's salvation – it was his Nemesis – it destroyed him.'[41] Sutherland's scathing remarks, quoted above, can be seen to be Froude's vengeful farewell to the comfortable and admired life he might have led if he too had not been 'destroyed' by Anglicanism, particularly the version of it practised by Hurrell and John Henry Newman before his conversion. Instead of becoming a successful and worldly clergyman certain of advancement, he has chosen to write a book expressing scorn at such a career, the result of which is certain to be ostracism from the conforming community. Froude and Sutherland are both defiant and a little self-pitying.

Regarding what ought to be the separate question of morality, there is further ambivalence on Froude's part. On the one hand, it is shown to be wrong for Markham and Helen to flirt and kiss and move towards adultery. The denouement seems to punish them. While dallying in a boat on the lake, they fail to notice that Helen's child has caught a chill; the child dies as a result, and Helen and Markham part, each to die shortly afterwards of a broken heart and a bad conscience. On the other hand, their mutual attraction is represented, with understanding and a lack of overt criticism from the narrator, as a natural phenomenon obeying a law of nature as compelling as any moral law could be. If orthodox Anglican readers found in this novel a good deal of unpalatable criticism of the alleged falseness and outdatedness of their religious beliefs, they, and others less orthodox, were also faced with a moral determinism likely to cause them at least as much alarm.

It is more or less the same dilemma with which George Eliot was to burden her heroine Maggie Tulliver in The Mill on the Floss (1860). George Eliot, a much more skilful novelist than Froude, had gone through the same phases of belief and doubt as Froude, moving beyond him into agnosticism while retaining a strong ethical sense. Neither Maggie nor Stephen

Guest is married and there is no child to complicate matters further; never-theless, when they float down the river together each has a prior engage-ment or understanding with someone else. While Stephen argues that they cannot and should not deny nature's law, which has brought them together in magnetic attraction despite their attempts to resist, Maggie refuses to consummate the relationship on the grounds that they must obey the moral law which says they should not seek happiness at the cost of others' unhap-piness. No solution being possible, since all four protagonists are aware of the situation and the human damage is therefore irreparable, George Eliot resorts to a tragic resolution in the death of Maggie when the Floss floods.

In *The Nemesis of Faith*, while with one voice Froude insists that Sutherland's loss of firm religious belief leaves him inevitably open to sin, in this case adultery, with another voice he busily undermines the moral-ising tendency. Much is made of Helen's lack of love for her husband; he, in turn, a necessarily shadowy figure, is described as dull and complacent, even culpable because he leaves his wife and daughter for long periods in Sutherland's care so that he can pursue his business elsewhere. In 'Confessions of a Sceptic' Markham states that to force a husband and wife to stay together if they become antipathetic towards one another is as reasonable as 'to lecture oxygen and hydrogen on the duty of continuing in combination when they are decomposed by galvanism'. They may, he continues, 'be *forcibly* held together in juxtaposition by external restraint; but combined they arc not'. Of the progress of the lovers towards consum-mation the narrator, picking up Sutherland's chemical metaphor, says, 'The two metals are melting fast in the warm love fire; they are softening and flowing in and out, vein within vein, a few more degrees of heat, and then . . .'[42] The dots are Froude's. He solves the problem of what will happen next with the catastrophe on the lake.

Whereas Sutherland's religious travails mirror Froude's exactly, this love story is wholly imagined, though not original. Even more closely than George Eliot in *The Mill on the Floss*, Froude borrows plot and leading idea from Goethe's *Elective Affinities*, in which the magnetic attraction of chem-ical compounds is explicitly applied to human relationships. Goethe estab-lishes a double attraction, with husband and wife each being drawn towards a house guest. Tragedy occurs when one mutually attracted pair take to the lake with a child who drowns while in their care. Guilt and death follow, but so subtly and objectively does Goethe describe the various relationships that it is impossible to draw any simple moral or causal conclusion. Human relationships, indeed, are seen to be far more complex and intractable than the chemical analogy deliberately employed to describe them.

Froude had been introduced to Goethe's writings by Carlyle, who translated *Wilhelm Meister's Apprenticeship* in 1824 and sang Goethe's praises throughout *Sartor Resartus*. Late in life Froude recalled his reading at Oxford in the early 1840s, beginning with the discovery of Carlyle's works in 1842: 'Goethe had been Carlyle's teacher. Oxford knew nothing of Goethe, knew nothing of modern languages or modern literature outside England.' On the question of religious doubt, Goethe made his contribution to Froude's thinking: 'How conquer doubt, asks Goethe. By argument never, by action always.'[43] Carlyle, as Froude knew, had taken from Goethe the phrase 'Do the duty that lies nearest thee' and used it as his comforter in times of spiritual doubt.[44]

In 1852 Froude was to translate both *Elective Affinities* and *The Sorrows of Young Werter* (*Die Leiden des jungen Werthers*) for a volume of *Novels and Tales by Goethe*, published by Bohn early in 1854. His name did not appear on the title-page, where R. Dillon Boylan is described as the translator of most of the stories. Bohn's preface announces that the 'gentleman well known in the literary world' who is responsible for *Elective Affinities* does not wish his name to appear, as 'it is possible that exceptions may be taken to some of the statements contained in this production of Goethe'.[45] It is equally possible that Froude's own name on the title-page might have raised eyebrows in those who associated it with the scandalous *Nemesis of Faith*. Certainly his friends advised him to remain anonymous on this occasion. Kingsley wrote to the Oxford philologist Friedrich Max Müller in May 1852 thanking him for

> the excellent advice you gave [Froude] *not* to put his name to his translation of Werther & the Elective Affinities. In the present tone of English bigotry & touchiness (half right, half wrong) it would have hurt both him & them. Now he is regaining credit fast with the Philistines.[46]

In subsequent letters to Max Müller, Kingsley commented further on Froude, who was by this time his brother-in-law. With *The Nemesis of Faith* in mind, he observed that, 'thanks to the artificial stall-feeding at Oxford', Froude 'took the distemper of Werterism about seven years later than he ought, & of course, more violently than most men'. The reference is to Werter's melancholy, unhappy love for an engaged woman, and ultimate suicide, a final act also contemplated, but avoided, by Markham Sutherland. Kingsley continues in robust language, declaring that if a man 'chooses to have the [spiritual] diarrhoea in public, as Froude had', he must 'take the consequences of so offending the public nose'.[47]

Carlyle also used frankly physical language when giving his opinion of the novel to John Forster on 4 April 1849. He thought it would be chiefly of interest to struggling clergymen:

> Froude's book is not, – except for wretched people, strangling in white neckcloths, and Semitic thrums [loose threads], – worth its paper and ink. What on Earth is the use of a wretched mortal's vomiting up all his interior crudities, dubitations, and spiritual agonising belly-aches, into the view of the Public, and howling tragically, 'See!' Let him, in the Devil's name, pass them by the downward or other methods, in his own water-closet, and say nothing whatever![48]

As Carlyle regularly used lavatorial language – mostly, indeed, with reference to his own works – his comments should not be taken as unfriendly towards Froude. Several newspapers, however, were extremely unfriendly. The burning of the book ensured that *The Nemesis of Faith* became an object of curiosity beyond Oxford. Emerson was soon musing in his journal that Thomas Hobbes's *Leviathan* had been burnt at Oxford in 1683, and now Froude's book had met the same fate. 'When, how, & by what authority', he asked, 'was the "Nemesis of Faith" burned?'[49] The *Morning Herald* and *Standard* newspapers carried hostile notices, the latter under the headline 'Exposure of a Blasphemous Book'. Froude was stung into replying, insisting in a letter to the *Standard* published on 9 March that the novel was 'a work of pure fiction', intended to show 'a person of weak mind' cast adrift from his upbringing and beliefs. 'An obvious moral', he wrote, 'is the consequent shipwreck of the entire spiritual nature'.[50] It was the defence he was to use in his preface to the second edition, not an entirely truthful one, and logically rather weak, as Henry Crabb Robinson recognised when he read the letter to the *Standard*. In his opinion it was very poor & rendering it difficult how to defend him on high ground, for his apology is that his tale is one of a weak mind and that he does not express his *own* opinions! I finished the Nemesis – the latter part is a tragic history, an ill constructed romantic story.[51]

Robinson felt sympathetic towards Froude nonetheless, pitying his poverty and the loss of the Hobart job. There were others who were kinder to the book than the *Herald* and the *Standard*. Robinson himself reviewed it mildly in the *Christian Reformer*, as did Frank Newman in the *Prospective Review*. In a notice in the *Examiner* in April, Forster reproduced Carlyle's rhetoric about men strangling in white neckcloths, and blamed Oxford Puseyism for Froude's distress.[52] Radicals rejoiced in the book's tendency to undermine orthodoxy. Delighting in its anti-Church elements, Holyoake announced in his secular paper, the *Reasoner*, in April that his friend the radical publisher James Watson had 'added this remarkable work to his Eclectic Library for special lending'. It could be had for a 'nominal charge' by those able to call in at the newspaper office. For country readers Holyoake produced extracts of 'striking passages' on the Tractarian Movement to show 'what is, strangely enough, passing beneath the tranquil surface of Oxford University'.[53] Robert Chambers wrote privately to Alexander Ireland his opinion that *The Nemesis of Faith* was too mixed in its messages to be of much help to the radical or humanist cause:

> I have been reading the Nemesis of Faith – a terrible outflowing of a creed-harrassed spirit, but likely to do more harm than good, because full of prejudice and error on the other side. The author must be a very strange person.[54]

Much the most sympathetic review of the novel was written by Mary Ann (soon to be known as 'Marian') Evans in her friend Charles Bray's *Coventry Herald and Observer*, where it appeared on 16 March 1849. She empathised absolutely with the spiritual torments of Sutherland, having gone through her own painful passage of losing faith in orthodox religion and being cold-shouldered by her brother Isaac and by her father, whom she was now devotedly nursing through his last illness. She opens her short notice with a piece of heightened rhetoric expressing her sense of the book's value:

On certain red-letter days of our existence, it happens to us to discover among the *spawn* of the press, a book which, as we read, seems to undergo a sort of transfiguration before us. We no longer hold heavily in our hands an octavo of some hundred pages, over which the eye laboriously travels, hardly able to drag along with it the restive mind: but we seem to be in companionship with a spirit, who is transfusing himself into our souls, and is vitalizing them by his superior energy . . . The books which carry this magic in them are the true products of genius, and their influence, whether for good or evil, is to the influence of all the respectable results of mere talent and industry, as the mighty Nile to the dykes which receive and distribute its heaven-fed waters. Such a book is *The Nemesis of Faith*.[55]

While conceding that the work is uneven in quality, she points out the need for it to be taken seriously as a sign of the times:

Its trenchant remarks on some of our English conventions, its striking sketches of the dubious aspect which many chartered respectabilities are beginning to wear under the light of this nineteenth century, its suggestive hints as to the necessity of recasting the currency of our religion and virtue, that it may carry fresh and bright the stamp of the age's highest and best idea – these have a practical bearing, which may well excite the grave, perhaps the alarmed attention of some important classes among us.[56]

Mary Ann had been flattered to receive a copy of the novel, addressed to the translator of Strauss and sent via Chapman. Froude now sent 'a charming note', thanking her for her review, and asking her to reveal her identity. Cara Bray, who reported this to her sister Sara Hennell on 23 March, added, 'Poor girl! I am so pleased she should have this little episode in her dull life, but I suppose she won't continue the correspondence.'[57] On 18 April Mary Ann wrote to Sara herself, acknowledging her loneliness as she awaited her father's approaching death and referring with enthusiasm to both *The Nemesis of Faith* and *Shadows of the Clouds*, saying the first made her feel, with the speaker in Keats's sonnet 'On First Looking into Chapman's Homer', 'like some watcher of the skies/ When a new planet swims into his ken'.[58]

The short notice in the radical *Westminster Review* offers its support to the novel and its protagonist, whom it describes as 'scrupulously conscientious – a man of faith in an age of insincerity' who is disheartened by the inconsistencies he finds in the profession of clergyman. The reviewer shrewdly notes that the story of the burning 'will save Mr Chapman no inconsiderable amount of advertising; and will tend to lend an *éclat* to a remarkable biography'.[59] Sales must indeed have been healthy, for Chapman brought out his second edition in the space of a few months, adorned with the defensive preface and bearing the title-page description of the author meaningfully altered to 'J. A. Froude, MA, late Fellow of Exeter College'. Froude's earlier publisher, John Ollivier, thought it worth exploiting his author's new notoriety by advertising *Shadows of the Clouds* in the *Publishers' Circular* on 1 June no longer as by 'Zeta', but as by 'J. A. Froude, MA, Author of *The Nemesis of Faith*'.[60]

Everyone read the work, from the evangelical Gladstone, who noted it in his diary on 11 April, a day on which he also indicated that he had scourged himself, as was his habit when he suffered from feelings of guilt, to the liberal (and libertine) Richard Monckton Milnes. Milnes was among the few to recognise the influence of Goethe on Froude. He also, along with Robinson, Newman, Clough, and Carlyle, saw the romantic aspect of the story of Froude's rich and forbidding father cutting him off financially, together with the loss of the Hobart job and the Oxford fellowship:

> It is a sort of religious, anti-religious *Wilhelm Meister*, and balances itself between fact and fiction in an uncomfortable manner, though with great ability, and has caused the poor man to lose his Fellowship and a college in Van Diemen's Land, and to fall into utter poverty. We call ourselves a free people, and what slaves of opinion we are after all![61]

Romance, if often of a gloomy kind, certainly seemed to follow Froude. Cara Bray was probably hopeful that her plain-looking friend Mary Ann might hit it off with Froude, with whom she had so much in common. Bray, who liked to collect radicals and outcasts and invite them to stay, hurried to befriend Froude, who visited Coventry, meeting Mary Ann on 7 June, a week after the death of her father. When the Brays took Mary Ann to Geneva for a holiday, Froude was planning to be one of the travelling party, which left London on 11 June. Instead, as Bray remembered in his autobiography, Froude sent a letter by Chapman to say 'that he was going to be married, which we thought a sufficient excuse'.[62]

The marriage, to Charlotte Grenfell, sister of Charles Kingsley's wife, took place in October. Like everything else in Froude's life, it was an event fraught with problems (and the marriage was not to be a happy one). Kingsley and the Grenfells were unenthusiastic about Froude's notoriety and lack of either financial support or career prospects. Though it was generous of Kingsley to offer him refuge when staying in Oxford became impossible, he probably did not envisage that the visit would last two months; nor would he have chosen for his wife's sister to fall in love with Froude. Knowing that his reputation would be tarnished by his association with his young friend, Kingsley wrote, somewhat melodramatically, in reply to an anxious letter from his mother:

> Pray for me that I may keep unspotted . . . Froude is no atheist, no man less so . . . Neither is he an infidel, not even a mere Unitarian, though he has very strong views about our blessed Lord's divinity, while he admires & loves his character & the revelation wh[ich] he believes was made through him . . . The sentiments in Froude's book are *not* his own: they are those of too many men, alas! now. It is a spiritual tragedy, that book, wh[ich] is most fearfully true; & he wrote it to shew what must be the end of a man, who too weak for action, destroyed his own moral sense by daring & morbid speculation. I think he was most mistaken in writing it – that it is too deep in its plot to be generally understood, & so do good, while the doubts wh[ich] it states will act poisonously on the minds of those who are already unhealthy, & I think & hope that he is beginning to see that.[63]

This was an echo of Froude's chosen defence, though Kingsley, having received that New Year's Day letter about Froude cutting a hole in his heart and writing with the blood, can hardly have believed that the sentiments were not Froude's. He added, to reassure his parents, that he would 'either get rid of Froude, or leave Lynmouth immediately', so as 'not to remain in his company one day longer than the common courtesies of life require'. The letter is undated, but must have been written towards the end of April, for on 1 May Froude wrote to his friend Elizabeth Long that he had just left the Kingsleys, who had shown him great kindness when, 'not agreeing with me and scarcely knowing me', they had invited him to stay. He later discovered that 'each day's post' brought Kingsley letters 'of reproach, of menace, of exhortation, all on my account'.[64]

The Grenfells, wealthy and aristocratic, appear to have opposed their daughter's marriage for a while, though they may have thought it a preferable fate to the one she was contemplating when she met Froude at the Kingsleys' house, namely that of converting to Roman Catholicism and becoming a nun. At any rate, the engagement was not a smooth one. Froude himself possibly blew hot and cold in his feelings for Charlotte; moreover, he had to face the pressing question of earning a living before he could marry anyone. On this front, too, he chopped and changed. Like his friend Clough, he impressed people by his charm and intelligence and won their sympathy for his loss of a career. Friends and strangers alike made suggestions and offered support, financial and moral. One of these was Samuel Darbishire, 'a gentleman of wealth and influence in Manchester', who, though he had never met Froude, offered 'to receive me into his house as a tutor to his son till further opportunity should present itself'.[65] Darbishire was a solicitor, a Unitarian involved in the running of Manchester New College, and a friend of the Gaskells. He had previously employed both James Martineau and Frank Newman as tutors to his children, and may have heard of Froude's situation through one or both of them. It was agreed that Froude would spend the summer tutoring his teenage son Vernon.[66]

Meanwhile, however, well-intentioned observers were pulling Froude in a different direction from either marriage or live-in tutoring. The young Oxford scholar Friedrich Max Müller read *The Nemesis of Faith*, as did his benefactor Chevalier Bunsen, Prussian ambassador to Britain, Biblical scholar, and leading Protestant thinker. Bunsen wrote to Max Müller from his official residence in Carlton House Terrace on 22 April:

> Yesterday evening, and night, and this morning early, I have been reading Froude's 'Nemesis of Faith', and am so moved by it that I must write you a few lines. I cannot describe the power of attraction exercised upon me by this deeply-searching, noble spirit: I feel the tragic nature of his position, and long have I foreseen that such tragical

combinations await the souls of men in this island-world. Arnold and
Carlyle, each in his own way, had seen this long before me. In the
general world, no one can understand such a state of mind, except
so far as to be enabled to misconstrue it.[67]

Thinking Froude might yet be saved for Christianity, if not for the Church
of England, Bunsen continues:

It is presumptuous to intrude into the fate and mystery of life in the
case of any man, and more especially of a man so remarkable; but
the consciousness of community of spirits, of knowing, and endeavouring after what is morally good, and true, and perfect, and of the
yearning after every real disciple of the inner religion of Christians,
impels me to suggest to you to tell him from me, that I believe the
spasm of his spiritual efforts would sooner be calmed, and the solution of the great problem would sooner be found, if he were to live
for a time among *us*, I mean, if he resided for a time in one of the
German Universities. We Germans have been for seventy years
working as thinkers, enquirers, poets, seers, also as men of action, to
pull down the old and to erect the new Zion.[68]

Bunsen is not thinking of Strauss and his followers, but of friends of his,
theologians at Bonn and Halle who were working at reconciling religion
with philosophy by means of 'liberal Christian investigation'. Let Froude
study under Rothe, Brandis, and Bleek in Bonn, and Erdmann and Tholuck
in Halle. 'I will gladly give him introductions to all of these.' Bonn, in
particular, would do him good:

He certainly needs physical change and invigorating. For this the
lovely Rhine is decidedly to be recommended. With 100*l.* he could
live there as a prince. Why go off to Van Diemen's Land? I should
always be glad to be of the least service to him, still more to make
his personal acquaintance.[69]

Max Müller did as he was asked, reporting back to Bunsen on 9 May
that he had seen Froude, who would be in London soon and would be
honoured to meet and talk to Bunsen. He added his own observations about

the factions which were seeking to gain control of Froude's soul, as if he were some modern Faustus. 'It would be very sad', he wrote, 'if talents such as Froude's fell into the hands of English Radicals, Chartists, and Unitarians, who are already opening their arms for him.' For his part, Max Müller thought Froude might become a kind of ambassador for modern German thought *not* of the Straussian, radical, rationalist variety:

> If men like Froude, who know the English nation, could show the practical results of German investigations and give them to the people not as a foreign, but as a native product, it might be possible for England to complete its reformation . . . Froude is . . . a little steamship, that need not fear the salt water, but he wants more ballast, and that he must fetch from Germany, or he will suffer shipwreck.[70]

By 22 May Bunsen had seen Froude twice and decided that he was 'a man of genius' and that Germany, 'especially Bonn', was the place for him.[71] The money for Froude's trip was to be put up by Monckton Milnes, who offered it anonymously via Bunsen. Froude did not find out until many years later who his benefactor was; he wrote to Milnes after the latter had become Lord Houghton, thanking him for his kindness, and saying that the offer had given him confidence in himself for the first time.[72]

Froude was sent £100 with the promise of a further hundred to follow; it was understood that he would spend two years studying theology in Germany. On 7 May he told Elizabeth Long that he was going to Bonn with 'the best introductions'. 'I shall get so wise in Bonn: as a first step let my beard and mustachios grow, and fall my hair over my shoulders, and wear a long coat, and talk in great long words', he joked.[73]

This was bravado. He did not go. Much later he recalled that at their meetings Bunsen had been kind, pious, and eloquent. A touch of irony enters his praise of Bunsen's 'rich stream of solid learning' on Lutheran theology, the atonement, free will, 'and all the rest of it'. At times, Froude remarks, he might have been listening to Augustine or to Luther himself, but in the end he felt overwhelmed. To describe Bunsen's effect on him he borrows Carlyle's famous rhetoric in *The Life of John Sterling* (1851) about listening to Coleridge talk. 'I felt as a bucket might feel', says Froude, 'under a pump which is full to the brim, the stream which continues to pour into it splashing over and washing itself away.' He returned the £100 to his 'unknown well-wisher, and went down to Manchester'. Here he joined the Darbishire family and had hopes of a job editing the *Manchester Guardian* through the efforts of Frank Newman.[74] On 20 June, Henry Crabb Robinson met Froude among other 'heretical notabilities', including Newman, at one of Chapman's parties. He found the thirty-one-year-old Froude 'quite a young man with a pleasing countenance and manners, those of a young Oxonian, quite gentlemanly'. Froude told him that he had found work in Manchester 'which relieves him of all embarrassments of a pecuniary kind'.[75]

The Darbishires introduced Froude to the leading Unitarians and other literary people in Manchester; through them he met members of the Martineau family, Geraldine Jewsbury, and the Gaskells. He cut a striking figure. Geraldine described him ten years later as having been very handsome, with 'a strange elfin beauty' and eyes which 'never looked at you, though they *saw* you'.[76] Elizabeth Gaskell wrote about him in fascinated detail in August 1849:

> Mr Froude is domesticated at the Darbishires' till October, when he is to be married . . . If any one under the sun has a magical, magnetic, glamour-like influence, that man has. He's *'aut Mephistopheles aut nihil'* [either Mephistopheles or nothing], that's what he is. The [Darbishires] all bend and bow to his will, like reeds before the wind, blow whichever way it listeth. He smokes cigars constantly; Père, Robert, Arthur, Vernon (nay, once even little Francis), smoke constantly. He disbelieves, they disbelieve; he wears shabby garments, they wear shabby garments; in short, it's the most complete taking away their own wills and informing them with his own that ever was . . . I stand just without the circle of his influence; resisting with all my might, but feeling and seeing the attraction.[77]

This account of Froude's magnetism is all the more interesting when one thinks of his own ambivalent response at Oxford to the mesmeric attributes of John Henry Newman. A few months after this Mrs Gaskell was passing on an account she had heard of Emerson's view of Froude as a 'languid gentleman at Oxford' who seemed to say 'nothing is new, nothing is true, and it does not signify'.[78] No wonder he intrigued people, if he reminded them of both Faust and Mephistopheles.

Elizabeth Gaskell was not alone in noticing the effect he had on the Darbishire family. Harriet Martineau, whom he met at this time, told her friend Fanny Wedgwood in January 1850 that she liked Froude and his new wife, adding:

> The Darbishires' respect and affection for him remain unabated by further knowledge, while there is, happily, less of the *rage for him* that I regretted in the summer. Since his marriage, they have of course seen less of him; but their interest, though more sober, is as genuine as ever.[79]

Froude's arrival at the Darbishires', with his charm, vulnerability, and strength of personality, had a particular effect on their daughter Marianne, who fell for him. Froude, in turn, unsure whether the Grenfells would allow him to marry Charlotte, whom he had known for only a few months and from whom he was now parted, may have felt attracted to Marianne. Something – perhaps the possibility that Charlotte might be jilted – galvanised the Grenfells into agreeing to, and setting about the arrangements for, the wedding. On 7 August Marianne Darbishire wrote to her sister that Froude was to be married and would live nearby.[80] Froude himself told Clough on 20 September that the wedding would take place on 3 October, and that he had taken a house in Manchester:

> I very much admire Manchester, that is, the Darbishire section of it, – and as I conquered my wife from Romanism and a convent, there can hardly be a more healthy atmosphere (moral I mean) to transfer her into.[81]

Froude planned to take a few private pupils and try his hand at writing. His financial position was not so dire as everyone had imagined. Though he was not to be forgiven by his father or reinstated as a recipient of family money until December 1852, Froude had saved £150 from his tutoring for the Darbishires and had £50 of his own at the time of his marriage. Charlotte brought £300 a year, and the Froudes were able to manage with this and the £120 or so that he began to earn annually from writing articles for *Fraser's Magazine* and for the *Westminster Review* after Chapman bought it in 1851. All this he told Clough in May 1852, in answer to anxious inquiries about the minimum income on which one could marry, Clough being inclined, though with much wavering and delay, to get married himself.[82]

Unitarian Manchester did not please Froude for long, nor he it. The rumour mill started working there as it had done in Oxford and London after the burning of the book. On a visit to Liverpool in October 1849 Henry Crabb Robinson attended a party where 'Froude's history was of course talked of'. Mr Darbishire was said to have discovered that Froude had never been destitute but had £400 a year which his family could not touch; Charlotte was reported to have £500 a year. In Manchester a couple of days later Robinson met Mrs Darbishire herself, who told him, with perhaps understandable pique, that Froude's wife was 'not haut[e] forme or young' and had 'not given up Romanism'.[83] On 25 November Froude wrote in disgruntled terms to his Oxford friend Max Müller:

> I shall not stay long in Manchester. The Unitarians here, partly from dislike of my books and partly from a foolish jealousy of an Oxford man coming down and putting out their lights, show me a cold shoulder, and even look coldly on the Darbishires on my account.[84]

Once an Oxford man, always an Oxford man, he was finding, despite his self-propelled exile. Clough was experiencing the same thing, now that he had taken up his post at University Hall, newly opened in Gordon Square. 'Here I am', he wrote to Tom Arnold on 29 October 1849, breakfasting and dining with 'my eleven undergraduates (that should be 30 and I hope will be some day)'. He was gloomy about the future, however, believing that 'in the end I shall be kicked out for mine heresies' sake' by the 'Sadducees' (Unitarians) who ran the place. 'For intolerance, O Tom, is not confined to the cloisters of Oxford or the pews of the establishment, but comes up like the tender herb – partout.'[85]

In a sense neither Clough nor Froude ever got over his rejection of – and by – Oxford. In September 1850 Froude left Manchester for a secluded part of Wales, where he began his life's work, a comprehensive history of the English Reformation which was to be published in twelve volumes between 1856 and 1870. His choice of subject was partly personal; as ever moved by a strong spirit of opposition, he set out to defend Henry VIII and Elizabeth as upholders of the true Protestant faith against the 'story' he had been told by Newman and others 'at Oxford', namely that the

Reformation in England was 'the most unfortunate incident which had destroyed the unity of the Church', that it had been 'a rebellion against divinely given authority' and 'a schism promoted by corrupt and tyrannical princes, carried out by unprincipled and priestly renegades'.[86] Froude's first published words on the subject were to be printed by Chapman in the *Westminster Review* in a series of long essays on Mary Stuart (January 1852), Mary Tudor (January 1853), and John Knox (July 1853).

Froude soon came to regret *The Nemesis of Faith* and his doubts about the Articles. In 1858 he hoped to be appointed to the Regius Chair of Modern History at Oxford, but before he could even apply he needed to be rehabilitated by his old college. On 15 March 1858 he wrote to the Rector of Exeter College asking for his support:

> I venture to tell you . . . that I have long most deeply regretted my conduct. Long ago I made the only expiation in my power in buying up the copyright of the book which gave so just offence. I was young when it was written. I was carried away like many others by the excitement of the Continent in 1848.
>
> I have been punished by nine years suspension of confidence, and I have spent that time in hard labour at Modern History – not, as I hope, without effect. I shall direct my publisher to send you a copy of the third and fourth volumes of my History, which have just been published. They will I believe make clear the purpose with which they have been written, which is nothing more and nothing less than to clear the English Reformation and the fathers of the Anglican Church from the stains which have been allowed to gather on them.
>
> If I ever return to Oxford it will be with the object of defending the Church of England from all enemies within and without.[87]

The professorship went to someone else on this occasion (though Froude was finally appointed in 1892, at the age of seventy-four), but Froude now signed the Articles and was accepted back as a member of Exeter College.[88] He remained outside academia, however, and in practice his relationship with the Church of England never extended beyond respectable church-going. He was prepared to write – anonymously – for Chapman's radical *Westminster Review*, and did so regularly from 1852 to 1857, but he was also keen to put a distance between himself and the 'infidel' book Chapman had published, hence the buying back of the copyright to prevent Chapman from issuing a third edition. When Chapman was going through one of his most serious financial crises in 1854, he asked Froude if he could be the publisher of the *History of England*. It was not, from Chapman's point of view, an unreasonable request, as he had commissioned Froude's historical articles for the *Westminster Review* and no doubt thought that these would form a part of the larger work. His letter, which has not been found, may have been tactless; Froude's reply was certainly direct:

> With regard to my *History* which you suppose to be identical with that of which I have spoken to you, your mistake, I suppose, is not intentional, but it is not less real. It will consist of six volumes (if I complete it), the first two of which will contain the reign of Henry the Eighth, the second two the reigns [of] Edward and Mary, the remaining two that of Elizabeth. The four first volumes will, with the notes and appendices, take ten years . . . But at all events, neither I nor any other writer of a book which he hopes to be valuable would compromise the prospects of it by committing the issue of it to embarrassment and crippled resources. I do not say this to wound you, but you must know as a man of business that there is but one course under circumstances of this kind. That no doubt, however, may remain in your mind, I may tell you that my book arose, in its present form, from the offer of a large collection of rare and unpublished MSS, which alone induced me to undertake the task at all. These MSS you did not possess and could not possess them, and you are rather unreasonable if you suppose that I was to abstain from writing a book with which you had no connexion whatever, when I was offered a large price for writing it, because I could not offer it to you to publish for me.
>
> You speak of [a] heretical book which was refused by the publishers: but the *Nemesis* was never refused and you do not pretend that you have lost by it. If my *History* proves valuable, the value of the copyrights which you already possess of my historical articles will more than indemnify you for any loss which you may suppose yourself to have experienced. If it does not prove valuable, you have escaped a bad speculation. The MSS relate exclusively to the reign of Henry VIII, and are of the greatest value. They were placed in Parker's hands

by the collector, and Parker was commissioned to find a writer capable of embodying them in a new history.[89]

Chapman thus had to swallow having his business affairs described, accurately enough, as 'embarrassment and crippled resources', while also being turned down as publisher in favour of John Parker of 445 Strand, proprietor of *Fraser's Magazine* and giver of those publishing parties which rivalled Chapman's at 142. Froude was, as he said, obliged to print with Parker, who had been asked by Sir Francis Palgrave, Keeper of the Records, to offer Froude access to the State Papers of Henry VIII if he would write the history.[90] On his many visits to London to consult the collection, Froude stayed with Parker.

It is not surprising that Froude kept Chapman at a slight distance now that he had regained ground with the Philistines, as Kingsley put it in 1852. Yet his temperament and circumstances ensured that on the one hand he was always regarded with suspicion by the orthodox, while on the other he could never align himself wholly with the unorthodox. Though he was brutal in turning Chapman down over the *History* in 1854, he refused to join James Martineau and others who were trying to wrest the *Westminster Review* from Chapman at that time, preferring to continue his contributions. It was Marian Evans (as she now called herself) who had encouraged Chapman to solicit an article from Froude when she was helping in September 1851 to plan the first number of the *Westminster* under Chapman's ownership. She had been fascinated by Froude; after he had changed his mind about going abroad with the Bray party in June 1849 on the grounds that he was going to marry instead, she wrote to her friends from Geneva in October, responding to the news of his wedding. In this letter she makes a clever intuitive allusion to Froude as both Faust and Mephistopheles. The reference is to the scene in Goethe's *Faust* in which Mephistopheles borrows Faust's doctor's gown to preach wisdom and morality to a young student, adding a cynical and undermining interpretation of his own to unsettle the naïve young man:

It is good that Froude should marry a respectability – only if he preach the new word at Manchester I hope he will preach it so as to do without an after-explanation and not bewilder his hearers in the manner of Mephistopheles when he dons the doctor's gown of Faust.[91]

Froude was pulled in opposite directions all his life. *The Nemesis of Faith*, like its author, is a strange piece of work. Its publication by Chapman was a phenomenon which preoccupied the literary and religious worlds for several months. If Chapman was not much good at the financial management of his publishing business, he certainly had a good eye for writers. This was to be proved beyond doubt when he chose as his chief assistant on the *Westminster Review* – which he set about trying to buy as early as 1849 – his anonymous translator of Strauss, the shrewd commentator on Froude and his novel, and a woman now freed by the death of her father to leave Coventry and make a career in London, namely Marian Evans.

3

Chapman, Marian Evans, and the Westminster Review (1851)

Exhausted after her father's death at the end of May 1849, Mary Ann Evans crossed the Channel on 12 June with Charles and Cara Bray, but without Froude. They travelled through France and northern Italy, and on 25 July the Brays came home, leaving their friend in lodgings in Geneva where she planned to spend the winter recuperating, reading, and deciding what to do next. Earlier in the year she had begun translating Spinoza's *Tractatus Theologico-Politicus* with Chapman in mind as the probable publisher; in December she answered an inquiry from him about her progress, sent on to Geneva by Bray. Chapman had been offered a translation of Spinoza's *Ethics* by an American, Samuel Hitchcock, which he did not wish to accept if Miss Evans's translation was likely to be finished soon – two works by the humanist philosopher being too many to put before a suspicious reading public all at once. Mary Ann told Bray to assure Chapman that he was 'absolved from observing any delicacy towards me about Spinoza or his translators', as she had given up the work some months before.[1]

Spring 1850 saw Mary Ann back in England but still unsure what to do and where to go. She spent some weeks living with each of her married siblings in the Midlands. Though her sister Chrissey was welcoming, she was preoccupied with her husband and children. Isaac, the model for the unforgiving Tom Tulliver in *The Mill on the Floss*, was hostile. He was embarrassed and irritated by his younger sister's religious unorthodoxy, intellectual precocity, and general desire to be independent. As she wrote ruefully to Sara Hennell from his house in Coventry on 11 April, some 'envious demons' had driven her 'across the Jura to come and see people who don't want me'. She was determined, she said, to pack a carpet bag and become 'a stranger and a foreigner on the earth'. Then, climbing down from such melodramatic heights, she asked Sara to find out what Chapman charged for lodgings at 142 Strand. For the time being, the Brays rescued her from her uncongenial relations by inviting her to spend the summer with them. After a visit from Chapman in October, she went for two weeks to the Strand as a trial run for a longer stay, returning to the Midlands at the beginning of December with the intention of taking up residence permanently at number 142 in January 1851. At Chapman's regular Friday evening gathering on 29 November she had met Eliza Lynn, a 'literary lady', she told the Brays, whom she wished to emulate by making her way in London, supplementing the £90 a year inherited from her father by translating and reviewing.[2]

On his visit to Coventry in October 1850 Chapman was accompanied by Robert William Mackay, whose book *The Progress of the Intellect, as Exemplified in the Religious Development of the Greeks and Hebrews* Chapman had published in June. The translator of Strauss was the right person to give a sympathetic review to this historical analysis of religious thought with its optimistic view that divine revelation progresses along with general human development, adapting itself to the state of knowledge of particular cultures at particular times. As Mary Ann pointed out in the review she did write, the importance of the book lay in its 'recognition of the presence of undeviating law in the material and moral world'. She saw that Mackay's emphasis on progress shifted the focus away from difficult questions of creed and dogma towards an optimistic belief in the future of human endeavour, intellectual and spiritual.[3]

Chapman managed to place her review of Mackay in the January 1851 number of the *Westminster Review*, the radical quarterly he was keen to take over from its current proprietor-cum-editor, William Edward Hickson. No one had ever made the *Review* profitable, but that sobering fact did not put Chapman off any more than it had deterred his many predecessors. The *Westminster* had been founded and financed by Bentham and James Mill in 1824 with a view to providing an organ for the radical political movement agitating for electoral reform. As Bentham put it, the ruling class or party (the Tories) 'had its instrument' in the shape of the *Quarterly Review*, and the '*sub-ruling* or *co-ruling* few' (the Whigs) had the *Edinburgh Review*. It was therefore 'high time the subject many' had a voice to represent their interests among the serious periodical press.[4]

For its first twelve years the journal was run by Benthamite Utilitarians advocating practical reforms. Though it sold about 3,000 copies a quarter at the height of Reform Bill fever in 1831–2, the usual sale was nearer 1,200, not enough to break even. Rich men of radical opinions were found from time to time to inject cash – Colonel Thomas Perronet Thompson in 1828, Sir William Molesworth in 1834 – but there was never enough in the long run.[5] John Stuart Mill, who took over as editor and proprietor in 1836 and opened the *Review* to original thinkers who were not Benthamites – men like Carlyle, Thackeray, Monckton Milnes, and Leigh Hunt – continued to make a loss. As he wrote more than thirty years later when trying to muster financial support for the *Westminster* under Chapman's long stewardship, the periodical had never been financially viable and never would be:

> The West. Review has been since its first establishment the organ of the most advanced radical party in England both as regards politics & religious speculation; & it was for a very long time the only organ in which anything of a very decidedly liberal character could appear in print, & is still the only one in which articles of its length can appear. It has been consistently of such (what are commonly called 'extreme') opinions that it has been impossible to obtain a sufficiently large circulation to make it profitable. It has often been carried on at a pecuniary loss, & it is still not without great difficulty that the editor is able to manage it.[6]

Hickson, who bought the *Westminster* from Mill in 1840, was financially independent, having retired from his family's successful shoemaking business. He held on for eleven years, losing money, paying only ten guineas for each article while his rivals offered at least twice that amount, and saving money further by writing a large proportion of the articles himself.[7] The *Review* closely reflected his particular interests: electoral reform, secular education, and sanitary matters. James Martineau wrote on religious subjects and his fellow Unitarian W. R. Greg contributed a celebrated piece on prostitution in July 1850. Mill collaborated with his wife on an essay on the enfranchisement of women for the July 1851 number. Otherwise, the writers employed by Hickson lacked distinction and the subjects lacked variety. By the time he was ready to sell the *Review* in 1851, Hickson had been cheated by the false accounting of his publisher George Luxford and was exhausted by the uphill effort of keeping the journal going against the odds.[8]

Financial support had come recently from an eccentric philanthropist, Edward Lombe, who lived in Florence but owned a huge estate in Norfolk. Hickson collected the rents on his behalf, reporting to George Combe of Edinburgh in January 1851 that £7,000 had been paid up by Lombe's tenants in the space of two hours.[9] Lombe, though generous, was a hard taskmaster, as Hickson had found, and as Chapman was shortly to discover. He was happy to give money for articles in the *Westminster*, but only for his own pet subjects, and only if the writer agreed in detail with his particular views. These were robust, to say the least; they included a wish to have the peerage abolished, a hatred of the established Church, and a desire to see education made wholly secular (in which aim he agreed with Combe).

Laying down the conditions on which he would transfer his support to Chapman's approaching custodianship of the *Westminster* in a letter of May 1851, Lombe declared with a characteristic sweep that he wanted 'abolition of Primogeniture & Entails' and 'suppression of the Established Church – Universities (O[xford] & C[ambridge]) – the Grammar & Endowed Schools – with application of their Funds to State Purposes'.[10] A month later, with Chapman's arrangement to buy the *Westminster* for £300 and take over fully in October now final, Lombe confirmed that he would be happy to co-operate with Chapman on the same terms as hitherto with Hickson, 'namely to pay £50 per number for a Great Article of some 50 pages upon subjects selected by me – & treated according to my way of thinking'.[11] Chapman needed all the financial help he could get, but he paid a heavy price in time and energy trying to keep on the right side of the tyrannical Mr Lombe.

He did, however, have the best of assistants in the person of Mary Ann Evans, or Marian, as she signed herself for the first time in a letter to Chapman of 4 April 1851. She still used the name Mary Ann when writing to members of her family, while to the Brays and Sara Hennell she went by the nickname 'Pollian', but on her move to London in January 1851 to pursue a journalistic career she chose the more adult name Marian.[12] As it happens, this letter, written from the Brays' home in Coventry, was an attempt to put an end to an embarrassing quarrel between herself and the two female inhabitants of 142 Strand, Susanna Chapman and Elisabeth Tilley. The disagreement might have ended the *Review* partnership with

Chapman before it had properly begun, with incalculable consequences for her future personal life and public career, if not for his.

1851 was probably the most important year in the life of both Chapman and Marian Evans. He bought the *Westminster Review* and gathered round him an extraordinarily talented group of writers; she gained writing and editing experience which proved invaluable for her later career as a novelist, as well as extending her social circle beyond that of the Brays and meeting, through Chapman, the man with whom she would share her life. It happens that Chapman's diary for 1851 survives, where all the others except that for 1860 have disappeared.[13] So often visible only in glimpses from the letters of his authors, as in the case of Froude, Chapman lays himself bare in these diaries, which are almost Pepysian in their frankness and detail. We know at every turn what Chapman was feeling during 1851.

What he was feeling on 1 January as he took stock of the year just gone by was this:

> I open the record of this new year with a sad retrospect of the last one, – sad in regard to the trying difficulties I have gone through pertaining to my business, sad in regard to the wretchedness I have endured through my affections, sad that I have wasted much time and seem to have made no intellectual progress, – and saddest of all that I have made *others* sad, and have not at all profited by this year, in the very vigour of my manhood, to become a better man.[14]

The business troubles had to do with his loss of advantage over other publishers during 1850 after the bumper year 1849, when he had been Putnam's chosen importer and co-publisher of American books. Whereas he had about 140 books on his 1849 list and was able to take out eye-catching advertisements in the *Publishers' Circular*, the number went down to below seventy in 1850, with a severe retrenchment in advertising to match. This was the year he was forced to reduce the price of Emerson's *Poems* to four shillings and that of *Representative Men* to five shillings.

The disappointment at his lack of intellectual progress reveals an important aspect of Chapman's character. Like Dickens and Lewes, to name but two of his acquaintances who made their way in the Victorian world of letters by their own efforts, he had none of the advantages, social or intellectual, of a university education. He taught himself by reading widely and keeping up

86

with advanced thinking in philosophy, theology, history, and science. It was his aspiration to contribute to his age's progress and to his own reputation by succeeding as an original thinker and writer, though he was obliged in the end – partly in response to the tactful but firm comments of Marian Evans – to accept that his talents lay more in enabling others to make their contributions to original thinking than to do anything useful by his own pen. Nonetheless, he could not resist spending time and energy engaging in epistolary discussions with authors who found his thinking muddled. James Martineau, for example, though pleased that Chapman was taking over the *Westminster*, confessed in June 1851 that if Chapman were to edit the *Review*, it would be 'conclusively ruined':

> He is an enterprising Publisher and a clever man: but it is his misfortune that he does not know his own limits; and is ambitious of a literary function, for which he is not qualified.[15]

The references in Chapman's diary to the wretchedness he has suffered through his 'affections', the making others sad, and the regret that 'in the very vigour of my manhood' – he would be thirty on 16 June 1851 – he had failed to become a better man, all relate to his sexual relationships. His wife Susanna is mentioned in negative terms throughout the diary. She is said to be conventional in her religious views, unfairly jealous of the children's governess and Chapman's mistress Elisabeth Tilley, and now of Marian Evans too. Chapman complains of her importunate requests for him to share her bedroom, which he does for a while, 'with a struggle', from 2 May.[16] Susanna's greatest disadvantage was her age. 'Susanna's birthday', Chapman notes on 27 August. It was her forty-fourth. Under the same date he records that he has twice had sexual intercourse with Elisabeth Tilley during the previous night. The running total of these occasions, noted meticulously throughout the diary, had now reached fifty-four since the beginning of the year.[17]

Susanna, though understandably jealous of Elisabeth, seems to have been more or less reconciled to the domestic triangle, claiming her marital rights from time to time and causing arguments sometimes, but generally putting up with a situation she could do little to change.[18] On one occasion, 19 May, Chapman describes an angry outburst to which he responded, unusually for him, with sarcasm:

I proposed to buy an Iron Safe for the business which was met by a torrent of invective about my 'reckless extravagance'. She was silenced by my remark that I thought she had better assume the management of the business in order to ensure having matters ordered conformably to her views.[19]

Chapman did not love his wife; he did not believe that unhappy marriages should be indissoluble, though the law decreed so. His simple solution was to follow his own desires with Elisabeth (and in 1859 with another young woman, Johanna von Heyligenstaedt), and to promote, in his publications and in the *Westminster Review*, advanced opinions on marriage as on other subjects. He eventually parted from Susanna in 1863 and was soon cohabiting with another 'Mrs Chapman', with whom he moved to Paris in 1874.[20] For the time being, though, he lived at 142 Strand with Susanna, his children Beatrice and Ernest, some clerks, and several paying guests, with Elisabeth acting as governess to the children and housekeeper to the establishment. A few of Chapman's circle knew of the arrangement, but most did not. It is inconceivable that devout Unitarians like James Martineau would have published with him if they had known, or that a respectable elderly bachelor such as Henry Crabb Robinson – who often recorded scandal and gossip in his diary, resorting to shorthand for the purpose – should have visited Chapman's soirées regularly. Robinson never jotted down any suspicions about Chapman's domestic circumstances.[21]

Marian Evans, however, entering the household in January 1851, soon became aware of the sexual tensions and found herself adding to them before long. On Wednesday 8 January, according to the diary, Chapman met her at Euston Station at three p.m. She herself wrote immediately to the Brays to assure them that she had arrived safely and that her room was comfortable. She reported that among the guests were an American Mr Jarvis ('evidently a noodle'), a female cousin of Chapman, and William Ballantyne Hodgson, headmaster and educational reformer, one of Martineau's Manchester friends, whom Chapman hoped to persuade to become a sleeping partner in the publishing business.[22] The very next day finds Chapman recording, in one of many passages scored out at an unspecified later date:

Had a very painful altercation with Elisabeth the result of her groundless suspicions hence I have been in a state of unhealthy excitement all day. She gave notice at the dinner table that she intended to leave in the Autumn.[23]

Since Elisabeth had nothing to fear from poor Susanna in the way of attracting and keeping Chapman's attention, it is clear that she was jealous of the new female arrival. Though Marian was plain-looking and in that respect hardly a rival for Elisabeth, she was formidably clever. Her approval of Chapman's ideas and plans flattered his sense of his intellectual abilities, with the result that this socially gauche young woman of thirty-one quickly upset the fragile balance of the household. Chapman played one woman off against the other, with Susanna siding on the whole with Elisabeth as the devil she knew. There were tiffs and arguments about the piano Chapman helped Marian to choose, especially as he was soon spending hours in her room listening to her play Mozart. Then he began to take German lessons from her, which caused an outburst from Elisabeth. On 22 January there was a silly business about which of the three women was to accompany Chapman on a walk.[24]

All the while Chapman was considering whether to publish a novel, *Realities*, by Eliza Lynn, which painted a frank picture of the free sexual mores among a group of theatrical people. After listening to Mozart on 12 January, Chapman took Marian to call on Eliza 'in the hope of inducing her to cancel some objectionable passages'. As he wrote with sweet reasonableness in the diary:

> I said that such passages were addressed [to] and excited the sensual nature and were therefore injurious; – and that as I am the publisher of works notable for the[ir] intellectual freedom it behoves me to be exceedingly careful of the *moral* tendency of all I issue.[25]

Susanna, Elisabeth, and Marian all supported his stance. As Eliza Lynn refused to drop the offending passages, Chapman declined to publish *Realities*, which was eventually brought out by Saunders & Otley at the author's expense.[26]

On 18 February Chapman describes how Susanna and Elisabeth have compared notes 'on the subject of my intimacy with Miss Evans' and have concluded, as he continues in a passage rescued from deletion,

> that we are completely in love with each other. – E. being intensely jealous herself said all she could to cause S. to look from the same

point of view, which a little incident (her finding me with my hand in M.'s) had quite prepared her for. E. betrayed my trust and her own promise. S. said to me that if ever I went to M.'s room again she will write to Mr Bray, and say that she dislikes her.[27]

Two deleted symbols relating to Marian on 19 January suggest that some intimacy took place between her and Chapman on that date. Certainly the women of 142 Strand thought so, for it was soon decided that Marian would have to leave. The diary falls silent for several days; pages are cut out. On 24 March Chapman observes:

> M. departed today[.] I accompanied her to the railway. She was very sad, and hence made me feel so. – She pressed me for some intimation of the state of my feelings. – I told her that I felt great affection for her, but that I loved E. and S. also, though each in a different way. At this avowal she burst into tears.[28]

So much for Marian's first attempt at living independently in London. She returned to the welcoming Brays in Coventry with nothing decided about the future. The purchase of the *Westminster Review* was not definite and Marian's role not yet defined, but Chapman had given her a task: she was to compile an *Analytical Catalogue of Mr Chapman's Publications*, a list of his chief publications to date with summaries of their contents and occasional critical remarks where she strongly approved of a particular book. For example, she praised Frank Newman's *Phases of Faith*, describing it as 'valuable, not only as the religious history of a distinguished mind, but also as containing important considerations on the general influence of Christianity'.[29] Though Marian was still vulnerable on the subject of her lack of physical attractions – when Chapman visited Coventry at the end of May 1851, he noted how she 'wept bitterly' when he spoke of female beauty[30] – her pride reasserted itself when she corresponded with him about books. Asking his opinion on 9 May of her account of Martineau's *Rationale of Religious Inquiry* for the *Catalogue*, she wrote with self-protective irony and growing self-confidence: 'Pray be candid – that is the first, second and third thing I require, though I am a woman and seem pettish. You know you must allow me to criticise your criticism.'[31]

*

In spite of her banishment to Coventry, Marian and Chapman had a lot to correspond about in the spring and summer of 1851. First, there arose a suggestion for her to prepare an abridgement of the Strauss translation. It came from Edward Lombe, who wrote to Chapman out of the blue on 13 March asking how many copies remained unsold and offering to relieve him of the stock in hand and take 'all the risks' of publishing an abridgement.[32] Chapman apparently replied enthusiastically, suggesting that Lombe might also be interested in supporting a cheap edition of works by Theodore Parker and Charles Hennell and mentioning that he was thinking of starting a radical periodical. Lombe's response was to ask the cost of the reprints and to say that if the periodical was to be theological in any respect he could have nothing to do with it, for 'I am ultra liberal in all matters of Politics, Philosophy & Religion'. He added that he had been supporting the *Westminster Review* under Hickson as long as it published articles to suit him, hinting, however, that Hickson was not proving entirely satisfactory.[33]

Chapman was delighted about the Strauss abridgement and lost no time in asking Marian if she would undertake it for £100, to be paid by Lombe.[34] He also saw the opportunity to take over the *Westminster Review* with Lombe's backing, not thinking, perhaps, that the peremptory Lombe would be quite as difficult with him as he was with Hickson whenever he considered that his wishes were not being carried out to the letter. Lombe's correspondence with Combe at this time accuses Hickson of spinelessness and duplicity. 'The Secretiveness of Mr H is such that in all probability we shall part', he wrote on 10 May. 'I did not support the W. R. merely for a few Fancy Articles but upon system to make it the Exponent of my Opinions & Convictions.' Hopeful of greater obedience from Chapman, he declared himself ready to support him as the new proprietor.[35]

Inevitably the relationship came to a sticky end after several months of a correspondence in which Lombe made impossible demands and threats, interspersed with tempting money promises, while Chapman, out of his depth, replied evasively and defensively. The £100 for the Strauss had to be sent back in December, as Lombe felt he had been cheated. Chapman had indeed been too presumptuous, pressing Lombe to support his other reprints as well as the Strauss. His besetting fault as a publisher was to attempt to use money donated for a particular purpose in other ways, according to his publishing needs. Lombe complained to Combe on 15 November: 'In Spring I spoke to him ab[ou]t Strauss – & at once he recommended Baur – Parker &

Hennel[l] in all only £2000!!! *modest.*' In the same letter he complained of Chapman's interpretation of his intentions vis-à-vis the *Westminster*:

> I promised my support to the W. R. on the old condition of retiring when I liked or of being dismissed at his pleasure – this . . . he converts into a *promise* of £200 a yr.[36]

Chapman's blunder here was to advertise to other well-wishers from whom he was seeking financial aid for the *Review* that Lombe was willing to give £200 a year, when it ought to have been clear from Lombe's letters that, though prepared to help out each quarter, he would only stump up money for individual articles which were written to his satisfaction. Combe received another complaint about Chapman a few days later:

> Now then for Mr Chapman – I shall be extremely cautious in entangling myself with him for he has shown very strong symptoms of a desire to hook me into extensive obligations.[37]

Lombe wanted critical articles on the hereditary peerage, the established Church, the Universities, the courts, and medical institutions, all of them subjects Chapman was also keen to see tackled. It was certainly unrealistic of Lombe to think that such articles could all be fixed up in one go, but he was a man in a hurry, partly through temperament, partly because he was in poor health. As for the £200 a year, tactlessly broadcast to others by Chapman in order to encourage them to be generous too, that was not intended as a regular subscription, as Lombe told Combe:

> I am not a general but a special purpose man – & they who desire support from me must be content to take my Opinions & my objects with my Dollars or they will have none.[38]

Chapman could hardly complain that Lombe had not made his conditions plain from the start; on 4 June he had spelt out his requirement that articles be written to his satisfaction, otherwise, as had been the case with Hickson, he would terminate the agreement. He added, reasonably but rather superfluously given the nature of the relationship between the funder and the funded, that 'the other party' was 'equally free to cut the connexion' at any time.[39] On 10 July Lombe told Chapman frankly, 'I am rather a hard task-master – "an austere man" – giving my horses plenty of oats – but making them work well.'[40]

When Hickson called at number 142 on 1 May 1851 to ask if Chapman was 'still disposed to purchase' the *Westminster Review*, he was able to give Chapman information acquired at first hand about the eccentricity of his benefactor. After beating the asking price down from £350 to £300, Chapman inquired about Lombe, and was told that he gave support only for 'special articles on special subjects'. Hickson divulged that Lombe's income was some £14,000 a year, that he was about forty-eight, 'was not on speaking terms with his father for many years', and had not been in England for twenty-five years.[41]

Chapman did his best, with Marian Evans's help, to find someone to write the desired article on the hereditary peerage for the first number of the *Review* under his direction, that for January 1852. They had no success. Frederick Oldfield Ward, a friend of Lewes's and writer on sanitary matters, was asked on 7 October, but 'declined on the ground of differing from Mr Lombe in toto, and that he wishes to devote his energies to the Sanatory [sic] Question', as Chapman noted in his diary. On 8 October, the day on which Chapman completed his purchase of the *Westminster*, Marian Evans reported to Charles Bray that since Ward, 'the man of the Sewers', had turned them down, 'we are going to try Carlyle for the peerage'.[42] Two days later Chapman recorded that he had walked to Chelsea with Marian, 'and left her while I called on Carlyle', who also declined to write the article. The same day, 10 October, Carlyle, in an effort to help Chapman, wrote to Robert Browning in Paris describing the visit from the publisher of 'Liberalisms' and 'Extinct-Socinianisms' whose aim, as Carlyle put it, was to 'bring out a Review, liberal in all senses, that shall charm the world':

> He has capital 'for four years' trial', he says; an able editor (name can't be given), and such an array of 'talent' as was seldom gathered before. Poor soul I really wished him well in his enterprise, and regretted I could not help him myself, being clear for silence at present. Since his departure I have betho[ugh]t me of you! There you are in Paris, there you were in Florence, with fiery interest in all manner of things, with whole libraries to write and say on this and the other thing! The man means to pay, handsomely; is indeed an *honest* kind of man, with a real

enthusiasm (tho' a soft and slobbery) in him, which can be predicated of very few.[43]

Browning, who knew Lombe from his time in Florence, replied that he had already spoken to Chapman during a visit to London in the summer. Chapman had (optimistically) told him 'how he had got in some measure rid of his *Lombago*, under which he must have been stiffened past even writhing'.[44] As it happens, Browning had been asked by Lombe, after a conversation in Florence in March, if Carlyle himself would be prepared to be subsidised by Lombe on terms rather freer – as befitted his celebrity – than those he sought to impose on Hickson's and Chapman's writers. Lombe wrote:

> In conversation yesterday you mentioned something concerning Mr Carlyle that much struck me – That he had once hinted to you how agreeable it would have been to him if any Publisher had consented to make him an annual arrangement – leaving him free to write when the fit came on.
>
> I am not in the Profession – but if at any time Mr Carlyle felt disposed to accept Two Hundred a year upon a similar understanding – I shall be most happy to enter into such an engagement & in such manner as he may please to dictate.

On hearing of the offer, Carlyle had wisely declined.[45]

Chapman did manage to get Martineau – referred to as 'Jemmy' in Lombe's letters – to write the article intended by Lombe to criticise Christianity; it was not, of course, to Lombe's taste, being a discourse along liberal Unitarian lines called 'The Ethics of Christendom'. Martineau, a regular contributor to the *Westminster* under Hickson, had been earmarked by Lombe for this essay before Chapman took over, but had refused. As he explained to Hickson on 14 February 1851, he 'could not possibly accede' to the proposal without doing violence to his convictions:

> [Lombe] asked me for a systematic attack on the '*Morality of Christianity*'. It is something astonishing to be first treated as a man whose whole life is a lie; and then be invited, in virtue of this, to discuss questions of Morals![46]

The article was left unwritten while Chapman and Hickson negotiated the sale of the *Westminster*. Martineau was not only one of Chapman's authors; as a well-known Unitarian who professed liberal and progressive views while remaining a religious believer, he was too influential for Chapman not to court him for the new *Westminster Review*. He was sent an early draft of the Prospectus in June 1851. Chapman had begun writing it immediately after agreeing terms with Hickson at the beginning of May; at the end of the month he went to Coventry for two weeks with the purpose of getting Bray's support for the *Review* and persuading Marian to return to London in the autumn to be his helper and co-editor. It was agreed that she would, if he could smooth things over with Susanna and Elisabeth in the meantime. She also stipulated that her editorial role be kept secret (hence his leaving her outside while he visited Carlyle in October and Carlyle's reporting to Browning that the editor could not be named). They discussed possible contributors, starting with a number of Chapman's own authors, to whom the draft Prospectus, finished by Marian in early June, was sent. Frank Newman, Froude, W. R. Greg, Mackay, and Hodgson were therefore among the recipients, as well as Combe and the *Westminster*'s last-but-one editor, John Stuart Mill.[47]

Martineau thought the Prospectus 'ill-written and poor in substance', as he told Hickson. He feared Chapman would be offended that he could not bring himself to praise it.[48] Marian was certainly offended, telling Chapman on his return to London from Coventry on 9 June that she found Martineau's response cold. In the same letter she advised Chapman on how to handle the inevitable questions about the editorship:

> With regard to the secret of the Editorship, it will perhaps be the best plan for you to state, that for the present *you* are to be regarded as the responsible person, but that you employ an Editor in whose literary and general ability you confide.[49]

This plan suited Chapman, with his literary ambitions; it also suited Marian, who enjoyed anonymity, partly from natural diffidence and fear of failure, and partly because female editorship was unheard of at this time. Though fated often to be controversial in her views and actions, she had no desire to thrust herself into the public eye or shock the conventional.[50] Perhaps she was born some generations too soon. Her early loss of faith, her pursuit of an independent career, and soon her courting of social exile by living with a married man occurred at a time when even men suffered for deviations from the norm, as is evident in the careers of Froude and Clough, and when divorce was difficult or even impossible to obtain.

Martineau thawed sufficiently to write the article on Christianity for the January 1852 number of the *Westminster* after all, but not to write it to Lombe's dictation. The latter wrote to Chapman on 10 November 1851 in ominously jocose mood, saying he was waiting with anxiety to see if 'Jemmy' would be 'up to the mark'.[51] Exasperated with Chapman on several counts by this time, he told Combe on 20 November that 'as a Pastor Martineau cannot do justice to my views on X [i.e. Christian] ethics – it will be all fudge – but I shall pay for it & then cut the connexion'.[52] On 13 February 1852 Chapman complained to Combe that he had received no money from Lombe; a month later, after Lombe's sudden death, he wrote more in sorrow than in anger:

> I was quite independent of him at the time of his death, and have not received aid from him to the extent of a shilling, but have lost a fearful amount of time in correspondence with him – often of a disagreeable kind. He did not even pay for Martineau's Article.[53]

Chapman's optimism and fundamental good nature saw him through this sorry episode, but his lack of common sense and his incorrigibility prevented him from learning from the experience, which was to be repeated in future years with other would-be benefactors, though none of them as eccentric as Lombe.

Once the purchase of the *Review* was certain and Chapman had charmed Marian Evans into swallowing her pride and agreeing to return to the Strand at the end of September, he set out to appeal to two kinds of interested parties: potential backers and possible contributors. Some correspondents fitted both categories. Combe, Mackay, Martineau, Newman, and Hodgson were men of at least comfortable means, and all agreed to support the *Westminster* in some way, whether by subscription, donation, or writing articles for nothing. Chapman's printer George Woodfall promised £50 a year, and Combe's friend T. H. Bastard, an educational reformer, was prepared to pay for some articles.[54]

The summer and autumn were spent in wooing influential thinkers like

Carlyle, Mill, and Combe, with mixed success. Carlyle wished Chapman well, but would do nothing more than recommend others. Combe interested himself from the start. He agreed to be Chapman's first subscriber (of £20),[55] sent advice in several long letters, and valiantly defended Chapman in his equally copious correspondence with Lombe, who, while treating Combe's phrenological ideas with sarcasm, approved of his practical activities on behalf of secular education in Scotland, and sent him money towards lectures and pamphlets on the subject. Combe agreed to write for the *Westminster Review* without payment; his 'Secular Education' appeared in the July 1852 number. Unlike Martineau, Combe was encouraging about the draft Prospectus, while sending detailed suggestions for its improvement.[56]

He also wrote at length to Lombe on 25 May, describing a recent interview with Chapman, whom he had found 'open and candid'. Chapman's intention was to 'take natural religion, natural morality, and the laws of Nature physical and moral as the basis of his operations: but he will avoid rudely shocking public opinion'. The list of contributors included 'all the ablest and most advanced thinkers and writers' of the day. Combe had only one fear for the project:

> His grand difficulty, as I told him, and as he acknowledged, will consist in the impossibility of finding able writers who will act on a uniform and self-consistent plan. They are all able Guerilla Chiefs, but no General on earth could reduce them to a Squadron, capable of acting from a fixed basis towards a series of objects.[57]

This was a tactful attempt to make Lombe understand that his own pet subjects might not always be treated as he wished; if you want the best writers, Combe implied, you must let them have their head. Chapman's solution, he reported, was to have two departments in the *Review*, one labelled 'Independent', under which heading views might be expressed for which the editor would not be held responsible. (The January 1852 number did have an 'Independent Contribution', an anonymous article on political parties in France, but Chapman and Marian soon dropped the division as unworkable.) Chapman 'did not name the Editor, but he says he will be an able Man'.[58] Combe was later let into the secret of the editorship, as were other contributors who found themselves corresponding with Marian about their articles. Though Combe himself was hoping to influence the *Review* in the direction

of his own thinking, based on the reading of character by craniological inves-
tigations with a view to introducing practical reforms in educational and
other institutions, he was more flexible and patient than Lombe, accepting
that other reformers had different priorities and seeing the need for them all
to pull together. This was the basis of his support for the *Westminster*.

Combe also offered Chapman useful advice about the legal and business
part of his arrangements – how to protect himself against losses while ensuring
that subscribers got something in return for their investment. The advice
was not always followed, and Combe became as exasperated as Lombe and
others as he saw Chapman fail to keep clarity in financial matters. In
September he rebuked Chapman for copying one of his letters to another
correspondent without permission, but he thought Chapman more fool than
knave, and continued to defend him to Lombe, assuring him on 28 November
that Chapman was not dishonest, but merely lacked precision in his running
of the business.[59] By this time Combe was falling out with Lombe on his
own account. Lombe was making ever more peremptory demands of him in
connection with the Scottish education question. Combe, though not a
churchgoer, was not an atheist either, a fact of which he reminded Lombe
in a letter of 27 November calculated to offend, while remaining perfectly
polite. Combe intended to show Lombe that he was his own man and no
one's creature:

> Apparently your ultimate aim is Atheism; and you would use me as a
> means of arriving at it; not the most direct means perhaps, but still
> calculated in your estimation to pave the way for it. This is the infer-
> ence I draw from your last letter. My Lecture . . . was delivered before
> your letter reached me, and I am glad that it expresses so strongly my
> views. From it, you will be able to judge whether these meet your appro-
> bation. If they do, I am ready to proceed [to publish the lecture with
> financial support from Lombe]. If not, I beg to mention that Mr George
> Jacob Holyoake, Editor of the Reasoner, is *the man* who, so far as I
> know, would act most in accordance with your convictions. He is a
> very able man, & an uncompromising Atheist.[60]

Lombe took offence, and the correspondence with Combe came to an abrupt
end in January 1852, shortly before Lombe's death. Combe had shown great
forbearance under Lombe's repeated attempts to bully him. He was, after all,

not a young publisher or editor eager for support, but a man in his early sixties who had been a successful lawyer, the owner of a family brewery, and the author of a best-selling book, *The Constitution of Man*, first published in 1828 and reissued several times over the years, with a sale of 80,000 copies in Britain alone by 1848.[61] Combe was the undisputed leader of the phrenological movement, and had managed the difficult trick of remaining largely respectable in Edinburgh society despite espousing this science of the brain founded on a deterministic view of human nature. Following the pioneers of phrenology, Franz Joseph Gall and Johann Kaspar Spurzheim, Combe believed that by observing the size of various organs in the brain which phrenology divided into faculties under the headings 'Affective' (expressing emotions) and 'Intellectual', one could come to an accurate understanding of an individual's moral and intellectual nature, its strengths and weaknesses. Among these faculties were Acquisitiveness, Amativeness, Benevolence, Combativeness, Constructiveness, Destructiveness, Firmness, Love of Approbation, Secretiveness, Self-esteem, Veneration, and Wit. The affective organs – many of them shared with animals – were to be found at the back of the head, with Amativeness placed at the bottom of the skull, while the intellectual organs (Comparison and Causality, for example) occupied a position higher up, at the top of the head, in the 'coronal' region. All this Combe ascribed to 'natural law'.[62]

Though he was attacked for materialism leading to atheism, Combe retained his faith in a benevolent, if distant, deity. He believed that the understanding of a person's make-up could be used for moral improvement through education and increased self-knowledge and for the amelioration of poverty and ignorance among the working class in particular. He favoured penal reform, opposing corporal and capital punishment in *Remarks on the Principles of Criminal Legislation, and the Practice of Prison Discipline* (1844), and advocating education for the reform of a prisoner's mind rather than punishment for his body. Combe's independent wealth, his happy marriage in middle age to Cecilia Siddons, daughter of the actress Sarah Siddons, and his own large organ of self-esteem allowed him to go his own way regardless of what others thought. On Sundays he and his wife drove intrepidly about Edinburgh in their carriage instead of going to church. 'The neighbours are accustomed to our profanity, and do not trouble us', he told a friend in 1848, 'but we are *the only* individuals apparently who venture on such a desecration, as they call it, of the Lord's day.'[63]

Undoubtedly there is a comic element in Combe's dedication to his theory. He drew up phrenological charts of everyone he met, though in 1852 he found Carlyle a difficult subject because of the thickness of his hair. He had studied the young Queen Victoria through opera glasses when he found himself opposite the royal box at a performance of *I Puritani* in July 1838. This is how he summed her up in his notebook:

> The coronal region is remarkably broad and rather high, particularly in the regions of Conscientiousness and Firmness. The middle region, comprising Veneration and Hope, seemed full; Benevolence, Imitativeness, and Ideality were rather full. The anterior lobe seemed broad but not long from behind forward. The lower or perceptive organs were large, those of Form and Language very large.
>
> I infer from these imperfect data that the queen has very considerable force of character, and is not a stranger to irascibility; but she has great powers of self-command. She has a very favourable combination of the propensities and sentiments; and she will possess energy combined with tact and good sense. She will be firm, decided, and upright.[64]

This was on the whole a rather accurate prediction of what Victoria, who was not yet twenty when Combe observed her, would turn out to be like as a monarch. Sometimes, however, his 'discoveries' about character bore the marks of the blindingly obvious; he was no less likely than anyone else to form an opinion from conversation and ordinary observation, and could be swayed by stereotypical expectations. For example, he decided on a visit to Holland in 1834 that in the Dutch 'the coronal region, and the organs of the domestic affections are large, and one sees everywhere cleanliness, order, and propriety'.[65] Still, as an educational and prison reformer Combe was a force to be reckoned with, and while some critics publicly or privately derided the phrenological framework, a number of influential people sought his advice and expertise. Charles Bray was a disciple, addressing Combe as 'master' in his letters and using phrenological observation when employing servants or deciding on worthy recipients of his philanthropic schemes in Coventry. In the autobiography he wrote in old age he remembered, with a touch of self-irony, how he had gone to London in the 1830s after reading Combe on phrenology, 'had my head shaved, and a cast of it taken that I might examine the skull of the man whose character I knew best'. He also bought a hundred casts of interesting skulls from James Deville, the leading phrenological manipulator and cast-maker in London, at whose shop-cum-museum in the Strand Bray had undergone the investigation of his own cranium.[66]

Others less eccentric than Bray turned to Combe for assessments of their children, particularly when they had awkward or rebellious sons. The liberal MP and anti-Corn Law agitator Richard Cobden asked about his son in July 1850; Combe wrote at length about the boy's large organs of Combativeness and Destructiveness, and his tendency to indulge in 'animal pleasures', for which 'careful training' was required. Cobden replied gratefully, saying he had passed on Combe's letter to his son's schoolmaster.[67] The royal family also sought his advice, inviting him to Buckingham Palace in 1846 to examine the heads of the royal children. In October 1850 Albert, visiting Edinburgh with the rest of the family, held long discussions with Combe about the constitution of the Prince of Wales and the direction his education should take. Dr Ernest Becker, secretary to Prince Albert and tutor to his son, spent three months in Edinburgh during the winter of 1850–1 studying phrenology with Combe. Albert and Becker were worried about the boy's 'violent & selfish dispositions', which they hoped to correct.[68] On a lighter note, Combe visited Buckingham Palace again in May 1852 to examine the heads of the little princesses Vicky and Alice, who talked flippantly of 'bumps'. Combe asked them who had made their brains and skulls. 'God', they replied. 'Precisely so', he said. 'Now whatever God made should be treated with respect. The word "bump" is intended to be ludicrous; let us therefore call them organs.' The girls agreed.[69]

During a visit to London in May and June 1851, the versatile Combe divided his time between visiting Buckingham Palace to consider the appropriate education for the heir to the throne with his father and tutor and calling in at 142 Strand to discuss plans for the radical *Westminster Review* with Chapman. He lost no time in assessing his new acquaintance phrenologically. Combe's analysis, based partly on craniological observation and partly on the impression Chapman's conversation made on him, was recorded in his journal for 21 June, after his second meeting with Chapman:

His anterior lobe is too short for much mental power, altho' well developed in the knowing organs & also full in the reflecting. Benev[olence], Ideality, Imit[ativeness], Wonder & Veneration seem largely, or fully developed, but Conscientiousness appeared to me less. The temperament is Bilious, lymphatic, nervous. I have less hope of his making a first rate work of it than when I last conversed with him.[70]

In September Combe was in London again visiting the Great Exhibition in Hyde Park. His journal records that on the evening of 5 September 'Mr John Chapman & his Wife' called on him to discuss the *Review*. Chapman gave him a revised version of the Prospectus, which Combe was sorry to see still lacked decisiveness about its objects:

It announces every thing in an empirical form, without stating a foundation in nature for any thing . . . Mr Chapman's own brain, a short anterior lobe, is, I think the cause of this. His wife, I am told, reads & decides on the M.S. offered to him for publication, & her anterior lobe is longer & in Causality better developed than his; but she has a large Secretiveness.[71]

Between the June and September meetings with Chapman, Combe had been a visitor at the Brays' house in Coventry. There, on 29 August, he recorded his impressions of Bray himself and of his long-term house guest, Marian Evans:

The whole party are superior and interesting persons. Mr Bray is a Ribbon manufacturer about 40; a Phrenologist and convert to the natural Laws, with an excellent intellect, bilious, nervous, lymphatic and sanguine temperament, excellent coronal region, but great Comb[ativeness] and Destruc[tiveness] and very deficient Concentrativeness. He is proprietor of the Coventry Herald, which he uses as the organ of the new philosophy and its applications, so far as public opinion will allow him to go.

Miss Evans is the most extraordinary person of the party. She translated Strauss's work 'Das Leben Jesu' from the German, including the Hebrew, Greek, and Latin quotations in it, without assistance; and it is said to be admirably executed. She has a very large brain, the anterior lobe is remarkable for length, breadth, and height, the coronal region is large, the front rather predominating; the base is broad at Destruc[tiveness]; but moderate at Aliment[iveness], and the portion behind the ear is rather small in the regions of Comb[ativeness] Amat[iveness] and

Philopro[genitiveness]. Love of approb[ation], and Concentrativeness are large. Her temper[ament] is nervous lymphatic . . . She shewed great analytic power and an instinctive soundness of judgment. We had a great deal of conversation on religion, political economy, and political events, and altogether . . . she appeared to me the ablest woman whom I have seen . . . She is extremely feminine and gentle; and the great strength of her intellect combined with this quality renders her very interesting.[72]

After this glowing assessment of Marian's intellectual qualities, it is hardly surprising that Combe's doubts about Chapman's inferior ones should have resurfaced on his return to London. By December Combe, back in Edinburgh, was complaining of Chapman's tactlessness in broadcasting the names of certain supporters who did not want to be publicly associated with the *Westminster Review* – Combe's friend Robert Chambers, for example, whose publishing firm might be disadvantaged by the connection and who (on account of the widespread suspicion that he was the author of *Vestiges of Creation*) was already under constant scrutiny in Edinburgh, 'as the saints are watching every opportunity of convicting him of a leaning to infidelity'. Combe's hopes for the success of the *Review* were kept alive by his admiration for Marian Evans and his knowledge of her close involvement. As he told Chapman frankly:

I would . . . very respectfully recommend you to use Miss Evans's tact and judgment as an aid to your own. She has certain organs large in her brain which are not so fully developed in yours, and she will judge more correctly of the influence upon other persons of what you write and do, than you will do yourself.[73]

Marian had already begun to use her tact and judgment to good effect with Chapman. When he took Susanna to Coventry for a weekend in September to finalise arrangements for Marian's return to the Strand at the end of the month, she spoke to him about his role. He noted the conversation in his diary:

Miss Evans thinks I should lose power and influence by becoming a writer in the Westminster Review, and could not then maintain that dignified relation with the various contributors that she thinks I may do otherwise.[74]

All summer she had been corresponding with him about the *Review*, becoming increasingly confident as she found him amenable to her suggestions. In particular, she advised and encouraged him as he struggled to involve a reluctant John Stuart Mill in the fortunes of the *Westminster*. The jointly drafted Prospectus, criticised strongly by Martineau and more mildly by Combe, met with an extremely frosty reception from Mill. Naturally he took a close interest in the fate of his old journal. Indeed, Hickson, though already in discussions with Chapman about the purchase of the *Review*, had hoped to persuade Mill to take it on himself for a second time. It was only after Mill's reply of 29 April, declining either to buy or to edit the *Westminster*, that Hickson called on Chapman to agree terms.[75] Mill hoped that Hickson would sell to someone with good radical credentials; for reasons not made clear, he was 'not sure nor do I think it likely, that I should be disposed to work for Chapman'.[76] When the latter wrote on 21 May to request an interview with him, Mill replied that he would be 'happy to give an opinion' on anything to do with the journal 'in which I have always taken & still take much interest', but it must be by correspondence, 'as I am much engaged at present, & living out of town'.[77]

On receiving the draft Prospectus, Mill sent his criticisms on 9 June. These were uncompromising:

> The Prospectus says, that the Review is to be distinctly characterised by 'certain definite but broad principles': but instead of laying down any such principles it contains little else than details of the measures which the review will advocate on the principal political questions just now discussed in the newspapers. The only sentence which seems intended for a declaration of principles is that forming the third paragraph – & this, so far from 'distinctly characterising' any set of opinions or course of conduct, contains nothing to distinguish the review from any liberal or semi liberal newspaper or periodical, or from anybody who says he is for reform but not for revolution . . . By the statement that 'reforms to be salutary must be graduated to the average moral & intellectual growth of society' I presume is meant (though I am by no means sure of the meaning if any) that the measures of a government

ought never to be in advance of the average intellect & virtue of the people – according to which doctrine there would neither have been the Reformation, the Commonwealth, nor the Revolution of 1688, & the stupidity & habitual indifference of the mass of mankind would bear down by its dead weight all the efforts of the more intelligent & active minded few.[78]

There is more in the same merciless vein, after which Mill says he cannot promise to be a contributor: 'My willingness to contribute even occasionally to the West[minste]r under any new management would entirely depend on the opinion I form of it after seeing it in operation.'[79] Marian, with whom Chapman consulted about this onslaught and the best way to respond to it, 'heartily wished' that they had thought over the Prospectus more carefully before sending it out: 'Everything has been too hurried. But you will say "After meat, mustard" – your wisdom comes too late. Still the moral is not useless – *Caution* for the future.'[80] She followed this up on 15 June with a set of detailed corrections to Chapman's draft reply to Mill, mainly aimed at making it more incisive. She advised him to 'leave out the dashes, which weaken instead of strengthening the impression on the reader' and to write 'that, I am convinced' instead of 'I am convinced that'. She also thought that telling Mill that his advice had been 'gratefully received' sounded 'too much like a craving for alms'; better to write 'duly valued'.[81]

Whatever Chapman finally wrote, it drew from Mill another severe reply on 20 June, once more on the grounds that the plans were not bold enough. Mill recalled the days of the *Westminster Review* under Bentham and his own father James Mill:

The reason you give for what you very truly call the air of conservatism in the Prospectus, is intelligible; but does not seem to me to render advisable the use of expressions giving the idea that the West[minste]r no longer wishes to be considered as professing extreme opinions. The review was founded by people who held what were then thought extreme opinions, & it is only needed as an organ of opinions as much in advance of the present state of the public mind as those were in advance of its then state. Anything less is but child's play after the events of the last three years in Europe [following the revolutions of 1848] & besides, every intermediate position is fully occupied by other periodicals.[82]

Mill wanted the journal to be a truly radical organ, which it did become again under Chapman, despite the pusillanimous Prospectus. Chapman felt bruised by all the criticisms – from Martineau, Combe, Mill, and Frank Newman, who also complained of the Prospectus – and thought Mill's letters 'cold' and 'half sarcastic'.[83] Nevertheless, he persevered in his efforts to gain at least the good will of his distinguished correspondent. Mill agreed to read a revised version of the Prospectus, giving his view on 17 October that it was an improvement, but still not the 'simple & plain expression of the plan & principles' which he would have liked to see. Thawing by a degree or two, he concluded: 'The first number will show what meaning the writers attach to the word Progress, & how far the review will be an organ of it.'[84]

For the time being, Mill was not prepared to do more than criticise from the sidelines. Fortunately, Chapman's sanguine temperament prevented him from retiring hurt from the fray. He continued to petition Mill politely from time to time, and was rewarded with an article on philosophy for the October 1852 number of the *Review*. Much later, in 1867, Mill generously lent Chapman £600 at no interest to enable him to continue during a particularly serious financial crisis.[85] In 1851, however, Mill was in a generally savage mood, and Chapman was by no means the only recipient of strong letters. Mill told Hickson in June, apropos of the article he and his wife Harriet had written on the enfranchisement of women, that he would not accept any editorial changes to its text, reminding Hickson that this was the only condition under which he ever consented to write. In October he expressed his strong disagreement with Hickson's article 'Life and Immortality' in clear, logical, brutal terms: 'You cannot expect me to like an article of which the conclusions are so opposite to mine; & as I do not think that they admit of being supported by good arguments, this implies that I think yours fallacious.' He pointed out errors in Greek quotations, and made much the same stylistic criticism which Marian Evans had made to Chapman in June about his reply to Mill. 'Your article', Mill tells Hickson, 'loses altogether in appearance of strength by the capitals and italics. Italics are bad enough but Capitals make anything look weak.'[86]

Though Mill had always been cool and rational – Carlyle wrote in 1835 of his great esteem for him, 'but to love *him*? It were like loving the 47th of Euclid'[87] – he had by this time become completely estranged from friends and family because of perceived slights towards his wife. They had only recently got married, in April 1851, after twenty years of being in love; Harriet Taylor had been in an unhappy marriage until the death of her husband in 1849. Mill was sensitive to rumours about their relationship before John Taylor's death, though it appears to have remained platonic throughout that time. Now he feared that his marriage laid him open to renewed gossip, and his response was to withdraw from society. He lived in Greenwich with Harriet and neither visited nor invited visitors – hence his remark to Chapman on 23 May that he would not meet him personally to discuss the *Westminster Review*, explaining that he lived 'out of town'.

Whatever the much maligned Prospectus had looked like when first sent out in draft to Martineau, Combe, and Mill, it was still, as they all noted, a rather feeble document on its final appearance in December. It seems that Marian Evans had not been able to influence Chapman very much in the preparation of this declaration of his aims. The final wording was surely more his than hers. Chapman's desire for a wide readership, with the solvency which would come with it, overcame his radicalism in the paragraphs which followed the announcement that he was to be the new publisher and that the *Review* was to have unnamed 'newly-appointed Editors'. The prose has his flabbiness of style, not Marian's sharpness, and the document strikes the cautious note to which Mill had so cogently objected. It begins reasonably enough, if hardly briskly:

> The fundamental principle of the work will be the recognition of the Law of Progress. Nevertheless, in the deliberate advocacy of organic changes, it will not be forgotten that the institutions of man, no less than the products of nature, are strong and durable in proportion as they are the results of a gradual development, and that the most salutary and permanent reforms are those which, while embodying the wisdom of the time, yet sustain such a relation to the moral and intellectual condition of the people as to ensure their support.[88]

This opening should have been followed by a brief account of the areas of discussion to be covered in the *Review* and a promise to commit the enterprise to the cause of progress while at the same time allowing writers of different religious and political views an airing in its pages, particularly in the independent section. The second paragraph does try to do this, but, lengthy and convoluted, it fails to be either clear or informative:

> Convinced that the same fundamental truths are apprehended under a variety of forms, and that, therefore, opposing systems may in the end prove complements of each other, the Editors will endeavour to institute such a radical and comprehensive treatment of those contro-verted questions which are practically momentous, as may aid in the conciliation of divergent views. In furtherance of this object, they have determined to render available a limited portion of the work, under the head of 'Independent Contributions' – for the reception of articles ably setting forth opinions which, though not discrepant with the general spirit of the Review, may be at variance with the particular ideas or measures it will advocate. The primary object of this depart-ment is to facilitate the expression of opinion by men of high mental power and culture who, while they are zealous friends of freedom and progress, yet differ widely on special points of great practical concern, both from the Editors and from each other.[89]

Chapman's lack of intellectual clarity was not the only problem. He felt unable to express to the full the radicalism he wished to promote, particu-larly in religion. His dilemma was that he was still known as the 'Unitarian' publisher who had taken over from Green; a number of his authors and, more significantly, many of the purchasers of his books were Unitarians, British and American. He could not risk alienating them by advertising too radical an agenda on religion, and he therefore tried to distance the Prospectus from complete 'infidelity'. Copies were circulated among his Unitarian acquaintances – Greg, Martineau, and others whom he wished to have as subscribers and contributors to the *Review*. Henry Crabb Robinson had sight of it too. He describes the conversation on 28 October at his friend Mrs Reid's house, as the assembled Unitarians discussed the Prospectus, 'which professes to set out on the principle of Progress & has an independent depart-ment for the insertion of opinions not those of the editors'. Robinson's conclusion is that the plan, and the editors' avowal of having 'sound negative views' – an implied admission that they have none affirmative – satisfy me that this Rev. will be devoted to the spread of infidelity, tho' not so coarsely perhaps as the Leader. It will however drive the Prospective out of the field – or at all events the Prospective and the Westminster cannot issue from the same *officina*.[90]

The *Prospective Review*, run completely on Unitarian lines and published by Chapman, did, as Robinson predicted, go under as a result of Chapman taking over the *Westminster*, though it limped on until February 1855. Robinson's mention of the *Leader* is telling. This was a truly radical weekly paper begun in March 1850 by G. H. Lewes and his friend Thornton Hunt, son of Leigh Hunt. The Hunt family had famous radical credentials. Leigh Hunt had been the friend of Shelley and Byron, and with his brother John had spent time in prison from 1813 to 1815 for a 'libel' on the Prince Regent in their newspaper, the *Examiner*. Now Thornton, a Chartist and active member of the Friends of Italy movement, set up the *Leader* to advocate social, political, and religious reforms. He was responsible for the political half of the paper, recruiting Holyoake and W. J. Linton, among others on the extreme wing of the radical party, while Lewes looked after the part devoted to literature, theatre, and the arts.

Lewes was also a seasoned contributor to the *Westminster Review* under Hickson, having written for it since 1840 on subjects including French drama, Shelley, and Spinoza. He attended Chapman's soirées, and was well known in London's radical circles. Indeed, he embraced the Shelleyan principles of free thinking in religion and free living in sexual matters, condoning, and even encouraging, his wife Agnes's adultery with his friend Thornton Hunt. When he set off in November 1849 for Edinburgh, Manchester, and other large towns to drum up support for the *Leader*, Agnes was already pregnant with the first of her four children by Hunt. Edmund Lewes, registered by Lewes as his own son, was born in April 1850, two weeks after the launch of the *Leader*. Agnes already had three sons by Lewes himself.[91]

The radicalism embraced by the *Leader* was uncompromising. In December 1849 Lewes drafted a Prospectus which was a good deal bolder than Chapman's for the *Westminster*. The *Free Speaker*, as the paper was entitled at this preliminary stage, would endorse 'the Sacred Right of Opinion and the Right to its *Free Utterance*'.[92] In Edinburgh he obtained promises of subscription from

Combe and Chambers; from Manchester he wrote to Thornton Hunt at the beginning of December that he had met Dr Hodgson, Geraldine Jewsbury, and Manchester's most notorious visitor Froude, all of whom were willing to support the paper in some way, though Froude, it was noted, had no money.[93]

Froude, for his part, wrote to Kingsley about this meeting with Lewes, describing the plan for the *Leader* and delivering an unflattering opinion of Lewes (as well as of Manchester society):

> We get along here, among coughs and colds and influenzas, and fog and smoke and blackguards and fools, and the one or two wiser men, tolerably. A great specimen of the blackguard I met the other day . . . It was Lewes. He is agitating for assistants in the great work of the destruction of prejudices of all sorts by a weekly paper (this is strictly confidential), a pious crusade in which my help was wished for, and in which yours too will be thankfully accepted.
>
> They pay twice the price for articles of any other weekly paper. They have got I think all the best of the working *clever writers* in London – the staff of *Punch* and of the *Spectator*, etc. – and mean to go ahead in religion and politics. I have no doubt it will be very clever and successful as far as money goes, but I declined working in such a cause with people I didn't know, and I might have added didn't respect. *Thackeray is one.* I fancy there are many of them pretty well tired of working with the gag in their mouths, and this is to be [their] spurt for freedom.[94]

These remarks exhibit Froude's peculiar way of facing both ways at once. It is hard to tell whether he approves of the idea of the *Leader* or not, though his disdain for Lewes, Thackeray, and the bohemian *Punch* set is clear enough. The description of Lewes as a 'blackguard' may just be a careless exaggeration following on from his denigration of Manchester society. It may refer to Lewes's enthusiasm and a certain thrusting social manner unattractive to the Oxford man. It is also possible that Froude had heard of Lewes's free marital arrangements, and disapproved of them. In addition, Froude is no doubt mindful of Kingsley's conservatism in religious matters, and adapts his tone accordingly. 'Chapman', he continues, 'told me, when I spoke of the Review, that Lewes would work at it. I said I wouldn't work with Lewes, so there we came to flat issues.'[95] It seems from this that already in late 1849

110

Chapman was considering starting a radical journal, though he was not yet negotiating actively for the *Westminster Review*.

Froude continued to speak and act somewhat disingenuously as far as the *Leader* was concerned. Despite his antagonism towards Lewes, he did contribute to the early issues of the paper. Two short 'Political Fables', 'The Lions and the Oxen' and 'The Farmer and the Fox', and three further fables, 'The Parable of the Bread-Fruit Tree', 'Compensations', and 'The Cat's Pilgrimage', appeared between 30 March – the opening number – and 20 July 1850. These addressed, in the oblique allegorical manner of the genre, questions of evolution, the supplanting of old beliefs by new, and the futility of a Faustian reaching after unattainable knowledge.[96] Froude also had a letter published, above his own signature, on 6 July. It was a voluntary contribution to the debate on the marriage laws being conducted in the pages of the *Leader*, whose editorial position was to agitate for greater freedom of divorce. Froude came in on the side of conservatism in this case, claiming support from, of all things, the very Goethe novel he had imitated with such notorious results in *The Nemesis of Faith*. Of *Elective Affinities* he says here that Goethe's aim is to show that 'the right way was not the way of self-indulgence, but of self-control' – which is to attribute to Goethe a single-minded purpose which the novel's ambiguity of tone refuses to endorse.[97]

In matters of religion, however, Froude, still smarting from his own treatment by the Church of England as represented by the Sub-Rector of Exeter College, declared himself at this time keen to attack Anglicanism alongside the *Leader*. Late in 1850 the Pope restored a Roman Catholic hierarchy in England, causing great controversy. Carlyle noted on 23 November that there were speeches in Parliament and daubings on walls bearing the legends 'No Popery!', 'Burn the Pope!' and 'Kick the Pope's bottom'.[98] The *Leader*, though as an advocate of free thinking hardly a supporter of Catholicism, could not resist attacking the Church of England for its intolerance on the Catholic question; the issue was a major subject in its pages for several months. Froude, who would later be the apologist for Henry VIII's break with Rome (and would re-sign the Thirty-Nine Articles himself), was delighted at this point to encourage the *Leader*'s onslaught. He wrote to the despised Lewes in February 1851 in friendly and vehement terms:

> If the Roman Catholics are bullied I hope to see them resist, keep their
> titles & take the consequences. It would utterly checkmate good John

Bull, who has so long gone without Religion himself, that the notion of suffering for it except in Novels or History has become entirely inconceivable to him. Can't you stir them up to it? The Church of England is the great lie which we must get burnt up; and I would help the Catholics to fire & faggot if I could.[99]

Perhaps the key word to explain Froude's strength of feeling here is 'bullied'; he associated the Church of England with the various authorities who had bullied him as a child and young man, namely his father the Archdeacon, his brother the Tractarian, the teachers and pupils of Westminster School, and the clerical Sub-Rector of his college.

Word reached Max Müller and Bunsen that Froude was writing for the *Leader*. 'F. must have gone mad', the latter wrote in alarm on 15 May 1850, 'or have been far more so politically than I imagined.' The *Leader*, he heard, was '*red and raw!*' Max Müller replied that he had not seen the paper and did not believe Froude to be the author of any 'red and raw' articles, but merely of a literary piece.[100] Such responses to the *Leader* serve to put in context Chapman's desire to keep the *Westminster* from attracting opprobrium, while still sticking to radical principles. Froude was happy to write for Chapman, contributing an admired essay on Mary Stuart to the first number under Chapman's control and continuing to write regularly until 1857. When he collected his periodical articles to republish them in two volumes in 1867 under the title *Short Studies on Great Subjects*, he was willing to acknowledge the *Westminster Review* as the source of several of the essays, but gave no original source of publication for the *Leader* pieces.

Unlike Froude, Lewes was not ashamed to be associated with both the *Leader* and the *Westminster*. During the summer of 1851 he and Chapman met several times; on 1 August they went to the theatre together.[101] In June Marian Evans, still in Coventry and not yet personally acquainted with Lewes, noticed that 'the names of Thornton Hunt, Lewes, Linton and several more' had appeared in the *London Gazette* as a result of the dissolving of their partnership in the 'Leader Newspaper Company' – which seemed, she thought, 'a presentiment of failure'.[102] The principals regrouped, selling the paper to the wealthy radical Edward Pigott, who ran it at a loss until it folded in 1860.[103]

Meanwhile, Chapman thought of Lewes for an article on modern novelists for his first number in charge of the *Westminster*. He had already tried

Thackeray, to whom Thornton Hunt introduced him on 12 June. On that occasion Thackeray had joked that he 'wanted to buy at the "trade price" some of my "atheistic" publications', Chapman noted in his diary. A couple of days later he asked Thackeray to write the article. The characteristic reply was 'that he, from his position, could not criticise his contemporaries, and that the only person he could thoroughly well review, and cut up would be himself!' Thackeray was sensitive about the 'rivalry and partisanship' which was being stirred up between him and Dickens, mainly by Dickens's pugnacious friend John Forster. He suggested Chapman should try Charlotte Brontë, who was visiting her publisher George Smith in London at this time.[104] When Chapman put this idea in a letter to Marian Evans, she replied that the same objection would apply to the author of *Jane Eyre* as to Thackeray: 'She would have to leave out Currer Bell, who is perhaps the best of them all.'[105]

Chapman next asked Marian to do the piece herself, but she declined, feeling that she would have enough work to do acting as co-editor and writing large parts of the regular 'Summaries' of recently published literature, English, American, French, and German, which were to be an innovative feature of the new *Westminster Review*. She agreed that Lewes was a good choice for the modern novelists article.[106] On 27 August Chapman recorded a meeting with Lewes on the subject. Though they were on good terms, the two men had very different temperaments; Chapman, who took himself seriously as an intellectual, privately expressed his disdain for Lewes, his superior in intelligence, knowledge, and experience, but a man who wore his learning lightly and did not take himself too seriously:

> [Lewes] seems to have no idea of treating the subject which shall exhibit a definite purpose in the Article and since conversing with him about it, it has occurred to me that Froude would be a much more appropriate man. I suggested that he should give the characteristics of each of the leading Novelists, describe their relative and intrinsic merits, erect a standard of Criticism whereby to judge them with a view of elevating the productions of the Novelists as works of Art and as refining the moral influences. If more were claimed from the Novelist the best of them would accord more. But Lewes is a 'bread scholar' and lacks that enthusiasm of thought and earnest purpose which I must alone seek for in Contributors to the Westminster.[107]

Chapman arranged with Lewes for a review by Marian Evans of W. R. Greg's *Creed of Christendom*, which had been published by Chapman in March, to appear in the *Leader* in September. The diary for 23 September notes: 'Lewes called in the afternoon to express his high opinion of Miss Evans's Article in the Leader.'[108] On 6 October, with Marian once more permanently installed at 142 Strand, Chapman 'had a long walk' with her in Hyde Park, after which they called at William Jeffs's bookshop in the Burlington Arcade on Piccadilly to ask him to lend them French books for the *Review*.[109] There they bumped into Lewes. Marian Evans recorded the meeting briefly in a letter to Charles Bray on 8 October: 'I was introduced to Lewes the other day in Jeff[s]'s shop – a sort of miniature Mirabeau in appearance.' The allusion is to Lewes's short stature and pockmarked face.[110]

It was a quiet, apparently unpromising beginning to the friendship between her and Lewes which was to develop into love, though not before she had fallen unrequitedly in love with another man, a friend of both Chapman and Lewes. Herbert Spencer, living and working at *The Economist* office opposite Chapman's house, was a close friend of Lewes, a contributor to the *Leader*, and a new author on Chapman's publishing list. In January 1851 Chapman brought out Spencer's first book, *Social Statics, or the Conditions Essential to Human Happiness Specified, and the First of Them Developed*, usually referred to by its short title, *Social Statics*. As the longer title suggests, this was a natural successor to the Utilitarian philosophy of Bentham and the Mills, with its emphasis on social conditions and human happiness. Spencer was an optimist, believing in a 'natural law' of human adaptation and progress; in many ways, his theory was the equivalent for human society of the theory of evolution for the plant and animal world soon to be expressed definitively by Darwin. Like John Stuart Mill, Spencer valued the freedom of the individual to make self-interested choices where these did not disadvantage others. He favoured reforms in education and in political representation; he also thought that the sexes should be treated as equal in law and in fact and that the training of children should be done through persuasion and reasoning rather than punishment.

The book, which Lewes admired, praising it in the *Leader* on 22 February 1851 as comparable to the work of Spinoza,[111] was not immediately successful, though Spencer's articles in the *Westminster Review* were soon to earn him the respect of liberal political and social commentators and of Darwin himself.

114

John Chapman, photograph (probably taken in middle age).

Susanna Chapman, 1850s.

John Buonarotti Papworth's architectural drawings for the rebuilding of 142 Strand, done in 1832 for John Wright, wine merchant and tavern keeper. The drawing of the front elevation shows four floors, though five were eventually built. The ground plan shows the shop at the front at street level, with a bar in the middle and the staircase leading to the upper floors; at basement level the capacious wine cellar stretches under the pavement at the front, with the kitchen, scullery, larder, and 'maids' W.C.' at the back.

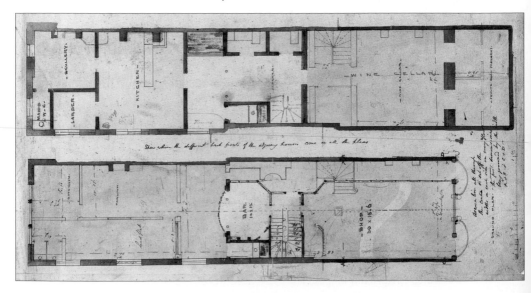

The front of Somerset House facing the Strand, with adjacent houses. No. 142 is the building on the extreme right of the picture, rising one floor higher than its neighbours.

The back of Somerset House, overlooking the Thames, with Waterloo Bridge in the foreground. The engraving, which dates from 1847, before the Thames was embanked, shows the terrace where Marian Evans and Herbert Spencer used to walk and talk, using Chapman's key, during their close relationship in 1852.

Marian Evans, painted in February 1850 by her Swiss landlord, François D'Albert Durade, shortly before she returned to England to begin her journalistic career with Chapman.

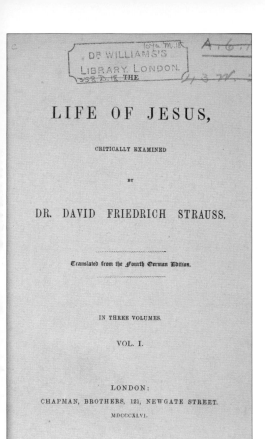

THE

LIFE OF JESUS,

CRITICALLY EXAMINED

BY

DR. DAVID FRIEDRICH STRAUSS.

Translated from the Fourth German Edition.

IN THREE VOLUMES.

VOL. I.

LONDON:
CHAPMAN, BROTHERS, 121, NEWGATE STREET.
MDCCCXLVI.

Title-page of Mary Ann Evans's anonymous translation of David Friedrich Strauss's *Life of Jesus*, published by Chapman when he was briefly in partnership with his brother Thomas. This copy is George Eliot's own, given to her life's partner G. H. Lewes, whose library was presented to Dr Williams's Library after his death by his son Charles Lee Lewes.

Title-page of Marian Evans's translation of Ludwig Feuerbach's *Essence of Christianity*, published by Chapman just after he moved his business from 142 Strand to King William Street in June 1854. This is the only book she published under her own name.

THE

ESSENCE OF CHRISTIANITY.

BY

LUDWIG FEUERBACH.

Translated from the Second German Edition,
BY
MARIAN EVANS,
TRANSLATOR OF "STRAUSS'S LIFE OF JESUS."

LONDON:
JOHN CHAPMAN,
8, KING WILLIAM STREET, STRAND.
MDCCCLIV.

Charles Dickens, by
Daniel Maclise, 1839.

T. Hosmer Shepherd,
'Holywell Street,
St. Clements. With One
of the Old Signs –
The Half Moon', 1853.
Holywell Street, leading
off the Strand nearly
opposite number 142,
was picturesque, with its
medieval buildings, but it
was also dirty, crowded,
and notorious for its
pornographic bookshops.

Photograph of J. A. Froude
on a carte-de-visite given to
Thomas and Jane Carlyle.

Title-page of Froude's controversial
novel, *The Nemesis of Faith*, published by
Chapman in 1849. Froude resigned his
fellowship at Exeter College, Oxford,
after the book was burnt publicly by
the Sub-Rector of the College.

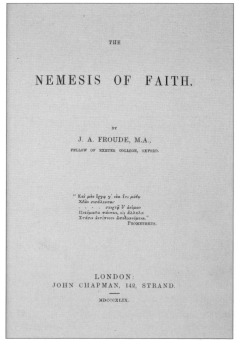

THE

NEMESIS OF FAITH.

BY

J. A. FROUDE, M.A.,
FELLOW OF EXETER COLLEGE, OXFORD.

" Καὶ μὴν ἔργῳ γ' οὐκ ἔτι μύθῳ
Χθὼν σεσάλευται·
. . . . . . σκιρτᾷ δ' ἀνέμων
Πνεύματα πάντων, εἰς ἄλληλα
Στάσιν ἀντίπνοον ἀποδεικνύμενα."
PROMETHEUS.

LONDON:
JOHN CHAPMAN, 142, STRAND.
MDCCCXLIX.

University College London, designed by William Wilkins and opened in 1828 to offer a university education to students who were not members of the Church of England. A number of professors at UCL, including Frank Newman, published their books and articles with Chapman.

Spencer had known that it would be difficult for an unknown writer to publish a serious sociological work with radical tendencies. Like everyone else with a book of this kind to place, he approached Chapman, telling his father in March 1850 that he had made an appointment at 142 Strand:

I am to read him part of the manuscript. Judging from the attitude he takes, I expect there will be considerable difficulty in getting the book published. He speaks of his position as being such that he dare not speculate; and that the question would turn more upon the degree of dependence he could place upon my ability to meet the cost, supposing the book should not pay. He says, moreover, that from his past experience of philosophical books, it is probable that the more highly he thought of it the less hopeful he should be of its success.[112]

Since Chapman's finances, always precarious, had been badly affected by the loss of the American agency, his pessimistic prediction was more than merely tactical; it was justified by his experience. A few days later Spencer reported another meeting, at which Chapman had told him that his printer George Woodfall was willing to give Spencer two years' credit on the cost of printing, which was to be borne by Spencer, not Chapman. Looking back on the arrangement more than fifty years later from his position as the most respected British social philosopher of the nineteenth century, Spencer gave Chapman full credit for taking him on, even on these terms:

The moral of these facts is that in the absence of a sympathetic printer, and a sympathetic publisher (for Chapman was anxious to bring out the book), and in the absence of this partial security I was enabled to give [money owed to Spencer for his railway engineering work], the book would not have been issued at all.[113]

Chapman not being in a position to advertise it widely, and Spencer's name being as yet unknown, *Social Statics* made little immediate impression. Lewes's praise in the *Leader* may have been the only notice taken of it. In May 1851 Chapman asked Spencer to write a piece for the *Westminster* on the population question; it was eventually finished for the April 1852 number.[114] He now became acquainted with Marian Evans. She was soon accompanying him to the theatre, for which he was given free tickets in his capacity as drama critic of *The Economist*, and where they were sometimes joined by Lewes, who reviewed plays for the *Leader*.[115] During 1851 Spencer was frequently at number 142, where Chapman and Marian teased him about his 'eligible bachelor' status. He wrote in mock-serious phrenological terms to a friend:

> I doubt not you would have greatly enjoyed being a party to the *badinage* that has been carried on at my expense by Chapman and Miss Evans (the translatress of Strauss) for these two months past. They have taken upon themselves to choose me a wife; and the various arrangements and delays in effecting an introduction have, as you may suppose, afforded subject-matter for much mirth. The affair was put into their heads by the inquiry the young lady made as to the authorship of 'Social Statics' – whether Herbert Spencer was a real or an assumed name &c &c. So on the strength of the lady's admiration for the book, and all other circumstances seeming as they thought suitable, I was startled by the information that they had found a wife for me. Some fortnight or three weeks ago the introduction took place. I cannot say that my inclinations at all endorsed their theory. My objection – at least the chief one – is a somewhat unusual one. The young lady is in my opinion too highly intellectual; or I should rather say – morbidly intellectual. A small brain in a state of intense activity, is the best description. Moreover she seems pretty nearly as combative as I am; and has, I fancy, almost as much self-esteem.[116]

Soon enough Marian was hoping he might think of marrying *her*; she would have been discouraged if she had seen a letter of Spencer's in April 1851, in which he took stock on the eve of his thirty-first birthday. 'I am a bachelor still', he wrote to a male friend, 'and as I see no probability of being able to marry without being a drudge, why I have pretty well given up the idea.'[117] He meant that in order to marry he would have to sacrifice his philosophical vocation to a career which would pay better than writing articles for *The Economist* and the *Westminster Review*. He never made that sacrifice, remaining a bachelor all his long life.

If the appearance of *Social Statics* went largely unnoticed, another book published by Chapman in January 1851 achieved an immediate notoriety almost matching that of *The Nemesis of Faith* in 1849. This was *Letters on the Laws of Man's Nature and Development.* One of its authors was Harriet Martineau, an experienced writer on social and political affairs who had, twenty years earlier, impressed Lord Brougham, the Whig politician and architect of the 1832 Reform Act, by the grasp of political economy demonstrated in her illustrative tales. She had brought out several books with different publishers; on 6 November 1850 she asked one of them, Edward Moxon, if he would publish the *Letters*, acknowledging that the work was 'daring to the last degree' and that 'the public wh[ich] certainly *is* ready for such works, may not be *your* public'.[118] Moxon took the escape route thus offered to him, and declined, whereupon Harriet turned to Chapman. In this latest work she was compounding her sins in the eyes of the orthodox by completely abandoning her Unitarian beliefs for a materialist position. She had dispensed with the idea of a divine power, replacing it with a faith in the mesmerism which she was convinced had saved her life in 1844. Her co-author was Henry George Atkinson, a young man of private means, thirteen years her junior, whom she had met at the time of her mesmeric cure. He was a practitioner – she recommended Tom Arnold to seek mesmeric treatment from Atkinson for his acute stammer[119] – and a man of weak intellect but handsome looks and plenty of charm. According to Chapman, writing in 1859, a wealthy philanthropist from Leicester who had endured amputation under mesmerism offered £10,000 to set up a mesmeric hospital, which Atkinson refused because of disagreements with the chief physician involved in the concern.[120]

The *Letters* shocked the conventional by their uncompromising rejection of God and immortality, expressed with a paradoxical fervour which had London echoing with the witticism, said to have originated with Douglas Jerrold, 'There is no God, and Harriet Martineau is his prophet.' Marian quoted it in a letter to the Brays on 15 February 1851 in which she remarked on the fuss caused by the publication of the *Letters*.[121] Some months later the authors called at 142 Strand. Marian Evans told Sara Hennell about the visit, describing Atkinson in amused phrenological terms:

> Mr Atkinson wrinkles up his forehead horizontally and draws in his lips – has a good anterior lobe, but I should think it is not well fed with blood. I honour Harriet Martineau for her powers and industry and should be glad to think highly of her.[122]

Others were horrified. Harriet's female neighbours in Ambleside and Grasmere, including Mary Wordsworth and Mrs Arnold, 'have thought it right to decline intercourse with Miss Martineau', as Elizabeth Gaskell told a correspondent; Charlotte Brontë was upset by the book's 'avowed Atheism and Materialism'.[123] Henry Crabb Robinson, a friend of the Wordsworth and Arnold families, found the book less offensive than they did, but he thought it 'unwise'. He saw that Harriet Martineau had inexplicably become the 'pupil' of the preposterous Atkinson for the purpose of the *Letters*, which were in the form of questions by Harriet and answers by Atkinson. The book was flawed by a fatal lack of logic. It was a strange mixture of uncompromising atheism and naïve credulity – 'clairvoyance assorted with all the wildest pretensions of Mesmerism & Phrenology'. Though disliking this publication of Chapman's, which was talked about in scandalised tones by his London Unitarian friends as well as the Church of England circle in the Lake District, Robinson continued to call in as usual at 142 Strand. Here he was introduced in February 1851 to Marian Evans, 'translator of Strauss – no recommendation to me, certainly, but the contrary'. 'And yet', he added in his diary, 'there was something about her which pleased me much both in look and voice.' They talked about the Martineau-Atkinson book, which Marian described as 'studiously offensive'.[124]

Marian reviewed the *Letters* in the *Leader* on 1 and 8 March 1851, showing respect for Harriet Martineau's spirit of honest inquiry but criticising the unquestioning acceptance of clairvoyance by a woman who had rejected religious faith as irrational. Atkinson is treated with some asperity in the review, which ends with a quotation from one of his more ridiculous oracular remarks: '"When a Ghost appears on horseback and in armour", Mr Atkinson remarks, "we must conclude the horse and armour to have ghosts as well as men."'[125]

Chapman had done it again; he had published a scandalous book, though this one was intellectually inferior to the works by Strauss, Frank Newman, and Froude which had previously caused a stir in the literary world. The Atkinson-Martineau book had no lasting influence, but it was, in its way, a sign of the times, at least inasmuch as it addressed, if foolishly, the same large questions of belief and unbelief which were being raised by Chapman's other authors. Moreover, Harriet Martineau – if not her young friend Atkinson – was a name to be reckoned with. She and Chapman began an important author-publisher relationship in 1851, which was to last for seven years before

Chapman, like so many of Harriet's acquaintances and enthusiasms, fell from favour. The cause was his handling of the finances of the *Westminster Review*, which she undertook to support at a critical time, subsequently coming to the conclusion that he had used her money dishonestly.

But this is to anticipate. Chapman's task during 1851 was to prepare for the first number of the *Review* under his management. Through hard work and co-operation from May to December, he and Marian Evans assembled an impressive group of writers for the January 1852 number. The ex-Unitarian politician W. J. Fox, who had written the opening article in the *Westminster Review* on its first appearance in 1824, now led off the new number under Chapman with 'Representative Reform', a piece on the extension of the suffrage. The naturalist Edward Forbes wrote on shellfish, W. R. Greg on the relation between employers and employees, and Froude on Mary Stuart. James Martineau contributed the Lombe-displeasing article 'The Ethics of Christendom', Frank Newman discussed Continental theories of legislation, and Lewes sent in an article on Julia von Krüdener, an eighteenth-century German 'coquette and mystic', instead of the much-discussed piece Chapman had wanted on modern novelists. Marian Evans and Herbert Spencer shared most of the new section at the back, the analytic summary of recently published books headed 'Contemporary Literature of England', with Lewes doing the contemporary literature of France, the veteran *Westminster* reviewer Jane Sinnett covering German literature, and the American R. W. Griswold reviewing American books.

At almost a pound per published page, Chapman's rate of pay was generous, nearly matching that of the *Edinburgh Review*; Lewes earned £40 for thirty-eight pages on Shakespeare's critics in the *Edinburgh* in 1849, for example, and £22 for twenty-seven pages on Goethe in the *Westminster* in 1852.[126] Unfortunately, the other side of the balance sheet looked rather different. Where the *Edinburgh* seems to have had a circulation of about 9,000, Chapman, despite the excellence of his writers, could manage only about 1,300, as Marian told Combe in June 1852. The circulation was much as it had been in Mill's time; radicalism simply did not sell so well as more orthodox quarterly journalism. Chapman was losing about £100 a month.[127] Small wonder that he was soon asking friends like Harriet Martineau to help.

At the end of 1851 Chapman was about to fulfil his dream of owning and editing an important radical journal. Financial problems aside, he was buoyant. During the next few months he would go into battle against the large publishing houses in the cause of free trade in books; his editorial partnership with Marian Evans flourished; as he had published Marian's translation of a radical German work, *The Life of Jesus*, in 1846, so he now arranged for Harriet Martineau to translate the work of another influential European writer, the French social philosopher, Auguste Comte.

4

Radical Reviewing and the Battle of the Booksellers (1851–2)

It was fortunate that Chapman was able to persuade Susanna and Elisabeth to accept Marian Evans once more at 142 Strand. After the busy summer of correspondence between London and Coventry about Chapman's plans for the *Westminster Review*, Marian returned to London permanently on 29 September 1851. For the next three months her letters, and Chapman's diary where it has not been cut, give a sense of the excitement, hard work, and fun of life at number 142. Chapman gained the support of an intelligent and witty woman whose organ of Conscientiousness more than made up for the deficiency in that region which Combe had observed in Chapman himself. Marian threw herself into the job of negotiating with contributors, using her powers of persuasion where necessary, as with Combe, and even on occasion drafting the outlines of a subject for the designated contributor, as in the case of the long-planned article on Christian ethics by James Martineau.

Marian's role brought her into contact with all the progressive writers of the metropolis. Her letters to her good friends the Brays ring with the joys of her new London life. Though she was in a sense only a backroom figure, her intellectual command of a wide range of subjects soon won her the respect and admiration of people – mainly men – far more prominent than she was at the time. Her stay at 142 Strand launched her career; though her novel-writing was not to begin for another five years, the unconscious preparation for it began with her shrewd accounts to the Brays and Sara Hennell of human nature as she encountered it in London and with the articles she wrote for the *Review* she helped to edit. Chapman could not have managed without her. His negotiations with subscribers to the *Review*, his continuing publishing business, and the large amount of visiting and being visited which he undertook in the interests of both concerns, not to mention his love of socialising for its own sake, would have defeated even a man of Chapman's energy if he had not had an active and decisive lieutenant. Marian and Chapman both took Combe's advice of 7 December to heart, namely to use her tact and judgment in the running of the *Westminster Review*.

During her first week back, number 142 was full of visitors. Chapman's diary for 29 September 1851 noted the arrival (from Manchester) of Dr Hodgson and his wife as well as that of 'Miss Evans'. A few days later Hodgson accompanied Chapman to visit W. J. Fox, the ex-Unitarian minister who had contributed to the *Review* in its earliest years. They 'had a long conversation with him on the educational movement', Chapman recorded. Fox read the new Prospectus and agreed to write the article on 'National Representation' for January 1852, on condition that Chapman supplied him with the facts. On Sunday 5 October Marian joined Chapman and the Hodgsons at dinner in the Camberwell home of William Ellis, an educational reformer and close friend of George Combe.[1] Ellis had been an associate of Bentham and the Mills; like Fox, he had contributed articles to the original *Westminster* in the 1820s. A wealthy businessman, he founded and supported several schools intended to educate working-class children on the Socratic method (and without resort to corporal punishment).[2] Marian's first impression of him, as recounted to Charles Bray, was that he was 'very good, but a bore'. She revised her opinion a few days later, when Ellis attended one of Chapman's soirées; 'Mr Ellis was more agreeable – really witty', she told Sara Hennell on 9 October.[3]

Wednesday 8 October was a red-letter day for Chapman. In the morning he completed the purchase of the *Westminster Review* from Hickson by paying the agreed sum of £300. That evening he held his soirée, attended by Ellis, the Hodgsons, the economist Joseph Kay, the celebrated Edinburgh scientist Sir David Brewster (inventor of the kaleidoscope), Harriet Martineau's cousin Richard Martineau – representing, as Chapman noted, 'the Unitarian element' – and the Swedish novelist Fredrika Bremer, who was staying at number 142 on her way home from a successful visit to America.[4]

Marian first reported to Bray her disappointment in this famous Swedish woman:

> I don't know how long Miss Bremer will stay, but you need not wish to see her. She is to me a repulsive person, equally unprepossessing to eye and ear. I never saw a person of her years who appealed less to my purely instinctive veneration. I have to reflect every time I look at her that she is really Fred[rik]a Bremer.[5]

After talking to her at the party, however, Marian withdrew her first harsh impression, conceding that

> Miss Bremer was more genial than I had seen her – played on the piano and smiled benevolently. This morning at breakfast, she told me a very pretty story – all the prettier for her broken English ('The young man had to make his *fate*.') Altogether I am beginning to repent of my repugnance.[6]

Such guarded and critical initial responses to new acquaintances, softened by subsequent meetings, occurred several times as Marian absorbed new experiences at a fast rate. It happened with Ellis, with Fredrika Bremer, and, at least as far as physical appearance was concerned, with Lewes when she met him on 6 October. She fired off daily letters to her friends in Coventry, giving rapid sketches of the people who came and went at 142 Strand. Among the visitors, many of them in town to see the Great Exhibition at the Crystal Palace before it closed on 11 October, was the author of *Vestiges of Creation*. 'Robert Chambers called yesterday', she told Cara Bray on 3 October; he was 'a plain Scotchman with a strong Doric accent and small twinkling eyes'.[7]

One of Chapman's house guests was Rufa Hennell's father Robert Brabant, a self-important doctor and Biblical scholar whose personal acquaintance with David Friedrich Strauss had led to Rufa beginning the translation of *The Life of Jesus* which Marian took over on her friend's marriage to Charles Hennell. Marian's sharp comment to Cara on 3 October 1851 that 142

Strand was 'only just exorcised of Dr Brabant' can be explained by an episode which had followed Rufa's wedding in November 1843. Having acted as bridesmaid, Marian was invited to stay at Dr Brabant's Devon home as a kind of replacement daughter; she explained to Cara at the time that Dr Brabant, making 'rather a learned pun', had christened her 'Deutera, which *means* second and *sounds* a little like daughter'.[8] She had been delighted by his flattery of her learning, but unfortunately the doctor's blind wife and vigilant sister-in-law found the relationship inappropriate and Marian's visit came to an abrupt end. Marian herself confided in Chapman about the embarrassing episode, as did Rufa, who blamed her father.

Chapman, thus taken into the confidence of the two young women, wrote down the story in his diary in June 1851:

> Mrs Hennell repeated exactly what Miss Evans had told me previously as a great secret . . . that in 1843 Miss Evans was invited by Dr Brabant . . . to visit his house and to fill the place of his daughter (then just married) . . . she went, the Doctor liked her extremely, and said that so long as she had no home she must consider his house as her permanent home. She in the simplicity of her heart and her ignorance of (or incapability of practising) the required conventionalisms gave the Doctor the utmost attention; they became very intimate, his Sister in law Miss S. Hughes became alarmed, made a great stir, excited the jealousy of Mrs Brabant . . . Miss Evans left. Mrs B. vowed she should never enter the house again . . . Mrs Hennell says Dr B. acted ungenerously and worse, towards Miss E. for though he was the chief cause of all that passed, he acted towards her as though the fault lay with her alone. His unmanliness in the affair was condemned more by Mrs Hennell than by Miss E. herself when she (a year ago) related the circumstances to me.[9]

The account gains piquancy from the fact that Chapman had himself recently been the object of Marian's romantic enthusiasm in circumstances which were similar in terms of his encouragement of her attention, though different in that Chapman was a handsome young London publisher with a free attitude to love and marriage, not a respectable elderly scholar living in Devizes. Marian's remark to Cara about the house being 'exorcised' of Dr Brabant represents an understandable feeling of vengefulness towards the conceited man who had made a fool of her eight years earlier. Eliza Lynn, who found herself in the same situation as a flattered young guest at Devizes in 1847, took her revenge on Brabant in an autobiographical novel of 1885, *The Autobiography of Christopher Kirkland*, in which she refers sarcastically to 'the learned and fastidious Devise'. She adds, expressing, not for the first time, her jealous disapproval of George Eliot:

> Dr Devise was a man who had extreme fascination for some people. One of our greatest celebrities, when in the Ugly Duck stage of her existence and before she had joined her kindred Swans, had wanted to dedicate her life to him.[10]

Despite her feelings of resentment towards Dr Brabant, Marian was polite to him for Chapman's sake, as he was likely to be a subscriber to the *Westminster Review*. His sister-in-law, Miss Hughes, was too; she promised £20, as Marian recorded on 13 October 1851.[11] Before returning to the country Dr Brabant 'very politely took me to the Crystal Palace, the theatre, and the "Overland Route" [a moving diorama of the overland route to India being shown in a Regent Street gallery]', she told Charles Bray on 4 October. She visited the Great Exhibition for the last time on its final day, Saturday 11 October, 'to hear the final God save the Qu[een]'.[12]

The Exhibition, the brainchild of Henry Cole and Prince Albert, had been a great success, attracting over six million visitors during its five-month existence. Queen Victoria went more than once; the Duke of Wellington attended the opening on 1 May, his eighty-second birthday; Thomas Cook ran cheap excursion trains; and a number of industrialists and landowners paid for their employees to visit.[13] Chapman went several times during the summer, accompanying – on different days – Elisabeth, his children, his brother Thomas on a visit from Glasgow, 'the Coventry party' of Marian Evans, Sara Hennell, and Charles Bray when they spent a few days in London in August, and a number of other friends and acquaintances.[14]

Though the Exhibition was blamed by publishers, including Chapman, for a downturn in book sales, it brought visitors to London in large numbers. Chapman's boarding house was therefore busy, especially with Americans. Horace Greeley, editor of the *New York Daily Tribune*, lodged at number 142 from early May to late July.[15] He sent back regular articles to the paper, including an early piece, 'Counsel to the Sea-Going', dated 6 May, which contained the following advice:

> Whatever may be wise at other seasons, never think of stopping at a London hotel this summer unless you happen to own the Bank of England. If you know any one here who takes boarders or lets rooms at reasonable rates, go directly to him; if not, drive at once to the house of Mr John Chapman, American Bookseller, 142 Strand, and he will either find you rooms or direct you to some one else who will.[16]

As Chapman's financial dealings with American publishers had been in a precarious state since the ending of his arrangement with Putnam two years earlier, he needed the income from the boarding house to tide him over a number of bad moments. 'Much disappointed', he wrote on 8 September,

> by the non arrival of remittances from America. Had it not been for the loan of £90 from the boarding house I could not have met the £200 due on Saturday. This ever recurring monetary difficulty is a painful addition to my many other anxieties, and I see no immediate prospect of deliverance from it.[17]

The diary tells the same story the following month. On the very day he signed the contract for the *Westminster Review* with Hickson, Chapman noted once more that the 'non-arrival of remittances from America is embarrassing me extremely'. The next day, 9 October, he went to Cavendish Square to call on the secretary of the Chemical Society, which had rented two rooms at 142 Strand at £55 a year until April and which still owed £63:

> He promises it in a few days, wh[ich] in the meantime alas is no relief to me. I have desired the assistants to postpone the execution of foreign orders for the present, wh[ich] is a very painful step to me. – I have consumed £220 lent me by Woodfall, and am yet in the same pressing difficulty.[18]

This was the moment when Chapman, beset on all sides by financial problems but optimistically drumming up support for the *Review*, annoyed Lombe with his unauthorised boasting about the promised help of that wealthy gentleman. On 10 October he sent out, along with the much-criticised Prospectus, a circular to interested parties. It began:

> MR CHAPMAN hopes to confirm and extend the influence of the Review, as the chief organ of liberal opinion, by engaging the co-operation of the highest talent and culture; and, being aware that this can be permanently secured only by a regular system of remuneration, he proposes to pay all contributors at the rate of £12 12s. per sheet. As, however, he is not in a position with regard to capital to bear the whole weight of the enterprise, in addition to the large payment he has already made for the copyright, he relies on those who, concurring with him in his aims, have the ability to further them pecuniarily, to aid him in carrying on the work with the thoroughness necessary to its adequate success.

The circular continues with the information that the current circulation of the *Review* is 1,000, not enough to allow him to break even, but rather, as he calculates, likely to leave him £500 a year short. He therefore asks his friends and supporters to advance him 'such sums as may be convenient to themselves, in the form of loans, to be repaid at the end of four years', by which time he hopes that the circulation will have risen sufficiently to yield a profit. The sum needed to see him through for four years, £2,000, 'has already been reduced to £1,200', he concludes the document, 'by a donation of £200 a year from EDWARD LOMBE, Esq.'[19]

It was this statement which set the cat among the pigeons with Lombe, and also with Combe, who was caught in the middle, hearing from Lombe every other day that Chapman was a cheat and replying in Chapman's defence, while at the same time urging Chapman to eat humble pie in his letters to Lombe. Chapman should, he advised on 28 November, write 'calmly' to Lombe, 'renouncing all claim to £200 a year for general purposes' and 'accepting of his gifts for particular articles as he proposes'.[20] Chapman, though respectful towards Combe, thought he could win Lombe round by the sheer quality of the *Review* under his management. He wrote cheerfully to Combe on 26 November after receiving the first warning of Lombe's anger:

On the whole I do not fear any permanent difficulties with Mr L.; he seems to me fitful and capricious, but I believe he is heartily interested in the Review, and I am persuaded the January number will please him. I believe, at bottom, he is more annoyed that he is not the sole pecuniary support of the Review, than that I have published his name as a Contributor. He did not wish me to adopt the plan of paying the writers of Articles generally, and I incline to think the independent course I have taken has disappointed him.[21]

While Chapman was raising subscriptions – £200 from R. W. Mackay, the same from his printer George Woodfall, and smaller amounts from Combe, Brabant and his sister-in-law Susan Hughes, Frank Newman, Combe's nephew Robert Cox, and some others[22] – Marian was noting the articles for the January number as they came in, as well as preparing her own work for the first issue, the round-up review of contemporary literature which was to appear at the end of the number. 'My table is covered with books', she told Cara Bray towards the end of October, 'all to be digested by the editorial maw – I foresee terribly hard work for the next 6 weeks.'[23] She was due to spend Christmas with the Brays, but had to write to them on 23 December to say she could not be with them until Saturday 27 December:

Dear Friends

Alas! the work is so heavy just for the next three days – all the revises being yet to come in and the proof of my own article – and Mr Chapman is so overwhelmed with matters of detail that he has earnestly requested me to stay till Saturday. I cannot refuse – but it is a deep disappointment to me. My heart will yearn after you all.

It is the first Christmas day I shall have passed without any Christmas feeling. On Saturday – if you will have me – nothing shall keep me here any longer. I am writing at a high table on a low seat in a great hurry. Don't you think my style is Editorial?

Ever dearest Friends
Your loving
Marian.[24]

*

The main rivals with which the new *Westminster* went into battle were the other two quarterlies, the *Edinburgh* and the *Quarterly*. The *Edinburgh* for January 1852 carried its usual number of eight long articles, mainly addressing historical and political subjects and written by contributors of some note in their day. Henry Rogers, an adversary of religious scepticism in general and of Frank Newman in particular,[25] reviewed the complete works of Descartes; W. J. Conybeare, another Church of England apologist, wrote combatively on recent controversies in the Church; and Thomas Erskine May, known to posterity for his authoritative volumes on parliamentary procedures, discussed recent legislation. There were also articles on copyright arrangements between Britain and France, church music, and the ordnance survey of Scotland. The January number concluded with an essay on 'the expected reform bill' recently announced by the Prime Minister, Lord John Russell. This was written by one of Chapman's authors, W. R. Greg, an ex-Unitarian who had owned a mill until he became almost bankrupt in 1850 and who now supported himself by writing articles for *The Economist*, the *Edinburgh Review*, the *Westminster*, and even the Tory *Quarterly*. His stance towards reform was that of a cautious progressive; in the *Edinburgh* article he welcomes the prospect of further extension of the suffrage, but warns against 'demagogues and agitators' who might rouse 'the mass of the people' to foolish or violent action.[26]

In the equivalent issue of the *Quarterly*, that for December 1851, Greg appears again, writing on 'Highland destitution and Irish emigration', an account, supported by pages of statistics, of the aftermath of the potato blight of 1846–7.[27] Greg's company on the *Quarterly* includes Francis Egerton, Earl of Ellesmere, on Prussian military memoirs, the traveller and art expert Lady Eastlake on physiognomy in fine art, and the elderly Tory lawyer and statesman John Wilson Croker, who contributed two long articles to the journal he had helped to found in 1809. The second of these is a characteristically pugnacious piece on the recent *coup d'état* of Louis Napoleon, in which Croker adroitly combines pride in the superiority of British representative government over French despotism with a warning against the extension of that representation promised by Lord John Russell's reform measures, the subject of Greg's article in the *Edinburgh Review*.

Though the readership for each of these large journals was different, tending to divide along political lines, with the Whig-liberal *Edinburgh* nearer to the *Westminster* than the ultra-conservative *Quarterly*, the

Westminster did compete with the other two on literary and intellectual terms, as was observed by a number of magazines and newspapers which included a digest of the quarterlies in their round-up columns. Chapman and Marian had prepared a set of striking articles, attractively varied in subject matter, for the most part written with verve as well as with the earnest reforming intention promised in the Prospectus, and covering a significantly wider field than its rivals. The number consisted of nine substantial articles, followed by the new surveys of recent publications in Britain, America, Germany, and France.

Fox wrote the opening piece on Lord John Russell's proposed reform agenda. Like Greg in the *Edinburgh*, he was measured in his advocacy of reform, pointing out that even the great Reform Act of 1832 excluded most of the 'operative classes', but reassuring anyone afraid of a revolutionary uprising in Britain that there were 'controlling forces' enough – royalty, the House of Lords, and the Church of England – to guard against too much democracy.[28] Fox's carefully reasoned call for further political reform, and the studied avoidance of controversy, fulfilled that part of Chapman's agenda which was designed to appeal to a wider constituency than the radical readers of the *Leader* or Holyoake's *Reasoner*.

The second article is a light-hearted but informative piece on 'shell-fish, their ways and works' by Edward Forbes, Professor of Botany at King's College London. Greg provided the third article, thus featuring in all three quarterlies at once – in each case anonymously, as was the journalistic custom. This one was on the 'relation between employers and employed'. Greg presents the subject, somewhat elaborately, as the last of the three battles 'appointed to humanity', the first being man's taming of nature, the second the liberation of man from slavery, and this last – yet to be won – the battle with 'an imperfect and diseased condition of that social world of which we form a part', namely the relations between employer and employee in a recently industrialised society.[29]

Froude's long article on Mary Stuart follows, presented as a review of three books on the subject. Froude chooses to answer in detail the exaggerated attack on Queen Elizabeth by the French historian F. A. Mignet, an apologist for Mary. Froude writes with panache and imagination, telling the complicated story of Mary's intrigues and marriages with brio. Already giving evidence of the influence on him of the Carlylean school of history, with its placing of the historian in the middle of the action, observing at close quarters, empathising, and exclaiming at events 'as they happen', Froude concludes the episode of Mary's husband Darnley's death with 'God forgive her and all of us!' After quoting some incriminating letters of Mary to the Queen of Spain, he asks:

> What was to be done with such a woman – who would keep no faith except when it suited her convenience, and whose indomitable spirit could neither be crushed nor gained except at the price of what could not be given it – its own way?[30]

This long narrative essay is the most striking in the volume. Clough thought it too crowded, and Froude agreed, telling his friend that the editor had 'clipped the canvas'.[31] Even after clipping, however, the article, at forty-six pages, was the longest in the number. Nonetheless, Marian and Chapman were keen to keep Froude's undoubted narrative talent in the service of the *Westminster Review*. He wrote on sixteenth-century English voyagers in July 1852, and on Mary Tudor in January 1853; these articles, with the one on Mary Stuart, formed the basis of the great historical multi-volume work on Tudor England which made his name a few years later. In October 1852 he wrote on a topic close to his heart, the Oxford Commission set up to investigate the affairs of his alma mater, Oxford University, with a view to its reform.

Another of Chapman's authors, Frank Newman, contributed a lively essay on theories of legislation in France, Germany, and Britain. The article Chapman had wanted on modern novelists, the one which Thackeray and Marian Evans had declined to do, did not appear from Lewes's pen. His contribution on the society flirt-turned-mystic Julia von Krüdener is not one of his best pieces; it bears signs of haste and probably confirmed Chapman in his relatively low opinion of Lewes's pretensions to serious reviewing. Lewes begins in lively and uncompromising vein:

> Who believes in a fifth-act conversion? . . . See into what an error Dickens has fallen with 'Dombey and Son'! There, in old Dombey, he has given us an incarnation of pride. As usual with Dickens a *charac-teristic* is substituted for a *character*, and we have pride in place of a Man.

This expression of disbelief in the unexplained conversion Dickens claims for Mr Dombey at the end of the novel is used as the prelude to a rather perfunctory discussion of the life of Julia von Krüdener and her too-credulous French biographer Charles Eynard, who is taken to task for exaggerating the extent of her saintliness after her religious conversion.[32] Lewes ends his review with a throwaway line about not having space and time to look at other historical examples of conversions from scepticism to religion, from a selfish life to a philanthropic one.

After Lewes comes Martineau with his essay, 'The Ethics of Christendom', so long awaited by an impatient Lombe, an eager Chapman, and a curious Marian Evans. As long ago as August 1851, while she was still in Coventry, Marian had drafted for Chapman a letter respectfully telling Martineau what was wanted:

> The future Editors of the Westminster desire that the article in question should contain an impartial inquiry into the moral spirit and code of the primitive Christians as embodied in the New Testament, conducted on true principles of critical investigation and with entire freedom from conscious or unconscious predisposition to accommodate the phraseology of the Gospels and Epistles to the expression of modern ideas, or to use them with an esoteric meaning.[33]

Warming to the theme, the translator of Strauss – herself as well qualified to write the essay as Martineau – continued to instruct him:

> An article such as they desire would show that Jesus contributed no new element to ethics, that the emphasis which he gave by his teaching and life to certain true principles was partly counteracted by his misconceptions concerning his own mission and the divine government in general derived from his Jewish culture, and by the false views and expectations which he consequently communicated to his followers, and that the beneficial effect of his character on Christendom has been chiefly due to the substitution of the ideal for the historical.

Despite the radicalism of this account, she emphasised that the aim was not that the author should write merely negatively about Christianity (which Martineau would hardly be inclined to do in any case), but rather that, while showing 'what Christianity has not done and cannot do for us', he should 'do full justice to the positive side and endeavour clearly to define what we really owe to Christianity as a stage in the religious development of the race'.[34]

Chapman noted in his diary for 9 September 1851 that Martineau had replied agreeing to write the article, 'but skillfully evading my question as to the meaning he attaches to the words "divine and permanent" in Xty' [christianity]. Martineau was careful not to commit himself to an essay which might be construed as antagonistic towards Christian faith. Chapman expressed his frustration in his diary: 'I wish I could nail him to an unequivocal confession of faith.'[35] The confession of faith he and Marian wanted was in effect an expression of informed and respectful scepticism. As Marian told Chapman in July 1852, she could not accept Martineau's Unitarianism, however liberal. 'Not that I mean to decry him', she wrote; 'I simply mean that I can't see things through spectacles of his colour.'[36]

The article, when it came, proved hardly more to the editors' taste than to that of its intended paymaster Lombe. Partly a learned discussion of the early history of Christianity from St Paul to Luther, followed by an account of the particular course of religious history in Britain from seventeenth-century Puritanism to nineteenth-century Tractarianism and the recent rise of Roman Catholicism, it is also a declaration of Martineau's own belief that 'the fundamental idea of Christendom may be described to be, *The ascent through Conscience into communion with God*'.[37]

Martineau's contribution – too believing for the editors and radical readers but probably not orthodox enough for some others – is followed by the 'Independent Contribution' on current French politics, prefaced by a declaration of the editors' dissent from its conclusion that a modern utopia would be achieved if the French socialists gained power.[38] Marian's own piece, most of the survey of 'Contemporary Literature of England', runs to forty-one pages and covers a wide range of recent publications. 'Literature' is understood in the widest sense in this innovative section, which sets the new *Review* apart from its quarterly rivals. The section opens with an appreciative critique of Carlyle's latest work, *The Life of John Sterling*, a sympathetic biography of a friend who had died young after giving up his career as a clergyman, partly through ill health and partly through doubts about Church of England doctrine. Marian praises the book as a 'labour of love'; Carlyle 'shows us his "sunny side"', she notes, after the ill-tempered fire-breathing of *Latter-Day Pamphlets* (1850).[39] More strong writing of the kind in which she was to excel in her full-length articles for the *Westminster* from 1854 appears in this section, which deals with books of travel, physiology, ethnology, zoology, and theology. She shows particular mastery of the last of these topics. Of John Henry Newman's *Lectures on the Present Position of Catholics in England* she writes:

> They exhibit an insight into character, a readiness in finding the 'Sesame' that will unlock the sympathies, and a sort of imperturbable blandness in argument, which are the chief secrets of proselytism. Add to this a very rare literary charm – a style at once easy and finished, a masterly power of simplifying the abstruse, of fetching the aptest illustrations from the fireside and the market-place, and of delineating the various phases of society by the light of a lambent, not too scorching, satire, and it is no wonder that many who differ *toto coelo* from Father Newman in opinion should find a fascination in his pages.[40]

The review continues with a striking statement of Marian's scepticism about religious faith, both Catholic and – with a Froude-like sideswipe – Anglican:

> Catholicism, though destined (in our belief) ultimately to yield before the principles which were involved in the great movement of the sixteenth century, as the plant lies folded in the germ, may yet win many triumphs over the spurious Protestantism that itself exemplifies the very assumption of infallibility against which it so loudly inveighs, like a barking dog infuriated at the sight of its own image . . . But the moral spirit of Father Newman's lectures is by no means equal to their literary merit. We rather marvel at the writer's ingenuity than feel impressed by his earnestness, and we turn away from the book with the same sort of relief that we have experienced in leaving the incense, the fretted roof, and the artificial lights of a cathedral, for the free pure air under the unintercepted light of heaven.[41]

After these magisterial pronouncements, notable for the imaginative use of metaphor and the implied belief in evolution in matters theological, the sections which complete the January number – Griswold's survey of American literature, Jane Sinnett's of German publications, and Lewes's of French books – strike the reader as mere journeywork. On the whole, however, Chapman and Marian succeeded in raising the average standard of writing far above the level it had stuck at under Hickson; the articles were sharper and more varied in topic, and, with the inclusion of the surveys, covered a much wider field than either the old *Westminster* or the rival quarterlies.

Friendly journalists like Lewes in the *Leader* and Holyoake in the *Reasoner* welcomed the *Westminster* under its new management. Lewes hails its appearance as 'a literary event', and praises its variety and excellence. The editors are congratulated on not succumbing to heaviness or exclusiveness, 'the two perils besetting Mr Chapman's path', but Lewes misses 'the boldness such a review ought to adopt' and advises Chapman not to 'fall into vague routiniary orthodoxy'. After all, he argues, just as Mill had done on reading the Prospectus, 'the orthodox *have* their organs already'.[42] Holyoake, on the other hand, revels in drawing attention to the comparisons hostile observers were making with the *Leader*, to which he was a contributor. He quotes in the *Reasoner* for January 1852 the attack on both the *Leader* and the *Westminster* by the *Church and State Gazette*, which accuses both of atheism and warns readers that the *Westminster Review* has 'fallen into the hands of a publisher' whose principal writers are known for their unorthodoxy.[43]

Lewes and Holyoake between them neatly illustrate Chapman's dilemma: to embrace atheism or out-and-out religious scepticism would be to lose valuable readers and subscribers (and therefore both sales revenue and much-needed investment) from the progressive wing of Christianity, while to court such readers by means of cautious, respectful articles would alienate true radicals and lay Chapman open to charges of cowardice or mere orthodoxy, a position already catered for, as Lewes and Mill pointed out, by other journals.

Combe wrote from Edinburgh on 16 January saying he had not yet read the new number, but his wife and house guest, the actress Fanny Kemble, liked it, as did Robert Chambers. 'Have you heard', Combe added, 'that it was voted out of the Select Subscription Library here a few days ago, by a large majority?' He went on to explain that the library's members were 'rigid Calvinists, & my surprise is great how it ever got into that Library'.[44] Henry Crabb Robinson, who had predicted that the *Westminster* would be an organ of infidelity, was agreeably surprised. Without knowing who the author was (though he soon found out), he singled out Martineau's article as the best in the volume. (He also pronounced Lewes's essay on Julia von Krüdener 'delightful'.)[45] He was happy to accept an invitation to the Monday soirée at number 142 on 19 January, where he met 'a very attractive party', more 'German' than 'free thinking', he was relieved to find. Two translators of Goethe were there, John Oxenford and 'a Yankee worshipper' named Godwin. Susanna Chapman took part in the conversation, speaking, Robinson records, 'half in jest and half in earnest against Göthe'.[46]

Marian Evans was struck by the disparate views expressed by friends of the *Westminster*; she was learning an early lesson about the difficulty of pleasing people. She wrote to Sara Hennell on 21 January:

> It is amusing enough to compare the diverse and contradictory opinions given by people and journals on every single article in the Review. Mr Johnson agrees with you in having an antipathy to James Martineau – therefore won't read the article. Herbert Spencer has tried and can't. Crabbe [sic] Robinson thinks it splendid – is shocked that the article on France should be in the same cover, whereas Mr Hodgkin of the Economist – a great man though you may not know it – thinks the 'Ethics' good for nothing, and the article on France the best of all.[47]

To Combe she wrote a few days later that no response to the new number had been received from Lombe, but that she and Chapman agreed with Combe that Martineau's article would probably 'not appear to him a suitable investment of his "dollars"'. Her own view follows:

> The article is certainly very far from being what was hoped for . . . , and is still farther from being broad enough for its title, but it contains a few valuable ideas which want enforcing and which gain at least as much by the *prestige* as by the style of the writer.[48]

She shows her awareness here of the custom of letting the authorship of articles be widely known, in despite of official anonymity, in cases where the editors are conscious of the pulling power of certain names.

By July Marian was commenting wryly to Chapman himself on the impossibility of running a journal without 'Editorial compromise' and on the mistake of starting a separate independent contribution, which section she and Chapman now dropped:

> Martineau writes much that we can agree with and admire. Newman ditto, J. S. Mill still more, Froude a little less and so on. These men can write more openly in the Westminster than anywhere else. They are amongst the world's vanguard, though not all in the foremost line; it is good for the world, therefore, that they should have every facility for speaking out. Ergo, since each can't have a periodical to himself, it is good that there should be one which is common to them – id est, the Westminster. The grand mistake with respect to this plan is the paragraph in the Prospectus which announces the Independent Section and which thus makes the Editors responsible for everything outside that railing – Ah me, how wise we all are après coup.[49]

She was right about the talent of the writers, and prudent to see the need for a broad editorial strategy. Nonetheless, as was inevitable, the *Review* did not break even financially. Combe recorded meeting Marian on 3 June, when she told him that Chapman was losing £100 a number, selling only 1,300 copies where he needed to sell 1,700 each quarter. On 6 July Combe had 'a long interview' with Chapman himself, coming away with a gloomy view of the state of Chapman's affairs – both the *Westminster Review* and the publishing business – and more than ever convinced of his 'want of business talent'.[50] In September Combe was staying with Bray in Coventry, where this was the chief topic of conversation. Bray, knowing that Chapman was the only hope for progressive writers with books or articles to place, tried hard to defend him, but failed to convince the phrenologist, who continued 'to be of opinion that Mr Chapman is deficient in business talent, in conscientiousness, & in real depth of intellect':

> He has great ambition, Benevolence, & a sympathy with liberal views, but transcendentally rather than practically. Mr Bray said that 5 friends have lent him £100 each, & the printer & Stationer of the Westminster Review have advanced him £500 on the security of the copyright of it, & that with these sums he will go on. I prophesied

that he will need more aid within two years. Mr Bray hopes he may make a fortune; yet he sees his defects.[51]

It would be no surprise to find the careful Scot more accurate in his prediction than the Panglossian Coventry man.

With so much work going into the launching of the *Review* during 1851–2, it is a wonder that Chapman found any time for his publishing business, yet he was extremely busy in that department. One venture in particular stands out as an example of Chapman's strengths and weaknesses as a publisher. This was the plan to publish an abridged translation of the six-volume *Cours de philosophie positive* by Auguste Comte, a social theory designed to embrace a modern, industrial, post-theological age of scientific progress. Like Strauss's *Life of Jesus*, Comte's work caused controversy because the author dispensed with orthodox religion, seeking to explain all phenomena as subject to undeviating laws of nature, from the laws of mathematics through those of physics, chemistry, and biology to the laws of 'social physics' governing human society. Comte undertook to describe the historical progress of each of the sciences, culminating with the science of man, for which he coined the word 'sociology'. His philosophy was welcomed by progressive thinkers in Britain, among them Mill, Lewes, and Harriet Martineau.

Lewes had first shown his knowledge and appreciation of Comte in his popular *Biographical History of Philosophy* (1845–6). Now he contributed a series of articles expounding the positivist philosophy in the *Leader* during 1852; Bohn published these as *Comte's Philosophy of the Sciences* in September 1853. Meanwhile, Harriet Martineau, her interest stimulated by reading Lewes's *Biographical History*, wished to undertake a condensed translation of the six volumes.[52] Chapman published her *Positivist Philosophy of Auguste Comte, freely translated and condensed by Harriet Martineau* in two volumes in November 1853.

Since Chapman had taken the risk of publishing the notorious *Letters on the Laws of Man's Nature and Development*, which had lost Harriet the friendship of her neighbours in the Lake District and the respect of her brother James and other Unitarians, he was the obvious person to approach with the idea of translating Comte. Chapman's diary for 19 April 1851 notes that he has received a letter from her on the subject. No agreement was reached at this time; Chapman was busy appeasing the women of his household, corresponding with the banished Marian Evans, and planning to take over the *Westminster Review* with the help of Edward Lombe and others.[53] As Lombe had offered to pay for an abridgement of Marian's translation of Strauss only a month earlier, Chapman thought he might be equally inclined to support a translation of Comte. He seems to have made an indirect appeal, to which Lombe replied with cautious enthusiasm on 10 May, declaring that he had 'always wished to see [the positivist philosophy] in an English dress'.[54] For the time being, however, Lombe restricted his active generosity to sending £100 for the Strauss.

Chapman's diary for 9 August gives evidence of his strengths when seeking support for his radical publishing ventures – boldness and persistence – and also of his chief weakness – an opportunism which alienated those on whose financial backing he depended. He had returned in his correspondence with Lombe to the idea of a translation of Comte, this time making his wish explicit. The diary entry reads:

> Rec[eive]d a letter from Mr Lombe in answer to my letter enquiring if he would assist in the publication of an abridgement of Comte's 'Philosophie positive' and in which I enclosed a letter on the project addressed to me by Miss Martineau.

Chapman notes that Lombe has enclosed with his reply an order on his London bankers to transfer £500 'to the credit of Miss Harriet Martineau in support of a great Literary work'. This was an act of generosity and a piece of good fortune beyond even Chapman's sanguine expectations, yet he could not resist making a further proposal to Lombe about the use of the money. Even a benefactor less touchy than Lombe might be expected to object to Chapman's suggestion. 'I acknowledged the receipt of the Draft', Chapman adds in the diary, 'but proposed to him (Mr L) that he should only contribute what may prove to be needful in the case, in order that he may help in other works'. Chapman notes that he has specified a cheap reprint of Theodore Parker's *Discourse of Matters pertaining to Religion*, which Lombe had already declined to support in his letter of 10 May.[55]

What possessed Chapman to make this suggestion to a man who had made it plain in every letter since the first on 13 March offering to bear the costs of an abridged edition of Strauss that the most vehement of his many strong objections to the status quo related to religion? Just when Chapman was wooing Lombe as a potential subscriber to the *Westminster Review*, he unleashed his correspondent's (admittedly excessive) fury by not resting content with his generosity about the Comte. Lombe replied on 18 August:

> You must forward my Letter to Miss Martineau without delay – It is for that Lady to express her pleasure on the subject in question . . . It was a great liberty – & a still greater blunder to detain a letter confided to you for a third party – nor as a matter of business was it quite correct.[56]

As Browning was visiting London that August, Chapman wrote to him, asking for a meeting, partly to discuss plans for the *Westminster Review* and partly to talk about Browning's idiosyncratic neighbour in Florence. He read out Lombe's letter, whereupon Browning seems to have fanned the flames: 'He said that he thought I had acted rightly and that Mr Lombe's letter was quite uncalled for', Chapman wrote in his diary on 23 August. Thus fortified, Chapman replied to Lombe on 27 August 'rebutting his reproofs &c &c'.[57] The very next day Harriet Martineau, also in London on a visit to the Great Exhibition, called at 142 Strand. She was 'delighted' that Lombe was prepared to support the translation and agreed to Chapman's proposal 'that she should appropriate the £150 as remuneration for the abridgement of Comte, and should devote the remainder to its publication'.[58] This was certainly more in the spirit of Lombe's intention than the smuggling in of a cheap reprint of Parker.

Perhaps Chapman's letter to Lombe of the previous evening contained this new suggestion – his side of the correspondence has not survived – for matters seem to have quietened down for a while. Harriet Martineau's accounts for 31 August show that she had received the £500 and invested it immediately in '3 per ct. Annuities'.[59] She described the transaction in her autobiography, written only four years later in anticipation of imminent death, though not published until 1877, the year after her actual death:

> Mr Chapman, who had been trying to track me, overtook me with a wonderful piece of news. Mr Lombe, a Norfolk country gentleman,

and late High Sheriff of the county, had for many years been a disciple of Comte, and had earnestly wished to translate the 'Positive Philosophy', but had been prevented by ill health. He was a perfect stranger to me, and residing in Florence; but, hearing from Mr Chapman what I was doing, he sent me, by him, a draft on his bankers for 500*l*. His obvious intention was to give me the money, in recompense for the work; but I preferred paying the expenses of paper, print, and publication out of it, taking 200*l* [actually £150] for my own remuneration.[60]

Things might have proceeded smoothly from here, with all parties – Harriet, Chapman, and Lombe – in agreement about the use of the money. Harriet expected the work to take eighteen months to two years. She did, accordingly, finish it in time for publication in November 1853. But a complication arose which, though not of Chapman's making, was not handled well by him. On 13 September 1851 his diary records the arrival of a letter from one of his doubting clergymen, W. M. W. Call, whose politically radical volume of poems, *Reverberations*, Chapman had published in 1849. (Call was to renounce his living in 1857, the year in which he married Rufa Brabant, whose first husband Charles Hennell had died in 1850.[61]) Call's letter announces that he has done an abridged translation of half of Comte, 'and he intends to compress the whole into 2 volumes, – precisely what Miss Martineau proposed to do'. Chapman hurried to tell Harriet, thinking she would give up her plan on hearing the news.[62]

He reckoned without Harriet Martineau's determination and sense of her own prominence in the literary world. She 'does not like to relinquish the task', he noted on 16 September.[63] He consulted his editorial adviser Marian Evans, who was still staying with the Brays in Coventry though planning to return to the Strand at the end of the month if Susanna Chapman and Elisabeth Tilley did not change their minds about allowing her back. Marian replied in some detail, giving a respectful but cautious opinion of Harriet's merits, weighing up the question of priority and fairness, and noting (indirectly and tactfully bearing in mind the identity of her correspondent) that Harriet Martineau's name on a title-page was considerably less of a draw since the publication of those atheistic-mesmeric *Letters* written with Henry Atkinson:

I think Call's plan – of a *condensed* translation – the best possible in the hands of a person having the requisite judgment and power of writing. It is true that Harriet Martineau's style is admirably adapted for the people, clear, spirited, idiomatic, but I should have less confidence in the equal fitness of her calibre of mind for rendering a trustworthy account of Comte's work. I should augur much greater depth in Call – knowing nothing of him, however, beyond his poetry and a letter or two. But, as Miss M. intimates, the question of what you are to do in the matter turns upon this other question – Does Call's version fulfil the conditions demanded by her and Mr Lombe's views? – is it one fitted for circulation among the people? *That* you can only ascertain by stating the whole case to him – as I suppose you have done. If he had the prospect of seeing his work ushered into the world by Mr Lombe's £500 he would perhaps not object to send a specimen to the parties interested. It would be a shame for his labour to be wasted if it be of the right kind. Miss Martineau disclaims any egotism in the affair, but she evidently thinks no one can be so fit for the work as herself. This I doubt – nor do I think her name in the title-page would be of much value now – at least not more than 'a graduate of Oxford or Cambridge' as the case may be.

Find out the quality of Call's translation if possible – and if it be satisfactory use your influence on his side – of course with all possible delicacy towards Harriet Martineau, who after all is an admirable woman worth twenty of the people who are sniffing at her.[64]

On being asked for his views, the modest Call told Chapman he was willing to pass on the three volumes he had already abridged for Harriet Martineau to use 'as part of the abridgement to be published by me', according to Chapman's diary on 24 September.[65] Call did not wish his name to be given, even to Harriet Martineau, presumably because he was still a practising clergyman and liable to be severely criticised for translating a doctrine inimical to religion. Chapman told Harriet on 8 October that his anonymous correspondent was willing to let her have the sections he had already prepared to use as she saw fit. Call, he said, relinquished all claim on money for his work, except a share of any surplus which might occur if the book more than covered its costs. Chapman, showing his decency and natural kindliness, made a point of letting Harriet know that Call's income was 'very small'. 'I feel very sorry for him', he concluded. Finally, Chapman put all decisions about the use of the £500 in Harriet's hands.[66]

It is not clear whether Harriet did use Call's material. Since she made no mention of his contribution in either her preface to the translation or her autobiography – though in both she describes Lombe's and Chapman's part in its publication – it may be that she made no use of it at all. If that is the case, it is all the more unfortunate that George Combe, meaning well as always, informed Lombe in a letter of 5 October 1851 that Chapman had told him 'that a translation of the work contemplated by Miss Martineau is already half printed under the auspices of a bookseller', so that 'your generous contribution of £500 will not be needed'.[67] Lombe replied indignantly, accusing Chapman of treating Harriet and himself 'shabbily', and referring to Chapman's original idea of using some of the money to reprint Parker's *Discourse* as 'a fraud attempted upon Her & a great liberty taken with me (& my money)'. He told Combe he had long wished to 'serve and oblige' Harriet, 'because she is from Norfolk' and because of 'the excellence of her earlier works'. He also hoped to 'divert' her from mesmerism and 'such stuff'. But he thought Chapman a liar and a cheat, and told Combe he might have to break off his relationship with him.[68]

Combe found himself defending Chapman against Lombe's accusations of cheating, both over Comte, the labour of which, as Lombe now saw, might be halved if Harriet used Call's version, and over the Strauss abridgement, which he had intended to subsidise only if the whole of the original three-volume edition of 1846 was already sold, which it was not. Finally, and most damagingly for Chapman's plans, came the advertising of his name as a regular subscriber of £200 a year to the forthcoming *Westminster Review* in Chapman's tactless circular of 10 October. Exasperated, Lombe threatened to withdraw his support for all three ventures and even to set his lawyers on Chapman.[69]

The result was that of all the money promised or sent by Lombe, only the £500 for Harriet Martineau's abridgement of Comte was safe, and that only because it was now in Harriet's hands, not Chapman's. Apart from the financial aspect, Lombe was excited about the Comte project, writing in high spirits to Harriet herself on 27 November, introducing himself and praising her willingness to do what he had 'not the power or the energy to attempt'. 'Grâce à vous Madame', he wrote, 'we shall dose the Parsons well – & give the Popular Mind substantial food'.[70] Meanwhile, Chapman saw that he would have to send back the £100 for the Strauss abridgement, which fortunately Marian Evans had been too busy to begin, and, more seriously, to release Lombe from any regular obligation towards the *Westminster Review*. He was hurt by Lombe's accusations, as he made plain in a letter of 3 December which he copied to Combe. He admits that he ought to have asked Lombe's permission before using his name on the circular for the *Review*, but denies dishonesty and saves his pride by absolving Lombe of all responsibility before Lombe can humiliate him further:

I hereby renounce my claim upon you for pecuniary assistance in any form; since I find you utterly distrust me and impute to me motives inconsistent with the honesty and uprightness of a gentleman, there is nothing left for me but with this letter to close our correspondence. I enclose a receipt from the translatress of Strauss for the £100 which you remitted me on account of the abridgement which she has engaged to make, and now remain, free of all responsibilities in reference to your commissions, Your obedient servant, John Chapman.[71]

Combe, now himself in dispute with Lombe over his speeches on Scottish education, told Lombe on 8 December that Chapman's actions had been indiscreet rather than dishonest, but it was too late.[72] Even if Lombe had been willing to reconsider, his death on 1 March 1852 put an end to any possibility of Chapman getting money out of him. Chapman had been thoughtless. He was foolish to try to use money intended for Strauss and Comte for other purposes as well, but he was no peculator. If he had intended to enrich himself, he would not have undertaken to publish so many books which had no hope of making him a profit, or to take on the radical *Westminster*, which had never made money for any of its owners. As it was, he was prepared to work from morning till night for little or no financial gain in order to further the radicalism in which he believed. His fault was to think that it did not matter whether donations were used precisely as the donors intended. Again and again he found that it did matter to the donors themselves.

On this occasion those who were working most closely with him – Marian, Harriet, and Combe – thought Chapman more sinned against than sinning. Harriet carried on with the Comte, giving both Chapman and Lombe due credit in her preface to the translation and in her autobiographical account in 1855. There she noted that after Lombe's death she appointed 'two trustees' to oversee the proper use of the invested £500. These were Henry Atkinson and Marian Evans.[73] Harriet's feelings towards Chapman were warm. She recounts in the autobiography that she stayed at 142 Strand for several weeks after the Comte abridgement was published towards the end of 1853. During this visit 'Mr Chapman obtained for me a first-rate regular Chancery-lane desk' with 'a singularly convenient slope, and of an admirable height for writing without fatigue', which she found infinitely superior to the flat table she had used hitherto.[74] Chapman is referred to as 'my friend' here; three years later, in 1858, Harriet broke with him on grounds not very different from those of the eccentric Mr Lombe.

The appearance of the *Positive Philosophy* was greeted with suspicion by the orthodox and with pleasure by the liberal and radical press. Lewes, whose own explanatory account of the Comtean philosophy had recently appeared with Bohn, wrote in the *Leader* on 3 December 1853: 'In the whole range of philosophy, we know of no such successful abridgement.'[75] Mill, who had been one of Comte's earliest admirers in Britain, refused to review Harriet's abridged translation for Chapman. He was still resisting most of Chapman's requests to write for the *Westminster*, and he disliked Harriet personally, probably because she was known to have gossiped about his relationship with Harriet Taylor before their marriage in 1851. Mill wrote to his wife in January 1854 that he would turn down Chapman's request. 'I don't like to have anything to do with the name or with any publication of H. Martineau', he wrote. This, coupled with his rejection of Comte's more recent work, a dogmatic system of secularised religion complete with humanist 'saints' and calendars, meant that he could not write warmly about either Comte or his translator. He was aware that 'as Chapman is the publisher, he doubtless wishes, & expects, an article more laudatory on the whole, than I sh[oul]d be willing to write'.[76]

Chapman and Marian had some difficulty in finding a reviewer, as the latter confided in a letter to Sara Hennell of 18 November 1853. An appreciative article finally appeared in July 1854, probably by the leading English positivist Richard Congreve.[77] Years later Chapman stated that James Martineau had wanted to review his sister's translation for the *Westminster*, whereupon Chapman, fearing another hatchet job on his estranged sister like his devastating review of the Martineau-Atkinson *Letters* in the

Prospective Review under the title 'Mesmeric Athesim' in 1851, insisted that if he accepted a review from James, he must be allowed to preface it with a paragraph disclaiming editorial responsibility for its views. Martineau refused, no doubt to Chapman's relief, and so did not on this occasion exacerbate the already broken relationship with his sister, who never forgave him for his sarcasm towards her belief in mesmerism and her relationship with the charlatan Atkinson.[78]

It appears that Chapman, after all the trouble over this Comte translation, eventually made a small profit on it, though in the absence of his business accounts it is impossible to say how much. Harriet Martineau wrote to him in March 1853 from her Ambleside home suggesting a print run of 1,500 and offering £300 of the original £500 towards publication costs.[79] The book was put on sale at eight shillings a volume. It was agreed that Comte should receive a share of any profits, as Harriet told Holyoake in April 1853, but it was not until 1856 that the sale justified sending him any money. In October of that year, hearing that Herbert Spencer was about to visit Paris, Chapman asked him to take a share of the proceeds to Comte. 'The sum was under twenty pounds', Spencer recalled in his autobiography.[80]

The early months of 1852 were taken up not only in launching and establishing the *Westminster Review* under new management and encouraging Harriet Martineau as she translated Comte, but also in a battle between discounting booksellers, led by Chapman, and the powerful union of large booksellers and publishers, the Booksellers' Association, headed by the long-established and respected firms of John Murray and Longmans. The affair brought Chapman into close co-operation with Dickens and Gladstone, among other famous writers and politicians. His name appeared regularly in the pages of the daily press; he was supported by the *Leader*, the *Athenaeum*, and *The Times* itself in his clash with the Association over the question of free trade in books. As with everything he did, in public or in private, Chapman threw himself into the affair with gusto, though his chief assistant at 142 Strand was less enthusiastic. 'Mr C. up to the ears in a business affair all about Bookselling and discounts', she told Sara Hennell on 31 January, 'which things grate horribly on my ears'.[81]

The Booksellers' Association had met at Exeter Hall in July 1850 to tighten up the regulations governing trade discounts. Henceforth booksellers were obliged to sign an undertaking not to discount new books by more than ten per cent. Anyone who refused had his trade ticket taken away and was publicly advertised as an underseller, with the result that publishers stopped supplying him with their books. Henry Bohn, among other discounters, fell into line after this meeting, but Chapman refused. He went on the attack by announcing in the *Westminster Review* in January 1852 that he deemed the rule not to apply to imported books, in which he specialised. He would therefore continue to sell American imports at a larger discount than ten per cent. The Booksellers' Association summoned him to a meeting, removed his ticket, and 'duly placarded' the fact 'in the shops of the metropolis', with the result that 'the majority of the publishers now decline to supply him with their publications', as Chapman wrote in his comprehensive article on the book trade, 'The Commerce of Literature', published in the *Westminster* in April 1852.[82]

The article, which Chapman immediately reprinted as a pamphlet, *Cheap Books, and How to Get Them*, deals not merely with his own experience, of which he writes in the third person and without naming himself, but with the larger questions involved. The costs of paper and printing, the destruction of competition by the restrictive practices of the Booksellers' Association, and the unfair advantage given to larger booksellers are, he argues, inimical to the desirable outcome of cheap books, a commodity as important for the education of the population as a cheap loaf is for feeding it. Nothing less than 'the progress of civilization' is at stake; free trade in books is in principle no different from free trade in other commodities.[83]

The newspapers took up the argument, some siding with the Booksellers' Association, partly, no doubt, because they depended for revenue on publishers' advertisements in their pages, while others, including *The Times*, came out in favour of free trade. Chapman, not content with writing his powerful article, sent letters to newspapers, to famous authors, and to Members of Parliament asking for their support. On 5 April he reported to Combe, an ardent believer in free trade, that his article was 'creating some stir'. John Murray and William Longman had written to *The Times* to defend the Association, but at the same time a number of other publishers were deserting its ranks. 'I have received a letter from Messrs J. W. Parker and Son to say they have withdrawn from the Association. Bentley preceded them, so I am sure to break it up', wrote Chapman.[84] Murray was nettled by the movement thus begun by Chapman. His letter to *The Times* on

2 April described the undersellers as 'solitary upstarts' trying by means of discounts to 'filch away the customers from old established houses, and thus to carve out for themselves a short road to opulence'.[85] However, with Chapman gathering support from prominent people, the Booksellers' Association decided to put the question to the Lord Chief Justice, Lord Campbell, promising to abide by his decision. Campbell, aided by his committee of two, Henry Hart Milman, Dean of St Paul's, and George Grote, reformer and historian of Greece, received deputations and submissions from both sides and issued his judgment on 19 May.

Meanwhile Chapman lobbied and organised. He wrote to W. E. Gladstone on 8 April, appealing to his known support for free trade and to his sense of fair play. Murray and Longman, he wrote, were claiming that the object of the Booksellers' Association was to 'maintain the solvency of the trade'. The irony of this remark was not lost on Chapman, whose own trade was now, as ever, on the brink of insolvency:

> I, for one, should feel extremely obliged for such considerate protection, could I but discern the dangers from which I am shielded; but it seems to me that the system adopted has rather a petrifying effect. It 'puzzles the brain' to find out how, by fettering the enterprise of men, they are enabled more effectually to pay their debts.

Referring to the streets in which Murray and Longman had their businesses, both famous in the history of publishing, Chapman concluded with an adroit compliment to Gladstone. 'I am convinced', he wrote, 'that though the ghost of protection may still haunt Albemarle Street and Paternoster Row, it will not overcome the strong sense of England's ablest thinkers'.[86]

It is highly likely that Chapman knew in advance that Gladstone would support him, for the latter had suffered from his publisher John Murray's boycott of the underselling firm of Bickers & Bush in connection with Gladstone's translation of Farini's *Roman State*, published at the end of 1851. Gladstone had been in correspondence with Murray over the boycott's damage to sales of his book, and was not satisfied by Murray's explanation that he was bound by the regulations of the Booksellers' Association not to deal with Bickers & Bush.[87] Gladstone therefore readily heeded Chapman's summons, sending a letter of support and even raising the bookselling question during a speech to Parliament on 12 May, while Lord

Campbell's committee was still considering the case.[88] Murray and Longman were embarrassed by this public opposition by a leading politician. Longman wrote on 22 May to assure Gladstone that 'although I felt myself called on to say a few words in favo[u]r of the publishers, it was my particular wish to avoid treating your statement with any want of respect'. He asked if he might meet Gladstone to discuss 'the future conduct of the Trade'.[89] By this time, Lord Campbell had pronounced.

Chapman, always sanguine, had been certain of success. He told Combe in confidence on 15 March that his determination, announced in the January number of the *Westminster*, 'to supply American books 25 per cent lower than heretofore' had involved him in 'so serious a contest with the booksellers and publishers that I may say my whole time has been absorbed in ascertaining my strength, preparing for the battle and fighting'. Though he was a David taking on a Goliath, he was confident of winning, not least because the editor of *The Times* had assured him of his support if Chapman would supply him with 'the materials for the battery'. Accordingly it was agreed that as Chapman was preparing the facts and figures for his *Westminster Review* article 'The Commerce of Literature', he would pass these on to *The Times*, so that it could enter the fray as soon as the April number of the *Review* appeared.[90] This explains how *The Times* carried knowledgeable articles and letters on the subject from the very beginning of April.

Chapman was not relying on Gladstone and *The Times* alone. Letters of invitation to a meeting at 142 Strand on 4 May were sent to about fifty well-known writers. Among them were Chapman's own authors and supporters: Chambers, Combe, Forbes, Fox, Hickson, Lewes, Mackay, Mill, Newman, Crabb Robinson, and Spencer. Carlyle, Dickens, Wilkie Collins, Henry Cole, George Cruikshank, Leigh Hunt, and Professor Richard Owen were other celebrated writers on the list. A number of them attended; the rest sent letters of support which were first read out at the meeting, then published in Chapman's *Report* of the proceedings, and finally quoted widely in the press.[91]

Chapman's greatest triumph was to persuade Dickens to chair the meeting. Marian Evans, watching from close quarters, sent this great news to Charles Bray on 17 April. Chapman had called on Dickens the previous day, along with Richard Bentley, who had defected from the Booksellers' Association to join the free traders, and 'found him very straight-forward and agreeable', she reported. Five days later she told Combe that 'the agitation in the Bookselling business' was going on 'with increasing vivacity'.[92] Not only *The Times* and other daily papers, but also the weekly *Athenaeum* and *Leader*, the trade journal, *Publishers' Circular*, and the gossiping *Critic*, reported throughout April and May on the progress of what the *Athenaeum* called 'the battle of the books'.[93]

The meeting on 4 May was well attended by luminaries. Marian Evans sat at the back of the room recording the proceedings for the benefit of her Coventry friends, to whom she described the occasion the following day. Mindful of Charles Bray's keen amateur interest in phrenology, she described the great men accordingly. Firstly, she sketches the chairman:

> Dickens in the chair – a position he fills remarkably well, preserving a courteous neutrality of eyebrow, and speaking with clearness and decision. His appearance is certainly disappointing – no benevolence in the face and I think little in the head – the anterior lobe not by any means remarkable. In fact he is not distinguished looking in any way – neither handsome nor ugly, neither fat nor thin, neither tall nor short.[94]

Next she describes Chapman himself, known to her in all his weakness but still admired for his compensatory gifts: 'Mr Chapman read his statement very well and looked distinguished and refined even in that assemblage of intellectuals.' The statement consisted of material from Chapman's *Westminster* article and his letter to Gladstone; he stressed the need to extend the principle of free trade won by the repeal of the Corn Laws in 1846 to embrace the book trade.[95] Letters had arrived from those unable to attend; these included Carlyle, Chambers, Combe, Gladstone, W. J. Fox, Cole, Mill, Leigh Hunt, and the veteran anti-Corn Law agitator and MP Richard Cobden.

Among those who were present, Marian singles out Charles Knight, the experienced publisher of cheap educational books, for special mention. He is 'a beautiful elderly man with a modest but firm enunciation', who 'made a wise and telling speech which silenced one or two vulgar, ignorant booksellers who had got into the meeting by mistake'. She also describes Richard Owen, celebrated professor of anatomy and discoverer of dinosaur remains, speaking 'in his silvery bland way' about the negative effects of the trade restrictions on scientific books, and sporting 'a tremendous head'. F. W. Newman also spoke well, as did Dickens's friend George Cruikshank.

Summing up the occasion and her wish for the success of the resolution taken at the meeting to present the agreed case for free trade to Lord Campbell, she expresses the hope that

> poor Mr Chapman will have a little time to attend to his business which is needing him awfully – in fact his private affairs are wearing a melancholy aspect. However he has worked well and in a good spirit at this great question and has shewn a degree of talent, and power of mastering a subject which have won him general admiration.[96]

Her hopes were not to be fulfilled. Though Lord Campbell ruled in Chapman's favour, with the consequence that the Booksellers' Association met on 28 May to disband itself, Chapman found himself on no 'short road to opulence', to echo Murray's letter to *The Times*, as a result of his fine victory. Not only did free trade in books increase competition, thus allowing others as well as himself to offer discounts – a result he considered perfectly fair – but the defeated publishers, though no longer an Association, continued to boycott him in practice, if not in principle. He told Gladstone in July that his business had been 'seriously damaged by the wilful obstructions of the defeated but powerful booksellers'.[97] Carlyle had foreseen this, telling his German friend Joseph Neuberg at the end of May that Chapman had 'gained his cause, so far, with unexpected speed', but adding, 'I can prophesy a very muddy troubled lake to fish in, for long years henceforth, to the vehement man'.[98] (Neuberg would soon get to know Chapman well; he lodged at 142 Strand during the coming winter,[99] and he contributed some articles to the *Westminster Review* on European subjects. In 1855 he became a rival of the 'vehement' Chapman in an affair of the heart.)

Chapman's books did not sell well; nor did the *Westminster Review*. He calculated in August that he had sold only 1,050 copies of the July number, and 2,370 of the January and April numbers combined – not nearly enough to break even. He told Combe, hoping to induce him to offer more financial help, that he planned to reduce payment for articles for the *Review* from £12.12.0 to £10 a sheet. Combe did what he could by refusing or deferring payment for his own articles, but he saw that helping Chapman's finances would be a long and costly business for anyone rash enough to try. 'Want of business talent' in Chapman was his diagnosis, which would 'render all temporary assistance ineffectual for good'.[100]

This was true enough, though even a better businessman than Chapman would have been unable to run the *Review* at a profit. As Mill, no enthusiast for Chapman, pointed out when he was drumming up support for the *Westminster Review* in the 1860s, all of the journal's previous owners had made huge losses. The difference was that Chapman, unlike Bentham, Molesworth, Hickson, and Mill himself, had no private income to prop up the venture. One consolation for the aspiring Chapman was that he gained some fame through his efforts. As the friendly *Leader* (in the person of Lewes) declared on 22 May:

> The old system is no more; – slain, to say the truth, by the energy and skill of John Chapman, who brings into the trade the feeling of a literary man, the far sight of a philosopher, and the public spirit of a leading reformer.[101]

Yet only five days later Marian replied ruefully to Cara Bray's letter of congratulation on the victory over the Booksellers' Association:

> You talk of poor Mr Chapman's laurels – alas, alas, he is suffering the most torturing anxiety, advertising for a partner in half-despair . . . The immediate difficulty is how to pay the authorship of the next number of the W. R. – a sum of £250! . . . He sits in the shop the greater part of the day now, and is about to part with Mr Beveridge, as a step in retrenchment.[102]

'Sitting in the shop' means exactly that: Chapman was working as a shop assistant in his own business in order to save on salaries for hired help. Only five months after the publication of the first number of the *Westminster Review* under his ownership, he was in trouble financially. And yet Chapman survived. Thirty-five years later, in 1887, he was once again in correspondence with Gladstone, who had by this time served three terms as Prime Minister. Chapman was now living in Paris and was 'married' to Hannah Macdonald (though Susanna was still alive and no divorce appears to have been arranged), but he was still editing the *Westminster Review*. His editorial policy at this time was to support Gladstone's efforts to bring in Home Rule for Ireland. He wrote to invite Gladstone to contribute to the *Review*:

> I need hardly say that if at any time you should feel disposed to make use of the Review for the publication of a paper from your own pen – either with or without your name attached to it – it would be cordially welcomed, and would greatly strengthen the position of the *Westminster* as the leading organ of the distinctively liberal cause.[103]

This letter was written from the National Liberal Club near Whitehall, where Chapman stayed on his visits to London. On 11 December 1887 he wrote from his home on Avenue Kléber in Paris to thank Gladstone for the paper he had sent, a letter of five pages which appeared, with Gladstone's signature, in the *Westminster* for January 1888.[104] Nothing, it seems, could deter Chapman from his chosen profession, despite chronic poverty and improvidence over a period of forty years. No wonder Marian Evans, though all the while acutely aware of his shortcomings, thought him heroic at the time of the battle of the books.

5

The Struggle for Survival (1852–4)

The summer of 1852 saw Chapman nearly sink into bankruptcy, despite the apparent success of his battle with the booksellers and the admiration he had won among important people for the stand he had taken. He pinned his hopes on Combe's willingness to use his considerable influence to bring in new financial backers for the *Westminster Review*. Letters exchanged during July and August between Combe and Bray, the Brays and Marian Evans, and Marian and Combe show that Chapman was lucky to survive the summer financially. On 14 July Susanna Chapman intervened on her husband's behalf with an unfortunately ill-judged letter to Combe defending Chapman against criticism of his handling of business affairs. She describes his lack of a business education, his liking for 'the best paper and the best printing', his choice of 'ornamental covers etc. which are much admired but do not increase the number of copies sold', and his misfortunes with employees. 'Two of them have left in his debt', she writes. Her husband's (mis)adventures with the changing law of copyright in the matter of Emerson's works – not his fault – are recounted, followed by praise for Chapman's dedication:

> He is industrious beyond any man I ever knew; he generally goes to bed at ten and rises at 5, takes a showerbath and works till breakfast time; he has great energy; often when the assistants have said it was impossible to get a case packed by a certain time, he says it must be

possible and by urging and superintending and assisting, the impossible is performed.

Finally, Susanna remarks that 142 Strand itself makes a loss, despite its use as a boarding house; with a rent of £400 a year, and rates and utilities making up another £100 or more, it represents yet another drain on her husband's stretched resources.[1] Combe's comment in the margin of this well-meant but hardly persuasive document is brief and to the point: 'Her own letter shows that Mr C has no adequate business talent. He must get into a line for which he is fitted before he can succeed.'[2]

Much more helpful to Chapman than Susanna's effort was Marian Evans's continued faith in him and Combe's strong faith in *her*. Marian spent a difficult summer, carrying out her editorial duties from Broadstairs, where she took seaside lodgings to escape from the London heat and from where she sent anguished but proud love letters to the unresponsive Herbert Spencer. 'You curse the destiny which has made the feeling concentrate itself on you', she wrote in July after Spencer had visited her on the Kent coast; 'I can be satisfied with very little, if I am delivered from the dread of losing it.'[3] At the same time she was corresponding with Combe, trying, with limited success, to persuade him that Chapman's business affairs were not as hopeless as he believed and that he deserved the full support of all friends of progress and reform. 'The maintenance of his position as a publisher is of importance on other grounds than personal ones', she wrote on 16 July.[4]

Marian also worked on her old friend Charles Bray, prevailing on him to join her in urging Combe not to give up on Chapman, who had already visited Coventry to put the state of his financial affairs before Bray. Aware that Chapman often failed to impress male acquaintances and was in general not his own best advocate, she undertook that task herself, writing to Bray on 14 July:

Mr Chapman wrote me word yesterday that he was going to you a second time to 'explain his explanation'. I trust your benevolence and fellow-feeling, or rather your sense of the importance, on other grounds than personal ones, that his position should be maintained will enable you to bear these visitations with patience. Of course, I am in great anxiety about him, and what is worse, I can do nothing.

155

I have had a letter from Geo. Combe today containing the same hope-less opinion as the one you forwarded to me. I am surprized that you and he think so ill of Mr C's affairs. My impression was that the busi-ness was in a thoroughly promising condition apart from the need of temporary assistance in capital.[5]

Chapman visited Bray three times during July, finally succeeding in face-to-face conversation where, as usual, he had failed to persuade in corre-spondence. Marian's reply later in the summer to a comment by Cara Bray acknowledges his epistolary faults, while defending his sincerity:

The sentence you quote is a good specimen of Mr Chapman's skill in 'the art of sinking', not in poetry, but in letter-writing. But it is nothing worse than bungling. He feels better than he writes.[6]

Between them Marian and Chapman persuaded Bray to write to Combe defending Chapman and asking Combe to encourage his friends to give financial support. Combe's reply of 18 July acknowledged that Chapman had 'a great deal of scheming talent, and the most anxious desire to act practically', but 'I cannot discover in him the *power* to fulfil his own good intentions'. He agreed with Bray about the importance for the progress of 'advanced opinion' that the *Westminster Review* be kept going, but could not see how Chapman was to do it 'except by finding a partner who can supply the two elements of capital and business talent, in which Mr C. is now deficient'. For this reason Combe could not in conscience ask Cobden 'or any other friend' to help in so unpromising a case.[7]

Bray tried again, hoping to dispel Combe's doubts by describing a new plan to keep the *Review* afloat. Knowing Combe's respect for Marian Evans's ability, he took care to mention her name as a supporter, though of course she was not in a position to offer financial help:

My dear Sir

Excuse my troubling you again. Probably the view you take of Mr Chapman and his affairs is the correct one, but what I have to say is independent of any difference of opinion on this score. I wish to keep the Westminster in *our* hands – viz: in yours and mine and Miss Evans's et hoc genus omne, and my proposition is, that it be made

over to 10 of us, for 100£ each. If in a given time, say two [or] three
or 5 years, Mr Chapman is able to redeem it, let him have the option
– if not it would belong to us – and by that time, under present
management, and as it is now going on, it would be worth that money.
Is this practicable? Mr C. says that 1000£ would keep him up permanently – if so, all the better for our cause, and the Review could not
be in better hands – if not, it will probably keep him up long enough
to ensure the success of the Review and we get that for our money.
If I were a capitalist I should not mind the risk, because to keep the
Review *right* is so important.

I shall be from home for a week, when perhaps you will tell me
what you think of my plan. I think the literary men who now write
for the Review would gladly take a share in it and perhaps help to
keep it up till it became a property.[8]

Combe, while agreeing that no one else could do better with the
Westminster Review, especially since much of the real editorial work was
done by the impressive and competent Miss Evans, and aware of the danger
of the *Review* falling into the hands of its less radical, Unitarian supporters,
was not convinced of the financial sense of Bray's suggestion. His scepticism sprang from his recognition, not only of the fact that no radical periodical ever made a profit, but also that the case was complicated by
Chapman's owning a publishing business which also ran at a loss and which
Chapman failed to keep separate from the affairs of the *Westminster*. He
made a note on the back of Bray's letter which reads 'Answered thus':

If a practical scheme can be found for preserving the Review in the
hands you mention, I should contribute £100 and ask friends to join
in raising £1000 but your scheme is not a practical one. Mr C. is
insolvent in his general business and the Review is still a source of
loss, in my opinion of £400 a year. To give Mr C. £1000 would be
simply to cover his general deficiencies perhaps for 2 years, when it
would be all lost, and the persons to whom the Review was conveyed
would be liable for its debts, and when Mr Chapman again stood still
they would be called on to pay those claims and take the whole
concern into their hands.

If by re-imbursing Mr C. in the £350 paid by him for the Review, disconnecting it from his general business, and applying the £650 remaining of the £1000 to it, it might be carried on for 2 years, and I should be ready then to allow him to buy it back on refunding the £350 and intermediate loss; but this would leave no remuneration for him and Miss Evans as editors. It they were paid £100 a year each, the loss would be £600, and the £1000 would suffice only for one year. Were the Review taken out of his hands entirely we should lose the advantage of his connection. In short I do not see any way to a practical solution of the difficulty.[9]

The puzzle could not be solved unless a large benefactor appeared on the scene, which is what happened, out of the blue, in December 1852, when Samuel Courtauld, silk manufacturer, Unitarian, and supporter of liberal causes, '*volunteered* to interest himself' in 'the affairs of Chapmandom', as Marian reported to the Brays.[10] Courtauld gave Chapman £600, it appears, which enabled him to carry on for another year or so.[11]

As a matter of fact, Combe's comments about remuneration for Chapman and Marian in his letter to Bray were wide of the mark. Chapman paid himself no salary, and Marian merely received food and lodgings for her services, as is evident from her interesting and wide-ranging letter to Chapman from Broadstairs at the end of July. James Martineau had been offering advice about the conduct of the *Review*, presumably with the aim of making it a thoroughgoing Unitarian journal, or at least of ensuring that it did not offend its Unitarian readers by its more radical articles. Marian was keen to counteract any influence Martineau might exert on Chapman during her absence from London. She disliked Martineau's beliefs and thought him excessively egotistical. Chapman is scolded for not listening to her advice on how to deal with Martineau and the equally prickly Mill, who was at last writing an article (on moral philosophy) for the October number of the *Review*:

As to Martineau, there is no doubt that he will write – 'Self-interest well understood' will secure that. Pray, how came you to tell him that J. S. Mill was going to write? I have told you all along that he would flatly contradict Martineau and that there was nothing for it but to announce contradiction on our title-page. I think M. is right as to the 'idea' of a quarterly, but it is plain that the Westminster can't realize that 'idea'. However, if I were its proprietor and could afford to make it what I liked, it should certainly not represent the Martineau 'School of thought'.[12]

After making a number of suggestions about articles and writers for the *Westminster*, she launches into an analysis of the choices facing its editors, prefacing this with the throwaway remark 'When you can afford to pay an Editor, if that time will ever come, you must get one', and in the process giving bold expression to her own views on religion:

> If you believe in Free Will, in the Theism that looks on manhood as a type of the godhead and on Jesus as the Ideal Man, get one [i.e. an editor] belonging to the Martineau 'School of thought', and he will drill you a regiment of writers who will produce a Prospective on a larger scale, and so the Westminster may come to have 'dignity' in the eyes of Liverpool.
>
> If not – if you believe, as I do, that the thought which is to mould the Future has for its root a belief in necessity, that a nobler presentation of humanity has yet to be given in resignation to individual nothingness, than could ever be shewn of a being who believes in the phantasmagoria of hope unsustained by reason – why then get a man of another calibre.

The only other course, she concludes, is the one they are currently following, namely 'that of Editorial compromise', thus keeping Newman, Froude, Mill, and Martineau – all of them 'amongst the world's vanguard', though in different ways – on the grounds that if they cannot each have a periodical to themselves, they can at least have 'one which is common to them – id est, the Westminster'.[13]

Having returned to London at the end of August and overseen final arrangements for the October number, Marian spent two weeks in Edinburgh as Combe's guest, followed by a few days in the Lake District with Harriet Martineau. She reported herself 'in clover' in the Combes' elegant house; 'between the beauty of the weather and the scenery, and the kindness of good people I am tipsy with pleasure', she told the Brays on 12 October, though she could not resist making fun of her host's propensity to mistake monologues for conversation:

The talk last night was pleasant enough, though of course all the interlocutors besides Mr Combe have little to do but shape elegant modes of negation and affirmation like the people who are talked to by Socrates in Plato's dialogues – 'Certainly, that I firmly believe' etc.[14]

For his part, the good-natured Combe committed a description of this visit to his journal, one which had none of the roguishness of his guest's account:

Miss Marian Evans, aged 32, who assists Mr John Chapman in editing the Westminster Review, has been our guest for a fortnight, & has left us this day. She is a distinguished linguist, including Greek, Latin & Hebrew, German, French & Italian; an admirable musician; and is mistress of all the philosophies of modern times; & is a good political economist; also knows art well. She is thoroughly feminine, refined, & Lady-like. Her brain is large, the anterior lobe & coronal region predominating. Temp[eramen]t nervous lymphatic; pleasing but not pretty.[15]

The October number of the *Westminster* was a strong one. 'We shall make a respectable figure after all', Marian had written with relief to Sara Hennell on 25 September.[16] They had Froude on the Oxford Commission (looking into matters at the University), Mill on philosophy, Forbes on botany, and Chapman's engineer cousin – also John Chapman – on 'our colonial empire'. This John Chapman had patented improvements to the hansom cab, collaborated on an early prototype of the aeroplane, and planned India's first railway in the 1840s. He had written *The Cotton and Commerce of India* in 1851. When he visited his much younger namesake at 142 Strand in November 1852 to watch the funeral procession of the Duke of Wellington, Chapman's daughter Beatrice, aged eight, thought this uncle, as she later recalled, a 'country looking gentleman, very wise and kind'.[17] The hard-working female editor, however, did not count this John Chapman's article among the best in the number; she had complained to Sara on 2 September that she had 'a great, dreary article on the Colonies by my side asking for reading and abridgement'.[18] Even after she had pruned it, the published article amounted to thirty-seven pages, longer even than Froude's or Mill's contributions.

Also in this October number was an article on the philosophy of style by Spencer, one on the Duke of Wellington by Greg, and a striking piece by Lewes, 'Goethe as a Man of Science', which was later incorporated into his *Life of Goethe* (1855). Lewes himself gave a puff to the whole number in his *Leader* column on 2 October, declaring:

> It is a matter of general remark, that the *Westminster Review*, since it passed into MR CHAPMAN's hands, has recovered the importance it acquired when under the editorship of JOHN STUART MILL. It is now a Review that people talk about, ask for at the clubs, and read with respect. The variety and general excellence of its articles are not surpassed by any Review.[19]

Heartening praise for the editors, though unfortunately not likely to affect the financial position of the *Westminster Review* and its owner.

The wealthy businessman who stepped in providentially to help, Samuel Courtauld, was one of Chapman's large circle of Unitarian acquaintances. He was the head of the well-known family firm of silk manufacturers and an ardent reformer in religious and social matters. Elizabeth Whitehead, later Malleson, who remembered with sympathy how ill-matched Chapman and his wife were, knew the family well. She noted in her autobiography that Courtauld was generous to those he thought could make a difference in the battle to improve society. He was a supporter of Bedford College for women, campaigned against the compulsory payment by dissenters of Church Rates, and had bestowed an annuity of £400 on W. J. Fox in 1847 to enable him to run for Parliament as a radical.[20] Courtauld's partner, his nephew Peter Alfred Taylor, attended parties at 142 Strand, and with his wife Clementia often invited Chapman and Marian Evans to his home. The Taylors were radical Unitarians and chief among the group of influential people who supported the cause of freedom for Italy, and in particular its charismatic leader Giuseppe Mazzini. In 1847 Taylor was co-founder and first chairman of the Society of Friends of Italy; Clementia helped Mazzini to raise money for the education of poor Italian children in London by holding bazaars and soirées.[21]

It was natural that exiles from repressive regimes in Europe should seek out radical periodicals to promote their interests. In the early 1850s the

Leader was full of articles by and about Mazzini, the French exiles Louis Blanc, Pierre Leroux, and Alexandre Ledru-Rollin, the Russian Alexander Herzen, the Hungarian Lajos Kossuth, and a number of German refugees, including Gottfried Kinkel, whose thrilling escape from a life sentence in the fortress of Spandau was welcomed in the *Leader* on 16 November 1850 with a celebratory poem by the Chartist poet George Hooper.[22]

Chapman, too, was keen to champion the cause of freedom in post-1848 Europe. Invitations to his Monday soirées were sent to a number of exiles. Marian reported on one of them to Sara Hennell on 21 January 1852: 'I was talking and listening for two hours to Pierre Leroux'. She described him as 'a dreamy genius', who expounded his idealistic views of Liberty, Equality, and Fraternity at length. 'He is in utter poverty', she noted; 'going to lecture – autrement il faut mourir – has a wife and children with him'. In the same letter she told Sara of the plan to get the most famous exile of all to contribute to the *Westminster Review*: 'We are trying Mazzini to write Freedom v. Despotism. Don't tell, of course.'[23] On 24 March Marian crossed the Strand to the Freemasons' Tavern in Covent Garden to attend a meeting of the Friends of Italy chaired by F. W. Newman and addressed to loud cheers by Mazzini, who denounced the Papacy and the French and Austrian forces occupying Italian soil. 'I *did* go to the *conversazione*', she told Clementia Taylor, who was fast becoming a good friend, 'but you have less to regret than you think. Mazzini's speeches are better read than heard.'[24]

While she admired Mazzini's bravery – he frequently travelled incognito to Italy though under sentence of death there and at risk of spies and assassins everywhere he went – Marian did not fall under his spell as the Taylors and others had done. Jane Carlyle, for example, had been a Mazzini enthusiast from her first acquaintance with him in 1840, when she had helped him to find lodgings in Chelsea.[25] Her husband was more sceptical, though he had written a famous letter to *The Times* in June 1844 attacking the Home Secretary, Sir James Graham, for authorising the Post Office to open Mazzini's letters. The Post Office had interfered at the request of the Austrian authorities, and Carlyle spoke for the nation when he described this violation of a man's privacy as quintessentially un-English and an act 'near of kin to picking men's pockets'.[26] Nevertheless, he kept slightly aloof from the circus surrounding Mazzini. He excused himself from attending the first Friends of Italy meeting, held on 11 February 1852, to which Jane

Carlyle went along with a number of prominent liberal-minded Londoners. Carlyle quotes with amusement her description of the occasion:

> Mazzini's Soirée, which my Wife attended, along with Clough and some other male and female disciples of good figure, was 'perfectly successful' after its kind: a very harmless meeting; properly a kind of *Lecture*, with fringings of coffee (*voluntary* coffee): Lecture wh[ic]h M. *read* in the most artless manner, 'with candles *between* him and the little slips of paper', and as practically as a grocer's bill, – since to be seen (by me not to be read) in the public Papers, – and listened to with[ou]t commentary, except of feet and hands by a believing auditory of the youthful middle-classes near a thousand strong.[27]

If Marian Evans failed to be charmed by Mazzini's quaint spoken English, the Carlyles adopted it with glee, peppering their letters with Mazzini-isms such as 'thanks God' and 'upon *my* honour'; Jane reported his description of a dinner menu in 1865 (when he had lived in London for nearly thirty years) as 'a crushed Fish; some conspicuous Bird – Goose – what shall I say? A viscous fabric, and a Pie whatever!'[28] Carlyle, though generous with his help when Mazzini first arrived in London, had tired of his conspiratorial ways and left him to Jane, but he recalled late in life being amused by Mazzini's 'curious bits of Exile London-and-Foreign life, and his singular *Italian*-English modes of locution'.[29]

Marian may have thought that Mazzini wrote better than he spoke, but the article he produced for the *Westminster*, published in April 1852 in the second number under Chapman's ownership, was a rambling affair. Entitled 'Europe: Its Condition and Prospects', it covered twenty-five pages with vague pieties about the past, present, and future of European politics. Marian reported to Charles Bray on 17 April that Greg had pronounced it 'sad stuff – mere verbiage', an opinion from which she did not dissent.[30] She probably did not know that Mazzini had written the article in French and had it translated into English, which no doubt contributed to the oddness of the style, though the abstract, romantic, religiose content is Mazzini's own.[31] Mazzini did not become a regular contributor to the *Review*, though he wrote two more articles on Italy for Chapman, in 1857 and 1867, after Marian Evans had left the *Westminster*.

In spite of his huge popularity, as shown by the numbers who turned up to his soirées and wished to meet him or have a scrap of his writing – in December 1852 Marian sent off a scribbled note Mazzini had written to Chapman about his *Westminster* article to an avid autograph hunter in Edinburgh[32] – Mazzini always struggled financially. This was the case with most of the political exiles, even those who managed to get jobs as tutors or governesses or as contributors to newspapers and journals. The Carlyles were instrumental in helping one of Mazzini's colleagues, Aurelio Saffi, get an invitation from Chapman to write in the *Westminster Review*. Jane Carlyle prompted her husband in August 1852: 'Would you write a little recommendation to Chapman for Saffi, who can get no trace of pupils and who wishes to try article writing'. Whereupon Carlyle wrote persuasively to Chapman the following day, recommending Saffi, who was commissioned to write an article on religion in Italy.[33]

The money troubles of the exile who was to become more famous even than Mazzini, Karl Marx, make Chapman's difficulties during the summer of 1852 look like small beer. As luck would have it, Chapman was the man Marx hoped would help him out, by discounting bills for him until money due for articles published in a New York newspaper arrived, and possibly also by publishing an English translation of *The Eighteenth Brumaire of Louis Bonaparte*, a topical work Marx had written about Louis Napoleon's *coup d'état* at the end of 1851. He could hardly have chosen a worse moment to turn to Chapman for financial aid. No relationship ensued, and Marx wrote nothing for the *Westminster Review*.

He and Chapman did meet, however. Chapman's diary records that on Sunday 27 July 1851 he went with his brother Thomas, visiting London for the Great Exhibition, to dine at Mr and Mrs Johnson's house in Hackney, where they 'met Freiligrath and a Herr Merks, another exile'.[34] Freiligrath, a colleague of Marx's on the banned Cologne newspaper, the *Neue Rheinische Zeitung*, had made useful English contacts on previous visits to London. He was now staying with his friend Andrew Johnson until he found accommodation for himself and his family.[35] On his first stay in London in 1846–8, Freiligrath, a revolutionary poet who earned his living working for his family's business, had found a job with the City firm of Frederick Huth & Co., one of several merchant banking businesses set up in London by German families, such as the Barings and the Grotes, in the eighteenth century. He had met and corresponded with Monckton Milnes and Edward Bulwer Lytton, who helped him find work; on the outbreak of the revolution in Europe in 1848 he had hurried back to Germany to take part. Now, with the return of repressive regimes throughout Europe following the collapse of revolutionary parliaments, he fled once more to England in May 1851, preceded by an article in the *Leader* in February entitled 'Pleasures of Prussian Citizenship. The impending Expulsion of the Poet Freiligrath'. In July 1852 he joined Oxford & Co., a firm of dealers in East Indian silk.[36]

The *Leader* article had appeared thanks to Chapman, whom Andrew Johnson visited at 142 Strand on 8 February 1851 'to request my aid in getting a paper into the "Leader" concerning Freiligrath', as Chapman noted in his diary. Wanting to help, he wrote to the *Leader*'s political editor, Thornton Hunt, a vocal supporter of Mazzini and other European radicals.[37] Chapman and Johnson had known one another at least since 1845, when Chapman published Schelling's *Philosophy of Art*, translated by Johnson, in his Catholic Series.[38] As well as being an enthusiast for German literature, Johnson had been a bullion clerk at the Bank of England since 1849.[39] He published two books in the 1850s, *Some Observations on the Recent Supplies of Gold; with Remarks on Mr Scheer's Letter to Sir F. Baring* (1852) and *Currency Principles versus Banking Principles; being Strictures on Mr Tooke's Pamphlet on the Bank Charter Act of 1844* (1856).

Through his banking connections Johnson was able to help Freiligrath find a job in 1852, and he was useful to Chapman too. Chapman's diary for 1851 shows that Johnson attended soirées at number 142 in January and April. He was called in to help Chapman balance his books on 10 February, and the latter was 'gratified to find' that he approved of the plans for the *Westminster* when the two men met on 25 May. On the same day Johnson took Chapman to meet Freiligrath, newly arrived from Germany.[40] In August Johnson was asked, along with Herbert Spencer, to read the much-criticised draft Prospectus.[41] Being keen to introduce the innovative 'Contemporary Literature' section to the *Westminster*, which would include surveys of recent French, German, and American literature, Chapman thought Freiligrath would be a good person to write on German literature for the *Review*. When Johnson and Freiligrath visited him on 11 June 1851, the latter responded positively to his request.[42] In the event, nothing appeared by Freiligrath, though Johnson offered to ensure that the 'Article on Foreign Literature' Freiligrath had agreed to write would be 'in good English'.[43]

Relations between Johnson and Chapman, meanwhile, continued to be good well into the 1860s, with Johnson writing in the *Westminster* a review of Mill's *On Representative Government* in July 1861, an article entitled 'The Depreciation of Gold' in January 1864, and some pieces in the 'Contemporary Literature' section in 1867 and 1868.[44] It appears that Johnson knew about Chapman's relations with Susanna and other women. Elisabeth Tilley visited him and his wife in 1851, and eleven years later, when Chapman was on the verge of leaving Susanna and setting up home with his current mistress, a young German opera singer, Johanna von Heyligenstaedt, Chapman, by now a qualified doctor, was considering moving to the country with Johanna and asked Johnson's advice, which he reported to Johanna in March 1862:

> His opinion is strongly against my going into the country with a view to practise my profession. As he says, if I do that I must be prepared to live what is called 'respectably', to conform to present ideas in respect to my social life, as he does, and to forego all expression of my real convictions: to go to church and seemingly to acquiesce in all the superstitions of the stupidest old ladies with whom I may come into contact. A nice life that would be – would it not? I hope thou wouldst hate me if I so degraded myself as to live it.[45]

Marx, who had settled in London in August 1849, was introduced to Johnson very soon after Freiligrath's arrival in mid-May 1851. On 28 May the latter wrote to Marx to say that Johnson had got hold of a ticket to show his friends round the Bank the following week. 'Perhaps your wife would also like to see it and to hold a banknote for a million pounds in her hand', Freiligrath added.[46] Soon Marx was using the Bank of England as his surrogate address; in October 1852 he told Engels to send any *important* letters to him care of Andrew Johnson, the Bullion Office, Bank of England.[47] He was also borrowing money from Johnson and hoping to use Chapman as another unofficial banker from whom he could get credit on presentation of letters from Charles Dana, editor of the *New York Daily Tribune*, for which Marx wrote regular lively essays on British current affairs (helped by Engels, who sometimes wrote them for him and often translated Marx's German draft into English).[48] In February 1852 Freiligrath suggested Marx try either the German publisher Trübner, of Paternoster Row near St Paul's Cathedral, for this purpose, or – preferably – Chapman, as 142 Strand was nearer to Marx's lodgings in Dean Street, Soho.[49] The following day, 18 February, Marx told Engels that Johnson was 'the only Englishman to whom I can turn when *in extremis* – and I hover constantly on the brink'. Engels was supplying him with articles for Dana, and Marx was desperate for copy to send to New York so that he might get some credit. 'I must chivvy you about the *Tribune* since I am myself being chivvied daily by Johnson', he wrote on 23 February.[50]

By August 1852 Marx was in a bad way. His landlady was 'pestering' him for the rent money, and he had been forced to write to Johnson asking him to 'discount a bill on the *Tribune* for me'. Freiligrath, trying to help, reported that he had spoken with Johnson on Marx's behalf, but that Johnson was unwilling to be the medium of a bill to be discounted by Chapman, as he (Johnson) would then be under an undesirable obligation to Chapman.[51] In any case, as we know, Chapman was in no position to do anyone a financial favour, given the state of his own affairs that summer. Still, however tight his own finances were, they were not as dire as Marx's, with a family to keep on small earnings and handouts from Engels and the possibility of eviction or even starvation at any moment. By 8 September this fate was staring him in the face. His wife Jenny was ill, as was one of his daughters:

I cannot call the doctor because I have no money to buy medicine. For the past 8–10 days I have been feeding the FAMILY solely on bread and potatoes, but whether I shall be able to get hold of any today is doubtful . . . I have not written any articles for Dana because I didn't have a PENNY to go and read the papers.

Engels immediately sent him £4 to bail him out.[52]

If things had been less difficult for both Marx and Chapman at this time, they might have come into closer and mutually rewarding contact. Marx had recently dashed off his witty *Eighteenth Brumaire of Louis Bonaparte*; his fellow exile Wilhelm Pieper was translating it into English, as Marx's English was not yet completely idiomatic. There was a 'prospect', he reported to Engels on 2 September, 'of its being published in English by a London bookseller'.[53] That bookseller was surely Chapman. As it was, the work, like so many of Marx's writings in the 1850s, remained unpublished, and Chapman and Marx went their separate ways.[54]

Struggling to survive though he was until Courtauld's money gave temporary relief in December 1852, Chapman took on a new office helper for the *Westminster Review* in the autumn of that year, possibly a replacement for one or other of the unsatisfactory clerks mentioned by Susanna Chapman in her pleading letter to Combe. This was a young man of twenty called William Hale White. Like Newman, Froude, and Clough before him, he was in flight from a proposed career in the ministry, in his case not in the Church of England but in the independent Congregationalist church. Born in Bedford in 1831, the son of a radical Nonconformist bookseller, Hale White was brought up as a member of the town's Bunyon Meeting. The sect practised public expressions of conversion in front of the whole congregation. Hale White's father, William White, was liberal and gave up his Calvinism in 1851 after reading and admiring Carlyle's works advocating a non-denominational spirituality; but the son had first to go through the boyhood misery of fearing himself damned and enduring with strong feelings of guilt a sham 'conversion' in the meeting house, then being sent to a theological college in Hertfordshire, and finally, in 1851, beginning a course of training as an Independent minister at New College in the St John's Wood area of London.[55]

Here Hale White, though fearful and ultra-sensitive, rejected the theological bullying of his teachers. With two other students he rebelled against the Principal's strict interpretation of scripture. In his work of autobiography-as-fiction, *The Autobiography of Mark Rutherford*, published anonymously in 1881, he gave full vent to the resentment he felt about this defining episode in his life:

> We used a sort of Calvinistic manual which began by setting forth that mankind was absolutely in God's power. He was our maker, and we had no legal claim whatever to any consideration from Him. The author then mechanically built up the Calvinistic creed, step by step, like a house of cards. Systematic theology was the great business of our academical life. We had to read sermons to the President in class, and no sermon was considered complete and proper unless it unfolded what was called the scheme of redemption from beginning to end.
>
> So it came to pass that about the Bible . . . we were in darkness. It was a magazine of texts, and those portions of it which contributed nothing in the shape of texts, or formed no part of the scheme, were

neglected. Worse still, not a word was ever spoken to us telling us in what manner to strengthen the reason, to subdue the senses, or in what way to deal with all the varied diseases of that soul of man which we were to set ourselves to save. All its failings, infinitely more complicated than those of the body, were grouped as 'sin', and for these there was one quack remedy. If the patient did not like the remedy, or got no good from it, the fault was his.[56]

As J. S. Mill had been rescued from a mental breakdown resulting from a forced education of Benthamism by reading the poetry of Wordsworth and Coleridge, so now Hale White was saved from a surfeit of Calvinism by reading *Lyrical Ballads*. According to 'Mark Rutherford', Wordsworth's 'real God is not the god of the Church, but the God of the hills, the abstraction Nature, and to this my reverence was transferred'.[57] This discovery went a small way towards softening the blow that fell on him when he and his fellow students were expelled in March 1852 for daring to question the New College theology. Hale White was supported by his father, who wrote and printed a pamphlet in his defence, *To Think or Not to Think*, and who received a letter from Kingsley, supporting White's stance but expressing an anxious wish that young men like his son would stay within the Christian tradition and not be swept into the arms of Straussism, Transcendentalism, or 'Mr John Chapman's *Catholic Series*'.[58]

Hale White was never swept into the arms of Chapmandom, but it was Chapman who helped him find his feet. At first, as he recalled, Hale White was 'adrift, knowing no craft, belonging to no religious body, and without social or political interest'. In September 1852 he got a teaching post at a school in Stoke Newington, but stayed only one night, during which he suffered a fit of terror and loneliness which made him give up the job before he had begun it. He escaped to a friend's house in North London.[59] It was at this point, in October 1852, that Hale White was taken on by Chapman and became Marian Evans's fellow lodger at 142 Strand. He wrote about this episode in his life several times, first in a convolutedly oblique form in *The Autobiography of Mark Rutherford*; then in a newspaper article protesting at John Cross's over-reticent biography of George Eliot (*Athenaeum*, November 1885); in another article responding to the news of Chapman's death (*Athenaeum*, December 1894); in an essay for the *Bookman* in 1902, 'George Eliot as I Knew Her'; and finally in the autobiographical notes he wrote for his children near the end of his life, published as *The Early Life of Mark Rutherford* just after his death in 1913. The last two accounts, written long after the deaths of both George Eliot and Chapman, are the most frank in their description of Chapman and his establishment, though they make no mention of Elisabeth Tilley or her role in Chapman's life, which Hale White may not have known about. He did know, however, that Chapman held liberal views on marriage and divorce, for Chapman made no secret of them.

In the wake of the schoolmastering fiasco, Hale White thought of trying for work with a publishing house. After visiting several publishers without success, he called at 142 Strand. He knew that Chapman published and sold 'books which were theologically heretical'; this may well have been attractive to someone recoiling from an unforgiving religious creed. The autobiographical notes describe the encounter with Chapman:

> As the New College council had tested my orthodoxy, so Chapman tested my heresy and found that I was fit for the propagandist work in No. 142 and for its society. He asked me if I believed in miracles. I said 'Yes and no'. I did not believe that an actual Curtius leaped into the gulf in the Forum and saved Rome, but I did believe in the spiritual truth set forth in the legend. This reply was allowed to pass, although my scepticism would have been more satisfactory [to Chapman] and more useful if it had been a little more thorough.[60]

Hale White moved into a room at the top of the house; as he remembered in his *Bookman* essay on George Eliot, she had 'a dark room at the end of a long dark passage', while his own room, 'the quietest I have known in London, or out of it, was over hers, and looked across the river to the Norwood hills'.[61] He found Chapman, or 'Wollaston', as he called him in the fictionalised account by 'Mark Rutherford',

> a curious compound, materialistic yet impulsive, and forever drawn to some new thing; without any love for anybody particularly, as far as I could see, and yet with much more general kindness and philanthropy than many a man possessing much stronger sympathies and antipathies. There was no holy of holies in him, into which one or two of the elect could occasionally be admitted and feel God to be

there. He was no temple, but rather a comfortable hospitable house open to all friends, well furnished with books and pictures, and free to every guest from garret to cellar. He had 'liberal' notions about the relationship between the sexes. Not that he was a libertine, but he disbelieved in marriage, excepting for so long as husband and wife are a necessity to one another. If one should find the other uninteresting, or somebody else more interesting, he thought there ought to be a separation.[62]

It is an intriguing sketch with its secularised use of the terminology of the discarded theology – 'the elect', 'temple' – and its summing up of what Chapman was like – open, welcoming, undogmatic, and yet a man of surprisingly cool feelings towards the individuals in his family circle.

At first Hale White worked on the *Westminster Review*, correcting proofs among other things. Then Chapman gave him a task which, with his extreme reticence and quickness to take offence, he loathed:

I was soon taken off the *Westminster*, and my occupation now was to write Chapman's letters, to keep his accounts, and, most disagreeable, to 'subscribe' his publications, that is to say, to call on booksellers and ask how many copies they would take.[63]

He stuck it out until February 1854, hating his lowly status, worshipping Marian Evans for her kindness and her cleverness, but remaining almost invisible to her – there are no references to him by name in her extant letters. In *The Autobiography of Mark Rutherford* he tells a possibly made-up or at least elaborated story of Mark Rutherford making a mistake over the number of books he was to sell and misunderstanding the content of a letter he had been asked to write for 'Wollaston'. He falls 'a prey to self-contempt and scepticism'. In this state of mind he goes to 'Theresa's' (Marian Evans's) room to read proofs with her. When she discovers another mistake by him, he faints, awaking to find Theresa sponging his face with cold water. He unburdens himself to her, telling of his overwhelming sense of failure and 'sobbing convulsively' in her lap.[64] Whether this actually happened or not, Hale White never forgot Marian's kindness towards 'a mere youth, a stranger, awkward and shy'. He was determined to correct Cross's depiction of her at her death as a remote sibyl; hence his article

171

in the *Athenaeum* in 1885, in which he remembers her in her 142 Strand days as 'one of the most sceptical, unusual creatures I ever knew'. He describes her sitting in her dark room, 'with her hair over her shoulders, the easy chair half sideways to the fire, her feet over the arms, and a proof in her hands'.[65]

Hale White knew that Marian had translated Strauss. Despite his admiration of her, he could not, even as a young man suspicious of the religious teaching he had experienced and smarting from his ejection from theological college, follow her the whole way to religious scepticism. He was at the heart of radical, freethinking London, but it was not a natural home for him. A letter to his father of May 1853, written from number 142, expresses his unease in response to an anxious remark of William White's about the Chapman circle:

> With all that you say I most cordially agree, most especially with what you say about *cold negativism*. Mr Chapman is nothing so much of a negation merely as many of his books are, but I see, and must see infinitely more of this [heartless] emptiness both in books and men than I ever saw before, and this drives me back again to all my old eternal friends who appear more than ever perfect, and Jesus above them all. Granted that all that the Strausses, Foxtons, and Newmans have made out is correct – that there is no miracle . . . and so on, yet I turn round on them and say 'You cannot deceive my eyes' . . . If you feel in a book that the writer's *heart*, his own real truest thought is not present, there is no rest but a vague dissatisfaction and disquiet. But on the Bible I can repose.[66]

Foxton, listed here with Strauss and F. W. Newman, was another of Chapman's authors, an ex-clergyman with religious doubts who had published a book with Chapman bearing the revealing title *Popular Christianity: Its Transition State, and Probable Development.*

By the end of 1853 Marian Evans, though still running the *Westminster Review* with Chapman, had moved out of 142 Strand into lodgings of her own, and Hale White had no desire to stay either. He recalled that Chapman offered him a partnership in the business, which he wisely declined, and he left number 142 in February 1854 to take up a clerkship in the Registrar-General's office just along the road in Somerset House. Despite the proximity of his new place of work, it was the last he saw of Chapman and also, to his 'lasting sorrow', of Chapman's adored female assistant.[67]

During the winter of 1852–3 Marian became unsettled. Her health always suffered in London; she was prone to colds and headaches, and was told by Sir James Paget, an eminent physician to the Queen and friend of Combe's, that though she had 'a perfectly sound constitution – lungs and heart all right', she was 'a soft pulpy individual, certainly not fit for a Strand life', as she cheerfully told a new friend, Bessie Rayner Parkes, in July 1853.[68] She had come to hate her dark room at number 142, particularly in foggy winter weather. She lamented to Combe on 13 November 1852, shortly after her return from Edinburgh:

> Alas! for the pure air I was breathing with you a month ago. My room here has the light one might expect midway up a chimney, with a little blaze of fire below, and a little glimmer of sky above.[69]

By the end of January 1853 she was determined to find lodgings of her own. As she told Bray, 'Many reasons, besides my health, concur to make me desire this change', though she did not say what the other reasons were.[70] One was a feeling of dissatisfaction with the *Westminster Review* – a passing mood, as it turned out – but the chief reason was one she could not tell to anyone. The fact was that after offering her love to Spencer during the summer of 1852, she had become friendly with, and attracted to, his friend Lewes. From 22 November that year, her thirty-third birthday, when she mentions to the Brays that Lewes has been sitting in her room 'talking till the second [dinner] bell rings',[71] references to Lewes in her letters to her friends increase noticeably. She dropped tactical mentions of him into her accounts of her doings, knowing that the Brays disliked him and that Cara and Sara disapproved of his open marriage.[72] 'Lewes has been quite a pleasant friend to me lately', she writes on 11 April 1853; and a few days later:

> Mr Lewes especially is kind and attentive and has quite won my regard after having a good deal of my vituperation. Like a few other people in the world, he is much better than he seems – a man of heart and conscience wearing a mask of flippancy.[73]

If she wished to be intimate with Lewes, it would be easier if she moved away from the ever-busy 142 Strand. As Chapman needed her to be on hand to edit the *Westminster*, however, she was persuaded to stay a few months longer by his offer to let her have his own room, which was 'very light and pleasant', she told Bray on 18 March 1853.[74] She agreed to postpone her move until the autumn.

Marian's gloom about the *Westminster Review* related mainly to an altercation between Chapman and Combe – as Combe's chief correspondent about his articles for the *Review*, she was uncomfortably trapped in the middle – and secondarily to dissatisfaction with the January 1853 number, which she thought 'rather below *par*'. She had been unable to superintend the 'Contemporary Literature' section this time, as she had been called away to the Midlands by the death of her brother-in-law.[75] Her own relations with Chapman came under strain; having spent several months defending his business methods to Combe and Bray, she now found herself agreeing with the fastidious Combe when she saw how the standard of editing at the *Westminster* had dropped during her brief absence. Hale White later recalled that she had disagreed with Chapman at this time: 'I fancy that one of the reasons was, that she did not like his somewhat disorderly ways.'[76]

Chapman had incurred Combe's displeasure by his incompetent handling of the advertising of Combe's books. At the height of Chapman's solvency problems in July 1852, Combe had generously sent back the £23.12.6 he had been paid for his article on secular education, suggesting that the amount be credited against future advertisements for his books inserted in the *Westminster Review*. He expected to see such an advertisement in the January 1853 number, and lost patience with Chapman when it did not appear. Chapman apologised on 10 January, but blamed a blunder by one of his assistants (might this have been Hale White?), who misunderstood his instructions and omitted the advertisement. As was his wont, he continued at length with his excuses:

> In consequence of Miss Evans's absence (through the death of her sister's husband), I had all the proofs and revises of the entire Review to read with the exception of the 2 first articles; some of them entailed great labo[u]r and two such serious delays (Greg's was one) in consequence of the necessity of corresponding with their authors that the

printing was thrown very late, making night work essential to get the Review out at anything like the usual time.[77]

Combe was not mollified; he merely felt vindicated in his judgment that Chapman was a hopeless businessman. He first wrote an unusually sharp and wounding note expressing his regret 'that you have perilled your own happiness and the liberal cause by an overestimate of your own powers'. Then, on receiving a hurt answer from Chapman, he responded on 15 January with a six-page letter going over all Chapman's sins and omissions, right back to the Lombe affair at the start of the *Westminster* venture.[78] Chapman, possibly at the urging of Marian and Bray, who also became involved, put an end to this lengthy exchange by eating humble pie, though his unfortunate habit of self-excuse almost got the better of him even now:

I freely confess that I deserve your censure for my negligence for which I am very sorry, and will endeavour to avoid any further grounds for complaint . . . I had intended to vindicate myself (and hence my delay in writing) but on further consideration it seems to me that future acts will be better than present words.[79]

In her own tactful letters to Combe, Marian expressed her regret at the 'painful correspondence which has lately been going forward between you and Mr Chapman', while to Bray she confessed that she was 'utterly dejected' and was not surprised at Combe's anger. 'Still', she added, 'I am sorry for Mr C. Many a worse man incurs less blame.'[80] She continued to stand up for Chapman, and for Susanna, too, whom we glimpse in a letter to Cara Bray in April 1853:

The little Chapmans have whooping cough and from having been quite beautiful with healthy bloom they have become pale as death. I have an increasing regard for Mrs Chapman. Her character has shewn some admirable phases lately, and indeed I think both *he* and *she* deserve far more respect than you are disposed to give them.[81]

On the other hand, she was understandably upset at being so closely associated with a man who seemed to make so many blunders. It was a particular source of annoyance to her that, given their joint editorship of the

Review, she should sometimes be suspected of being the author of Chapman's letters. She swiftly put Bray right about this, betraying her unease about the conduct of the *Westminster* at this time, though she was still reluctant to join the chorus of criticism of Chapman:

> You seem to be under the very great mistake of supposing that I dictate Mr C's letters. I have nothing to do with their composition, and I must protest against being regarded as responsible for anything in the management of his affairs beyond the mere letter-press of the Review – and even that is not always what I will. Every conversation I have had with him on this affair of Mr Combe's has been painful. I am sorry for Mr Chapman, however, and I do not wish to dilate on his deficiencies.[82]

Bray helped to bring Combe round, too, by declaring that Chapman had '*very many* good qualities', though 'orderly business-like habits' were not among them. 'We must make the best we can of him – accept & acknowledge the good & what of the bad he cannot mend.'[83] Fortunately, Combe was prepared to do so. His support was to be needed the following year when another crisis occurred in the affairs of Chapmandom.

Meanwhile, things carried on as usual at number 142. The future novelist living there found plenty of opportunity to observe human nature and to write amusing descriptions of Chapman's temporary lodgers. She regaled Combe in February 1853 with an account of August Stamm, a German with radical religious views who had published a book called *The Religion of Action* (*Die Religion der That*):

> Dr Stamm has been domesticated at Mr Chapman's for some time. He has the most amiable social qualities, beautiful simplicity and purity of character and considerable attainments; but he is not, I think, destined to have much influence over other men. He would by no means concur in this negative clause; on the contrary he thinks himself a prophet. I ventured to tell him that a translation of a work beginning '*Völker der Erde, hier ist das Buch, nach dem ihr mit Verlangen eure Arme ausstrecht*' ['Peoples of the earth, here is the work for which you stretch out your arms with longing'], would be simply 'nuts' to our reviewers, but he was evidently incredulous. You will perceive

that he has no slight endowment of self-esteem, and this is unchecked by a fine sense of the ludicrous, without which even pure moral enthusiasm is apt to verge on the ridiculous in its manifestations. Still, Dr Stamm is a charming being, and wins everyone's good will. Perhaps his droll English has something to do with this, and his handsome face still more. His resources are very narrow, and he is determined not to return to Germany until its political condition is more hopeful.[84]

Stamm also caught the eye of others in Chapman's circle. Hale White noted his comic English and his attempts to interest Carlyle in his book, 'a materialistic gospel', according to Hale White.[85] Carlyle told Chapman in March that he had received a letter from Dr Stamm announcing that he intended to call on him – a letter which made Carlyle expect 'nothing less than *Elijah the Tishbite*', as Marian reported to the Brays.[86] And Clough, newly returned from a trip to America and hastening to renew contact with his London acquaintances, visited Frank Newman in October and found

a certain Dr Stamm, abroad on a mission to form a new Religious Union or League – he delivering himself of a sort of Anima Mundi Religion; Humanism I think they call it – F. Newman fraternizing from a Theistic distance.[87]

Clough called once more at 142 Strand, and was asked by Chapman to write the section 'Contemporary Literature of America' for the October number of the *Westminster*.[88] His friend Froude continued to be one of Chapman's star contributors, writing on Mary Tudor in January, John Knox in July, and the Book of Job in October 1853. These pieces were mainly offshoots of his research on the history of the Elizabethan age, sent to Chapman from the countryside in Wales, where he and his wife had moved after their unsatisfactory spell in Manchester. Though Froude wrote regularly for the *Westminster*, articles by him also appeared in *Fraser's Magazine*, whose owner, J. W. Parker, was to publish his *History*. He was willing, too, to write for the *Edinburgh* and even the Tory *Quarterly*, if they would accept his papers. In September 1853 he told a friend that the *Edinburgh* had rejected an article on Elizabeth, which was going to appear in *Fraser's* instead. 'The *Quarterly* and I could not after all hit it off', he wrote. Its editor, Walter Scott's son-in-law John Gibson Lockhart, 'has all the old Scotch Tory dislike of Elizabeth'. Meanwhile, he added, his piece on the Book of Job was coming out in the *Westminster*, and he was going to write on Spinoza for the *Edinburgh Review*.[89] In the event that article, which Marian Evans thought 'admirable in its account of Spinoza's doctrine', appeared, nearly two years later, in the *Westminster* rather than the *Edinburgh*.[90]

In January 1854 Froude's review of his fellow Oxonian Matthew Arnold's new volume of poetry appeared in the *Westminster*. Chapman had invited Arnold's brother-in-law, W. E. Forster, later a liberal politician and architect of the Education Act of 1870, to write articles on American slavery – 'the subject is just the thing now', wrote Marian Evans to Chapman in October 1852 – and 'British Philanthropy and Jamaica's Distress', both of which appeared in 1853.[91] In April of that year, Forster spoke to Chapman about accepting a review of Arnold's poems from Froude, but Chapman seems to have been reluctant, for Froude contemplated trying the *Quarterly*, which, in Arnold's opinion, expressed to his sister Jane, Forster's wife, was 'much to be preferred'.[92] Arnold was no enthusiast for radical reviewing, radical politics, or radical religion. He stood by as an ironic observer of his friends' travails, referring, for example, with amusement to Clough's erstwhile 'home', University Hall, as 'Doubting Castle'.[93] Yet his poems, particularly 'Empedocles on Etna', published in this 1852 volume, express the difficulties of religious belief and the misery of the divided mind. Froude was at first unable to place his review; it was December 1853, nearly a year after publication of Arnold's *Poems*, before its fate was finally decided. 'I heard last night from Froude', Arnold told Jane on 4 December, 'that Chapman had just written to him "begging for the article on me which he had twice refused"'.[94]

It is not clear why Chapman was reluctant to accept a review of Arnold's poetry. Perhaps he was afraid that the subject of religion was becoming altogether too prominent in the pages of the *Westminster*. Froude was contributing his articles on Elizabeth which included support for the Church of England during her reign; Martineau was writing an article on religion for almost every number, and Mazzini had expressed vague religious sentiments in his article on Europe. Though Chapman was happy to publish liberal anti-slavery articles by Arnold's brother-in-law, he had been cautious about accepting Forster's first article, on Quakerism. This enlightened young

Bradford mill owner, brought up a Quaker and now a non-denominational believer on the Carlylean model, had approached Chapman directly at the beginning of 1852:

> Dear Sir,
>   Ever since I have seen your prospectus of the *New Westminster*, I have wished to become a contributor to it. Both your prospectus and your public tempting me. Are you full for your second number – viz., your April number?

Forster offered Chapman a choice of subjects, including the history and future of Quakerism, F. D. Maurice's theology, or – hardly likely to be acceptable to Chapman – Spencer's *Social Statics*, which Forster intended to criticise for 'what seems to me a *reductio ad absurdum* of the *laissez faire* doctrine; at the same time acknowledging its great merits both as to style and matter'. Forster explained that he had already published a pamphlet defending the Quaker William Penn against an attack by Macaulay. Chapman accepted the proposed article on Quakerism. It helped that Forster did not want payment: 'My first paper I should wish you to consider as a subscription to your undertaking', he wrote.[95] Chapman printed this defence of Quakerism in the April 1852 number, but placed it in the short-lived section headed 'Independent Contribution' and prefaced it with an editorial disclaimer about its ideas being in some ways 'at variance with the particular ideas or measures' intended by the new *Westminster*.[96]

Froude himself was rather caught between stools, being rebellious and idiosyncratic enough to dislike all kinds of orthodoxy, yet at the same time yearning to be drawn back into its comforting fold. Arnold shrewdly remarked to Clough on their friend's split personality in this respect after he had met Froude while visiting Wales in the summer of 1853:

> I should like you to see Froude – quantum mutatus! He goes to church, has family prayers – says the Nemesis ought never to have been published &c. &c. – his friends say that he is altogether changed and re-entered within the giron de l'Eglise – at any rate within the giron de la religion chrétienne: but I do not see the matter in this light and think that he conforms in the same sense in which Spinoza advised his mother to conform – and having purified his moral being,

all that was mere fume and vanity and love of notoriety and opposition in his proceedings he has abandoned and regrets.[97]

Froude's feelings about the oppositional *Westminster* were to be tested in
the tussle for the journal which broke out the following year.

Lewes, though busy on the *Leader*, continued to do the regular round-up
of French literature in the *Westminster*, and also contributed longer articles such as those on Goethe in October 1852 and Charlotte Brontë's
Villette and Elizabeth Gaskell's *Ruth* in April 1853. He had been the first
critic to give intelligent praise to the unknown 'Currer Bell' when *Jane
Eyre* became the publishing sensation of 1847. He was so struck by the
novel that he persuaded J. W. Parker to let him review it in *Fraser's Magazine*,
and he also wrote to the pseudonymous author expressing his delight in
her work. She was impressed by his 'candid tone' of praise and criticism
(of its 'melodramatic portions') and entered a correspondence with him in
which they discussed the relative merits of romance and realism in fiction.[98]

She and Lewes corresponded intermittently, meeting in June 1850 when
the shy novelist visited her publisher George Smith in London; she was
touched on seeing in this bohemian man of the world a physical likeness
to her beloved sister Emily, who had died in December 1848. 'The aspect
of Lewes's face almost moves me to tears', she wrote; 'it is so wonderfully
like Emily's'.[99] In his article for the July 1852 number of the *Westminster*,
'The Lady Novelists', Lewes praised both Charlotte Brontë and Elizabeth
Gaskell for displaying 'deep feeling united to keen observation'. He
responded warmly again to both novelists in his April 1853 review of *Villette*
and *Ruth*, praising the sympathy and frankness with which Mrs Gaskell
deals with the subject of prostitution, and describing *Villette* as 'a work of
astonishing power and passion':

> Contempt of conventions in all things, in style, in thought, even in
> the art of story-telling, here visibly springs from the independent orig-
> inality of a strong mind nurtured in solitude.[100]

This is reviewing of a high order by an equally strong mind; Lewes's articles in the *Westminster Review* on recent fiction are characterised by their
open-mindedness and astuteness, particularly with regard to the sexual

mores or 'morality' represented in such novels, while most of his fellow reviewers were tut-tutting at the perceived boldness and crudity of novels by the Brontës and Mrs Gaskell.[101]

Lewes's friend Herbert Spencer was Chapman's chief writer on philosophy and social science. In his autobiography he remembered not only that Chapman was the only publisher who would consider taking on his first book, *Social Statics*, but also that he owed almost all his friendships to Chapman, starting in the late 1840s, before the move to 142 Strand:

> My only opportunities of meeting strangers occurred at the house of Mr Chapman (afterwards Dr Chapman) to whose evening parties I had already been once or twice while he lived at Clapton; and who had now transferred his publishing business from Newgate Street to a large establishment in the Strand, nearly opposite *The Economist* office. Here he gave his weekly *soirées*, which I from time to time attended.[102]

Spencer mentions meeting a number of literary women there, including Eliza Lynn, Marian Evans, and two young women who became close friends of Marian's in 1852–3. These were Bessie Rayner Parkes, daughter of the radical Birmingham lawyer who had given financial support to the Strauss translation and the author of a small book of poems published by Chapman in November 1852, and Bessie's friend Barbara Leigh Smith, campaigner for the education of girls and later co-founder of Girton College. Marian described this new friend to Sara Hennell in July 1852 as 'one of the *tabooed* family'. Cousins of Florence Nightingale, Barbara and her younger siblings were the illegitimate children of a wealthy liberal, Benjamin Smith, who supported universal education and the abolition of the slave trade. Barbara was to become Marian Evans's most sympathetic friend, and, like her, to have a romantic relationship with Chapman.[103]

At Chapman's Spencer also met F. W. Newman, whose 'very gentle manner suggested an angelic sweetness of nature', though 'if conversation passed into discussion, it soon appeared that he could become peppery enough'.[104] Conversation obviously did become discussion between the two men, for Henry Crabb Robinson recorded in his diary for 8 March 1852 calling at number 142 and being introduced to Spencer, 'the author of a strange book [*Social Statics*] lately published' by Chapman. He found Spencer 'in dispute with Newman', expounding a doctrine of 'Necessity & Materialism' which Newman disliked; Newman told Robinson that he found Spencer a 'disagreeable disputant'.[105] It was Chapman who had introduced Spencer to Lewes in 1850; the two men discovered a mutual interest in evolution, or 'the development hypothesis', as they called it, and became good friends.

Apart from Lewes, Spencer's closest acquaintance in Chapman's circle at this time was Marian Evans. Though Spencer was never in love with her, he spent so much time in her company in 1852 that, as she put it in a letter to the Brays in June, 'all the world is setting us down as engaged'.[106] Spencer recalled thinking her the most intelligent and gifted woman he had ever met, combining – uniquely, he believed – a 'capacity for abstract thinking' with a talent for 'concrete representation'. He described how they walked and talked at the back of number 142 in the early summer of 1852:

> In those days, before the Thames embankment was made, the southern basement of Somerset House rose directly out of the water; and the only noises on that side came from the passing steam-boats. From end to end, this basement is surmounted by a balustrade, and behind the balustrade runs a long terrace: at that time as little invaded by visitors as by sounds. The terrace is shut off by a gate from one of the courts of Somerset House. Chapman had obtained a key of this gate; whether by favour or by some claim attaching to his house, the back of which abutted on Somerset House, I do not know. Frequently on fine afternoons in May, June and July she obtained the key; and we made our way on to the terrace, where we paced backwards and forwards for an hour or so, discussing many things.
>
> Of course, as we were frequently seen together, people drew their inferences. Very slight evidence usually suffices the world for positive conclusions; and here the evidence seemed strong. Naturally, therefore, quite definite statements became current. There were reports that I was in love with her, and that we were about to be married. But neither of these reports was true.[107]

After Marian's unrequited declaration of love that summer, Spencer began to take Lewes with him when he visited her, till in due course Lewes stayed behind when Spencer got up to leave, and, to Spencer's relief, Marian, already attracted-to Lewes, transferred her affections to him.[108]

Spencer's articles in the *Westminster* and the *Leader* earned him his reputation as Britain's leading social philosopher. Like Comte in his own field, like Darwin in natural history and Marx in political and economic thought, he sought to bring his subject under observable natural laws. His article for the April 1852 number of the *Westminster*, 'A Theory of Population, deduced from the General Law of Animal Fertility', is a good example of this. Dealing with a number of recent books on physiology, Spencer attacks the question of population, its history, and its future, in his balanced, lucid style. There are two kinds of forces governing all life, he says, 'forces preservative' and 'forces destructive'; these opposing forces 'must perpetually tend towards equilibrium'. The 'lower' the life form, the less the ability to 'contend with external danger' and therefore the greater the fertility required to 'compensate for the consequent mortality; otherwise the race must die out'. Hence the profligate sowing of seeds in nature, so many of which never germinate. It was the theme at the heart of Tennyson's *In Memoriam* (1850) with its dramatic cry about Nature –

> And finding that of fifty seeds
> She often brings but one to bear,
> I falter where I firmly trod –

and Darwin was to tackle 'the vast destruction of seeds' most memorably in the chapter entitled 'Struggle for Existence' in *The Origin of Species*.

If lower organisms have to produce lots of offspring in order for any to survive, higher organisms, according to Spencer, having 'higher endowments' and 'much capacity of self-preservation', need a 'correspondingly low degree of fertility'. The world will not become overpopulated:

> From the beginning, pressure of population has been the proximate cause of progress. It produced the original diffusion of the race. It compelled men to abandon predatory habits and take to agriculture. It led to the clearing of the earth's surface. It forced men into the social state; made social organization inevitable; and has developed the social sentiments. It has stimulated to progressive improvements in production, and to increased skill and intelligence . . . After having

done all this, we see that the pressure of population, as it gradually finishes its work, must gradually bring itself to an end.[109]

The article on population was reprinted as a pamphlet, which Spencer sent to several acquaintances and scientific writers. At the meeting of the British Association for the Advancement of Science that summer the pamphlet came to the attention of a young biologist, 'then known to but few', as Spencer recalled. This was Thomas Henry Huxley, recently returned from a voyage on the *Rattlesnake*, which had been commissioned to survey the east coast of Australia. Huxley was the ship's assistant surgeon and one of its scientific investigators. He had been back in London since November 1850, with no permanent job and little money, waiting, in Spencer's words, 'for the needful grant' to let him publish the results of his researches on board. The two men met and became friends.[110]

It was probably Spencer who introduced Huxley at 142 Strand; Marian Evans mentions in letters to friends that he was 'the centre of interest' at Chapman's soirée on 23 February 1853.[111] The following November she told Combe that Huxley, 'a scientific man who is becoming celebrated in London', had been engaged to write 'the scientific department of the Contemporary Literature' section in the *Westminster Review* from January 1854.[112] This was a new departure, as Chapman explained in an editorial note in the January number. Instead of dividing up the section into notices of English, French, German, and American books as before, future numbers would group such notices under thematic headings such as 'theology, philosophy, and politics' (James Martineau's province), 'history, biography, voyages and travels' (Froude), 'belles lettres' (Jane Sinnett), and the new section, 'science'.[113]

Huxley was indeed becoming famous as a brilliant biologist, yet during 1853 he suffered from almost constant depression and frustration, from which he was relieved chiefly by Chapman's offer of regular journalistic employment. His education had been unorthodox, consisting of irregular schooling from the age of ten, followed by an apprenticeship to his medical brother-in-law and a free scholarship to study medicine at Charing Cross Hospital.[114] On graduating with prizes and medals, he joined the medical service of the navy in order to 'earn his bread', and spent four years, from the end of 1846 until November 1850, with the *Rattlesnake*.[115] During his time on shore in Sydney he became engaged to be married, and on his return set about publishing the results of his research on molluscs and other marine species and trying to get a lectureship which would earn him enough to marry his fiancée.

Though his papers appeared in *Philosophical Transactions of the Royal Society* and other scientific journals to praise from eminent scientists like Charles Lyell, Edward Forbes, and Richard Owen, and though he was elected a Fellow of the Royal Society and awarded a Royal Medal for Physiology in 1852, Huxley was unsuccessful in various bids for an academic post. He tried the universities of Toronto, Sydney, Aberdeen, Cork, and – most frustratingly – King's College London, where he thought he would succeed as he had the support of Edward Forbes. His disappointment and resentment appear in a letter to his sister in April 1853: 'I can get honour in Science, but it doesn't pay.'[116] Huxley despaired in 1853 of ever getting regular employment and being able to bring Henrietta, his fiancée of six years, from Australia. Letters between them took several months to arrive and showed the strain, with Huxley in constant fear that she would not continue to wait for his call. On 1 January 1854 he told her that he hoped never to go through another year like the one just passed, 'or I shall become altogether as the nether millstone'.[117]

His luck turned in 1854, when he was appointed to a lectureship at the School of Mines in Jermyn Street. He could now send for Henrietta, who arrived in May 1855; they got married in July after an eight-year engagement and nearly five-year separation. In the same year he became Fullerian Professor of Physiology at the Royal Institution. The start of his better luck, however, dates from Chapman taking notice of him during his year of terrible disappointments. Their extant correspondence opens with Chapman's letter of 12 August 1853 saying that he and Marian had 'read your article and shall be glad to print it; – in the next No. if we can find room'. Chapman goes on to suggest the paper could be shortened here and there; he has indicated in the margins some examples of phrases which might be dropped. 'The printers will not bless you as the most legible of writers!' he adds cheerfully, asking also that Huxley 'mark a line *down the side* of all passages which are *quoted*', in order to facilitate the printing process.[118]

'Science at Sea', a lively and controversial account of the voyage of the *Rattlesnake*, appeared in the *Westminster* in January 1854. Huxley does not let on that he was a member of the crew, but presents the article as a review of the *Narrative* of the voyage published by John Macgillivray, the chief naturalist to the expedition. He explains the importance of the vessel's commission to explore the inner and outer routes of the northern passage to Australia so as to chart a safe way for other ships to follow; he also gives a graphic picture of life on board ship and encounters with indigenous people, not taken from the account by Macgillivray, who, he says, for all the information he gives about *people*, 'might have been the Ancient Mariner, and his companions "blessed ghosts"'.[119]

Huxley draws on his own journal of the voyage to describe the hot rain falling on '150 men, shut up in this wooden box', with the decks 'utterly unventilated' and 'a sort of solution of man in steam' filling them 'from end to end'. He writes about the inhabitants of Papua New Guinea with their necklaces made of teeth and bracelets of human jaws and their general backwardness; yet he shows his radicalism in his ironic analysis of 'the blessings of civilization' which the white man is bringing them, namely 'labour, care, drunkenness, disease, and ultimate subjection and extinction'. Huxley also uses his anonymity to attack his erstwhile employer, the Admiralty, for its neglect of both the ship and its members. You might think, he says, that a ship being sent to the other side of the world with such an important scientific mission would be made properly seaworthy and be equipped with necessary works of reference, 'which are ruinously expensive to a private individual, though a mere dewdrop in the general cost of the fitting-out of a ship', but in the case of the *Rattlesnake*, 'her lower deck was continually under water during the voyage' and 'she sailed without a volume' on board. Finally, he takes verbal revenge on the refusal of the Admiralty either to pay for the publication of the researches carried out during the voyage or to promote any of its scientific officers.[120]

On the strength of this swashbuckling piece by London's rising scientific star, Chapman asked Huxley in October 1853 if he would write the regular science section he was introducing to the *Review*. Huxley's scrawl in reply says he would be happy to undertake the task. 'I have however to make one most bare & mechanical inquiry', he adds bluntly, 'to wit: What's the Pay?'[121] Chapman's answer of 26 October promises '£6.6.0 per number' for eight pages. Ever the optimist, he expresses the hope that 'the sale of the Review will enable me at no very distant date to pay at the "Edinburgh" rate – £1.1.0 per page'. Rather more prudently he adds, for the benefit of a new contributor to a cash-strapped journal, that Huxley should return the books supplied by Chapman for reviewing purposes.[122]

*

The first round-up of scientific publications done by Huxley appeared in the January number. It included a notice of Harriet Martineau's abridged translation of Comte's positivist philosophy, published by Chapman in December 1853, which Huxley compared favourably with Lewes's exposition of Comte brought out by Bohn a couple of months earlier. Huxley, understandably resentful about not yet having an academic post and inclined, as Marian Evans had noted in November, to '*paradox* and *antagonism*',[123] wrote sneeringly of Lewes's amateurishness. He was a man of book knowledge only, Huxley wrote, 'without the discipline and knowledge which result from being a worker', that is an experimental scientist.[124] This was particularly wounding to Lewes, who in his *Westminster* article on Goethe in October 1852 had shown his sympathetic awareness of Goethe's disappointment at having his scientific researches 'superciliously regarded as those of a poet dabbling in science'.[125] Now he was being treated to the same criticism by a new member of his own progressive circle. Lewes protested in the *Leader* on 14 January that he had been pursuing biological study, 'practically and theoretically', for eighteen years.[126]

Marian Evans, already close to Lewes and now living away from 142 Strand in lodgings near Hyde Park, saw the manuscript of the review in December 1853 and tried to prevent Chapman from publishing it as it stood. She wrote a series of letters to her co-editor, marked 'PRIVATE', in which she urged Chapman to use his editorial privilege with Huxley. She had read Lewes's book, and seems to have told Lewes about Huxley's criticism in the draft article. She wrote to Chapman in mid-December, suggesting that at least one critical remark could be refuted by Lewes, and incidentally showing that she was already sensitive about any gossip which might arise about her friendship with him:

Dear Friend,

May I beg that you will not send Mr Huxley's M.S. to the printer until you have seen me again? I have found out that he is in the wrong in his remark on the embryological doctrine at p. 33 of Mr Lewes's book, and also that the ridicule he throws on the remark about the gallionella ferruginea is not well founded. At all events I think you will wish for the sake of the Review as well as from your own sense of justice that such a *purely* contemptuous notice should not be admitted unless it be well warranted. The case is the more delicate as the criticism of Mr Lewes comes after the unmitigated praise of Miss Martineau. I hope to see you tomorrow afternoon.

How came you to mention to Miss M[artineau] that you saw the proof of Mr Lewes's book '*in Miss Evans's room*'? I think you must admit that your mention of my name was quite gratuitous.

So far you were naughty – but never mind.[127]

After visiting 142 Strand to speak to Chapman, she wrote again the next morning in distress that Chapman had agreed to remove this particular criticism but that the rest of the review, with its disdain for Lewes's pretensions to scientific expertise, was to stand:

It turns out that I have done Mr Huxley a service & Mr Lewes a disservice by shewing you that the criticisms of the former were open to a severe rejoinder. Now, the point which would have most clearly betrayed the arrogance & superficiality of Mr Huxley's review will be omitted, while his contemptuous dismissal of the book without any characterization will be retained. I am exceedingly annoyed at this, & wish that I had let his ungentlemanly sneers pass without remark. The misfortune is, that not having read the book, you are at Mr Huxley's mercy. If you had, I think you would have determined to expunge Mr Huxley's notice altogether & get some one who knows the book & can give an unbiased opinion, to write a substitute for it.

I think I ought to have a voice in the matter, in virtue of the share in the management of the W[estminster] R[eview] which I have had hitherto, & which does not cease till this number is out. My opinion is, that the editors of the Review will disgrace themselves by inserting an utterly worthless & unworthy notice of a work by one of their own writers – a man of much longer & higher standing than Mr Huxley, & whom Mr H's seniors in science & superiors both in intellect & fame treat with respect.

My reason for writing this is, that after I left you last night, I felt that I had done Mr Lewes a mischief when I meant to do him justice.[128]

This is the only time Marian sought to persuade Chapman by referring to her editorial rights; it is significant that she did so on behalf of the man whom she loved and whom she was probably already planning to accompany to Germany in the summer as his partner – hence the notice to Chapman here that she was giving up the editorial post she had occupied heroically for two years. Another private letter to Chapman followed, in which she expressed the opinion that the notice of Lewes's *Comte* now looked like being 'a regular "mess"':

> The only wise thing to be done in the case, as far as I can see, would be to leave it out altogether. You are not bound by any obligation that I know of, to review the book, since you go on a principle of selection not of universal registry, and certainly Mr Huxley's notice, mitigated or unmitigated, will be of no earthly advantage either to the Westminster Review or to its readers.
>
> So far as your duty is concerned in the matter I think reasons of delicacy would at once present themselves to the reader for your merely mentioning Mr Lewes's book as a manual containing a brief sketch of Comte's system interspersed with commentary and criticism. Do you really think that if you had been the publisher of Mr Lewes's book and Bohn the publisher of Miss Martineau's, Mr Huxley would have written just so? 'Tell that to the Marines.'[129]

Despite her robust efforts the offending review was published, with some detailed accounts of Lewes's mistakes, which Huxley calls 'marvellous errors', and a sharp tone adopted throughout towards Lewes's claim to be presenting up-to-date scientific knowledge.[130] Huxley continued to contribute both full-length articles and the scientific round-up to the *Westminster*. Chapman had offered him a lifeline when he was in the deepest despair. By mid-1854 he had enough secure lecturing to enable him to plan his long-delayed marriage, and he became so busy that he sought to reduce his regular commitment to the *Westminster Review*. Out of gratitude to Chapman and an unwillingness to let him down, he approached another up-and-coming scientist, John Tyndall, with a proposition that they should share the regular science section. He wrote to Tyndall on 17 October 1854 explaining what would be required:

> To give some account of the books in one's own department – is no particular trouble – and comes with me under the head of being paid for

what I *must*, in any case, do – but I neither will nor can go on writing about books in other departments, of which I am not competent to form a judgment even if I had the time. I wrote to Chapman, the publisher, to tell him this and he urged me to suggest some way in which I could still assist. I told him that if Sciences were divided into *Physico-Chemical and Natural History* divisions I would still supply the latter half of the Science Article – and I recommended him before going anywhere (*no more note paper, by Jove*) else, to apply to you to take the former. The total *amount* of stuff required is half a sheet; – the *pay* six guineas – (at least I used to get 12 for the whole sheet, but they may pay you extra as a Star –); the *duty* – to give an account critical, analytical, or anything else-you-please-ical, of the books sent you by Chapman. *Vide* as models of style &c., the luminous articles on contemporary Science which have distinguished the last three months of ye Westminster.[131]

Tyndall, having studied chemistry in Germany, had been appointed Professor of Natural Philosophy at the Royal Institution in 1853, and would become distinguished for his work on heat and light. He did not know Chapman personally, but had visited 142 Strand in April 1854 to see his American cousin, Hector Tyndall, who was lodging at Chapman's on a trip to Europe.[132] To Huxley's request he replied that he would be 'happy and proud' to be Huxley's colleague on the *Westminster*, but that current lecturing commitments meant he could not start for another six months. He asked about the arrangements:

Have you no voice in the choice of the books that you review? Why I thought that Chapman had been taken away by cholera and here I find him, to my great satisfaction, turning up again. I was rather dismayed to read of what I conceived to be his death in the coffee room of a hotel at Llanrwst; for, though I do not know the man, something of his that I have read has engendered within me a respect for him.[133]

The article by Chapman which impressed Tyndall was probably 'The Commerce of Literature' which began the fight with the Booksellers' Association in 1852; the mystery about his 'death' was cleared up in Huxley's reply:

Chapman who died of cholera was a distant relation of my man. The poor fellow vanished in the middle of an unfinished article which has appeared in the last Westminster, as his forlorn Vale! to the world.[134]

It was Chapman's cousin, the expert on India, whose article, a review of *The Sphere and Duties of Government* by Wilhelm von Humboldt, appeared in the October number of the *Westminster Review*, with Chapman's explanation of his cousin's sudden death while writing it.[135]

As for the choice of books, Huxley explains that 'you notice what you like, and what you do not, you leave undone, unless you get an editorial request to say something about a particular book'. On the question of when Tyndall could join him, he begs his friend to 'be a brick, and split the difference, and say you will be ready for the April number. I will then write and announce that fact to Chapman.' Tyndall agreed, and Huxley wrote with relief and a new happiness resulting from the recognition of his talents by both the scientific world and journalism (in the person of Chapman) and from his knowledge that Henrietta would soon be sailing from Australia to join him.[136] 'I'm not a miserable mortal now – quite the contrary', he writes, although he is troubled by chronic dyspepsia. He adds a poem about his 'absurd stomach':

> Towards that organ my feeling is the costermonger's towards his donkey –
> > 'I gives him hay, I gives him corn,
> > As much as he can chump off,
> > And then – if he don't cut along,
> > Vy! I cuts his precious rump off.'
> Now I give him hay and corn of the quality he likes – but he won't always cut along in proportion – and you know I can't 'cut his rump off' – that would be suicidal.[137]

And so Chapman gave an early boost to the careers of two of the most celebrated scientists of the nineteenth century. He ensured that the *Westminster Review* under his management was the leading non-specialist journal in the dissemination of scientific progress.[138] When the culminating work on evolution, Darwin's *The Origin of Species*, came out in 1859, Chapman was able to call on Huxley, Darwin's greatest champion, ready on his friend's behalf to 'sharpen up my claws and beak' in order to repel 'the curs which will bark and yelp', to review the work in the *Westminster Review*.[139]

In his letter of 17 October 1854, asking Tyndall to share the reviewing task, Huxley had mentioned that he had almost decided to give up writing for the *Westminster* altogether, 'because I feared there would be some interference in the management which I should not like. However the latter obstacle has come to nothing.'[140] He was referring to an attempt in the summer of 1854 by some of Chapman's creditors to wrest the *Review* from his hands. Huxley, coiner of the term 'agnostic' to describe his own position on religious questions (it fitted Chapman, Lewes, Spencer, and Marian Evans too), would have resigned immediately if the plan to oust Chapman had succeeded. For the takeover attempt was led by James Martineau, who, with other Unitarians, had become impatient with the predominance among the *Westminster*'s reviewers of a non-religious, or even anti-religious, stance. Chapman, having triumphed over the Booksellers' Association in 1852 and scraped through the same year without becoming bankrupt, now had to overcome a powerful faction among the rainbow coalition of his supporters and creditors. 1854 was another year of drama for the inhabitants of 142 Strand.

6

A Split in the Ranks (1854)

Towards the end of 1853 Chapman survived a fire and a robbery. On 30 September the printing office of Savill & Edwards, used by several journals in the Strand neighbourhood, burnt down. Marian Evans reported to Sara Hennell the next day that the *Westminster Review* had 'narrowly escaped the fate of the Leader, the Lit[erary] Gazette and poor Dr Vaughan's elaborate article on the Religious Tendencies of the Age, intended for the next number of the B[ritish] Quarterly'. Chapman was affected in a small way; he told Combe that the current number of the *Westminster* had had a 'very narrow escape from being all burnt; the type which was still standing was all destroyed'. Fortunately he had lost only £35 in the incident.[1]

Then on 3 November Marian described to Charles Bray how 'poor Mr Chapman' had just left her,

> looking fagged to death from having, as a bit of extra work yesterday, run along the Strand after a thief who had managed to get into the house and *out* of it again with £8 worth of plate!

The *Leader* carried an account of the episode and its aftermath:

> An impudent thief, who gave the name of Henry Devine, but withheld his address and occupation 'out of regard for his family', was brought up at Bow-street on Saturday, charged with stealing a quantity of plate

193

from Mr J. Chapman, the bookseller, 142, Strand. About two o'clock one day the housemaid saw the prisoner coolly walk down from the drawing-room, and out into the street; she called out to her master, who at once set off after him. The prisoner ran off at full speed, but Mr Chapman, attracted by the glitter of his own plate, with which the thief in his flight was now strewing the street, ran faster after him, and eventually tripped him up on his face on the pavement. On appearing before the magistrate, prisoner said, with the greatest effrontery, he 'merely took the plate to enable him to raise money sufficient to go to Australia, and intended to reimburse Mr Chapman when he got to the gold diggings'. He considered he had been very badly used by Mr Chapman, who, instead of offering him a glass of ale after his fall, had seized him by the throat, and nearly choked him. He considered 'such conduct anything but gentlemanly, but was willing to forget and forgive, if Mr Chapman on his part would do the same'.[2]

Such misfortunes were as nothing compared to the struggles to keep the *Westminster* in radical hands a few months later.

The year 1854 began, like its predecessor, with a protracted row between Chapman and Combe, with Marian once more caught in the middle. It had been agreed in June 1853 that Combe would write an important article on criminal legislation and prison discipline. Marian warned him then that there would be no room for it until the January 1854 number.[3] Combe told her cheerfully that she and Chapman could 'feel quite at ease about rejecting it, if found too phrenological and technical, for I shall print it as a pamphlet and distribute it, if you reject it, and thus my labour will not be lost'.[4]

Combe wished to address the topical question of the prison system, especially with regard to the cruel punishment of prisoners unable to do the hard labour required of them. New legislation was being contemplated by the Home Secretary, Palmerston. Combe's aim in his article or pamphlet, or article-cum-pamphlet, was to compare the systems adopted by different British prisons and by penitentiaries in America, Germany, and Spain; and he meant to persuade legislators of the usefulness of phrenological studies of prisoners in framing their new reforming laws. He managed to get the written support of leading physiologists like Carpenter and Owen, and doctors like his friend Sir James Paget and the progressive physician at the Middlesex asylum, Dr John Conolly.[5]

The piece grew too long for a mere article and it was soon agreed that, in addition to the *Westminster* article, a pamphlet was to be brought out, also by Chapman. Marian was given the job of reducing its hundred pages to thirty-two for the *Westminster*, where it would reach a wider public and appear in advance of the pamphlet. In November 1853 she had the delicate and, as she said, unpleasant task of telling Combe that there was now no room in the January number, and so the article would be held over until April 1854.[6] No doubt because of her fair and courteous dealings with him and the hard work she was prepared to do on his behalf, Combe accepted this further delay, but he exploded when Chapman asked him on 28 February if he would mind waiting for the July number. Combe wrote in exasperation, saying he had been patient for months while Chapman 'coolly consulted [his] own convenience', but now he would wait no longer. The pamphlet would be printed as soon as it was ready – and *not* by Chapman, whose 'style of managing business' did not suit Combe.[7]

Letters flew to and fro on the usual recriminating and self-excusing pattern. Marian herself almost lost her temper, writing firmly to Combe on 3 March: 'I beg you will not make me a referee in any matters relating to Mr Chapman, as I have nothing whatever to do with his affairs.'[8] Chapman published the article in the April number after all, and wrote with hurt pride but some dignity to Combe on 13 April:

> I am grieved that circumstances, chiefly beyond my control, have resulted in causing in your mind a considerable amount of dissatisfaction with respect to the publication of your article; but I trust you will derive some gratification from the knowledge that your views on Criminal Legislation have, by means of the Westminster, obtained an immediate and wide circulation on both sides of the Atlantic.[9]

Though she was determined to be fair to Chapman, Marian was surrounded by people who disapproved of him; to these were now added Lewes, angered by Chapman's publishing the damning Huxley review in January 1854. She was exhausted by having to hold the ring between Combe and Chapman, annoyed by her failure to prevent Huxley's mauling of Lewes, and she also had reason to be cross with Chapman on her own account. An agreement had been reached that she would translate Ludwig Feuerbach's *The Essence of Christianity* (*Das Wesen des Christenthums*, 1841) for his Quarterly Series;

in June 1853 the *Leader* had carried an advertisement for this and for an original work, 'The Idea of a Future Life', by 'the Translator of Strauss's *Life of Jesus*'.[10] Chapman seems to have pulled back from his promise to publish the 'Future Life' book, and to have refused her request for books to help her with it, which effectively meant she could not write it. She wrote angrily in December 1853:

> If I could do as I pleased I would much rather become myself a subscriber to the London Library and save both myself and you the trouble of speaking to you on the subject. But as this said work will occupy nearly the whole of next year and as I am to have no money for it – since the 'half profits' are not likely to have any other than a conceptual existence, a 'gedachtsein' – I don't see how I can possibly go to any expense in the matter.
>
> I bitterly regret that I allowed myself to be associated with your Series, but since I have done so, I am very anxious to fulfil my engagements both to you and the public . . . I would much rather that you should publish the work and *not* pay me than pay me and not publish it. I don't think you are sufficiently alive to the ignominy of advertising things, especially as part of a subscription series, which never appear . . .
>
> I have been making a desk of my knee so I fear some of my words may be illegible, which will be a pity because of course you can't substitute any half as good.[11]

The Feuerbach translation appeared in the Quarterly Series in July 1854; 'The Idea of a Future Life' did not materialise.

As Marian told Sara Hennell, who had agreed to read the translation in manuscript as she had the Strauss ten years earlier, *The Essence of Christianity* was 'the book of the age' in Germany, though she had little expectation of its effect in Britain. 'People here are as slow to be set on fire as a *stomach*', she wrote.[12] In Feuerbach's view religion is a psychological and imaginative necessity; mankind, aware of its imperfection, creates a perfect being to worship. What mankind is really worshipping is the perfection of its own species: '*Homo homini Deus est.*' The essence of Christianity is really 'the essence of human feeling'; the only divinity is 'the divinity of human nature'; 'God is the idea of the species as an individual'.[13] Feuerbach combines a

Straussian view of the Bible as a set of mythical texts with the Spinozan idea that the moral duty of mankind is to temper its natural egotism with altruism. The true object of our reverence, therefore, is our fellow human beings.

Marriage is the finest expression of such love and reverence, and exists, according to Feuerbach, wherever two people love one another, independent of the sanction of any church. To Marian Evans, in love with a married man who could not divorce his wife and contemplating spending her life with him, this secularised doctrine of love and duty could not have been more attractive. She had already studied Spinoza, beginning to translate his *Tractatus Theologico-Politicus* in 1849 with a view to its being published by Chapman; after finishing the Feuerbach, she turned in November 1854 to a translation of Spinoza's *Ethics*, which she did finish, but for which she and Lewes could not find a publisher.[14] The sanctification of purely human relations which she found in Spinoza and Feuerbach was to be represented fictionally in acts of kindness by characters in her novels, most notably by Dorothea Casaubon in *Middlemarch*, when she works through a night of selfish misery and jealousy to go out the following morning and visit Rosamond Lydgate in an attempt to save Rosamond's marriage. Marian told Sara on 29 April 1854, as she was putting the finishing touches to her translation of *The Essence of Christianity*, 'With the ideas of Feuerbach I everywhere agree.'[15]

Though she added that she would 'alter the phraseology considerably' if she were free to do so, she found Feuerbach's prose a good deal more congenial than the three dry volumes of Strauss. 'His text', she reported to Sara in February, 'is – *for a German* – concise, lucid, and even epigrammatic now and then'. Her dissatisfaction with Chapman at this time finds expression in a sharp postscript:

> It is such a comfort to have at least *one* person who can appreciate one's work. The dreariness of giving such a translation to Mr Chapman who neither knows what is in itself good English nor what is the difficulty of truly representing German![16]

The secret plan to accompany Lewes to Germany in the summer was probably complete by April 1854, when Marian told Cara Bray that she was hoping to take over the regular 'belles lettres' section of the *Westminster* from Jane Sinnett in July. She needed an income, and saw that she would earn little or nothing from the Feuerbach translation. The 'belles lettres' column would bring in £16.16.0 a quarter. In the event, Jane Sinnett begged Chapman not to take away her regular income, and she retained her position.[17] This turned out to be rather a good thing for Marian, as she began to write not journeyman round-ups of current literature for the *Westminster*, but original, incisive full-length articles on a wide range of subjects. Once she had removed herself first from the tiresome editorial work and then from Chapman's orbit altogether by going to Germany in July, she became free to exercise her skills in extended pieces of trenchant, influential writing.

Removal was on Chapman's mind too. He finally accepted that 142 Strand, for all its advantages of centrality and imposing appearance, was too expensive. Marian told Cara on 18 April that he had 'at length decided to leave his house at Midsummer'. There was the prospect that the Chapmans would become her neighbours in Cambridge Street, Hyde Park Square; Susanna viewed a house there, but it cost too much for her to take.[18] By 19 May Chapman had found a house to rent in Blandford Square, near Regent's Park. He had considered a larger one in Dorset Square, which he would have taken if Marian had agreed to 'become their lodger – but I could not make up my mind to this for sundry reasons, though on many grounds I should like it'.[19] She soon had to drop such disingenuous or secretive remarks, as the trip to Germany came ever nearer. She mentions Lewes in every letter to the Brays from now on, and on 27 May tells Charles Bray that she will not be living with the Chapmans as 'it is quite possible that I may wish to go to the continent or twenty other things'.[20]

In early June the Chapmans were preparing for their 'double removal', of themselves to Blandford Square and the publishing business to King William Street, leading north off the Strand near the Trafalgar Square end. A further change in the Chapman household was to take place; Elisabeth Tilley, for reasons which are not clear, was to leave. We have almost a last glimpse of her in Marian's letter to Sara on 3 June giving an account of the momentous move: 'A well-to-do brother of Miss Tilley's is come from Australia and will do something for her, I hope.' Marian wrote to Chapman from Germany a few months later, asking 'Has Miss Tilley sailed for Australia?'[21] The last word from Elisabeth herself came long after the exciting, often turbulent years at 142 Strand. In December 1878 she wrote from a boarding house in Heidelberg to the now famous George Eliot, commiserating with her on the death of Lewes.[22]

On 24 June 1854, almost seven years after he had moved in, Chapman left 142 Strand. Marian visited her friends in their new house in Blandford Square on 2 July; a week later she told Sara that she was preparing to go to 'Labassecour', Charlotte Brontë's fictional name for Belgium in *Villette*.[23] On 19 July she sent her last letter from Cambridge Street to her three Coventry friends, the Brays and Sara Hennell, not mentioning Lewes, but giving her address as 'Poste Restante, Weimar for the next six weeks and afterwards Berlin'.[24] It was the end of an era for her; though her connection with Chapman and the *Westminster Review* was by no means over, it entered a new phase as she began a new, happier life with Lewes. For Chapman the move from 142 was undoubtedly a wrench; we have no information about the reasons for Elisabeth Tilley's leaving, but that, too, was an important change for him, as was the loss from London of his intelligent friend, assistant, and adviser on the *Westminster Review*. Another difficult summer lay ahead of him; it was to test his resolve and his resilient nature to the limit.

Whatever savings Chapman made by leaving number 142 and moving to a smaller house, they were not enough to prevent him from becoming insolvent. His publishing business made a loss; since the fight with the Booksellers' Association in 1852, he had published very small numbers of books each year – the *Publishers' Circular* counts twenty-nine in 1852, twenty-three in 1853, and thirty in 1854. As Combe had predicted, Courtauld's money to save the *Westminster* had now been used up. Chapman was reduced to asking contributors who were normally paid for their articles if they would write for nothing – Froude replied to one such letter on 2 August, saying, 'I am very sorry for you', but 'I so largely depend on what I can make by writing that I shall not find it possible'.[25] Chapman called a meeting of his creditors on 4 August. Most of them – Courtauld, Harriet Martineau, and Barbara Leigh Smith's uncle Octavius Smith among them – agreed not to call in their money, so that Chapman could continue to run the *Westminster Review*, but James Martineau and W. B. Hodgson refused.[26]

Martineau, the leading Unitarian among the *Westminster's* reviewers, was becoming discontented with the number of articles appearing alongside his own contributions on theology which either expressed hostility to religious belief or merely ignored religion as a force in society. These articles included those written by Spencer, and Martineau will have been aware that Lewes, Huxley, Chapman, and Marian Evans were non-believers. The *Westminster*

Review was not, he felt, sympathetic to Christian, especially Unitarian, interests. Martineau, with his fellow Unitarians in the north of England – J. H. Thom in Liverpool, J. J. Tayler in Manchester, and Charles Wicksteed in Leeds, all of whom had been publishing their books with Chapman since he took over the business from Green a decade before – contributed regularly to the *Prospective Review*, the dedicated Unitarian journal, also published by Chapman. Indeed the four men edited it jointly.

With a circulation of about 500, the *Prospective* neither made nor lost money for Chapman, since its contributors were not paid. However, the small circulation and the narrowness of its subject matter and its readership alike, compared to the *Westminster*, worried the editors, especially as they saw the *Westminster*, which they liked to think of as 'their' journal, becoming, in their view, overly secular, even 'atheistic'. Of course, Chapman and Marian Evans would call it diverse, eclectic, inclusive, undogmatic, and liberal, as their well-meaning if clumsily expressed Prospectus had indicated. The *Prospective* looked unlikely to survive, as various changes were taking place in the careers of its chief contributors. In September 1853 Tayler left Manchester for London when Manchester New College finally moved south to share University Hall in Gordon Square with the hall of residence now presided over by W. B. Carpenter of University College. Tayler was too busy to write for the *Prospective* while the move was taking place; at the same time Thom was planning to withdraw from it through ill health.[27] The quality of the articles fell; Marian Evans wrote cruelly in August 1853 that she was 'positively revelling' in the current number of the *Prospective*:

> I have been dying with laughter over one passage in the article on Shak[e]speare which was made for Herbert Spencer and which I long to quote to him . . . James Martineau transcends himself in beauty of imagery in the article on Sir W. Hamilton, but I have not finished him yet.[28]

Martineau himself made a partial move to London early in 1854, when he began lecturing at Manchester New College in its new London home, travelling from Liverpool every two weeks for two days at a time. He was to move to a full professorship at the college three years later. On 3 July 1854 he complained to his erstwhile pupil, Richard Holt Hutton, also a contributor to the *Prospective Review*, that Chapman was turning the *Westminster* into 'the organ of his own egotism, and ever shifting thought, and not the expression of any consolidated and influential body of competent and consistent opinion'.[29] Martineau thought of himself as representing reason and liberalism; he was a progressive among Unitarians, many of whom found him too liberal for their taste. Compared to those at the other end of the broad spectrum of *Westminster* reviewers, such as Spencer, Huxley, and Lewes, he was, however, a traditionalist. Combe's words to Lombe in May 1851 about the difficulty, if not impossibility, of keeping together a heterogeneous group of thinkers, all believing their own opinion to be the true one, all 'Guerilla Chiefs' disinclined to follow one 'General', had proved prophetic.[30] Martineau's displeasure, as expressed to Hutton in July 1854, undoubtedly had personal and particular, as well as general, grounds. That month's number of the *Westminster*, in which his usual round-up of books on theology, philosophy, and politics appeared, carried the belated but very favourable review of his estranged sister Harriet's translation of the abominated positivist philosophy of Comte.[31]

Martineau later recalled that at the same time as he and his colleagues were trying to liberalise the Unitarian readers of the *Prospective Review*, they were becoming increasingly annoyed by the tone of the *Westminster*. Their initial hope was to merge the two periodicals under the *Westminster*'s name, but they saw that their influence would be nullified by the agnostic tendency which was predominant.[32] Their next plan was to try to buy the *Westminster Review* from Chapman. A fund was set up, probably in the early summer of 1854, attracting a number of subscribers from the liberal wing of Unitarianism and beyond. These included Froude's old employer, the Manchester solicitor Samuel Darbishire, W. B. Hodgson, W. R. Greg, and Walter Bagehot.[33] When Chapman was forced to declare his insolvency in early August, Martineau and his group saw an opportunity to take over the *Westminster* completely.

According to his own disgruntled account of how the takeover failed, Martineau and his friends were cheated of the opportunity:

> The proprietor and publisher of the 'Westminster' became insolvent, and the 'Review' – the most important of his assets – passed, with the rest of the estate, to the disposal of the creditors. Had it come into the market, and its value been tested by the offer of sale, a bid for it would have been made by the proprietors of the 'Prospective' with tolerable certainty of considerable increase to the dividend. With other of the creditors, I

was of opinion that this regular course ought to be followed. Receiving, however, no notice till the 3rd of August, of the creditors' meeting at 11 A.M. on the following day, we, who lived from two hundred to four hundred miles off, had no opportunity of taking part in the proceedings. A balance sheet was laid before the local attendants, from which the 'Westminster Review' was omitted; and, to induce the creditors to forego all claim upon it and leave it in the publisher's hands, a personal guarantee was offered of a definite composition by a friend whose security was perfect. The meeting closed with this proposal; but we absentees, disapproving of the management which had been resorted to, declined to accept the composition, unless a second meeting were called at which a vote should be taken after complete valuation of the assets. Instead of conceding this reasonable demand, the publisher's wealthy patron set himself to *buy off* the dissentients by payment in full of their claim on the estate. I refused to listen to such proposals; but I was left alone; and, as my debt did not warrant me in taking more than a secondary part, I gave no further expression to my dissent than by declining to accept any share in the composition, when it came to be distributed.[34]

Martineau's chief ally, and the only other refusenik, was W. B. Hodgson, the liberal educationalist, later a supporter of higher education for women, and friend and disciple of Combe. Though not a Unitarian, he had mixed with Unitarians during his time teaching in Manchester and was a close friend of Martineau. He now lived in Edinburgh. Hodgson had supported Chapman when he first bought the *Westminster* from Hickson, and wrote an article for the *Review* in 1853 on language teaching in schools, advocating the replacement of the classics with modern languages.[35] On his trips to London he stayed at 142 Strand. Crabb Robinson was introduced to him there in October 1853 and described him as 'a very clever-looking man' and a 'Scotch hard headed liberal'. Robinson invited Hodgson, Chapman, and W. B. Donne, a new contributor to the *Westminster*, to a breakfast party on 16 October.[36] Hodgson's feelings towards Chapman and the *Westminster* appear to have been friendly enough; in February 1854 he attended one of Chapman's soirées, at which he saw another of Combe's friends, T. H. Bastard, a financial supporter of the *Westminster*, Marian Evans, and a number of German exiles, including Freiligrath and Gottfried Kinkel, whose wife Johanna played the piano.[37]

By the summer of 1854 Hodgson had joined Martineau in his determination to get hold of the *Westminster*. He visited Combe in Edinburgh on 13 September to tell him about the plan, as Combe recounted in his journal:

> Dr Hodgson called and explained the circumstances of John Chapman's insolvency, and detailed a litany of selfish equivocations, not to say downright dishonesties, and incapacities, which did not surprise me, but confirmed all my recent experience of Mr Chapman & his mode of acting. He is offering 8p in the Pound to his trade creditors, stipulating that he shall retain the Review.[38]

On the same day, 13 September, Combe's nephew Robert Cox wrote that Hodgson was hoping that Martineau would edit the *Westminster* if they could acquire it. Cox had 'in a manner promised to go as far as £100', but had indicated to Hodgson that Combe might not have any 'loose funds at present'. Hodgson, he wrote, 'is very ill pleased with Chapman, whose Conscientiousness it appears does not cut a good figure'.[39]

Combe was recording a new development in his journal only two days later, namely the intervention of Chapman's 'wealthy patron' to pay off Hodgson and attempt to pay off Martineau. It was Samuel Courtauld once again. Combe muses on his motives for saving the day for Chapman and subjects Chapman one more time to phrenological analysis:

> Dr Hodgson writes to me that Mr Courtauld, John Chapman's friend and patron, has paid him (Dr H.) Chapman's debts to him . . . in full to avoid calling another meeting of creditors, or forcing Chapman into bankruptcy.
>
> There is truly a great deal more of benevolence than of conscientiousness and discriminative intellect in the world. Mr Courtauld is sacrificing his money apparently from the best of motives, to uphold Chapman as the organ of advanced opinions, without any perception of the inadequacy of the man to accomplish the end in view. Chapman is deficient in business talent, in conscientiousness, in knowledge, and in sound practical sense; he is a dreamer and a schemer; his leading motives are ambition and the love of the new; and his chief talents are a capacity for plausible talk, rendered easy by large Secretiveness, Love of approbation, and Wonder, acting unrestrained either by

Causality or Conscientiousness. Great efforts making to preserve the Westminster Review in his hands; and this, in my opinion, is an error of judgment. He is morally and intellectually incapable of taking the lead in the philosophy, religion, social economy, and science of the 19th century; and yet this is what he aims at. He must be editor as well as publisher; in short the great oracle of liberal opinions. He will fail again in a few years. He has much good nature, but ill directed.[40]

Despite his low opinion of Chapman, however, Combe not only stayed aloof from Martineau and Hodgson, but showed that his generosity towards the *Westminster* would not cease, though his hopes for its future were not strong. He had recently sent £20 towards the costs of the *Review*, and was now Chapman's creditor for a total of £35.12.0. Chapman addressed him carefully on 22 September, asking if Combe was content to remain in credit for that amount, since Chapman had avoided bankruptcy and was still in charge of the journal. Tetchily but decently, Combe agreed.[41]

Courtauld paid off Chapman's debt to Hodgson, which amounted to £466.7.10, including interest, as Hodgson told Combe on 15 September:

Finding me quite immoveable in my purpose to make Chapman choose between a second meeting of Creditors & the Bankruptcy Court, Mr C. has been compelled to remove me as an obstacle, otherwise insuperable, to the arrangement with the other Creditors.[42]

Martineau still refused to accept payment. He did not budge, and remained a creditor until he cancelled the debt when buying back the copyright of his *Westminster* articles in 1857.[43] Courtauld was shocked by Martineau's intransigence and by his 'coarse imputations of falsehood & injustice' against Chapman, 'recklessly indulged in upon authority of tea-table gossip'. On 13 November 1854 he sent Chapman a copy of a document addressed to Martineau:

I may take this opp[ortunit]y of informing you that as you have declined to either take the composition upon Mr Chapman's debts with the general body of the creditors, or to accept payment in full, thus refusing to allow him to discharge in any way his legal liability to you as his creditor – the amount of his debt to you £88.8.1p has been placed in my hands, to satisfy your claim, whenever you may demand payment, or think it right to accept it.[44]

With the support of Courtauld and others, Chapman was safe.

Martineau and his Unitarian friends now removed their business from Chapman. Henry Crabb Robinson observed in his diary in November 1854 that J. J. Tayler, holding 'melancholy views of the present prospects of religion' because the *Westminster Review* looked like being given over to 'the *Atheists*', was to 'leave Chapman as a publisher', though 'with no dislike for him personally'.[45] Martineau ceased to write for the *Westminster*. He and his friends set about founding a new periodical of their own which would succeed the ailing *Prospective* and have a broader base, beginning with the subscribers who had already expressed their readiness to back the takeover of the *Westminster*.

Martineau had been one of the *Westminster*'s strongest writers, for all the rhetorical flourish and exaggeration with which Marian Evans found fault, but Chapman, with a strong stable of loyal supporters and contributors, and new writers like Huxley, Tyndall, and Donne, kept the *Westminster Review* going at its high standard. Martineau's parting shot, as it were, was the notice he gave in his last round-up article in the October 1854 number to the translation of Feuerbach's *The Essence of Christianity*, just published by Chapman, not anonymously like the Strauss, but with the translator's name, 'Marian Evans', on the title-page. Since the writer, Feuerbach, the translator, Marian Evans, and the publisher, Chapman, all seemed to Martineau to represent the dangers of the age, he was at his most negative in his last piece for the journal:

> It is a sign of 'progress', we presume, that the lady-translator who maintained the anonymous in introducing Strauss, puts her name in the title-page of Feuerbach. She has executed her task even better than before: we are only surprised that, if she wished to exhibit the new Hegelian Atheism to English readers, she should select a work of the year 1840, and of quite secondary philosophical repute in its own country.[46]

It was certainly a sign of Chapman's fairness and openness that he printed this attack on his friend's translation, published in his own Quarterly Series. He had gone through a tortured summer trying to fend off bankruptcy and the loss of the *Westminster Review*. In a letter to Robert Chambers in October he confessed that 'the contest with Dr Hodgson and Mr Martineau' had been 'very painful to me', but he appears not to have shown his torment to other friends. Sarah Hennell reported to Marian in November that she had seen him the previous month:

> Mr Ch. came to our lodgings for one hour or two, looking very well, as if he could still thrive upon his misfortunes. Almost all his time was spent in reading to us a pile of manuscripts – being notes of the Hodgson and Martineau controversy about the Westminster.[47]

Living happily in Weimar with Lewes, Marian replied to Sara's commiseration on 'that disgraceful notice of Feuerbach' that she had not seen it, but that Lewes had read it in Weimar's library. She was more annoyed on Chapman's account than on her own. The review 'appears to be rather stultifying to Mr Ch. as publisher of the *Series*', she wrote, adding that she was very sorry for Chapman: 'Whatever may have been his mistakes I think he must have been hardly used by Dr Hodgson and J. Martineau.'[48] She was not alone in thinking this. Combe suggested by his refusal to join Hodgson in crowing over Chapman and by agreeing not to call in the money Chapman owed him that he disapproved of the pursuit of Chapman. And Henry Crabb Robinson, though anxious like his Unitarian friends that the *Westminster Review* was becoming dangerously freethinking, confided much the same opinion to his diary.[49]

Martineau and Hodgson may or may not have known that Harriet Martineau had lent Chapman £500 in April 1854, using the *Westminster Review* as security.[50] As she wrote in her autobiographical manuscript less than a year later, the arrangement had been her own idea. Early in 1855 doctors diagnosed a tumour which she and they thought would be fatal; accordingly she was making preparations for her autobiography to be published, by Chapman, immediately after her death. In the event she lived for nearly twenty more years, and the autobiography remained unpublished all that time. Her main aim in writing it was to justify her own conduct and beliefs, since she expected that her brother would spread a negative account of their relationship and of her work. Chapman and she were as close as two such different people could be at this time, writing confiding letters, each offering support for the other, with Harriet assisting Chapman financially and Chapman giving her comfort and practical help in her illness. Harriet was therefore keen to vindicate Chapman against the attacks of his enemies, whom she saw as her own enemies too, chief amongst them being her brother James.

This is Harriet's account in 1855 of the events of the previous summer:

It was a time of anxiety and sorrow. My good friend and publisher, Mr Chapman, had just failed, – in consequence of misfortunes which came thick upon him, from the time of Mr Lombe's death, which was a serious blow to the 'Westminster Review'. Mr Chapman, never in all our intercourse, asked me to lend him money; yet the 'Westminster Review' was by this time mortgaged to me. It was entirely my own doing; and I am anxious, for Mr Chapman's sake, that this should be understood. The truth of the case is that I had long felt, as many others had professed to do, that the cause of free-thought and free-speech was under great obligations to Mr Chapman; and it naturally occurred to me that it was therefore a duty incumbent on the advocates of free-thought and speech to support and aid one by whom they had been enabled to address society. Thinking, in the preceding winter, that I saw that Mr Chapman was hampered by certain liabilities that the Review was under, I offered to assume the mortgage, – knowing the uncertain nature of that kind of investment, but regarding the danger of loss as my contribution to the cause. At first, after the failure, there was every probability, apparently, that Mr Chapman's affairs would be speedily settled, – so satisfied were all his creditors who were present with his conduct under examination, and the accounts he rendered. A few generous friends and creditors made all smooth, as it was hoped; but two absent discontented creditors pursued their debtor with (as some men of business among the creditors said) 'a cruelty unequalled in all their experience'. One of their endeavours was to get the Review out of Mr Chapman's hands; and one feature of the enterprise was an attempt to upset the mortgage, and to drive Mr Chapman to bankruptcy, in order to throw the Review into the market, at the most disadvantageous season, when London was empty, and cholera prevalent, – that these personages might get it cheap. One of them made no secret of his having raised a subscription for the purpose. It was the will of the great body of the creditors, however, that Mr Chapman should keep the Review, which he had edited thus far with great and rising success; and his two foes were got rid of by the generosity of Mr Chapman's guaranteeing supporters.[51]

Though Harriet was hardly an impartial observer, being implacably hostile towards her brother and his opinions, and believing him to be motivated by spite towards her, she did wish to give a truthful account of the episode, and her assessment of the importance and intellectual, if not financial, strength of the *Westminster Review* in its early years under Chapman's ownership is perfectly accurate. (She had her reasons, when writing this account in 1855, for not including Marian Evans's name in the accolade she gave the editorial work on the *Westminster*.) Harriet adds that just at this time Chapman's cousin and namesake was suddenly struck down by cholera as he was writing his Humboldt article, and 'while my poor friend was suffering under the first anguish of this loss', another contributor, 'wrought on by evil influences, disappointed the editor of a promised article at the time it ought to have been at press'.[52]

John Chapman had died on 11 September, when things were touch and go with the ownership of the *Westminster Review*. Harriet was in London at the time, and she wrote to her friend Fanny Wedgwood on 17 September, naming the defaulting contributor as Greg, and saying that he had 'disappointed Chapman of an article, in the most selfish and saucy way, after having *promised* it, and when there was not a day to lose'. She herself was helping Chapman out by staying on in London a few extra days to write a second article – on the Crystal Palace in its new home in Sydenham – for the October number.[53] Chapman must have missed his industrious and judicious co-editor at this moment; he was now producing the *Westminster* on his own, in addition to fighting his survival battle with Martineau and Hodgson. In the same letter Harriet tells Fanny Wedgwood that Courtauld has stepped in to pay off Hodgson, supported by Octavius Smith, uncle of Barbara Leigh Smith, a philanthropic liberal, and the proprietor, in Herbert Spencer's words, of 'the largest distillery in England'.[54]

Meanwhile Harriet retained her mortgage on the *Westminster*, James and his friend having 'lost their scheme on the Review, and all future access to it'. In her delight at this happy outcome, she momentarily waxed generous towards her brother: 'I hope these subscribers [to the takeover fund] will set him up handsomely in the "Prospective", and let him try what he can do.'

Then she reverted to her usual sharpness on the subject: 'I wish him every possible facility and opportunity for working out his views and notions; and I wish it more as I see more plainly how bent he is on stealing other people's.'[55]

Harriet's view was that James was acting out of hostility towards her as well as out of annoyance with Chapman and the tendency of the *Westminster Review*; she wrote in 1858 of the 'pertinaceous efforts of certain creditors, who openly desired to wrest the review from the hands of its owner, & to upset the mortgage of it to me'.[56] Whatever the truth of this, the battle was not fully won until December 1854, when the dissidents finally accepted that Chapman would keep the *Westminster* and that it would not be merged with the *Prospective*.[57] Chapman had the financial support of Courtauld, Octavius Smith, and Harriet Martineau, and the moral support of these three and several more. Marian Evans sent her best wishes on 4 October, assuring Chapman that she could add Lewes's to hers: 'He shares my interest in the result of all the difficulties which you have indicated in your letters.'[58] Bray remained staunch, despite the doubts about Chapman which he and Combe felt. He wrote to the latter on 23 September criticising Chapman's poor management of money, but praising him for his hard work and determination; Hodgson, he thought, was wrong to 'take advantage of his debt to get the Review into his own hands & to make James Martineau editor'.[59]

Huxley, we know, would have stopped writing for the *Westminster* if Chapman had lost it to the Unitarians, and Spencer, though mostly out of London during the tussle over the *Review* and therefore not directly involved, would certainly have taken Chapman's side, given his often expressed gratitude to Chapman for publishing his books and articles when he was an unknown writer of daringly progressive views.[60] He spent several months in France and Brighton at this time, researching and writing his next book, *The Principles of Psychology* (1855). A gap occurred in his writing for the *Westminster*, as he became ill from overwork and took time off from August 1855 until January 1857. He recalled years later that when he recovered and offered Chapman an article to be called 'The Cause of All Progress', Chapman, thinking the title 'too ambitious', suggested 'Progress: its Laws and Cause', under which more modest heading it appeared in the April 1857 number of the *Westminster Review*.[61]

Combe emulated Solomon in keeping both factions reasonably happy by refusing to take sides when they pressed him for his support. Of those other writers for the *Westminster* who were less radical in one way or another than

Chapman's supporters while not embracing political, social, or religious ortho-doxy (which would have precluded their joining the journal's ranks in the first place), there were three contributors of some importance to Chapman: Greg, Newman, and Froude.

Greg had contributed two or three articles a year since 1842, when Hickson was in charge of the *Review*. He had written four weighty political articles for Chapman, on employment, Robert Peel, and the Duke of Wellington in 1852, and on the abuse of charity in January 1853. The article on Peel had particularly impressed Gladstone and the Oxford academic Mark Pattison, both of whom noted its effect on them in their diaries.[62] Though brought up a Unitarian, Greg had become a sceptic, as his book *The Creed of Christendom*, published by Chapman in 1851, demonstrated. He wrote regu-larly for the *Edinburgh Review* as well as for the *Westminster*, and had become interested in exile politics, particularly the Hungarian cause as represented by Kossuth. Greg seems to have been a difficult contributor; though Marian Evans respected him and reviewed his *Creed of Christendom* favourably in the *Leader*, she had an argument with him in December 1852 over his article on charity, when he was unwilling to modify a passage after she had pointed out some errors. 'He is so unused to editorial suggestion', she told Combe, 'that there is no alternative but to let the article stand in its present unsat-isfactory state or to reject it altogether'.[63] The article was accepted, but Greg may have felt annoyed at the *Westminster*'s two editors, both more than twenty years his junior, daring to find fault with his work.

He was a neighbour of Harriet Martineau in the Lake District, and the two were 'on friendly terms', as Marian reported to Combe during her brief visit to Harriet in October 1852.[64] Less than two years later Harriet was complaining of his arrogance when it became clear that he would follow Martineau in leaving the *Westminster*. In a letter to Chapman of 1 November 1854 acknowl-edging receipt of a cheque for £12.10.0, 'being a half-year's interest on the mortgage of the Westminster Review', she commented on him:

> Mr Greg piques himself on calmness & impartiality, whereas a more insolently prejudiced man does not exist. Look at his talk of 'secession' – as if you were not as much the dismisser as they the seceders![65]

Martineau and Hodgson had identified Greg as the best person to edit the new journal they now turned their attention to founding.

What would Frank Newman do? Mill thought he was 'terrified at anything like really free opinions'; his former pupil Walter Bagehot bluntly told Henry Crabb Robinson in January 1855 that Newman was 'essentially incapable of cooperating with anyone'.[66] Robinson himself, long a Newman watcher, who had seen him exercising a divisive influence at University College, University Hall, and Bedford College, yet admired and liked him, assumed in November 1854 that Newman would leave the *Westminster* along with the other dissidents. He was told as much by Greg, who visited him on 19 November to ask him to subscribe £100 to the new review.[67] But Newman went his own way. It was he who had alerted Chapman to the plan by Martineau and Hodgson to take over the *Westminster* – 'a godsend' which prevented Chapman from being taken by surprise, as Harriet Martineau said.[68]

Newman's experience of publishing his books with Chapman made him critical of his business methods, but he was not inclined to leave him. A letter of 23 August 1854 to Holyoake expresses his doubts, but also a slight hope that Chapman might mend his ways:

I think he clearly has deceived himself by a notion, that the bad sale of books in their earlier years is no clue to their after bad sale, & that it is a temporary loss necessarily encountered in giving them publicity. Hence he has gone on year after year estimating his stock at a pecuniary value which it *never* had, & only at last opened his eyes to what might, I think, have been long ago obvious . . . I think a publisher should above all things avoid to borrow on the credit of a stock the *whole* value of which is liable to be swallowed up in advertisement & agency. This is what I want to persuade him of for the future; but I fear, not with success.[69]

Critical of Chapman's too sanguine temperament and its effect on his business though he was, Newman refused to join Martineau. On 27 November he asked Martineau: 'Is any good purpose answered by my reading *either* document, Chapman's or yours?' He expressed doubts about the new journal, telling Martineau that his articles in the *Westminster* were excellent: 'You seemed to be less in trammels there than in the Prospective.' As for Greg as editor, Newman 'honour[ed] his energy & knowledge & excellent desires', but thought him too conservative in temperament to 'lead the left'.[70] Newman continued to write articles on politics, religion, and foreign affairs for

Chapman at the rate of one or two a year. He told Martineau in June 1855 that he had contributed an article on American administration to the April number and one on international affairs for July. 'I wrote them freely', he says, 'and indeed could not comfortably take money from Chapman in his present circumstances'. He would like to write for the new journal, to be called the *National Review*, too, 'if I am admissible, & if there is any prospect of its attaining a considerable circulation'.[71] He did write three articles for the *National*, beginning in 1857, but he remained primarily a *Westminster* reviewer.

If there was gossip and speculation about how Newman would react to the split, there was a good deal more about what the enigmatic Froude would do. He was universally considered the most valuable of the likely defectors, as his historical articles in the *Westminster* commanded widespread respect. 'If you keep Froude', Harriet Martineau told Chapman in November, 'I don't think your loss will be great'.[72] A number of observers expected him to be wooed away by Martineau. Marian Evans supposed in a letter to Chapman from Weimar on 15 October that 'James Martineau has won Froude over to his views and purposes'.[73] As late as 21 December Combe was told by the optimistic Hodgson not only that the new review would be 'backed by large capitalists' and so set out to rival the *Westminster* with Greg as its editor, but also that Martineau, Newman, and Froude were all 'going over to it'. Combe was gloomy about its prospects, on the sensible grounds that as 'one liberal Review has never hitherto paid its expenses', two could hardly be expected to prosper. He was sorry that 'the liberals are agreed in nothing except in a common dislike to certain prevailing doctrines in religion, politics, & social organism', having no 'counter doctrines to propose'.[74]

While expressing his sympathy with Chapman's troubles in August 1854, Froude had declined to write his articles for nothing. On 5 November, with letters and documents between the main parties to the dispute doing the rounds of the *Westminster* and *Prospective* circles, Froude wrote his hostile letter to Chapman. He was partly annoyed that Chapman had asked to publish the history of Elizabethan England Froude was writing, assuming a kind of right because he had been printing Froude's articles on the subject in the *Westminster Review*. Froude's answer to this was the painful remark about not entrusting his important work to Chapman's 'crippled resources' and the explanation that Parker was to publish it. He was also irritated by Chapman's unauthorised quoting from his letters, in particular the disclosure of Froude's comments on Martineau to Newman. 'The extract which you have now made, as you well know', he wrote, 'gives a very different impression of my opinion of Mr Martineau's conduct towards you, from what the letter really contains'. Chapman is accused of ungentlemanly behaviour:

> I may add that as far as I am able to judge you have most exceedingly wronged Mr Martineau in representing him as having stooped to private misrepresentation of you and your conduct for personal ends of his own. His language to me about you has been language rather of regret and disappointment at your having fallen short of the expectations which he had formed of you; and of remaining esteem for the many high qualities which he still recognized in you; and I do not think you do your cause any good by these recriminating defences of it.[75]

The letter to which this is a reply has not survived, but we know from the many extant examples of Chapman's self-excusing letters to those, like Lombe and Combe, who lost patience with him, what sort of letter it must have been.

It would seem, then, that Chapman must lose Froude. Yet the planners of the new *National Review* could not be sure of him. They were now finding for themselves that setting up a new periodical is no easy thing. They had secured promises of financial backing from Darbishire and other wealthy patrons, including Lady Byron, widow of the poet, who had become sympathetic to Unitarianism, but Henry Crabb Robinson was not keen to subscribe.[76] The publishing firm of Smith, Elder agreed to bring out the journal but pulled out in February 1855 when their request that the 'avowed Editor' should be a Church of England clergyman was turned down by the Unitarian subscribers.[77] Greg was, everyone agreed, too ambitious in his editorial plans, and his enthusiasm for Kossuth and the liberation of Hungary frightened some of the more conservative supporters.

One of the founders of the new journal, the forceful Walter Bagehot, tried to persuade Henry Crabb Robinson to contribute financially, writing on 8 February that it was essential not to let any of the support for the old *Prospective* be grabbed by the *Westminster* while the organisers of the new periodical delayed and argued:

> I hold it quite a mistake to suppose the Westminster will die of itself.

You are giving it the best chance of success – by not opposing it – by (as you will be obliged to do) relinquishing the Prospective – by therefore giving its sale to Chapman, to the enemy. You may kill the Westminster or drive it to terms and agonies – by starting an opponent, but if you allow it to hold up its head as the only organ in which liberal religious opinions can be expressed, it will live and thrive and propagate poison for a thousand years. The agitation we have begun will strengthen it. Chapman now boasts that he has smashed us and it is bread and meat, corn and wine to him. I hope you won't desert us.[78]

At the same time James Martineau reported to Charles Wicksteed on 18 February that the review was still not ready to enter the lists against the *Westminster*, having lost both its publisher and its editor, Greg having resigned on recognising that he did not have the full support of the subscribers and out of fear for his future position on the *Edinburgh Review*:

Having both staff and funds in readiness, and in the opinion of experienced publishers, an open field of unrepresented feeling and opinion between the heavy Whiggism and decorous Church-latitude of the Edinburgh on the one hand, and the atheistic tendency and Refugee-politics of the 'Westminster' on the other, – we proposed to start 'The *National* Review', of which I enclose a Prospectus. W. R. Greg undertook to be Editor, and all was ready for announcement; when through certain misunderstandings or mismanagements Greg lost his publishers, and fearing to compromise his relations with the Edinburgh, had not spirit enough to begin again with new people, and retired. His lavish notions had rather alarmed us, – and indeed himself; for on quitting the field he advised us to take up a more moderate scheme, – involving less outlay and requiring smaller returns. So now, in the third place, we revert to what in truth was our notion till Greg came in: a 4/- Review, of about 200 pages, – name as yet undetermined; Editor (with aid) R[ichard] H[olt] Hutton at a salary; contributors partly volunteers, partly paid on a certain graduated scale; the whole expense such as to be balanced by a sale of 1250.[79]

It is interesting to see Martineau, one of Chapman's severest scolders for his unrealistic notions about the finances of the *Westminster Review*, here wildly overestimating the readership for a periodical of a much narrower range.

In the event, the *National*'s circulation did not reach half the projected 1,250 in its first year; it bankrupted its replacement publisher Robert Theobald, and, despite being taken on in July 1856 by the large firm of Chapman & Hall, was wound up in 1864 after just under ten years of existence.[80]

Another problem was finding a name for the journal. Bagehot, who came in to share the editorship with his old school and University College friend Richard Holt Hutton, told Hutton as late as March 1855 that the title was not yet agreed on. Martineau 'cannot stand the Liberal and inclines to the English Quarterly', while Bagehot himself favoured the 'New Review'. By April the organisers had fixed on the *National Review*.[81] It is clear that even with its anti-atheist consensus, this new journal was as vulnerable to disagreements as ever the *Westminster* was. And still everyone wondered what Froude would do. He was certainly not committed to the *Westminster* by a sense of obligation or loyalty to Chapman. Bagehot hoped to get him for the *National*, but was unsure; 'Froude has no views of his own', he told Crabb Robinson in January; 'I own I cannot think Froude's co-operation at all essential – though his popular and effective style makes him most valuable as a contributor'.[82] In March Bagehot and Hutton were planning their first volume, but still did not know if Froude would write for them. 'I am not able to judge of the state of his feelings towards us', Bagehot confessed to Martineau.[83] By 19 April Bagehot had not heard from Froude; if he would write for them, 'we sh[oul]d do very well in Literature', he told Hutton.[84]

The first number of the *National* was published in July 1855 without a contribution from Froude. Despite his sharp words to Chapman, he did not defect, but carried on writing for the *Westminster*, both regular round-ups of history, biography, voyages, and travels, and long articles on history and philosophy, including the one on Spinoza with which Chapman opened the July 1855 number. He wrote in friendly terms to Chapman in May about the title of this article, even offering to fill the gap left by Martineau in the theology and philosophy department for the next two quarters, if Chapman was stuck. He wanted to know from Chapman 'who among learned men' was 'on our side'.[85]

Chapman had been quick to find a substitute for Martineau. In October 1854 he approached Mark Pattison, who agreed, though he mostly shared the section with his friend Henry Bristow Wilson, whom he introduced to Chapman, and who eventually took over the theology and philosophy round-up from Pattison. In 1854 Pattison was a Fellow of Lincoln College, Oxford (and later its Rector), and an ordained clergyman, though one who favoured liberalising the Church of England. His main interest was university education; during the 1850s and 1860s he wrote a number of articles for Chapman on education and religion, often comparing English and German scholarship in these fields. His friend Wilson was a practising clergyman in Huntingdonshire; like Pattison, he had liberal theological views.

Both men were, on the face of it, strange choices for Chapman to make. He may have been stung by the atheist, Comtist label being applied to him and the *Westminster* by the departing Martineau and his friends, and perhaps he wanted to show that the *Westminster Review* was genuinely eclectic rather than narrowly anti-religious. Chapman, always at his most confident when recruiting and advising new contributors, mounted his high horse a little when thanking Pattison for agreeing to undertake the philosophy and theology department. He told his new contributor on 30 October what was wanted:

> In originating these reviews of Contemporary Literature my wish has been, by securing articles truly elevated, intellectually and in moral *tone*, to exercise a wholesome influence on our current literature and to guide the reader to what is truly good. I leave to you the selection of books to be noticed.

On a housekeeping note, he asked Pattison 'not to cut the *tops* of the *foreign* books as they are merely borrowed' and to return all the books to Chapman when the article was finished.[86]

The *Westminster Review* continued to flourish, as Bagehot conceded ruefully to Hutton in February 1856:

> This last no. of the Westminster is very good. We shall go smash if we do not look out. I think Froude wrote the 'History' summary. I do *not* think the article on Heine Lewes's, it is not discontinuous or abrupt enough . . . It is a very good article, much better than anything we have this time.[87]

The article he singles out here, 'German Wit: Heinrich Heine', was the third outstanding piece of writing Chapman had received from Marian Evans, now living in Richmond as Mrs Lewes.

*

When Marian Evans sent her farewell note on 19 July 1854 to her Coventry friends, she had told only two people that she was going to Germany with Lewes. These were Chapman and Bray. Cara Bray and her sister Sara Hennell were offended that she had not confided in them, but also disappointed and a little shocked at the step she had taken. It took several months of awkward correspondence between them to put matters right with her oldest female friends.[88] Meanwhile, Chapman earned Marian's gratitude by writing to her almost immediately, asking her to contribute an article for the *Westminster* on Victor Cousin's book about the seventeenth-century French intellectual Madame de Sablé.[89] She wrote back warmly on 6 August, showing her appreciation of his thoughtfulness towards her and expressing sympathy with his financial plight:

Dear Friend

Your letter made me glad and sorry. It is the immemorial fashion of lady letter-writers to be glad and sorry in the same sentence, and after all, this feminine style is the truest representation of life. I was delighted to see your writing on the back of the letter which the Post-Beamter, like a conscientious man, refused to give me because I had not my passport in my pocket, and when at last I did get it, I opened it with all sorts of grateful, affectionate feelings towards you for having written to me so soon. But I was deeply saddened by what you tell me about yourself. I have always cherished the hope that you would work your way to independence by gradually paying off all debts and anything short of that I can never regard as a relief for you. But I think I am able to enter sympathetically into your whole position, and to estimate both your inward and outward difficulties, so you may rely on always having a fair appreciation from one person in the world, as well as a sisterly interest, which is perhaps less worth having. I shall be very anxious to know how things turn out – but I know you will write to me when you can.[90]

She could be sure that Chapman, with his views on love and marriage, would not play the hypocrite and turn his back on her, but she was less sure of others. Her last words in this high-spirited but nervous letter suggest an anxiety even about how Susanna Chapman might react to the news of her relationship with Lewes: 'Give my kind remembrances to Mrs Chapman, if she will accept them, and believe me always Your faithful and affectionate Marian Evans'.[91] To Bray she was more defensive (though she knew that he kept a mistress and illegitimate children and might surely hope that he, too, would avoid hypocritical expressions of disapproval); 'I hope you want to hear something of me', she wrote on 16 August. She was careful to add, probably for the benefit of Cara and Sara, that the great composer Liszt, director of opera and Kapellmeister to the Grand Duke of Weimar, lived openly with 'a Russian Princess', the married Carolyne Sayn-Wittgenstein, and was universally accepted as a 'Grand Seigneur in this place'.[92]

Working on her article while Lewes researched his biography of Goethe, and moving with him in the highest social and intellectual circles in Weimar, Marian was happy. She expressed her feelings less guardedly to Chapman than to any of her other friends. 'I am happier every day', she told him on 30 August. 'Affection, respect, and intellectual sympathy deepen, and for the first time in my life I can say to the moments [echoing Goethe's Faust in his desire for a moment to last longer] "Verweilen sie, sie sind so schön".'[93]

The two most important English-speaking residents in Weimar seemed just as welcoming as the Germans. 'Mr Wilson', Marian wrote in the same letter, was 'extremely polite and agreeable'. This was Thomas Wilson, whom she had met at 142 Strand in 1851. Another of Chapman's ex-clergymen who had lost his faith, he had resigned his curacy and left his subsequent teaching post at Bedford College on account of his heterodoxy. He now taught English at a school in Weimar, where he enjoyed the patronage of the Grand Duke and Duchess. Carlyle had helped him to the Weimar post. 'I sent this Wilson to the young Duchess of Weimar, at her request, for a grand "Institution" she has been setting up', he told a friend in May 1854, adding, 'he pleases greatly, as I expected'.[94] The other English speaker of note was James Marshall, who acted as secretary to the Grand Duke. Carlyle knew him too, describing him to his mother in 1853 as 'a little black cocknosed Irishman, who thro' many adventures has come to be an Official Gentleman *at Weimar*'.[95] Carlyle smoothed Lewes's path by writing a warm letter of introduction for him on 14 July, a few days before Lewes left for Germany with Marian:

Dear Marshall,
    Mr G. H. Lewes, whom I have long known, and whom everybody here knows as an ingenious brilliant, entertaining, highly gifted and

accomplished man and writer, will deliver you this little Note in Weimar, where he purposes to rest himself among you for certain weeks, or at least give up his heavier labours in favour of lighter and more genial. He has had on hand this long while, and I believe is far advanced in it, a *Life of Goethe*: what that will mean, in reference to his visit to Weimar, I need not suggest to you. I have promised that you will open all reasonable paths to him in those inquiries, and do for him whatso-ever you can in the way of friendly welcome, – which, for his own sake, you will soon find that he well deserves of you. He has a Card of mine for Eckermann [Goethe's erstwhile secretary]; Wilson he already knows: he speaks German, French like a native; has roamed and read in all directions, ancient and modern, grave and gay; and 'has not his tale a-seeking' (as the Scotch say), but on the contrary has it *ready*, in a pertinent and sprightly form, towards any man on almost any subject. Pray be good to him, all of you, while he sojourns in your old city.[96]

Carlyle had not known that Lewes and Marian were going to Germany together with the intention of living as man and wife. He soon found out, along with the rest of literary London – and literary Edinburgh too. Harriet Martineau, in London in mid-September helping Chapman against her brother and Hodgson, heard the news and wrote ungenerously (and inaccu-rately) to her friend Fanny Wedgwood:

Mr Lewes and his elder boys, and Miss E. are living at Weimar, – he writing Göthe's life. My notion is that L. finds it answer well to pick her brains for his own book and his boys' education, and so makes profit and pleasure agree. When will she find that out?[97]

Lewes's three boys were not with the couple; they were to know nothing of their father's relationship with Marian until 1859, when he was able to tell them at the same time that his companion was the author of that year's novel sensation, *Adam Bede*.

Meanwhile, Harriet Martineau ceased to have anything to do with Marian, reacting as she had done to other acquaintances who behaved in ways she disapproved of, including W. J. Fox, who had left his wife in 1834 to live with another woman, and Elizabeth Barrett on the occasion of her elope-ment with Robert Browning in 1846.[98] If she could break off a friendship with Elizabeth Barrett, who was legally married, she would certainly never countenance Marian Evans again, despite having liked her enough to invite her to her home and to make her joint trustee with Atkinson of the Comte fund in 1852. When writing her autobiography a few months after learning of Marian's relationship with Lewes, she made no mention at all of the woman who was so closely associated with the *Westminster Review* Harriet was determined to support, and with the cause of freethinking and free speech she herself so boldly espoused on every subject *except* relations between the sexes.

Lewes's and Marian's friends and acquaintances were agog with the news. Letters were exchanged, curiosity expressed, condemnation and excuses made among a wide circle of mainly reform-minded writers, many of whom feared that the cause of progress would be set back by this free sexual behaviour of two of its adherents. Carlyle, Combe, Chambers, Joseph Parkes, and others had their say, while Chapman and Bray were kept busy defending their friends. The chief source of news about Lewes and Marian was Robert Tait, a Scottish painter and pioneer in photography, who was visiting Weimar at the same time as the couple. A native of Edinburgh, who had moved to London, he was a correspondent of Combe, to whom he wrote on 28 August:

> Mr G. H. Lewis [sic] from London, & Miss Evans, are here at present and intend remaining for some 2 or 3 months longer. I called at their lodgings yesterday, but Mr Lewis was out. Their object, or at least his object, I believe, is to collect materials for a Life of Goethe.[99]

Combe noted on this letter that he answered it on 4 September, but he appears, against his usual practice, not to have kept a copy of this or any of his subsequent letters to Tait on the subject of Marian and Lewes. Tait's letters to him, however, survive. They gradually disclose, in response to Combe's questions, details of the arrangements of his fellow visitors. First he writes on 14 September from Dresden about his time in Weimar and his reaction to Chapman's as yet unresolved problems over the *Westminster*:

> I much enjoyed my visit to Weimar, and made various pleasant excursions with Mr Wilson and Mr Lewis. Miss Evans would have joined in some of these, but she happened then to be much engaged with an article for the Westminster; which she sent away the day I left. I have

been sorry to hear of Chapman's difficulties. I have often thought had his business been really well managed it might have grown into one of the largest & most influential. I have not heard that Miss Evans is a loser, – nor do I think it likely, – that is that she loses any money owing to her.[100]

Tait's next letter to Combe, written on 10 October after his return to London, gives a great deal of information about Lewes and Marian in response to 'your inquiries'. The subjects under discussion may have thought Weimar's two English speakers friendly and disinclined to baulk at their relationship, but Tait tells Combe that Wilson and Marshall were embarrassed by it:

The circumstances in which Miss Evans & Mr Lewes were living in Weimar, certainly excited remark & were the subject of frequent conversations between Mr Wilson & myself; & were the cause of considerable anxiety to Mr Wilson, who, being more a resident than they, would have been naturally disposed to be attentive & friendly with them.[101]

There follows Tait's long account of how he came to meet the couple, together with a verbal map of their lodgings, so that Combe could be in no doubt of the fact, which Tait had carefully deduced from his observation, that Lewes and Marian were living together in intimacy:

Before leaving England Mr Carlyle had told me that Lewes had gone to Weimar, & Mr C. had given him a note of introduction to Mr Marshall, who is attached to the Court there. I had heard, some time before, from Mr Chapman, that Miss Evans intended a visit to Germany; it had also occurred to me that they might have gone together, so when I arrived at Weimar and was told by the Ober Kellner [head waiter] at the Erb Prinz (the Hotel where I took up my abode) that a Mr Lewes & his 'Sister' were in Weimar, and came every day to the table d'hote, I immediately supposed it would be Miss Evans whom the Kellner had mistaken for a 'Sister'. Whether the Ober Kellner had been told that she was sister to Mr L., or had only thought so, I do not know; but I had reason to remark shortly before I left that that was still the impression of the waiter. Mr Lewes & Miss Evans on reaching Weimar had gone to this Hotel; remained there for two days, & then removed to lodgings.[102]

Tait visited these lodgings, at 62a Kaufgasse. He describes the layout of the three rooms:

The day of my leaving I was in two of these rooms; one was Mr L.'s bedroom – the other was their Common Sitting room, – out of which I observed Miss Evans to go by a door which I supposed led into her bedroom. To get to the sitting room it seemed necessary to go through Mr L.'s little bedroom: at least I was taken that way . . . and so was Mr Wilson on the occasion of the only visit he made to them. Mr Wilson's impression was there was no other way into the sitting room, or even to Miss E.'s bedroom beyond, than through Mr L.'s room.[103]

The only conclusion to be drawn from this is the one Tait draws:

The circumstances certainly are suspicious, as I cannot but feel; and though my impression of the character of the parties is not such as to counterbalance altogether the nature of the circumstances, yet I cannot entertain any other thought than that Mr Lewes will return before long to his wife & 6 children, to whom I have heard him express much attachment.[104]

The three youngest of the six children, as Tait soon learned from Carlyle, had been fathered not by Lewes, but by Thornton Hunt.

The letter finishes with a remark about the circumstances being particularly 'injudicious' of, and 'injurious' to, Marian, and a plea to Combe not to 'mention my name unnecessarily in connection with this subject', as it would be 'a hateful thing to be suspected of being a scandalmonger', and 'from my having been lately in Weimar I would be readily liable to suspicion in this case'.

For his part, Combe was already in correspondence with Marian's friends, trying to find out the truth. Cara Bray wrote defensively to Combe's wife on 23 September, saying she had 'not heard of anything dreadful happening to Miss Evans', but conceding that her friend had travelled to Weimar with Lewes.[105] Chapman replied non-committally on 4 October to an inquiry from

Combe that 'Mr Lewes and Miss Evans certainly went to the Continent together', he to collect materials for his biography of Goethe.[106] Four days later Bray was assuring Combe that Marian had not taken Lewes away from his family: 'I have heard that Mr and Mrs Lewes have not been man and wife to each other for some years.' He balanced on a knife-edge between seeming actively to support his friends' unconventional behaviour and condemning it, thus avoiding hypocrisy – just: 'Nothing that I have yet heard or know will make any difference to my conduct towards her, although I may regret what she has done as imprudent and as laying herself open to evil report.'[107]

Combe was not to be appeased. He was utterly confounded by this example of behaviour he viewed as immoral from the woman he so admired intellectually. She had been the chief reason for his keeping faith with Chapman and the *Westminster Review*; she had been a pampered guest in his house. His phrenological analysis of her as the possessor of a large organ of Conscientiousness had, he now believed, been proved wrong. 'We are deeply mortified and distressed', he told Bray on 15 November. With a last effort to explain behaviour so out of keeping with his sense of her, he added: 'I should like to know whether there is insanity in Miss Evans's family; for her conduct, with *her* brain, seems to me like morbid mental aberration.'[108] Like Harriet Martineau, Combe never addressed another word to Marian Evans. (His awareness of Bray's mistress and his children by her – a secret confided to him by Bray himself in September 1851 – did not prevent Combe from corresponding with, or visiting, Bray.[109])

Carlyle, who knew about Marian's role in the editing of the *Westminster Review*, though he had not met her, was also shocked, but he did not completely cut off relations with Lewes, whom he had known and liked for many years. Like all the others, he was inclined to blame Marian more than Lewes; indeed he thought Lewes justified in leaving Agnes after she had given birth to three children by Hunt between 1850 and 1853. But he could not condone the liaison, which was to him an undesirable sign of the times. He wrote with characteristic vehemence to his brother John on 2 November:

Lewes . . . has not only gone to Weimar, but is understood to have a 'strong-minded woman' with him there, and has certainly cast away his Wife here, – who indeed deserved it of him, having openly produced those dirty sooty skinned children which had Th[ornto]n Hunt for father, . . . Lewes to pay the whole account, even the money part of it! – Such are our sublime George-Sand Philosophies teaching by experience. Everlasting peace to them and theirs, – in the Cesspool, which is their home.[110]

Like Combe, Carlyle heard all about the Weimar arrangements from Tait, who had taken a number of photographs of Carlyle, his wife, his dog, his house, and his garden in July, and was now, in November, visiting Cheyne Row frequently to paint Carlyle's portrait, which he was to exhibit at the Royal Academy in 1856.[111] Tait now learned from Carlyle about Agnes Lewes's liaison with Hunt, and Carlyle learned from Tait about Lewes's new relationship with Marian. As Tait reported to Combe on 15 October, Carlyle had asked him when writing to Wilson or Marshall in Weimar to say that if he had known that

Miss Evans was going with Mr Lewes, not *a word* of introduction of any kind would he have ever given him; though at the same time, he was ready to bear testimony to his belief, that, in spite of these absurdities and immoralities, Lewes was a kindly, well-meaning, & veracious man in the main.[112]

Since the Carlyles had never met Marian, they were not required, as Combe was, to decide whether to keep or drop her acquaintance. They simply chose not to get to know her, but continued to be friendly towards Lewes; indeed Carlyle saw the *Life of Goethe* through the press for Lewes the following summer, and allowed it to be dedicated to him.[113]

The affair was interesting enough to observers on a personal level. Everyone feared for Marian's reputation; those who knew about Lewes's open marriage thought he would soon abandon her. Even Chapman stooped to declare to Robert Chambers that he hoped Lewes would 'prove constant to her; otherwise she is *utterly* lost'.[114] Joseph Parkes, whose daughter Bessie defied him by writing friendly letters to Marian in Weimar, assured her that Lewes would 'abandon Miss Evans as he had done his wife and others'.[115] Parkes was also among those progressives who saw the scandal as likely to do damage to their political cause. 'I was in a mixed *Literary* party last night', he told Bessie on 14 October, where everyone was speaking of the matter in some way – as almost insane on her part, & in respect to both as an injurious stigma on their general Liberalism; & socially odious. I cannot marvel. Indeed some of the set are without any principle – social or religious.[116]

It was unfortunate that the Lewes-Marian Evans affair should coincide with Chapman's struggles to keep the *Westminster* and the decision by some of his contributors to break away. Parkes, himself a Unitarian, drew the understandable but inaccurate conclusion that the Weimar business was in part responsible for the withdrawal of Martineau and his friends: 'By this event partly, & Chapman's [financial] embarrassment, the Writing Corps are sep-arating.'[117] Combe, who knew the whole story of the *Westminster* split and was therefore under no illusion that Marian and Lewes had anything to do with it, nevertheless saw that others would be likely to make a connection and that the orthodox would gladly seize on this example of behaviour by two unbelievers to suggest that faith was the only guarantee of morality. He told Bray on 15 November: 'T. Hunt, Lewes, and Miss Evans have, in my opinion, by their practical conduct, inflicted a great injury on the cause of religious freedom.'[118]

Bray was provoked into using some weasel words in reply. 'I quite agree with you in every word', he wrote. 'The cause of religious freedom has suffered lately in more ways than one – this scandal – Chapman's failure etc. Still a cause is not to be judged by its professors.' He went on, with almost comic earnestness (if indeed no irony was intended), to urge Combe to action:

> We want a good book or article on the subject of marriage and divorce. Could not you write one for the Westminster? *It would do great good just now.* Treat it physiologically, phrenologically, morally, socially, practically.[119]

Combe did not rise to this particular challenge.

Tait too commented to Combe on 22 October on the wider implications of the love affair:

> I look on these immoralities of professed liberals exactly in the same light in which you exhibit them: in my note to Mr Wilson I remarked

that one of the worst results of these gross irregularities (sh[oul]d they
be confirmed) would be that the orthodox would point to them as
illustrations of the tendencies of Westminster reviewing and 'enlightened liberalism'![120]

In all the surviving discussion of the affair, the focus is on Marian's immorality
and recklessness and on Lewes's open marriage, which was quite widely known
about, since he and Agnes had made no effort to hide it. Did Chapman and
Bray, with their own 'irregular' arrangements, feel a twinge of guilt at joining
in the high moral tone of the debate? Probably very few people knew about
Bray's mistress and children, as he kept them separate from his home life;
Combe's knowledge did not prevent him from talking in disapproving terms
of Marian and Lewes in his letters to Bray and expecting Bray's full agreement in reply. As for Chapman, though his difficult relationship with his
wife and his intimacy with Elisabeth Tilley were known to Marian, and therefore to the Brays and Lewes, very few of his other acquaintances seem to
have known. Elizabeth Malleson did, as we have seen, but William Hale
White, though living at 142 Strand, did not. A number of respectable and
religious people – Crabb Robinson, the Martineaus, Newman, and others –
might not have consorted with Chapman, supported him, and written for
him if they had had an inkling of his liberal practice in sexual matters,
though, as Hale White remembered, he made no secret of his *theory* that
marriage should be dissoluble if either partner became dissatisfied.

There remains a mystery about precisely how many people did notice
Chapman's domestic arrangements. His importance to progressives as a
publisher and editor may have outweighed their disapproval if they did know,
and so kept them silent on the subject. Nonetheless, it is striking that in all
the talk about Marian and Lewes in 1854, no surviving comment links their
behaviour to Chapman's or uses his irregular sexual relations as an example
of the dangers of radicalism and religious unorthodoxy. Only Joseph Parkes,
himself an unfaithful husband, it seems, hinted darkly in his letters to Bessie
that 'some of Mr Lewes's Colleagues or allies are no better than himself; &
my knowledge of them has made me very shy of their society'.[121]

Fortunately the two subjects of all this talk and correspondence were
spared hearing and reading it, though they were nervous about the inevitable
gossip; Marian worried about the reaction of her female friends and Lewes
knew that he was liable to be accused of abandoning his family. Marian's

rather reticent journal records on 11 October, 'A painful letter from London caused us both a bad night.'[122] The following day Lewes wrote to Carlyle, explaining that his marriage had long been over and that he was now separated from Agnes, though continuing to support her and the children (including those whose father was Thornton Hunt, as Carlyle noted). He did not at this stage volunteer any information about his relationship with Marian, but was obliged to do so on 19 October, after receiving a friendly letter full of 'noble sympathy' from Carlyle, endorsing the separation but wanting to know if certain rumours about his companion in Weimar were true.[123]

Lewes wrote joyfully, telling Carlyle what a 'delightful shock' he had felt on receiving the letter:

> I sat at your feet when my mind was first awakening; I have honoured and loved you ever since both as teacher and friend, and *now* to find that you judge me rightly, and are not estranged by what has estranged so many from me, gives me strength to bear what yet must be borne![124]

He went on to explain that his separation from Agnes was not caused by Marian, but he did not deny the liaison, though he declined to discuss it. Carlyle noted regretfully: 'No answer to this second letter.'[125]

Early in November Lewes and Marian moved to Berlin to spend the winter there. Before leaving Marian wrote to Bray naming him and Chapman as her two confidants and asking him to try to prevent inaccuracies becoming fixed in the minds of the *Westminster* circle:

> You know I am already suffering from imaginary words attributed to me, and I need not tell you that any real ones would soon get twisted and exaggerated, and be bandied about from Edinburgh to London. I decline to make *any direct* communication to *any* person about my private affairs except to yourself and those who are one with you, and to Mr Chapman. You know the truth about me, and I only ask of your friendship that you will state as much of it as you think proper to those who have any sincere interest in me.[126]

She was grateful to Chapman for giving her work for the *Westminster*; from October 1854 to January 1857 no number of the journal appeared without a substantial article by her, as well as some excellent critical round-ups of recent literature in the 'Contemporary Literature' section, which Jane Sinnett had now vacated. In losing his co-editor, Chapman had gained his best contributor. With Huxley and Tyndall doing the science section, Pattison and H. B. Wilson the philosophy and theology round-up, and Harriet Martineau, Froude, Newman, W. B. Donne (on politics and classical literature), and occasionally Lewes writing full-length articles alongside Marian, the *Westminster Review* in 1855 showed that it had survived the split in its ranks and was, if anything, stronger than ever. 'Martineau's Anti-Chapman', as Carlyle christened the *National Review* on its debut in July, could not compete.[127]

Indeed, Chapman had somehow achieved the distinct coup of getting an article from Carlyle himself for the January 1855 number. Though deep in researching and writing his multi-volume history of Frederick the Great and refusing all requests, he agreed to write a piece for Chapman on an obscure episode in German history he had come across in the course of his work. The article, 'The Prinzenraub: A Glimpse of Saxon History', begins in the characteristically robust and personal style of the famous historian of the French Revolution:

> Over seas in Saxony, in the month of July 1455, a notable thing befell; and this in regard to two persons who have themselves, by accident, become notable. Concerning which we are now to say something, with the reader's permission. Unluckily, few English readers ever heard of the event; and it is probable there is but one English reader or writer (the present reviewer, for his sins) that was ever driven or led to inquire into it: so that it is quite wild soil, very rough for the ploughshare; neither can the harvest well be considerable. 'English readers are so deeply ignorant of foreign history, especially of German history!' exclaims a learned professor. Alas, yes; English readers are dreadfully ignorant of many things, indeed of most things; – which is a lamentable circumstance, and ought to be amended by degrees.
>
> But, however all this may be, there is somewhat in relation to that Saxon business, called the *Prinzenraub*, or Stealing of the Princes, and to the other 'pearls of memory' (do not call them old buttons of memory!) which string themselves upon the thread of that. Beating about in those dismal haunted wildernesses; painfully sorting and sifting

in the historical lumber-rooms and their dusty fusty imbroglios, in quest of far other objects, – this is what we have picked-up on that accidental matter. To which the reader, if he can make any use of it, has our welcome and our blessing.[128]

Since absolutely no one but Carlyle could have written this, the customary anonymity of the *Westminster* reviewer was redundant in this case, which was all the better for Chapman and the *Review*. As Bray commented to Combe on 7 January, when chewing over the whole story of the split once more, this contribution from Carlyle was 'worth 50 James Martineaus or Dr Hodgsons'. 'Chapman', he added, 'in my opinion has conducted the Review better than it had ever been conducted before'.[129] This was nothing less than the truth. The *Westminster Review*, now safe from takeover, went from strength to strength, as did Chapman in the aftermath of the split and of the removal from 142 Strand. Several changes had occurred during the dramatic events of 1854, but the spirit of 142 Strand lived on in Chapman and his circle, particularly in his relations, personal and professional, with a number of 'strong-minded women'.

7

Chapman's Radical Women

The dynamics of Chapman's relationship with Marian Evans had changed from the early days in 1851, when Marian, awkward and insecure, had fallen unrequitedly in love with Chapman and was obliged to accept a platonic friendship in order to fulfil her agreed role as his assistant on the soon-to-be-purchased *Westminster Review*. Gradually during her time at 142 Strand she became in many ways the dominant partner; her intelligence, tact, and conscientiousness worked wonders with Chapman's supporters and contributors, most notably Combe. Her confidence grew as she advised and occasionally even lectured Chapman about his dealings with writers. He recognised her talents and often followed her editorial advice. Now that she was the object of scandal, the balance changed somewhat. She relied on his good offices on her behalf while she was in Germany, and she appreciated his offer of regular employment on the *Westminster Review*. With themselves and Lewes's wife and family to keep, both she and Lewes needed to earn as much as they could by writing for periodicals.

Gratitude for his personal support and recognition of her dependence on the *Westminster Review* for income combined to make her write warmly and respectfully to Chapman from Weimar and Berlin. Having sent off her first full-length article, 'Woman in France: Madame de Sablé', for the October 1854 number, she became anxious and depressed when Chapman failed to reply with thanks and praise. She confided to Sara Hennell in a letter written on 22 November, her thirty-fifth birthday, her fear that Chapman did not like the article, 'as he has said no word of satisfaction about it'; even more worryingly, 'though he had been urgent on me to write for the Review before, he has made no proposition to that effect since'. [1] Chapman was presumably so bound up in the fight to keep the *Westminster* that he found no time to write immediately, but by 7 December Marian had received another letter from him, and was soon corresponding about her next contribution, an account of a book on the court of Austria by Karl Vehse which appeared in the April 1855 number.[2]

It was a slightly stuttering start to her new role as significant contributor to the *Review*, though the first article, on Madame de Sablé, attracted some praise. Sara Hennell, painfully adjusting to the new situation, and confessing to Marian on 15 November that she had 'a strange sort of feeling that I am writing to some one in a book', expressed her admiration of the article's 'elegance and profundity'.[3] Henry Crabb Robinson, not yet aware of either the author's identity or her situation, wrote in his diary on 14 October that he was reading 'a charming Art[icle] on the French female *literary character* – Acute, entertain[in]g & yet wise'.[4]

The article gives a picture of Madame de Sablé's correspondence and table talk with Parisian politicians and intellectuals such as Pascal and La Rochefoucauld. It also makes a plea for nineteenth-century British women to be 'admitted to a common fund of ideas' as seventeenth-century aristocratic Frenchwomen were, while acknowledging that the social conditions under which Madame de Sablé lived were far from being a model:

> No wise person, we imagine, wishes to restore the social condition of France in the seventeenth century, or considers the ideal programme of woman's life to be a *mariage de convenance* at fifteen, a career of gallantry from twenty to eight-and-thirty, and penitence and piety for the rest of her days. Nevertheless, that social condition had its good results, as much as the madly-superstitious Crusades had theirs.[5]

In July 1855 the literature round-up has a very different look from the usual mediocrity of the long-serving Jane Sinnett's contributions. Marian has taken over the section, which positively sparkles with her trenchant criticisms of recent fiction. Of Charles Kingsley's *Westward Ho!* she writes:

Mr Kingsley, unhappily, like so many other gifted men, has two steeds – his Pegasus and his hobby: the one he rides with a graceful *abandon*, to the admiration of all beholders; but no sooner does he get astride the other, than he becomes a feeble imitator of Carlyle's *manège*, and attempts to put his wooden toy to all the wonderful paces of the great Scotchman's fiery Tartar horse. This imitation is probably not a conscious one, but arises simply from the fact, that Mr Kingsley's impetuosity and Boanerges' vein give him an affinity for Carlyle's faults – his one-sided judgment of character and his undiscriminating fulminations against the men of the present as tried by some imaginary standard in the past. Carlyle's great merits Mr Kingsley's powers are not fitted to achieve; his genius lies in another direction. He has not that piercing insight which every now and then flashes to the depth of things, and alternating as it does with the most obstinate one-sidedness, makes Carlyle a wonderful paradox of wisdom and wilfulness; . . . still less has he the rich humour, the keen satire, and the tremendous word-missiles, which Carlyle hurls about as Milton's angels hurl the rocks. But Mr Kingsley *can* scold; he *can* select one character for unmixed eulogy and another for unmitigated vituperation; he *can* undertake to depict a past age and try to make out that it was the pattern of all heroisms now utterly extinct; . . . he *can* call his own opinion God, and the opposite opinion the Devil.[6]

Her chief quarrel is with Kingsley's narrow-minded anti-Catholic bias in this story set in Elizabethan England, but she also throws in with gusto an accusation that he has copied the denouement of *Jane Eyre*, and thinks his comic characters poor imitations of Walter Scott's.[7] She seems to have found in Kingsley an example of how not to do it when writing fiction.

Marian's confidence as a writer grew as she wrote her anonymous contributions for the *Westminster*. The relationship with Lewes brought her not only emotional happiness and congenial companionship but also the steady praise of a clever, experienced writer who recognised and generously encouraged his partner's literary talent. This was invaluable at a time when Marian had many social trials to endure. On their return from Berlin in March 1855, she spent six weeks of anxiety and loneliness in a boarding house in Dover while Lewes returned to London to see Agnes and his children and make arrangements for their financial and educational future. Marian worked at her Spinoza translation and took walks when the weather permitted, but her diary is full of references to headaches and depression, particularly after she had received a 'painful letter which upset me for work' on 9 April.[8] When she wrote to Bessie Rayner Parkes, she enclosed her notes in letters addressed to Chapman, knowing that Bessie's parents disapproved of their daughter's correspondence with her.[9]

On 18 April Marian came to London to join Lewes, first in lodgings in Bayswater, and a week later in more permanent lodgings in East Sheen, 'a charming village close to Richmond Park', south-east of London. Chapman was among the first to call on them, followed by Rufa Hennell. Marian made sure to tell Charles Bray about this visit by a respectable woman to a couple considered by many to have become social outcasts, though the predominant pattern of behaviour was for their acquaintances either to shun them both or to avoid visiting them while inviting Lewes, but not Marian, to their homes. 'Mrs Hennell called on me the other day, very kindly and nobly', Marian told Bray on 1 May. 'I respect her for it.'[10]

To Marian's delight Charles Bray came to see her and Lewes while he was in London in July. The visit was hardly an unqualified success. Bray did not like Lewes and resented his scepticism – even scorn – about phrenology as expressed in some trenchant *Leader* articles in the early 1850s. Marian's letter to Bray of 16 July indicates that the two men had argued on the subject when they met in East Sheen a few days earlier. She defends her partner against misunderstanding, and allows herself a dig at Combe, whom she knew to have expressed 'petty and absurd views about the effect on his reputation of having introduced me to one or two of his friends'.[11] Bray has apparently accused her of being influenced by Lewes's views into rejecting phrenology altogether. She responds vigorously: 'Mr Lewes begs me to say that he never meant to deny that size was a measure of power, *all other things being equal*, but simply to deny that size is an *absolute* measure of power.'[12]

Two of her female friends, Bessie Rayner Parkes and Barbara Leigh Smith, were determined to show their sisterly solidarity by writing to her. Bessie had to be warned not to address letters to 'Miss Evans', but to enclose them in envelopes addressed to Lewes, in order not to arouse the suspicion of their landlady, who had presumably been told that Marian was 'Mrs Lewes'.[13] It would be some time before Sara and Cara decided they could visit or invite their friend; the latter had even stopped writing to Marian while she was in Berlin. After a new overture from Cara in September

1855, Marian responded with an assurance of her unchanged feelings of friendship, adding some proud words about her relationship with Lewes and her sense of the injustice and in many cases hypocrisy of those who criticised and ostracised her:

> If we differ on the subject of the marriage laws, I at least can believe of you that you cleave to what you believe to be good, and I don't know of anything in the nature of your views that should prevent you from believing the same of me. *How far* we differ I think we neither of us know; for I am ignorant of your precise views and apparently you attribute to me both feelings and opinions which are not mine. We cannot set each other quite right on this matter in letters, but one thing I can tell you in few words. Light and easily broken ties are what I neither desire theoretically nor could live for practically. Women who are satisfied with such ties do *not* act as I have done – they obtain what they desire and are still invited to dinner.[14]

During the summer of 1855, while Lewes finished his *Life of Goethe*, which was to be published to general interest and acclaim in November, Marian worked at an article for the October *Westminster* which was to establish her literary credentials once and for all, while also offering a masterly analysis of the poor logic and intolerant ethics of a brand of evangelicalism currently making headlines in the form of influential sermons and books by the Scottish preacher Dr John Cumming. As if in unconscious preparation for this trenchant, witty essay, she practised her well-trained editorial skills on Chapman, who had sunk once more into bloated rhetoric in the first draft of an article he was writing for the same number, 'The Position of Woman in Barbarism and among the Ancients'.

Chapman's topic, though concerning the distant past in foreign countries – Greece, Rome, the Middle East, and China – was of close interest to both Chapman and Marian, given their personal circumstances and shared progressive views. In the published article Chapman discusses the practice of polygamy for men in some societies, the buying and selling of women among the ancient Hebrews, and the marriage and divorce opportunities for men – but not women – in ancient Greece and Egypt. Rallying cries for the liberalisation of the divorce laws in England and the right of women to keep their own property on marriage break through from time to time, as we might expect. In turning to consider the situation in ancient Rome, Chapman comments meaningfully on the Romans as

> a people among whom Woman finally rose to a position of respect and dignity which has never been surpassed, and acquired a legal recognition of her rights both of person and property; – a recognition still withheld from the women of England, even in the nineteenth century.[15]

The article ends with the hope that 'even England, the most persistent conservator of the feudal system, will ere long be so far inspired by the spirit of the Roman legislators as to adopt from them what may seem suitable to the genius and needs of her people'.[16] Chapman's aim was to add to the debate on the English divorce laws which had been given a boost by the establishment of a Royal Inquiry in 1853. He seized the opportunity to follow up with another article in the *Westminster* in April 1856, 'The English Law of Divorce', in which he scrutinises the first report by the commissioners to the inquiry, a stepping stone on the way to the passing of the Matrimonial Causes act of 1857.[17] The Act made divorce less complicated and expensive to attain and was a first step towards allowing women to plead for divorce on the same grounds as men, though full equality was not yet granted them. (Nor did the law allow Lewes to divorce Agnes and marry Marian.)

The two articles, as finally published, are among Chapman's best pieces of writing. Despite his personal interest in promoting radical change, he confines himself largely to a factual account of his subject, quoting from a wide range of acknowledged experts, such as James Mill on the condition of Hindu women and George Grote on Greece in the first article, and reports of divorce cases and legal findings in the second. He had clearly heeded many of Marian's criticisms of 'The Position of Woman', which she read in draft in June 1855, commenting extensively and forcefully in a letter in which she resumed her old role as adviser. She praised his grasp of detail and ability to give a clear account of factual evidence, qualities which had been evident in 'The Commerce of Literature', his admirable article setting off the fight with the Booksellers' Association in 1852. Marian begins her critical remarks of the draft with this strength – 'a decided faculty for *digesting facts* as evidence' – before turning to his weaknesses. 'Whenever you pass from narrative to dissertation', she writes, 'certain old faults reappear – inexactness of expression, triads and duads of verbs and adjectives, mixed metaphors and a sort of watery volume that requires to be reduced by evaporation'.[18]

A lesson in correct English follows. Marian does not spare her friend, having decided, she says, that he would prefer her to write 'as unceremoniously as I used to do in the old days'. She attacks those passages in which Chapman has aspired to fine writing while actually falling into cliché and wordiness:

> I have a logical objection to the phrases 'it *would* seem', 'it *would* appear', 'we *would* remark'. Would – under what condition? The real meaning is – it *does* seem, it *does* appear, we *do* remark. These phrases are rarely found in good writers, and *ought* never to be found.
>
> 'Suffice it to say' is the peculiar property of hack writers. Don't infringe on their domain . . .
>
> 'Progressive improvement' (2d page of manuscript) is a questionable phrase. You mean *gradual* improvement. To 'emerge from a catalepsy' is also questionable . . . 'Stepping stones' cannot be 'forged into fetters'.
>
> Your sentences would often be much improved by being broken up. That plan of linking propositions together into unvarying, long sentences gives your style a tough, gutta percha sort of consistency. It should be more brittle – as most clear and bright things are.[19]

In relation to the argument of the piece, she points out some chronological confusion in a passage about feudalism and suggests a few things to improve what Chapman himself has called a 'meagre' account of Greece. In spite of these faults, however, 'the article is very interesting and able'.[20] Chapman was dashed by her criticisms; that he took them to heart is shown by the changes he made before publishing the piece. Two days after this critical letter Marian wrote again, assuring him that the article was 'worth publishing', but stating as kindly as possible that, with all his merits, he was not a good writer:

> There is no reason for you to be desponding about your writing. You have made immense progress during the last few years, and you have so much force of mind and sincerity of purpose that you may work your way to a style which is free from vices, though perhaps you will never attain felicity – indeed, that is a free gift of Nature rather than

a reward of labour. You have plenty of *thoughts*, and what you have to aim at is the simple, clear expression of those thoughts, dismissing from your mind all efforts after any other qualities than precision and force.[21]

Marian's own article, 'Evangelical Teaching: Dr Cumming', follows immediately after Chapman's in the October *Westminster Review*. It begins with a sustained paragraph of wit, allusion, and carefully weighted comparisons, as if in practical illustration of the critical creed she had enunciated in response to Chapman's writing. Only someone who combined a gift for linguistic cleverness with a thorough acquaintance with religious fervour, Bible knowledge, and a reading and understanding of English, French, and German works of scholarship could have written so:

> Given, a man with moderate intellect, a moral standard not higher than the average, some rhetorical affluence and great glibness of speech, what is the career in which, without the aid of birth or money, he may most easily attain power and reputation in English society? Where is that Goschen of mediocrity in which a smattering of science and learning will pass for profound instruction, where platitudes will be accepted as wisdom, bigoted narrowness as holy zeal, unctuous egoism as God-given piety? Let such a man become an evangelical preacher; he will then find it possible to reconcile small ability with great ambition, superficial knowledge with the prestige of erudition, a middling morale with a high reputation for sanctity . . .
>
> Let him preach less of Christ than of Anti-christ; let him be less definite in showing what sin is than in showing who is the Man of Sin, less expansive on the blessedness of faith than on the accursedness of infidelity . . . In this way he will draw men to him by the strong cords of their passions, made reason-proof by being baptized with the name of piety. In this way he may gain a metropolitan pulpit; the avenues to his church will be as crowded as the passages to the opera; he has but to print his prophetic sermons and bind them in lilac and gold, and they will adorn the drawing-room table of all evangelical ladies, who will regard as a sort of pious 'light reading' the demonstration that the prophecy of the locusts whose sting is in their tail is fulfilled in the fact of the Turkish commander's having taken a horse's

tail for his standard, and that the French are the very frogs predicted in the Revelations.[22]

Just such a popular preacher is Dr Cumming, minister of the Scottish National Church in Covent Garden and author of such works as *Prophetic Studies* (1850) and *The Finger of God* (1853). Marian deplores his bigotry and ignorance, his assumption that all religious sceptics are necessarily immoral:

> The only type of 'infidel' whose existence Dr Cumming recognizes is the fossil personage who 'calls the Bible a lie and a forgery'. He seems to be ignorant – or he chooses to ignore the fact – that there is a large body of eminently instructed and earnest men who regard the Hebrew and Christian Scriptures as a series of historical documents, to be dealt with according to the rules of historical criticism, and that an equally large number of men, who are not historical critics, find the dogmatic scheme built on the letter of the Scriptures opposed to their profoundest moral convictions.[23]

Not only does Cumming ignore the historical and philosophical arguments of those writers whose works Marian Evans knew so intimately – Strauss, Feuerbach, and Spinoza – but his narrow creed encourages hatred and exclusiveness. According to Cumming's beliefs, 'a wife', she writes, 'is not to devote herself to her husband out of love to him and a sense of the duties implied by a close relation – she is to be a faithful wife for the glory of God'. Marian's principled unorthodoxy can claim to be more natural and human than Cumming's brand of orthodoxy:

> Happily, the constitution of human nature forbids the complete prevalence of such a theory. Fatally powerful as religious systems have been, human nature is stronger and wider than religious systems, and though dogmas may hamper, they cannot absolutely repress its growth: build walls round the living tree as you will, the bricks and mortar have by and by to give way before the slow and sure operation of the sap.[24]

Charles Bray wrote on 13 October to say that he and his friends and family had read the article and knew it was hers. 'No-one else *could* do it, altho' I sh[oul]d be pleased to think that we had another person who could do it.'[25]

238

Marian replied acknowledging authorship, but asking Bray to keep the secret. The article 'appears to have made an impression', she wrote. She had been asked by one correspondent to print it as a separate pamphlet 'for the good of mankind in general', but was keenly aware that if it were known that the author was a woman, its impact would be 'a little counteracted'. She added here a short sentence which has since been deleted, probably by John Cross after her death.[26] We may suppose it to refer to her relationship with Lewes, which would certainly put the author of the article into the category she so successfully demolished in its pages, namely that of immoral infidel, in the minds of many readers.

Marian was paid £15 for 'Evangelical Teaching'.[27] It was money well spent, as Chapman appreciated. During 1856 she published three long articles – 'German Wit: Heinrich Heine' (January), 'The Natural History of German Life' (July), and 'Silly Novels by Lady Novelists' (October) – as well as the regular round-ups of recent literature, in which she briefly reviewed, among other things, Browning's *Men and Women* and the third volume of Ruskin's *Modern Painters*.

'The Natural History of German Life', a review of two books on German social history by Wilhelm Heinrich von Riehl, ranges widely on the subject of class relations in various European societies. It also tackles the question of realism in art, taking to task 'our social novels', including those by Dickens, for their unrealistic presentation of the poor. 'The greatest benefit we owe to the artist, whether painter, poet, or novelist', she writes in a passage which came to have resonance in relation to her own novelistic practice, 'is the extension of our sympathies':

> Art is the nearest thing to life; it is a mode of amplifying experience and extending our contact with our fellow-men beyond the bounds of our personal lot. All the more sacred is the task of the artist when he undertakes to paint the life of the People.[28]

This was the critical ideal which informed her novel writing, from the 'Dutch realism' of the portrait of rural life in late eighteenth-century England in *Adam Bede* to the sympathetic understanding of the selfish egotist Casaubon and the uneasy religious hypocrite Bulstrode in *Middlemarch* and the representation of Jewish life and beliefs in *Daniel Deronda*. Marian's dislike of narrow evangelicalism, expressed in the article on Cumming, combined with her ever-sharpening ideas about why and where novelists went wrong in her last article of 1856, the very funny 'Silly Novels by Lady Novelists'. The idea for the article came from her reading a recent novel, *Compensation*, by Lady Chatterton. She noted in a letter to Chapman on 5 July 1856 that she had 'long wanted to fire away at the doctrine of Compensation, which I detest, considered as a theory of life'.[29] It was a subject she had dealt with briefly in her *Westminster* round-up for July 1855, where she had followed her filleting of *Westward Ho!* with a notice of *Constance Herbert*, by Jane Carlyle's friend Geraldine Jewsbury. This novel overtly illustrates the principle that nothing renounced 'for the sake of a higher principle' will prove 'to have been worth the keeping' by telling the story of three women who renounce their lovers out of moral duty, only to find, as Marian says, that the lovers were 'extremely "good-for-nothing" and that they (the ladies) have had an excellent riddance'. Renunciation, on this plan, would 'cease to be moral heroism, and would simply be a calculation of prudence', she concludes.[30]

On 20 July 1856 she offered Chapman an article on 'Silly Women's Novels', which she thought 'might be made the vehicle of some wholesome truth as well as of some amusement'.[31] In this article she is scathing about a number of novels by women, grouping individual examples into types or species, but does not commit an act of treachery against her sister writers in general. She is careful to explain that her criticisms do not undermine the role of novelist for women; on the contrary, she mentions Charlotte Brontë, Elizabeth Gaskell, Harriet Beecher Stowe, and Harriet Martineau as living women who have written fine novels. Her aim is taken squarely at bad novels, and her main objections, as in her other recent articles, are to confused or hypocritical moral doctrines and a lack of realism in fiction.

Like 'Evangelical Teaching', the article opens strikingly:

Silly novels by Lady Novelists are a genus with many species, determined by the particular quality of silliness that predominates in them – the frothy, the prosy, the pious, or the pedantic. But it is a mixture of all these – a composite order of feminine fatuity, that produces the largest class of such novels, which we shall distinguish as the *mind-and-millinery* species. The heroine is usually an heiress, probably a peeress in her own right, with perhaps a vicious baronet, an amiable duke, and an irresistible younger son of a marquis as lovers in the foreground, a

240

clergyman and a poet sighing for her in the middle distance, and a crowd of undefined adorers dimly indicated beyond. Her eyes and her wit are both dazzling; her nose and her morals are alike free from any tendency to irregularity; she has a superb *contralto* and a superb intellect; she is perfectly well-dressed and perfectly religious; she dances like a sylph, and reads the Bible in the original tongues . . . In her recorded conversations she is amazingly eloquent, and in her unrecorded conversations, amazingly witty. She is understood to have a depth of insight that looks through and through the shallow theories of philosophers, and her superior instincts are a sort of dial by which men have only to set their clocks and watches, and all will go well.[32]

Lady Chatterton's *Compensation* belongs to this mind-and-millinery species; in it a child of four and a half talks, as Marian says, 'in Ossianic fashion', telling his frowning grandmother that her forehead is 'like Loch Lomond, when the wind is blowing and the sun is gone in' and other such nonsense. 'We are not surprised to learn', she continues, that 'the mother of this infant phenomenon' is 'herself a phoenix'. As adept at Greek and Hebrew as she is at dancing, she is 'a polking polyglot, a Creuzer [a German writer on ancient religions] in crinoline'.[33]

Another species is 'the *oracular*', consisting of novels 'intended to expound the writer's religious, philosophical, or moral theories'. Too often, however, the authors are themselves ignorant in these fields:

To judge from their writings, there are certain ladies who think that an amazing ignorance, both of science and of life, is the best possible qualification for forming an opinion on the knottiest moral and speculative questions. Apparently, their recipe for solving all such difficulties is something like this: Take a woman's head, stuff it with a smattering of philosophy and literature chopped small, and with false notions of society baked hard, let it hang over a desk a few hours every day, and serve up hot in feeble English, when not required.[34]

Finally, whereas the oracular type is 'generally inspired by some form of High Church, or transcendental Christianity', the final type, 'the *white neck-cloth* species', represents 'the tone of thought and feeling in the Evangelical party':

241

This species is a kind of genteel tract on a large scale, intended as a sort of medicinal sweetmeat for Low Church young ladies; an Evangelical substitute for the fashionable novel, as the May Meetings are a substitute for the Opera.[35]

Such novels are just as likely to be silly, ignorant, and pretentious as their High Church counterparts. Most of these stories are set among the upper or middle class, whereas in real life many evangelicals belong to the lower classes. The amused and scathing critic here becomes an advocate of a more truthful kind of fiction:

The real drama of Evangelicalism – and it has abundance of fine drama for any one who has genius enough to discern and reproduce it – lies among the middle and lower classes ... Why then, cannot our Evangelical lady novelists show us the operation of their religious views among people (there really are many such in the world) who keep no carriage, 'not so much as a brassbound gig', who even manage to eat their dinner without a silver fork, and in whose mouths the authoress's questionable English would be strictly consistent?[36]

Marian acknowledges that women can write, and have written, good novels, using the experience peculiar to their gender to proper effect. She then sums up the talents required by either gender, making a checklist against which she was soon to measure her own first efforts at fiction:

No educational restrictions can shut women out from the materials of fiction, and there is no species of art which is so free from rigid requirements. Like crystalline masses, it may take any form, and yet be beautiful; we have only to pour in the right elements – genuine observation, humour, and passion. But it is precisely this absence of rigid requirement which constitutes the fatal seduction of novel-writing to incompetent women. Ladies are not wont to be very grossly deceived as to their power of playing on the piano; here certain positive difficulties of execution have to be conquered, and incompetence inevitably breaks down. Every art which has its absolute *technique* is, to a certain extent, guarded from the intrusions of mere left-handed imbecility. But in novelwriting there are no barriers for incapacity to stumble against, no external criteria to prevent a writer from mistaking foolish facility for mastery. And so we have again and again the old story of La Fontaine's ass, who puts his nose to the flute, and, finding that he elicits some sound, exclaims, 'Moi, aussi, je joue de la flute'; – a fable which we commend, at parting, to the consideration of any feminine reader who is in danger of adding to the number of 'silly novels by lady novelists'.[37]

'Silly Novels' was written during the summer of 1856; Marian had already decided, as her journal entry for 20 July indicates, to try fiction writing; her first story, 'The Sad Fortunes of the Reverend Amos Barton', was begun on 23 September.[38] Its setting is the everyday working lives of country people like Marian's own family; the date is around 1830, the time when she was growing up and when various religious trends – Methodism, Tractarianism, and Evangelicalism – rivalled one another in churches up and down the country. Her aim was to present imaginatively and sympathetically the struggles, virtues, and failings of characters who were *not* paragons, beauties, and polking polyglots, but ordinary people getting on with their lives.

Marian finished one more article for Chapman, on the eighteenth-century poet Edward Young, which appeared in January 1857. As luck would have it, Chapman, unaware of her decision to turn to fiction, wrote on 15 January offering, in his kindly, self-consciously flowery manner, to pay more for her articles in future:

Dear Friend,

Of course it is impossible to adopt any scale of remuneration whereby I could graduate the payments to contributors to the W. R. so that each writer may be rewarded according to his (*or her*) merit. Still there are cases where a departure from the rule usually acted on would be so obviously just that I can have no hesitation as to the propriety of treating them as exceptional. Your articles are so uniformly excellent that I desire to express my appreciation of their merit by paying for what you may hereafter contribute at the rate of £12.12.0 per sheet.[39]

It was too late. Lewes had sent off the manuscript of 'Amos Barton' to his own publisher, John Blackwood of Edinburgh, on 6 November 1856, saying it was by 'a friend'. Blackwood accepted the story, which was published serially in *Blackwood's Magazine* from January 1857; meanwhile, Marian had already started her second story, 'Mr Gilfil's Love Story', begun on Christmas Day 1856.[40] On 4 February 1857 Marian, now communicating directly with her publishers, wrote to John Blackwood's partner and brother, William, signing herself for the first time 'George Eliot'. She was lost to Chapman and the *Westminster Review*, though through diffidence about her abilities and fear of stirring up once more the scandal about the 'strong-minded woman' living with Lewes, she kept her authorship a secret from all her friends, including Chapman, and clung on to her chosen pseudonym as long as possible. Therefore she replied gratefully but evasively to Chapman's offer of 15 January:

> I am much gratified by the satisfaction you express in my contributions to the Westminster, & of course no expression of satisfaction is so agree-able as that which is conveyed in the eloquence of cheques. As long as the W. R. is in your hands & you are willing to have me as a contribu-tor, it will always have the precedence with me over every Review, both on the ground of old friendship & of the greater freedom which it gives to the expression of opinion.[41]

She and Chapman still visited and corresponded with one another; he wondered what she was doing, since she no longer wrote for the *Westminster Review*. She did offer to do an article on F. W. Newman, whose career and personality fascinated her, but in January 1858, four months after suggesting it, she wrote to tell him she was too busy. 'My inability is simply an inability to do two things at once', she wrote, without explaining what the other thing was.[42] (It was her first full-length novel, *Adam Bede*.) The friendship might have continued but for Chapman's lack of discretion and Marian's extreme sensitivity about keeping her secret. On 5 November 1858 Herbert Spencer visited her and Lewes at Richmond, where they now lived, bringing them 'the unpleasant news that Dr Chapman [Chapman had qualified as a doctor the previous year] had asked him point blank if I wrote the Clerical Scenes'.[43] She was angry with Chapman and also with Spencer, to whom the precious secret had been revealed in October 1856. To Chapman she wrote sharply after Spencer had told her the bad news, signing herself 'Marian Lewes', as was now her custom, but omitting the usual salutations:

I have just learned that you have allowed yourself to speak carelessly of rumours concerning a supposed authorship of mine. A little reflection in my behalf would have suggested to you that were any such rumours true, my own abstinence from any communication concerning my own writing, except to my most intimate friends, was evidence that I regarded secrecy on such subjects as a matter of importance. Instead of exercising this friendly consideration, you carelessly, certainly, for no one's pleasure or interest, and to my serious injury, contribute to the circulation of idle rumours and gossip, entirely unwarranted by any evidence . . . Should you like to have unfounded reports of that kind circulated concerning yourself, still more should you like an old friend to speak idly of the merest hearsay on matters which you yourself had exhibited extreme aversion to disclose? Marian Lewes.[44]

Rather uncharacteristically, Chapman did not reply. Marian's journal strikes a bitter tone on 30 November:

I may also note, by way of dating the conclusion of an acquaintance extending over eight years, that I have received no answer from Dr Chapman to my letter of the 5th, and have learned from Mr Spencer that the circumstances attending this silence are not more excusable than I had imagined them to be. I shall not correspond with him or willingly see him again.[45]

What a sad end this is to a relationship so close and so mutually fruitful during those eight years. Eighteen months earlier, in May 1857, Marian had written in high spirits to congratulate Chapman on qualifying as a doctor; her own fresh starts in life – the relationship with Lewes and the as yet undisclosed birth of 'George Eliot' – allowed her to feel an affinity with him. She addressed him as 'My dear M. D.', and wrote:

I do sincerely share in the joy you must be feeling. The sweetest of all success is that which one wins by hard exertion, and I am sure all who know you must admire the persevering energy with which you have worked your way through all difficulties to this new starting point in your life.[46]

In the same letter, treating him once more as her chief confidant in matters relating to her life with Lewes, she told him that she had at last informed her brother and sister that she was 'married'.[47] Now, a year and a half later, she could not forgive him his dogged curiosity about the authorship of *Scenes of Clerical Life*. When *Adam Bede*, published in February 1859, became that rare thing, a critically acclaimed bestseller, Chapman pressed Spencer once again about the authorship. He reviewed the novel himself in the *Westminster Review*, and was unable to resist hinting that the author might not be 'of the masculine gender'.[48] Lewes had written to him on Marian's behalf on 12 February to deny her authorship of *Adam Bede* categorically; though Marian herself had a bad conscience about this lie, Lewes felt justified by the famous example of Walter Scott's denial that he was the author of the Waverley novels.[49]

In his review Chapman gave Marian the kind of praise she would have appreciated if he had not interspersed it with verbal nudges and winks about the gender of the author and about his having guessed the reasons for the creation of fictional place names in the novel. 'Loamshire', he says, stands for the Midlands; as a Midlander himself, he recognises the authenticity of the dialect speech. His chief praise is for the realism, humour, and wise tolerance of 'George Eliot', and above all for the 'catholic spirit' manifested with reference to 'religious doctrine'.[50] He does not let any resentment of his banishment from Marian's acquaintance affect his judgment, but squarely claims that the novel is a work of genius. Chapman's article, though not very well written or structured, compares favourably with that in the *Edinburgh Review* by Caroline Norton, which, though equally admiring, consists mainly of plot paraphrase and long quotations strung together on some breathless remarks in praise of the novel's realism and humour.[51] The *Quarterly Review* missed a trick by not reviewing *Adam Bede* when it came out, only catching up with the George Eliot phenomenon in October 1860, when *Scenes of Clerical Life*, *Adam Bede*, and *The Mill on the Floss* were reviewed together by James Craigie Robertson, who used the fact that it was now generally known that 'George Eliot' was the unorthodox 'lady translator' of Strauss and the unmarried partner of Lewes to write a mean-minded piece, giving only grudging praise for some of the characterisation.[52]

Chapman approached Marian one more time in January 1860. As he had done with Froude, but more cautiously in this case, he asked permission to publish several of her *Westminster* articles in a separate volume:

I am aware that I gave you back the receipts which conveyed to me the entire copyrights in the articles, and therefore only ask your acquiescence in my republication of them with the understanding and agreement on my part that after paying the expenses of paper, printing, binding, advertizing and commission on publishing from the proceeds of sale I should divide the profit with you. The articles make altogether about 150 Westminster pages, and would not extend therefore beyond a small post 8vo volume which however I should have much pleasure in issuing. It would reflect equal credit on you and on the Westminster – No, not *equal* credit for of course it would be chiefly yours; and though the Volume would be small, I hope and believe you would derive some substantial advantage from its publication.[53]

He received no reply from his old friend. The more distant and, in truth, disliking Lewes apparently wrote a refusal on her behalf. His journal for 18 January notes: 'Chapman last night wrote a cool request to be allowed to republish Marian's articles from the Review, and offering her half profits. Squashed that idea.'[54]

No doubt Chapman was irritating to the Leweses. Marian was suffering tortures under the forced lifting of the pseudonym in the summer of 1859, when many friends and readers in addition to Chapman began putting two and two together, and also under the animosity of her brother since he had learned that her 'marriage' was not legal. Famous now, and earning large amounts from her fiction, she no longer needed Chapman or the *Westminster Review*. She had moved on. Yet Chapman's mistakes hardly deserved the dusty answer and the complete break which ensued. It was his fate to be written out of George Eliot's life in the biography written by her conventional, non-radical husband John Cross, who was embarrassed by the early radical beliefs and radical acquaintances of the woman to whom he had been married only a few months before her death.

The journalist T. P. O'Connor wrote, after Chapman's own death, of walking down the Strand with Chapman when the latter 'stopped at the bottom of Catherine Street, and, pointing to a house opposite, said that had been his house and shop'. O'Connor describes Chapman:

A strikingly handsome man Dr Chapman was. I did not know him till he was an old man, but even then he was beautiful. He was upwards of six feet high, had massive and at the same time beautifully-chiselled features; large, brown, soft, inscrutable eyes, a beautiful mouth, a beard, long, white, patriarchal; a carriage erect, dignified, impressive, and, above all, he had that indescribable quality called magnetism.

The two men talked of George Eliot, whereupon Chapman 'gave my arm an eloquent squeeze, and whispered, "You know she was very fond of me!"'[55]

And so she was until their lives took different directions. It would be difficult to say which had been more helpful to the other when they worked together at 142 Strand on the *Westminster Review*. But since hers was to be the career which eventually became more prominent, and hers the more lasting fame, perhaps we may say that, immensely useful to Chapman and the *Westminster* as Marian was, her debt to Chapman was greater than his to her, since he offered her a role which, as it turned out, was the perfect apprenticeship for the novelist she became.

Marian Evans's young friends Bessie Rayner Parkes and Barbara Leigh Smith had moved in Chapman's circle since he took over the *Westminster Review* in 1852. Both belonged to politically radical Unitarian families; Bessie had literary ambitions and Barbara was already active in the political and social sphere. They attended Chapman's soirées, where they got to know Marian Evans. Being respectively nine and seven years her junior, they admired her achievements on the *Review*. As feminists, they supported her when she began to live with Lewes, though neither of them liked or trusted him at first. Chapman published two slight volumes of poetry by Bessie (slight in bulk and in talent): *Poems* in 1852 and *Summer Sketches and Other Poems* in 1854. He also issued an anonymous pamphlet by each of the young women in 1854: Barbara's eighteen-page *A Brief Summary, in Plain Language, of the Most Important Laws concerning Women; together with a Few Observations thereon*, published in October, and Bessie's pamphlet of twenty-four pages, *Remarks on the Education of Girls, with Reference to the Social, Legal, and Industrial Position of Women in the Present Day*, which came out in November.

Between them, Bessie and Barbara were addressing two of the four main topics in relation to women's position in society which had begun to be discussed in earnest in the years since the Reform Act of 1832 had widened the franchise for men and removed a number of electoral injustices and inequalities. The enfranchisement of women had been advocated in the July

1851 number of the *Westminster* – shortly before Chapman took it over – by J. S. Mill and his wife Harriet Taylor. Mill would continue to agitate for votes for women in articles and books and, after his election to Parliament in 1865 as radical MP for Westminster, in bills put before the House of Commons. Success in this domain was deferred until after World War I. Many agitators thought that other wrongs of women needed to be righted before they could logically be expected to receive the vote; in particular, the laws of divorce and married women's property required to be changed to give women equal legal status with men. Even more important, in the eyes of many, was, as a prerequisite to the granting of such equal rights, the instigation of proper education, including higher education, for women.

Education was the subject tackled by Bessie Rayner Parkes in *Remarks*. It is an odd little document, bold and feeble by turns, not distinguished for its style or logical coherence, but striking a blow for women's right to education on the conciliatory grounds that they are by nature fitted to influence society for the better. The boldness occurs chiefly in two sections headed 'Physical Training' and 'Mental Training'. In the first, Bessie makes a plea for the establishment of gymnasia for women and against the wearing of corsets. She criticises the Pre-Raphaelite painters for their representation of women with 'skinny and ill-expanded corporeal frames'.[56] Bessie had first-hand knowledge not only of the paintings of Dante Gabriel Rossetti, Holman Hunt, and their circle, but also of their favourite model, the consumptive Lizzie Siddal, who spent several weeks in April and May 1854 in Hastings under the kind and watchful eye of Barbara Leigh Smith in her nearby Sussex farmhouse, where she, too, was painting with a group of female artist friends. Rossetti wrote frequently to Barbara at this time, thanking her for her help, and mentioning Bessie's kindness too. The two women were demonstrating their independence by socialising with Lizzie; as Barbara said in a letter to Bessie, 'Miss S', though very beautiful and 'poetic', 'is not a lady'. Her lover Rossetti 'wishes her to see Ladies and it seems to me the only way to keep her self esteem from sinking'.[57]

If Bessie advocates healthy, unrestricted bodies for women in her pamphlet, she offers a brave hostage to fortune in the matter of their mental training. First she points out that women have shown themselves fully capable of academic study – look at Mary Carpenter, the famous Unitarian teacher and educational reformer in Bristol, she says, and at Elizabeth Blackwell (her own cousin, though she does not say so), the first qualified woman doctor, who, though a graduate of New York, was British by birth and had recently visited London, where she walked the wards with eminent London doctors. Secondly, and in a passage even more controversial than the suggestion that women might qualify as doctors, she advocates uncensored reading for girls, even when the subject is sex. Young women are 'kept apart' from the works of Chaucer, Ben Jonson, Dryden, and Fielding 'as they might be from the plague or the cholera', she writes, adding, 'this subject of the relation of the sexes should certainly engage the attention of young women'. They should have 'all past and present literature fearlessly' opened to them. Even George Sand should be read.[58] (As a matter of fact George Sand was read by Elizabeth Barrett, the Brontës, and Jane Carlyle, though *she* borrowed one of the daring Frenchwoman's novels from the London Library in 1843 in the name of her male friend Erasmus Darwin.[59]) Finally, under the heading 'Social Intercourse' Bessie invites her readers' agreement that French-style marriages of convenience are a bad thing, as are all 'early and foolish marriages'. 'A much freer intercourse between people of different sexes will be absolutely necessary as a basis for noble matrimony than has hitherto sufficed', she claims.[60]

Chapman reissued Bessie's pamphlet in 1856, and in October 1858 it was mischievously attacked by W. C. Roscoe in the *National Review* on the trumped-up grounds that the passage on 'mental training' could be construed, as Marian Evans noted indignantly, as 'a recommendation for girls to read impure literature'.[61] Roscoe, though not completely reactionary in the matter of 'Woman' – the title of his article – accuses Bessie, whose name was now included on the title-page of *Remarks*, of exaggerating the feminist cause. He uses the now current term 'strong-minded woman' in a negative way, and, spotting the red rag Bessie had brandished in the form of advocating that women be allowed to read Chaucer, Fielding, and George Sand, runs at it in bullish fashion, claiming that Bessie's aim is to '*teach* young girls to study the sexual relations with these works for text-books'. He consoles himself, however, with the following reflection:

> Practically her recommendation is not a very dangerous one. Few people would send their daughters to attend the lectures of the Professor of Passional Influences who proposes to read George Sand with his pupils.[62]

Of the five recent works on women's position listed at the head of Roscoe's article, three were published by Chapman. This may be taken as evidence that in 1858 the writers on the *National Review* still considered Chapman (and the *Westminster Review*) their main rival and antagonist, and, more importantly, that Chapman was the chief enabler of progressive writers in this as well as every other field. Following his own hard-worked essay on the position of women in barbarism and among the ancients, published in the *Westminster* in October 1855, he had printed several more important articles on the woman question: his own 'English Law of Divorce' (April 1856); two articles by the veteran feminist, now aged seventy, Caroline Frances Cornwallis, 'The Property of Married Women' (October 1856) and 'The Capabilities and Disabilities of Women' (January 1857); and 'Female Dress in 1857' by Harriet Martineau (October 1857).

On the question of tight-lacing, Bessie followed her friend Barbara's example and practised what she preached, at least when she was out of sight of her own disapproving parents. The young women went on walking holidays together; not only did they abjure corsets but, on a trip to Germany, Austria, and Switzerland in 1850, they wore short boots with coloured laces and skirts cut four inches above the ankle to make walking easier.[63] In August 1854 they holidayed together in Wales, correcting the proofs of Bessie's pamphlet and bathing naked in mountain lakes. 'Fancy us going on like Grecian nymphs who had never had any sense of propriety', Bessie wrote happily to Barbara's sister. 'I felt positively an ennobled human creature' and 'sang a great many songs to Echo, who sang them back to me'.[64]

Bessie, like many other men and women in reforming circles, was enchanted by Barbara, a genuinely free spirit. She was beautiful in a large, unPre-Raphaelite way. Dante Gabriel Rossetti gave this frank description of her to his sister Christina in November 1853:

> Ah if you were only like Miss Barbara Smith! a young lady I met at the Howitts', blessed with large rations of tin, fat, enthusiasm, and golden hair, who thinks nothing of climbing up a mountain in breeches, or wading through a stream in none, in the sacred name of pigment.[65]

Everyone remarked on Barbara's golden hair, and many individuals and institutions had reason to be grateful for the happy coincidence in her of the possession of an independent fortune – 'tin' – and an enthusiasm for, and generosity towards, the causes of education and equality, both for the poor and working class, and for women, rich or poor.

Barbara's family, though Unitarian and politically radical – pro-reform, anti-slavery – like Bessie's, was different in one way. Though rich, it was not 'respectable'. Her father, Benjamin Smith, a radical MP and owner, with his brother Octavius, of the family brewery and distillery, financed various philanthropic ventures, including a non-denominational school for poor children in Westminster which he founded. He had five children, of whom Barbara, born in 1827, was the eldest, but he never married the children's mother. Anne Longden, a milliner, whom he settled in his property in Sussex, went under Ben's middle name, being known as 'Mrs Leigh'.[66] Anne died in 1834, aged thirty-two, and Ben took the upbringing of his young children upon himself. The girls were given an equal education with the boys, and each child gained financial independence at the age of twenty-one. Their friend Mary Howitt described the family after a visit to them in 1845:

> The father is the Member for Norwich, a good Radical and partisan of Free Trade and the abolition of the Corn-Laws. Objecting to schools, he keeps his children at home, and their knowledge is gained by reading. They have masters, it is true, but then the young people are left very much to pursue their own course of study. The result is good; and as to affection and amiability, I never saw more beautiful evidences of it . . . They have carriages and horses at their command; and their buoyant frames and bright, clear complexions show how sound is their health.[67]

Of Barbara's relations, only one of her father's sisters, Julia Smith, consorted with the 'tabooed family'. Cousins like Florence Nightingale and Blanche Smith (who married Clough in this summer of 1854) were not encouraged by their families to recognise the Leigh Smiths. Bessie, to her parents' consternation, worshipped her bold and beautiful friend, while William and Mary Howitt's daughter Anna Mary, a gifted artist, painted with Barbara when she stayed in Sussex. Anna Mary painted Barbara several times, representing her as Boadicea and Dante's Beatrice, among other heroines of love, war, and liberty.[68] In London Barbara took over her father's infant school when he gave her the title deeds on her twenty-first birthday in 1848. She moved it to Edgware Road in 1854, appointing Elizabeth Whitehead (later Malleson) to the post of head teacher. Elizabeth too was taken with the idea of discarding corsets for girls. 'How charming it would be to organise a regiment of stayless, free-thinking, free-stepping girls!' she enthused to Barbara shortly before the Portman Hall School opened in its new premises in November 1854. Boys and girls were educated together, and the social classes were mixed up too. George Combe's ideas on education were followed, with the emphasis on secularism and tolerance. One of Barbara's pupils was the crippled son of the Italian nationalist Garibaldi.[69]

Barbara was now living in Blandford Square. The Chapmans were her near neighbours after their move from 142 Strand to the same square in June 1854; Barbara's aunt Julia had become their lodger when it became clear that Marian Evans was not going to join them but was going to Germany instead.[70] During this summer of near-bankruptcy and of arguments with Martineau and Hodgson, Chapman prepared to publish Barbara's pamphlet. *A Brief Summary* was a concise, well-digested account of the laws, particularly the property laws, as they affected women, followed by 'a few observations thereon'. The material was a masterly boiling down to essentials of John Wharton's *Exposition of the Laws relating to the Women of England* (1853). The immediate impulse for Barbara's pamphlet came from the recent publication of another by Caroline Norton, who had been carrying on a one-woman crusade to expose legal injustices and regain custody of her children since 1836, when her husband had sued the then Prime Minister, Lord Melbourne, for adultery with Caroline. Melbourne was acquitted, but Caroline was vilified; her husband refused her access to her children. She petitioned Parliament on several occasions without success, and now put her case before the public once more with *English Laws for Women in the Nineteenth Century*. Barbara seized the moment to appear with a pamphlet making a calm, clear case for reform to support and counterbalance Caroline Norton's personal outcry.[71]

A Brief Summary, which appeared anonymously in October 1854, listed the chief differences in the law as it affected not just men and women, but, more tellingly, unmarried and married women. A single woman 'has the same rights to property, to protection from the law, and has to pay the same taxes to the State, as a man', she writes. (In a sideswipe she notes that this equality does not stretch to allow a woman with the requisite property qualifications to vote.) Her main point is that, having become an 'independent human creature' at twenty-one, a woman returns, if she marries, to being 'again considered as an infant'; she 'loses her separate existence, and is merged in that of her husband'.[72] This is patently unfair to women, who lose the right to their own property and earnings, while aspects of it are unjust to men, who become liable for their wives' debts, even those contracted before marriage. Barbara touches on the subject of divorce – much easier for men to achieve than women – but directs her attention mainly to the laws relating to women's property.

Chapman brought out a second edition in 1856; the pamphlet was taken up by the Law Amendment Society, founded by Lord Brougham in 1844 with the purpose of reforming outmoded laws; and Barbara herself followed it up with a petition to Parliament in March 1856. Brougham agreed to present the petition to the House of Lords and Sir Erskine Perry introduced it in the Commons. It repeated the chief points of *A Brief Summary*, begging Parliament to give legal protection to the fruits of women's labour and to ensure that 'in entering the state of marriage, they no longer pass from freedom into the condition of a slave'. More than 3,000 women signed Barbara's petition, including Marian Evans and Sara Hennell, with a number of prominent women, married and unmarried, at its head. Among these were Elizabeth Barrett Browning, Jane Carlyle, Elizabeth Gaskell, and Harriet Martineau, as well as Barbara, Bessie, the Howitts, and Julia Smith's friend Mrs Reid, founder of Bedford College.[73]

It was not only women who signed Barbara's petition, though she naturally asked as many as she could contact. A combination of hard work and personal persuasion went into compiling it. 'Received a charming letter from Barbara Smith, with a petition to Parliament that women may have the right to their earnings', Marian Evans noted in her journal on 16 January 1856. Barbara had written winningly from the Isle of Wight on 14 January, praising Marian's recent articles in the *Westminster Review*:

> Dear Friend! (by your permission granted under your hand & seal August 1855) I have thought a great deal of you & had a great deal of your society lately & write to thank you for it. Heine is capital, & so was Dr Cumming . . . I send you a copy of a Petition which I have set going & which has already been signed by H Martineau Mrs Gaskell Mrs Howitt Mrs Jameson &c &c &c. Will you sign if I send a Sheet & will you tell me any Ladies to whom I can send sheets, perhaps among Mr Lewes' friends there may be some. I had got an MP *not* W J Fox! no Lord as yet but a distant hope of one.[74]

Chapman did his bit too. The *Westminster Review* reproduced the text of Barbara's petition and a list of the first twenty or so subscribers in an article printed in October 1856, Caroline Frances Cornwallis's 'The Property of Married Women'.[75]

The bill did not reach a second reading. It was killed by opponents who pointed to a separate Divorce Bill then before Parliament which gave legal protection to women separated from their husbands.[76] The result of the latter agitation was the Matrimonial Causes Act of 1857 offering partial remedy for women's wrongs, while married women's property legislation was not passed until 1882. In 1869 a third edition of Barbara's pamphlet was issued by Trübner (Chapman having given up his publishing business by then). The *Westminster Review*, still edited by Chapman, gave it publicity in the form of a supportive notice by Sheldon Amos, Professor of Jurisprudence at University College London, who coupled it with J. S. Mill's efforts on behalf of women, in particular his book *The Subjection of Women*, also published in 1869.[77]

Barbara went on to provide money for the founding of an all-woman monthly journal in March 1858. *The English Woman's Journal* was co-edited by Bessie Rayner Parkes and Matilda Hays and published by their own company from offices in Cavendish Square. Following her marriage to a French doctor, Eugène Bodichon, in 1857, Barbara spent half of each year with him in Algiers, and half in London and Sussex, where she provided enthusiasm, energy, and a list of influential contacts, as well as the all-important 'tin', for the plan to offer higher education for women which eventuated in the founding of Girton College in 1869.[78] She had met Dr Bodichon in 1856, when her father took her to Algiers to restore her physical health, which had broken down as a result of her exertions, and her emotional health, which had suffered from her intense relationship with Chapman.

The summer of 1854 was significant for Barbara, as it was for Chapman. He left 142 Strand for Blandford Square, while Elisabeth Tilley went to Australia and Marian Evans to Germany with Lewes. He faced bankruptcy and revolt; but for the support of Harriet Martineau and eventually Sam Courtauld, he would have gone under. Even his robust health and optimism gave way under the strain early in 1855. Marian mentions it in a letter to Bray in April, and tells Cara Bray in October that Chapman 'has had a return of the dangerous symptoms in the lungs'.[79] As for Barbara, while writing her *Brief Summary* and spending time in Wales with Bessie in August 1854, she heard of the impending death from consumption of her former tutor, who had been in love with her. In November she received a proposal of marriage from James Joseph Sylvester, a middle-aged professor of mathematics to whom she had recently been introduced by the Howitts. 'No one can know you without being made better by the influence of your example', he wrote, 'and to love you is to love goodness of heart, generosity and all that ennobles our nature'. She turned him down gently.[80] Her own feelings were in turmoil, for she had begun an emotional relationship with her new neighbour Chapman some time before going to Wales with Bessie.

The affair took up a good deal of Barbara's energy, as well as Chapman's, at a busy time for them both. When Barbara showed signs of congestion in the lungs towards the end of 1854, Julia Smith took her to Rome for the winter. Marian Evans, hearing the news from Chapman himself, wrote from Berlin on 9 December that she could 'hardly imagine her an invalid', so 'bright and blooming' had she always been.[81] On her return to England in spring 1855, Barbara became involved with Chapman again. Their relationship came close to consummation in August and September 1855, as we know from a series of letters from Chapman to Barbara which have survived, while hers to him have not.

Chapman sent Barbara thirty-two letters between 8 August and 22 September, writing daily at times and sometimes twice a day. That his passion was reciprocated is clear from his detailed responses to points she had made in her (lost) letters to him. In the end, though clearly tempted by his proposal that they should live together, she decided, despite her independent-mindedness, declared dissatisfaction with the marriage laws, and defiant, even proud, sense of her own illegitimate status, to refuse him. Chapman's letters are extraordinarily intimate; they expose him more thoroughly than even his surviving diaries do. His faults are therefore on display at least as much as his strengths, yet it would be wrong to suggest, as some historians and biographers have done, that these letters prove him nothing but a rake, a rogue, and above all a gold-digger in his pursuit of Barbara.[82] That he was a womaniser is incontrovertible, but the partners we know about, Elisabeth Tilley, the young opera student Johanna von Heyligenstaedt, and his second 'wife', Hannah Macdonald, were far from rich. On the contrary, he supported them as much as he could out of his own straitened means.

Chapman writes first from London on Wednesday 8 August; Barbara has gone to Sussex, taking Anna Mary Howitt with her to recuperate from an illness.[83] He addresses her as 'my own Darling' and refers, as Professor Sylvester had done in his proposal letter, to 'the purifying and ennobling influence of your love'. The difference is that Chapman knows his love is returned, but also that Barbara is hesitating to live with him. He hopes she will not 'yield to misnamed prudence and expediency' and refuse him, and complains that at present they see one another only 'rarely and for such a short time'. He plans to meet Barbara the following Sunday in Hastings or Brighton, and tells her that Susanna and the children are going to Surrey on Monday, leaving him alone in Blandford Square. 'The safest for you of all plans', therefore, 'is to come to Town as often as you can allege a sufficient reason for doing so'. If she felt able to take her close friends Anna Mary Howitt and Bessie Rayner Parkes into her confidence, he could visit her in Sussex while they are staying with her. Otherwise, he suggests, he could take a furnished room in London for three months, so that they could spend '2 or 3 hours together most days'. Barbara herself has suggested renting a studio for her to paint in, where he might visit her in private. His longer-term plan is to let the Blandford Square house 'next spring' and take rooms for himself in London, 'where we could be together whenever you are in town'.[84] (Chapman carried out this plan in February 1856, even though he had lost Barbara by then. Marian Evans told Sara Hennell on 19 February that he had 'let his house in Blandford Sq. for a year' and that Susanna Chapman was living at Redhill in Surrey, while Chapman was 'devoting himself body and soul to his medical studies'.[85])

The first of these courtship letters ends with a question: 'Is N. still hovering about? I wish I may never see him again.' Chapman is referring here to his rival for Barbara's affection, Joseph Neuberg, the German businessman and friend of Carlyle who used to lodge at 142 Strand in the early days and who wrote occasionally for the *Westminster Review*. As subsequent letters make clear, Chapman had nothing to fear from Neuberg, for Barbara was annoyed by his attentions. On 15 August Chapman warned her that, to his 'disgust and vexation', Neuberg had told him he was going to Hastings 'to take up his abode some time for the benefit of his health. I know he'll persecute you.'[86]

The most personal parts of these letters return again and again to the question of when, how, and where they can meet, and whether Barbara, who has confessed to having a 'terror' of the 'Master Passion' (sex), is prepared to consummate the affair.[87] Chapman pleads with increasing urgency, and soon begins to link her lack of sexual experience with various symptoms she has confided to him of irregularity in her menstrual cycle. Sexual activity will alleviate her problems, he says. It is undoubtedly in his interests as the would-be consummator of his physical passion, though as a persuader, not a seducer, since Barbara is an adult who can, and does, make up her own mind. Yet this habit of discussing, and even prescribing for, her symptoms is not entirely a matter of convenience or prurience on his part. It is clear from his letters to others as well as Barbara at this time that he was seriously planning to pursue the medical career he had begun and abandoned as a very young man (he was only thirty-four now). He told Harriet Martineau in October that he had resolved to study medicine with the hope of graduating in 1857. He would continue editing the *Westminster Review* and publishing his own articles in it; these would now be largely on medical subjects, particularly women's health:

> I hope to be able to treat various subjects, important and interesting to the general reader, from the physiological side, and in a popular way. Physical Education, for instance – particularly of girls, and many questions bearing on health. The closing Essays of my projected series on Woman I always intended should draw largely on Physiology. Such articles would be sure, when republished with my name, to advance my professional interests and to bring me patients.[88]

In the event, his articles in the *Westminster Review* during the next two years did not constitute a series on women and physiology, but they did deal with current matters of legislation which concerned women and health: divorce and the founding of a Medical Council and Medical Register. In his letter to Harriet Martineau he announced his plan to 'discuss the question of divorce' and expounded his long-held views on the subject, though he knew from her reaction to the Lewes-Marian Evans liaison that she would not agree with him:

> I would have marriages rest on *mutual* consent alone. If a couple *mutually* wished to separate I would grant a divorce. If one wished a separation and the other did not, I would still grant a divorce but would, when no criminal conduct could be alleged, exact from the one seeking separation either an *immediate* compensation to the other in the form of payment of a fixed sum, determined according to

Thomas Carlyle, painted by Robert Tait and exhibited at the Royal Academy in 1856.

Title-page of the radical *Westminster Review* for January 1852, the first number issued under Chapman's ownership and his and Marian Evans's joint editorship. Together they revived the reputation of the *Review* as the best quarterly journal of literature; among Chapman's innovations were the sections on foreign literature and on science.

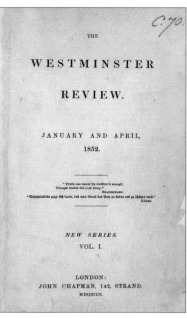

THE

WESTMINSTER

REVIEW.

JANUARY AND APRIL,
1852.

"Truth can never be confirm'd enough,
Though doubts did ever sleep."
SHAKSPEARE.

NEW SERIES.
VOL. I.

LONDON:
JOHN CHAPMAN, 142, STRAND.
MDCCCLII.

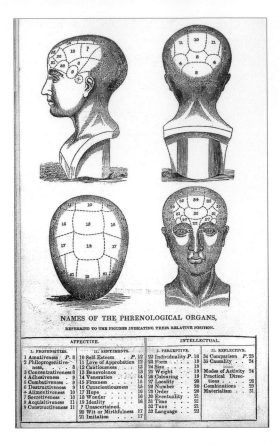

NAMES OF THE PHRENOLOGICAL ORGANS,
REFERRING TO THE FIGURES INDICATING THEIR RELATIVE POSITION.

AFFECTIVE.		INTELLECTUAL.	
I. PROPENSITIES.	II. SENTIMENTS.	I. PERCEPTIVE.	II. REFLECTIVE.
1 Amativeness . P. 8	10 Self-Esteem . . P. 12	22 Individuality P. 18	34 Comparison . P. 23
2 Philoprogenitive-	11 Love of Approbation 12	23 Form 19	35 Causality . . 24
ness, ... 8	12 Cautiousness . . . 13	24 Size 19	
3 Concentrativeness 8	13 Benevolence . . . 13	25 Weight 19	Modes of Activity 24
4 Adhesiveness . 9	14 Veneration 14	26 Colouring . . 19	Practical Direc-
5 Combativeness . 9	15 Firmness 15	27 Locality . . . 20	tions 28
6 Destructiveness 9	16 Conscientiousness 15	28 Number . . . 20	Combinations . 29
+ Alimentiveness 10	17 Hope 16	29 Order 20	Materialism . . 31
7 Secretiveness . 10	18 Wonder 16	30 Eventuality . . 21	
8 Acquisitiveness 11	19 Ideality 16	31 Time 21	
9 Constructiveness 11	? Unascertained.	32 Tune . . . 21	
	20 Wit or Mirthfulness 17	33 Language . . . 22	
	21 Imitation . . . 17		

Phrenological heads, frontispiece to George Combe's *Outlines of Phrenology*, 1836. This is the sixth edition of Combe's best-selling book about reading character from the contours of the head. Combe made phrenological observations of John and Susanna Chapman and Marian Evans, as well as the royal princes and princesses at Buckingham Palace.

sound & able. Mr. Chapman was busy preparing an amended prospectus, part of which he read to me, and I regretted to see that he has given effect neither to Mr. Milne's criticism, nor mine; and instead of boldly proclaiming principles founded in nature & pledging himself to their development, he announces merely "progress" without ~~~~ telling from what & towards what; and also his intention of finding out the middle term or essential idea in which contending parties of every class & sect agree. This will lead to mere words. I had a better opportunity of observing his head than formerly. His anterior lobe is ~too short for ~much mental power; altho' well developed in the knowing organs & also full in the reflecting. Benev. Ideality, Imit. & Veneration wonder seem largely or fully developed. But Conscientiousness appeared to me less. The temperament is Bilious, Lymphatic, nervous. I have less hope of his making a first rate work of it than I had when I had conversed with him.

A page of Combe's journal, giving his phrenological observation of Chapman in June 1851.

The opening of a letter from Susanna Chapman to Combe in July 1852, defending her husband against accusations of poor business management.

An extract from a letter to Chapman from the eccentric philanthropist Edward Lombe, written in Florence in July 1851; he calls himself a 'hard task-master', one who gives his 'horses plenty of oats', but only on condition that they 'work well'.

Photograph of the political exile Giuseppe Mazzini on a carte-de-visite given to Jane Carlyle.

Harriet Martineau, by George Richmond, 1849. Chapman published the controversial work she co-authored with Henry George Atkinson, *Letters on the Laws of Man's Nature and Development*, in 1851. She lent him money in 1854 to keep the *Westminster Review* in his hands.

Barbara Leigh Smith's cartoon of her friend Bessie Rayner Parkes on a walking tour in 1850. Chapman published feminist pamphlets by both Bessie and Barbara in 1854.

Portrait of Barbara Leigh Smith, from 1857 Madame Bodichon, by Samuel Laurence. Barbara was famous for her unconventional upbringing, her wealth, and her beauty, especially her red–gold hair. She and Chapman fell in love in 1854.

Photograph of Herbert Spencer,
1858, reproduced in his
Autobiography, 1904. Chapman
published Spencer's books and
articles on social matters;
Marian Evans fell unrequitedly
in love with him in 1852, while
she was boarding at 142 Strand.

Photograph of George Henry
Lewes, 1858. Lewes wrote for
the *Westminster Review*; Chapman
introduced him to Marian Evans,
with whom he went to Germany in
July 1854, after which they lived
together in London as a couple,
though Lewes was already married
but unable to divorce his wife Agnes.

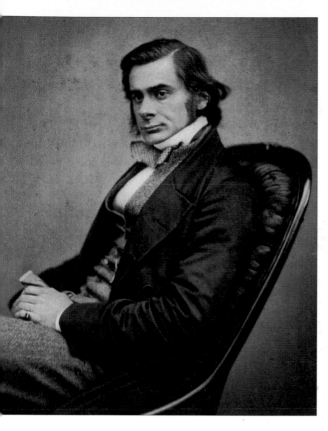

Photograph of Thomas Henry Huxley, 1857, reproduced in *Life and Letters of Thomas Henry Huxley*, ed. L. Huxley, 1900. Chapman gave Huxley's career a start in 1854 by asking him to contribute regular scientific articles to the *Westminster Review*.

Chapman's invention, the spinal ice-bag, advertised in the second edition of his book, *Diarrhoea and Cholera*, in 1866. Among those who tried the invention were Charles Darwin and John Stuart Mill.

DR. CHAPMAN'S SPINE-BAGS
(PATENT),
FOR
THE TREATMENT OF DISEASE
THROUGH THE AGENCY OF
THE NERVOUS SYSTEM,
BY THE APPLICATION OF
DRY COLD AND HEAT ALONG THE SPINE.

SPINAL ICE-BAG.

" The ICE-BAG, which has evidently been constructed with a great amount of thought, is divided into cells, and closed by a very ingenious clamp. Its arrangements enable it to be worn by persons moving about. The WATER-BAG consists of two parallel india-rubber tubes for the application of hot or cold water on either side of the spine. The bags are intended to enable the practitioner to carry out those 'vaso-motor nerve' views of the treatment of disease which were enunciated by Dr. Chapman in this journal July 18, 1863."
—MEDICAL TIMES AND GAZETTE, July 23, 1864.

The Spinal Ice-Bag, when applied in appropriate cases, is **soothing** and **agreeable**, as well as curative. (See Statements of facts, pages 12, 13, and 14 of this Circular).

SPINAL WATER-BAG.

Among the many diseases over which, by means of Dr. Chapman's discoveries, a remedial control has been acquired is the important group consisting of **Functional Diseases of the Stomach**, and comprising those hitherto incurable maladies—**Sea-Sickness**, and the **Sickness associated with Pregnancy**. For evidence that

Photograph of Chapman in old age, reproduced in the
Westminster Review in January 1895, shortly after his death.

circumstance, or security that a yearly allowance of suitable amount should be made.[89]

Harriet Martineau knew nothing of Chapman's domestic circumstances, including his love affairs and his desire to separate from Susanna; if she had, she would not have supported him financially or written her warm and confiding letters to her 'dear friend'. She took his wish to practise medicine at face value, accepting it as an expression of his genuine scientific curiosity and desire to alleviate mankind's ills. We have seen enough of Chapman's words and deeds to allow that he really was motivated by these admirable aims, whatever admixture of self-indulgence and self-interest also existed. Though many of the remarks in his letters to Barbara are embarrassing to read on these grounds, it would be an oversimplification and an injustice to sneer and snigger at his expression of particular interest in the ills of *womankind*.

The love letters discuss the details, provided by Barbara, of her irregular periods, headaches, and other physical ailments. Chapman, acting as medical adviser already, begins by prescribing hot baths with mustard, a steam bath to 'sit *over*', the avoidance of draughts, wearing horsehair socks, ensuring that her boots are not too tight, and going out riding every day for exercise.[90] On 20 August he reports that he has found the right kind of socks and some soft boots, which he will send her. Two days later he writes:

> I spent last night . . . in reading up our best authorities concerning the derangement of health from which you are suffering (you must know I possess several works on the practice of medicine).

He quotes from the medical works of various qualified doctors, showing his awareness of the differences of opinion within the profession and a personal tendency to embrace, or at least not to dismiss, homoeopathic methods. The letters to Barbara are in effect a rehearsal for his thoughtful article 'Medical Despotism', published in the *Westminster Review* in April 1856. 'There is a man of some repute at Hastings', he writes, a Dr Greenhill who, though orthodox, is worth consulting. 'Ashwell I see contends for the superior efficacy of walking to riding exercise with the precaution that it be never extended to fatigue.'[91] Samuel Ashwell was a doctor at Guy's Hospital and the author of *A Practical Treatise on the Diseases Peculiar to Women, illustrated by Cases, derived from Hospital and Private Practice* (1840).

Chapman took immense pains; he consulted doctors he knew in London, and wrote to Dr James Wilson at the famous water cure in Malvern, using the long-suffering Susanna Chapman's name so that he could 'give a full description of your symptoms', as he told Barbara.[92] He went to see Ashwell, who gave him mustard pills for her and recommended a 'Chamber Horse', 'a sort of elastic chair with air in which you move up and down' and which was supposed to have a beneficial effect on the womb. When Chapman mentioned the subject of 'marriage' to Ashwell (meaning sexual intercourse), Ashwell 'eagerly jumped at the idea', he reports.[93] This was convenient for Chapman, but it is worth noting that his suggested remedy for Barbara's ills is not a mere quack prescription like something in a Ben Jonson comedy, but one which noted medical authorities were also keen to recommend. If it all seems a little amateurish and too close to the chummy man-about-town world of London clubs, that is an inevitable consequence of the relatively undeveloped state of medicine in the nineteenth century and the fact that only men could qualify as doctors.[94]

Barbara was inclined to accept the idea of living with Chapman but, surprisingly perhaps, she favoured secrecy, whereas Chapman was for openness, including 'a frank announcement to your Father, brothers and sisters'. Then she could be 'really united with me' and 'look forward with joyous anticipation to becoming a Mother'. Otherwise, he wrote, following the advice given by most medical authors on the subject of women's health, her life would be 'but half fulfilled' and her health would not improve.[95] In the early days of September Barbara suggested that they should wait two years before becoming lovers completely; Chapman tried to dissuade her from such a delay. Then she put the case for a trip to Germany together, no doubt with her friend Marian's example of the previous year in mind. Chapman replied that he would like that 'immensely', but 'could not be away long I fear on account of the Review'.[96]

Chapman pressed her to consummate the affair immediately. If she did not wish to conceive yet, 'we might avail ourselves of Riciborski's [sic] law for a time'.[97] Adam Raciborski was a medical practitioner in France, author of works on puberty and menstruation, and advocate of a 'safe period' in a woman's ovulation cycle when conception would be least likely to occur. His ideas were quoted in some English works, including Edward John Tilt's *On Diseases of Women and Ovarian Inflammation* (1853), in which Chapman may have read about them if he had not read Raciborski's work in French, which seems likely given his misspelling of the name. (If they *had* consummated their affair using Raciborski's method, Barbara and Chapman might well have produced an offspring, as the female cycle was misunderstood by Raciborski and others who pronounced as 'safe' the unsafest part of it.[98])

By 1855 Chapman was thoroughly alienated from his wife, though he loved his children and spent as much time with them as he could. It is impossible not to feel sorry for Susanna, who turned forty-eight on 27 August 1855; she had long ago lost any physical attraction she might once have had for Chapman, and had been understandably querulous about his relationships with Elisabeth Tilley and Marian Evans. Since divorce was out of the question on both legal and financial grounds, she was at least as much a victim of the unhappy marriage as he was, though it appears that she would not have favoured a divorce in any case, since a social stigma would have attached itself to her in particular as a divorced wife. Chapman occasionally expresses annoyance with Susanna in his letters to Barbara, unfairly, given the impossibility of her situation. On 29 August he complains:

I cannot say that I value my present home at all; I experience much unhappiness there, and rarely any pleasure. I could enjoy the children infinitely more, if it were not for the cloud which is continually hanging over us, and the constant fear of some painful discussion. As soon as I enter the house whatever spontaneity and elasticity of spirit I may have desert me . . . I *shall* stick to the dear children, under all circumstances I count on having them much with me; but as your feeling in favour of secrecy seems very strong I presume it will be wisest for *me* to have a nominal home where S. and the children reside and where I shall often be with them.[99]

A week later he shows no sympathy with Susanna's concern for respectability:

What she would like would be that however much I might be with you she should continue to live in a house held in my name and which I should treat as mine. She does not object so much to my attachment to you as to its becoming known. In short love of approbation is her strongest feeling.[100]

The catalyst for Barbara's refusal, after she had engaged for nearly two months in detailed discussion, partial agreement, and planning for a future life together, was one Chapman had not foreseen. Knowing that her father had lived in just such an unconventional 'marriage' as the one he proposed to have with Barbara, he assumed that Ben Smith would approve, and so persuaded Barbara to tell him about their plans. Barbara did so, and reported back in mid-September that her father had told her to go to America if she wanted to practise her principles, as he did not at all like the idea of her practising them in England.[101] People are not always consistent, and Ben Smith may, for all his unorthodoxy, have shared the prevalent view that what was all right for a man in the matter of sexual relations was not all right for a woman. Or he may have felt that since such a view *was* prevalent, Barbara would suffer disproportionately in English society (as indeed she could see Marian Evans was suffering). He may simply have disliked Chapman, or thought him motivated chiefly by the thought of his daughter's 'tin'.

Barbara had been unsure what to do. She had temporised for several weeks while Chapman tried to persuade her, perhaps using her menstruation problems as an excuse to delay consummation even as Chapman deployed them as a reason to hasten it. Now she followed her father's advice, though not without pain. The last complete surviving letter in the series, written on 22 September from Hastings, where Chapman had taken temporary lodgings partly in order to be near her and partly because his own health had broken down again, expressed the hope that her father would come round or that Barbara would defy him. He signed himself 'Yours until death, J C'.[102] Henceforth Chapman and Barbara had no further intimate connection.

All the time this exhausting correspondence was going on, Chapman still ran his business and edited the *Westminster Review*. He also corresponded at length with his oldest radical woman acquaintance, Harriet Martineau, who was consulting him about her autobiography and planning to send him the finished draft; 'I dread the labour of having to read her volumes', he confessed to Barbara on 22 September. He and Harriet exchanged confidences about their health, and Chapman told her that he felt 'singularly lonely' in his 'long lingering troubles', which he suggested were only partly connected to the usual business worries.[103] On 27 September he was still in Hastings because of the recurrence of his lung problem, about which he was gloomy. The end of his relationship with Barbara had made him miserable; to Harriet he simply wrote a vague phrase about 'troubles having nothing to do with business' adding to his all-round sense of hopelessness.[104]

Harriet, convinced that she herself had only weeks or at the most a few months to live, entered sympathetically, if characteristically, into his troubles, wishing that he could share her 'philosophy', by which she meant either Comtism or mesmerism or both:

I sh[oul]d have liked to see you fairly through your present stage of questioning & sadness about the present conditions of human existence, & to have seen you landed on the firm ground of our philos[oph]y.[105]

This difficult, narrow-minded, and yet courageous and often kind-hearted woman liked her younger friend and publisher. She told him why:

I feel our friendship to be a very sincere one. I have found you less easy to know than I sh[oul]d have supposed from your unreserved nature or habits: & I have long seen that you are entirely misapprehended & undervalued by the saucy fellows who have given us so much trouble . . . I have long felt grateful to you for your aims & aids in behalf of free thought & speech, & I liked your frankness. Then came the fellows, & with it admiration of your temper under it. I now believe that if you can keep your health & spirits, & secure by strenuous prudence a fair field of action & speech for yourself, you may do great things in life.[106]

Harriet's remark about Chapman being 'less easy to know' than might have been expected from his open nature is a shrewd one. Even a reading of his private diaries and love letters leaves one unsure of the proportions of the different, often conflicting, elements in his character: energy, enthusiasm, ambition, foolishness, naïvety, frankness, self-interest. He seems at once ingenuous and disingenuous, intelligent and limited, generous and needy. Barbara Leigh Smith fell for him, as Marian Evans had done; the latter outgrew him, and Barbara in the end avoided a relationship about which she was not sure, unlike Marian in her happy liaison with the more dependable Lewes. Chapman's part in the relationship was not all bad. He did care for Barbara and for her health, and she had reciprocated his feelings and encouraged his advances. Even her close female friends, who knew all about the flurry of letters during August and September, did not blame him. Anna Mary Howitt wrote to him in a friendly tone on 1 October to reassure him that Barbara, though 'dreadfully distressed in mind', was 'really pretty well in body', and that her father and brother were showing some kindness to her after the eruptions caused by her revelation of her plans.[107]

Chapman did not bear grudges. He brought out a second edition of Barbara's *Brief Summary* at the beginning of 1856 and was happy to print the text of her petition on married women's property in the *Westminster Review* in October. His children attended Barbara's school during 1856, when Beatrice was eleven and Ernest nearly ten.[108] As Marian Evans noted in February 1856, he was now studying medicine in earnest. In future he would direct much of his still prodigious energy to promoting medical reform in the *Westminster* and, in due course, to writing medical books himself. Meanwhile, if his personal relationships with women were complicated and not always happy or creditable to him, he can fairly be praised for promoting their interests in the pages of the *Westminster Review* and in the pamphlets they themselves wrote for him to publish.

8

Dr Chapman and Friends

Harriet Martineau liked to have chaste but slightly flirtatious relationships with attractive younger men. Henry Atkinson, co-author of the infamous *Letters on the Laws of Man's Nature and Development* in 1851, was one such friend. Chapman was another. Their connection, as author and publisher, had become closer in 1854 when she took on the mortgage of the *Westminster Review* to save it from falling into her brother's hands, and she followed Chapman's business affairs with interest. She intended him to publish the autobiography she was writing during 1855, and was also inclined to confide in him about her health. In January 1855 she came to London to consult two doctors, Peter Latham, Physician Extraordinary to the Queen, and Thomas Watson. So alarmed was she about her symptoms, which included difficulty in breathing, that she anticipated death at any moment. In these circumstances she chose to stay with the Chapmans in Blandford Square, as she explained in her *Autobiography*:

> I felt it so probable that I might die in the night, and any night, that I would not go to the house of any of my nearest friends, or of any aged or delicate hostess: and I therefore declined all invitations, and took rooms at Mr Chapman's, where all possible care would be taken of me, without risk to anyone. There Dr Latham visited and examined me, the day after my arrival.[1]

Latham and Watson diagnosed enlargement of the heart, but they also thought that the tumour which was supposed to have been cured by mesmerism in 1844 had returned. Harriet, who prided herself on her unflinching honesty, was put in an awkward position, as she had published her account of the 'cure' in the *Athenaeum*, to the public disgust and dissent of her family. Still inclined to tell the world about the state of her health, but not wishing to admit that the tumour might not have been cured, she let it be known that the disease which was now so far advanced as to suggest that her death was imminent was solely the heart problem. Back in her home in Ambleside in September 1855, she confided in Chapman that she did not wish to give her brother James or her medical brother-in-law Thomas Greenhow the satisfaction of saying 'I told you so' about the mesmeric cure:

> The great, & constantly increasing enlargement round the waist is too much to be owing to the enlargement of the heart w[hic]h certainly exists; & it does not appear to be water. Dr Latham's opinion (& Mr Shepherd's here) is that it is owing to a very large internal tumour (itself a mortal disease, & certain to end in dropsy). It is *certainly not of* the same nature as the Tynemouth disease. As we fully know this, & as the heart disease is the primary, & still predominant one, we see no dishonesty in making no mention of the other.[2]

Chapman, in turn, offered his partial confidences to Harriet during his turbulent correspondence with Barbara Leigh Smith at this time, writing of his own poor health and hinting at personal troubles. He told her all about his plans to become a doctor as soon as was practicable. He began his studies at St George's Hospital in Hanover Square that autumn, reporting to Harriet on 19 November that he was 'working very hard each morning at dissections' and attending 'two lectures on Anatomy *every* day'. His interest in reforming the medical establishment, soon to be aired in his *Westminster Review* articles in 1856 and 1858, is already apparent. 'I am shocked', he tells her,

> at the wretched management and abuses which I find at St George's Hospital. The system of accepting the gratuitous services of the Surgeons and Physicians causes the patients to be only half attended to, while the students who pay large fees for clinical instruction are neglected

almost altogether. I hope the time will come when I shall be able to overhaul this business thoroughly in the W. R.[3]

In a long letter of 6 January 1856, Chapman talks of the importance of improving the general public's understanding of medicine and health, and of his hopes of furthering this understanding both in his treatment of patients and 'by my pen'. He announces proudly that 'the cleverest Physician at St George's Hospital, Dr Bence Jones, has taken me by the hands and offers to be of all the use he can to me'.[4] Jones presents an interesting contrast to Chapman in terms of their respective paths towards medical qualification and practice at a time when the study of medicine was rather a haphazard affair, though soon to be reformed and regulated by the creation of a Medical Council in 1858 and a Medical Register the following year. Chapman himself contributed in a small way to the modification of the Medical Act of 1858 by his powerful articles in the *Westminster Review*, in which he welcomed reform but warned that over-regulation by the state would put a dampener on medical research and experimentation without necessarily succeeding in its laudable aim of eliminating quackery altogether.[5]

Jones, a respected physician and Fellow of the Royal Society, had walked the wards at St George's as part of his training, as Chapman was now doing. But there the similarity ends. Jones was educated at Harrow and Trinity College, Cambridge, graduating in 1836 with the intention of becoming a clergyman. Changing his mind, he became a pupil surgeon at St George's, attended lectures at University College London, visited the famous German chemist Liebig, returned to Cambridge to take his MA (a formality), and was appointed a Fellow of the Royal Society in 1845 and physician at St George's in 1846. He published medical papers in the *Philosophical Transactions of the Royal Society* describing his study of the chemical composition of urine.[6] Jones's career was rendered successful partly by his genuine knowledge of his subject, gained at different institutions over a number of years, but also partly because of his public school background, Cambridge degree, and family connections.

Oxford and Cambridge conferred degrees in medicine, but as they did little to offer a proper medical education, most serious students of the subject in the first half of the nineteenth century spent time in Edinburgh, Paris, or the London hospitals, where proper courses in physiology, pathology, and materia medica were offered. As Chapman himself pointed out in his third long article on the subject, 'Medical Education', in July 1858, until recently Oxford did not require proof of attendance at any hospital in order to award a medical degree, while at Cambridge in the 1810s John Elliotson's examination had consisted of his reading out a thesis in Latin to a medical professor who made a few objections, also in Latin, to which Elliotson replied in the same language. Like so many others, Elliotson got his real medical training at Edinburgh. Though both Oxford and Cambridge had improved matters in recent years, much still needed to be done.[7]

Chapman's path towards qualification was inevitably different. He could not afford to study full-time, but had to keep on the *Westminster Review* and his troubled publishing business, writing one, two, or even three articles for each number of the *Review* in order to save on contributors' salaries, as he told Harriet in January 1856.[8] We know that he had spent a short time at St Bartholomew's Hospital in his late teens or early twenties, and another period studying medicine in Paris in 1842, and that when he married Susanna in Derby in June 1843 he described himself in the marriage register as a surgeon.[9] He now applied himself to study at St George's, but actually took his degree at St Andrews in May 1857, where he was examined in writing and orally over a period of three days. The reasons for his doing this are not clear. St Andrews was known to confer degrees, for a fee, on men who had not studied there, but the examination itself appears to have been as rigorous as at any other medical institution at the time.[10]

On Monday 27 April 1857 Chapman told Harriet about his plans. He was off to St Andrews the following Sunday to take his exams, intending to stay until Friday 8 May, when he would spend a week with his brother Thomas in Glasgow, then visit Edinburgh for a few days, after which he would call on Harriet at the end of May on his way back to London.[11] He wrote again from St Andrews on Saturday 9 May, describing the proceedings there:

There were 65 candidates for the degree; the examination, extending over three days, has been comprehensive and sufficiently severe. I believe many students have been or will be rejected. 8 had been 'plucked' [failed] up to last night. The fates of all will not be known until Monday. I received the degree yesterday evening.[12]

Chapman, being an experienced publisher and the proprietor of an important national journal, was given a warm welcome by writers and academics. 'I have enjoyed my visit here extremely', he writes in the same letter. 'The different Professors have been very kind and friendly – getting up very interesting parties for me every night'. He was a guest first of J. F. Ferrier, Professor of Moral Philosophy at St Andrews, and then, at Edinburgh, of Robert Chambers.[13]

The next thing was to gain a licence to practise from the Royal College of Physicians, which Chapman did in October 1857.[14] Harriet Martineau chided him on learning in July that he had found his first patient, but had not had the heart to accept a fee:

> Surely you will not be *weak* any more, after all the experience you have had, – & with so much depending on you! Surely it is your very first duty in life 'to make an honest penny'; & you have *no right*, after all that is come & gone, to make presents to your patients.

Her tone is genial, but she had a reason of her own for urging him to make some money; in all her anxiety about her health, she had been trying to settle her affairs, and wanted him to find someone else to take over her mortgage on the *Westminster Review* and return her £500.[15] Since patients were not immediately forthcoming, Chapman found himself employing his usual delaying tactics with Harriet, who eventually broke with him as acrimoniously as Lombe had done.

If he could not practise as a doctor yet through lack of patients, Chapman did put his recently gained knowledge of medicine to good use in his two *Westminster Review* articles in 1858. He also exhibited once more his ability to absorb and disgorge copious quantities of facts. In 'Medical Reform' in April he aims to catch the eye of MPs and government ministers as the Medical Reform Bill is progressing through Parliament. He claims that his article of April 1856 'contributed in no small degree to the defeat' of the earlier bill, which he had argued would stifle progress by over-regulation. Now he rehearses the (extremely complicated) history of medical practice from ancient times to the present day, giving details of the twenty institutions in the United Kingdom empowered to confer medical degrees and scrutinising their courses of study. These institutions include Oxford and Cambridge, the four Scottish universities – Aberdeen, Edinburgh, Glasgow, and St Andrews – London University, and the long-established London Colleges of Surgeons and Physicians.

Reforms, Chapman demonstrates, have as yet been partial and piecemeal, with a number of anomalies still in existence, especially with regard to the question of licences to practise and the geographical boundaries imposed by the terms of these licences. Jealousies between institutions have ensured that unjust privileges and exclusions have persisted, the most recent example being the vigorous resistance by the Royal College of Surgeons to the establishment of a medical faculty at the new University of London. 'Vested interests, by their very nature', he writes, 'are ever opposed to the spirit of Reform'. The current Medical Reform Bill, while admirable in its efforts to remove such monopolies and rivalries, is still too much inclined to maintain a connection between medical bodies and the state; Chapman advocates a complete severing of that connection.[16]

Though the Medical Reform Bill was passed with much of its proposed state regulation intact, Chapman's article does seem to have had some influence on the Government, as he claimed in the preface to *The Medical Institutions of the United Kingdom: A History exemplifying the Evils of Over-legislation*, a reprint of the *Westminster Review* articles which was published in 1870.[17] Early in 1858 he had made contact with Spencer Horatio Walpole, Home Secretary in Lord Derby's second Tory administration, which came to power in February 1858. The conduit to Walpole was the Colonial Secretary in the same administration, Derby's son Lord Stanley, to whom Chapman wrote on 29 March, sending an advance copy of the April article:

My Lord,

In fulfilment of my promise I have now the pleasure of submitting to your Lordship early sheets of my article on the Medical Institutions of the United Kingdom. The article consists of a history of these institutions, of their relation to the State, and of the evils which that relation has produced, – evils suffered by the public, the profession and by the medical bodies themselves.

I can scarcely hope that your Lordship will have time to read the article, but at all events you will, I venture to believe, serve the cause of wise legislation by placing it in the hands of Mr Walpole – commending it at the same time to his attention.

That Chapman had been promised such help by Stanley is demonstrated by the latter's note on the back of this letter, which reads: 'Chapman, Dr I have sent his art. on to Walpole with recomm. to attend to it.'[18]

Stanley was a valuable ally. Their relationship began now in all probability because Chapman had carried an article in the January number of the *Westminster* which attracted Stanley's attention. It was a piece by Lewis Pelly on the English in India. Stanley took a special interest in the subject, becoming the first Secretary of State for India in September 1858, when legislation was passed transferring control of that country from the East India Company to the Crown, an action deemed necessary in the aftermath of the Indian Mutiny of the previous year. A wealthy philanthropist with reforming, even radical, views on education, factory matters, sanitation, and religion, Stanley was prepared to finance the *Westminster Review* in order to have such views promoted in the public press, even though he served in a Tory administration.

For Chapman, struggling as ever and with Harriet Martineau asking for her £500 back, Stanley arrived in the nick of time with his loans and gifts for the cause of free thought and speech, beginning with a cheque for £50 for which Chapman thanked him the day after sending his medical article for Walpole's attention.[19] Chapman explained that he was trying to make up the amount owing to Harriet. He had promises so far of £50 each from Harriet herself, her cousin George Martineau, and her friend Erasmus Darwin, and £150 from a 'Great Unknown'.[20] This was J. H. Hippisley, a 'gentleman of independent means', who became a major supporter of the *Westminster Review* at this time.[21] Stanley summarised his reply to this second letter from Chapman as follows:

> The sum wanting is only £200. Others ought to bear their parts but sh[oul]d you fail in making up this deficit do not hesitate to apply again to me. The Rev must not be allowed to fall into hostile hands. When you have £150 more, I will find the last £50. But others sh[oul]d be tried first. I do not wish my *name* mentioned except to Miss M. or any one whom it may be important to secure & then privately.[22]

Good fortune had truly come along in the shape of Lord Stanley. Chapman, grateful on behalf of the *Westminster Review* and as determined as ever to promote reforming causes in its pages, was also ambitious to make his mark in medicine, and he thought Stanley might help him with this too. He was sufficiently encouraged by his new patron's expressed interest to seek a public position on the about-to-be-founded Medical Council, but was unsure of the best way to make his candidature known. As he told Stanley on 21 July in characteristically wordy style:

> Seeing that the Medical Bill passed through committee in the House of Lords last night, it occurs to me that perhaps I ought to state to your Lordship that as Mr Walpole possesses in my articles adequate data from which to form a judgment of my fitness for membership of the Medical Council I have not made any formal application to him to be appointed one of its members. Nor does he know I believe what are my professional qualifications, viz, M.D. of the University of St Andrews, and Licentiate of the Royal College of Physicians of London.
>
> Having your Lordship's sanction of my acceptance of the office if offered to me, I am of opinion, after full reflection, that it would be peculiarly suitable for me, and that it would enable me to be of considerable use to the profession; but trusting to Mr Walpole's appreciation of my medico-political knowledge and views, and feeling assured of the all-sufficiency of your Lordship's influence to secure my appointment if I am deemed deserving of it, I have remained passive – neither applying to Mr Walpole, nor seeking the influence of other persons disposed to interest themselves in my favour.[23]

After more expressions of gratitude to Stanley, the letter finishes with information he no doubt hoped Stanley would pass on to Walpole:

> The assurance of your Lordship's influence on my behalf 'on public grounds' is a source to me of great self-gratulation, and of course I prefer, if I should be appointed, that the appointment should be made on those grounds only. Therefore unless it is desirable that I should formally offer myself as a candidate I beg that your Lordship will not take the trouble to answer this note.
> One of the chief Medical Journals (the *Medical Gazette*) after thanking Mr Walpole and others, says, – 'Last and not least, we owe much of the present position of the Medical Reform question to the able writer of the article in the last *Westminster Review* on Medical Education, which we recommend to the careful perusal of our readers.'[24]

An earlier letter of Chapman's had been endorsed by Stanley, 'Will use influence to promote his views about Med. Council.'[25] The appointments to the Council had still not been decided by the middle of September, when Chapman sent Stanley four references written for him by respected practitioners, including his mentor at St George's, Henry Bence Jones, who 'stands pre-eminent in the country in his application of Organic Chemistry to Medicine' and 'has one of the largest consulting practices in London', as Chapman says. Another was Dr Robert Druitt, a medical officer of health at St George's and author of a standard textbook on surgery, *The Surgeon's Vade Mecum*, which had gone through several editions since its first appearance in 1839.[26] Chapman now feared he would not be chosen, and so it proved. On 6 December he thanked Stanley for his efforts and expressed his disappointment at not being elected.[27] He probably suspected – and was probably correct in his suspicion – that class snobbery was at work as well as wariness in government circles on account of his outspoken criticism of over-legislation. He had told Stanley in September that he had only one paying patient and that he feared he would not get a proper practice while he was editing the *Westminster Review*. 'Some eminent professional men in London', he wrote, 'actually deem it the best policy to conceal from their patients the fact that they write [for journals], even on professional subjects!'[28]

Stanley and Walpole were not the only prominent politicians with whom Chapman was corresponding. In his article on medical education in July 1858 he joined the chorus of voices criticising the handling of the Crimean War of 1854–6, particularly the neglect of soldiers' health and sanitation which Florence Nightingale had brought to the public's attention:

> The administrative imbecility which sent out that army, wretchedly officered, and lacking adequate supplies of food, clothes, shelter, and provision for the sick and wounded, roused the indignation of all England, – an indignation only appeased by sacrificing the Minister-at-War, and by the most strenuous efforts to remedy, as far as was possible, those appalling sufferings, which official negligence and ignorance had created.[29]

In November 1856 Palmerston's government had asked Florence Nightingale's friend, the MP Sidney Herbert (later Lord Herbert), to preside over a committee of inquiry into the sanitary state of the army. Herbert visited nearly every barracks and military hospital in Britain during 1857 and 1858, and delivered an interim report in August 1857; he was asked to continue with his inquiry when Derby's government took over in February 1858.[30]

A letter from Herbert to Chapman on 23 April 1858 shows that Chapman was thinking of carrying an article in the *Westminster Review* on the subject of the medical and sanitary conditions of the army during the Crimean conflict. Herbert writes:

> My dear Sir,
>
> I had intended calling upon you these last few days; but I have been confined to the house by influenza.
>
> I think the comparisons suggested by your correspondent between the administrative systems of the French & English Armies, would be of great value if we could get data upon the accuracy of which we could rely.
>
> But before drawing any conclusions from it, even supposing these data could be got, we should have to ascertain & to shew how far their practice agrees with their regulation.
>
> The administration of the French Army in the Crimea broke down as signally & much more inexcusably, at the end of the War, than ours did at the commencement. We failed at the beginning from inexperience; but we learned our business as we went on, though we didn't change the system. We merely learned by practice how to administer a bad system well.
>
> The French, on the other hand, began with a good system, & what their employés seemed to have learned as they went on was how regulations could be evaded, checks escaped from, & peculation committed with impunity. The soldier was robbed of his provisions in camp & of his comforts in hospital – a great loss by fever & more especially by typhus which was the consequence. But you could get no sufficient evidence of these results, notorious as they are both in the French & English Armies . . . I return the letter of your correspondent with many thanks.[31]

In the end Herbert himself wrote an article for Chapman on the subject. Entitled 'The Sanitary Condition of the Army', it appeared in January 1859, signed 'S. H.', and was reprinted as a pamphlet later in the year with his full name. Herbert wanted maximum publicity for his findings and his proposals for reform, which the armed forces had been resisting, much to his irritation, while his committee of inquiry was doing its work. It is a sign of the usefulness of the *Westminster Review* even to non-radical politicians as a channel for reforming ideas. When Derby's government failed in April 1859 and Palmerston came back in, Herbert was appointed Secretary of State for War.[32]

1858 saw the end of Chapman's friendship with Harriet Martineau. In January she answered Erasmus Darwin's questions about Chapman and the *Westminster Review* in terms intended to persuade him to contribute to the repayment of her £500 mortgage. The *Review*, she told him, 'still has the field to itself as the champion of free-thought'. Matthew Arnold had praised it, and Sir Charles Lyell 'is a very hearty friend of both the Review and the Editor'.[33] Having secured the promise of £50 from Darwin and the same from George Martineau, she was horrified to find out a few months later that Chapman had been less than frank with her about his debts. A fraught exchange of letters between them in June and July centres on Chapman's delay in repaying her – through George Grote, who had agreed to be their banker for the purpose. He was forced to concede that he had been obliged to remortgage the *Review* to Samuel Courtauld, who, with Octavius Smith, was still a creditor, but who had been advising Chapman to sell his publishing business for some time. Harriet felt that her own integrity had been undermined, as she had assured her friends, when urging them to contribute to repaying her mortgage, that Chapman had no other creditors.[34]

After receiving self-excusing letters from Chapman, Harriet declared herself unappeased. She reminded him on 16 July of her loyalty to him during hard times, and repeated her earlier assessment of his qualities, but concluded, as Lombe and Combe had done, that his lack of business acumen had led him to compromise his trustworthiness:

> All this gives me great pain. I have long respected some really great qualities in your character; – your admirable industry, – your bearing-up under protracted adversity, – your perseverance in study under circumstances w[hic]h w[oul]d have made many men reckless & self-indulgent; &, for the sake of these, & your amiable & friendly temper, I have been willing to get over your unfitness for business, & the drawbacks w[hic]h

belong to it. But your struggle with difficulties has been too long protracted, & you have given way in your weakest part. You have been unable, – while harbouring no evil designs, – to preserve your commercial honour, & your sincerity towards your best friends.[35]

The letter, begun without the usual greeting, ended in the same way, with a last complaint that Chapman was incapable of 'ordinary plain dealing'. Though he had received similar criticisms from others, Chapman still thought them unfair. He was stung into defending himself yet again; on 29 July he expressed his 'deep regret' that their friendship should come to 'this painful end', and he could not resist suggesting that her 'physical sufferings' had impaired 'the justness of [her] feelings and the clearness of [her] judgment'. Harriet, furious, got her niece Maria Martineau to write that she was insulted by this accusation, whereupon Chapman had the decency to apologise.[36] His apology was accepted, but Harriet's last word, on 6 August, was that she had lost confidence in him, and there was now 'nothing more to be said'.[37]

Courtauld, who had been urging Chapman to wind up the publishing business and release him since 1855, only hanging on because his fellow creditor, Octavius Smith, wanted Chapman to continue, also broke with him now.[38] Grote, acting as banker and Solomon, told Harriet on 4 June that he had spoken to Chapman, whose feelings, he was sure, were 'honourable'. A week later Grote suggested that Harriet had been overly severe in charging Chapman with misrepresentation, and on 22 June he went so far as to assert that Chapman had not been bound to inform her of his pecuniary arrangements with Courtauld. 'The peremptory view which you take of his proceedings is one in which I cannot concur', he wrote.[39] Whatever the rights and wrongs of the matter, Harriet's mind was not to be changed. Two more articles by her appeared in the *Westminster Review* – 'The Last Days of Churchrates' in July and 'Travel during the Last Half Century' in October 1858, but as Marian Evans told Bray on 13 October, 'the exchange of cheque and receipt is understood to be the last communication between her and the editor'. 'A pity for the Review', she added.[40]

Marian's assessment – a generous one considering Harriet had not maintained contact with her since the revelation of her relationship with Lewes – was correct. Harriet was a clever, shrewd, forceful writer, respected by all and still in demand by editors, despite her excursions into mesmerism, positivism, and 'spiritual atheism'. James Payn, a young writer whom she introduced to

Chapman and the *Westminster Review* – he contributed an article on ballads in January 1855 – later recalled the contradictions in her character. He saw that it was easy to caricature her as a fussy, dogmatic, deaf spinster with a tendency to fall out with erstwhile friends and damn them privately and publicly thereafter. These things were true, but she had, he wrote, a tender, earnest gravity that often 'nipped ridicule in the bud'. Robert Chambers, one of the sceptics, 'used to contend that Miss Martineau never wanted her ear-trumpet at all', not because she could hear without it, but 'because she did not care to hear what anybody had to tell her'. It was true that she was 'somewhat masterful in argument', Payn conceded, but she had a good deal of genuine kindness and even tolerance too.[41]

Naturally Harriet no longer wanted Chapman to publish her autobiography, but that had in any case to wait nearly twenty more years for publication when, to her astonishment, she did not die immediately, or even soon. The chief loss to Chapman was her clout in the pages of the *Westminster Review*. The withdrawal of her financial support (and Courtauld's) was luckily offset by the readiness of Stanley and Hippisley to step in. Marian Evans, who was to fall out with Chapman herself in November 1858 over his gossip about the authorship of *Scenes of Clerical Life*, expressed her sympathy with his troubles, including his final break with Harriet, in a letter of 11 October to Sara Hennell:

> I felt deep compassion for him yesterday. His health seems to be threatening again, and the load of anxieties he has to carry about his neck, while he is making efforts so strenuous and in many respects so disagreeable that few men would have the courage for them! That hideous Martineau-correspondence gave me almost a sick-headache only to think of.[42]

The *Westminster Review* continued to be strong, though it had lost its two best women writers, Marian Evans to novel writing and Harriet Martineau to disagreement. (She began writing almost immediately for the *Edinburgh Review*.[43]) Fortunately Chapman could still count on Herbert Spencer, Frank Newman, W. B. Donne, Mark Pattison, H. B. Wilson, and occasionally Froude and Huxley. New contributors in the late 1850s and early 1860s included W. M. W. Call, friend of Marian Evans and second husband of Rufa Hennell, who wrote on religious subjects, and from 1860 Frederic Harrison, a young

Comtist who caused a stir with his first article, 'Neo-Christianity', on the controversial *Essays and Reviews*, a volume of liberal and even semi-sceptical essays on religion by a set of clergymen and Oxford dons.[44]

Financially the *Westminster* was secured in November 1858 by Lord Stanley advancing Chapman £600, a loan which he converted into a gift in January 1860.[45] His generosity, and his explicit statement that Chapman could use the money 'as you think fit', that is, for the *Westminster Review* or the publishing business, allowed Chapman, as he gratefully acknowledged on 30 March 1860, finally to free himself of the albatross which the latter had been for several years.[46] He now sold the firm to George Manwaring. Though the transaction did not go smoothly, with Manwaring appearing not to have enough money to make the purchase and the disaffected Courtauld refusing to accept Manwaring's bill as payment for Chapman's debt to him, Chapman did finally rid himself of the loss-making enterprise.[47]

One of Chapman's last publications was a two-volume edition of *The Rise of the Dutch Republic* by the American diplomat and historian John Lothrop Motley. The letters from Motley to Chapman about the book's progress towards publication between August 1854 and March 1857 show the anxious, depressed Motley, already forty years old but so far unknown, spending months at a time in various European libraries and archives researching his major work on the Netherlands and relying on Chapman as his only hope of reaching an audience with the results of his study. He had visited London in May 1854 with the first volume of his history in draft and had tried to interest John Murray in taking it on. Murray declined, and Motley found Chapman willing to bring out his book, if he was prepared to contribute £250 towards the cost of printing. Motley's father agreed to put up the money, and Motley corresponded with Chapman from Switzerland and later Florence, where he held a diplomatic post. Chapman suggested that the book's format might follow that of Marian Evans's translation of Strauss; Motley expressed himself 'very willing to submit to your taste and experience'.[48]

Though there were delays in getting the book out, which worried Motley, he was grateful to Chapman, not least because Chapman sent proofs of the book to Froude in September 1855 with the intention that Froude should review it in the *Westminster Review*. Froude responded that he believed the writer would 'take at once a first place among historians', praise which Chapman forwarded to the delighted Motley. 'His warm expressions concerning my book have gone straight to my heart', he told Chapman on

18 November; 'to receive so high praise from a writer of such eminence is a ray of sunshine to one who has been toiling under ground, alone and in the dark for so many years'.[49] The book came out in the spring of 1856, and Froude's positive review appeared in the *Westminster* in April. Motley wrote to his mother that Froude's review was 'uncommonly well written and extremely flattering'.[50]

Harpers published the work in America, and Motley became famous. When he had finished another two volumes on the Netherlands in 1860, he visited London, where he received a note from John Murray, who expressed 'self-reproaches for his shortsightedness for having lost his chance of being my publisher, and his desire, if possible, to repair his mistake if I was not bound to any one else'.[51] Chapman was in the process of selling his publishing business to Manwaring, and in any case Motley, having part-paid for publication of his first two volumes, would not have felt obliged to offer Chapman his new volumes. Yet the story is a familiar one: Chapman gives a new writer his start, but cannot offer much, if any, financial reward; subsequently the writer, now well known, moves to a more prominent publisher.

Now that he had got rid of his publishing business, Chapman was free to concentrate on editing the *Review*, trying to build up a medical practice, and writing articles and books on medical subjects and on other topics of social interest, about which he corresponded at length with Stanley.

As might be expected, Chapman was generally on the side of experiment and innovation in medicine. This was demonstrated in his *Westminster Review* article in January 1859, reprinted later that year as a pamphlet of fifty-one pages, *Chloroform and other Anaesthetics: Their History, and Use during Childbirth*. Chloroform was a relatively new and still controversial painkiller for use in surgery and childbirth; as Chapman says in the pamphlet, both mesmerism and ether had been tried in recent years, James Simpson having first used ether for a birth in November 1847. More recently, Simpson and others had found chloroform more reliable, though some doctors disagreed, and many objected to the use of painkillers at all in childbirth. As Chapman pointed out, there were those, doctors and others, who invoked the passage in Genesis in which God, after the Fall, condemns women to suffer pain when bearing children. Chapman is scathing:

A section of the clergy was of course not wanting to vindicate the well-earned reputation of all priesthoods as the most powerful obstructives to human progress. One of their body declared chloroform to be 'a decoy of Satan'.[52]

For the July 1859 number Chapman worked hard at an article on 'The Government of India: Its Liabilities and Resources'. For this Stanley gave him a great deal of help, supplying him with parliamentary reports from his office as Secretary of State for India, and commenting on the article in draft.[53] As luck would have it, Stanley had to resign his post in mid-June, as Derby's administration went out and Palmerston's second administration came in. Chapman commiserated on 17 June, telling Stanley that he had the respect of all parties and classes for his work in office. He could not resist adding that he also felt

> some regret on personal grounds; for while my reasons for wishing for some public employment are as urgent as they were when I first spoke of the subject, I see no chance of their being complied with unless through your Lordship's kindness.[54]

Stanley, though out of office for the next seven years (he was appointed Foreign Secretary by Earl Russell in July 1866), continued to be close to the sources of political power. When a vacancy arose on the Medical Council in January 1861, Chapman used his connections with Stanley to try again. Sidney Herbert, now Lord Herbert of Lea, was also supporting him by informing the current Home Secretary, the reform-minded Sir George Cornewall Lewis, of Chapman's credentials.[55] It was a long shot, and unsuccessful. Meanwhile, Stanley's continuing help for the *Westminster*, financial and advisory, though known to Harriet Martineau, Courtauld, Octavius Smith, and others involved in the affairs of the *Review*, was kept secret from the wider public. It was well known that Stanley stood on the left of his party, with liberal views on many subjects, but the *Westminster Review* was a good deal more radical than Stanley could publicly acknowledge himself to be, particularly on the topic of religion. Stanley was careful about his religious scepticism; his diaries show that he did not go to church when living in London during parliamentary sessions, but did attend regularly when on his vast estate in Cheshire.[56]

In December 1859 Chapman got Stanley to read the draft of an article he was writing on 'Christian Revivals' for the January 1860 number of the

Westminster. A friend had told him it would 'give serious offence' to Christians, and Chapman wanted to ensure not that the article should not give offence, but that its facts and figures could not be rejected by those who inevitably would take offence. Stanley sent him some statistics on 'attendance at public worship'.[57] He was able to draw attention to the fact – shocking to many – that, according to the last census in 1851, only 800,000 or so of London's population of over two million attended church.[58] Stanley did not wish his help to be known; Chapman had to assure him on 20 December that he had 'burnt every word you have written – whether on the proofs or in notes – respecting the article'.[59] In a way Stanley now unofficially took on the role Marian Evans had once occupied; Chapman confided his problems with contributors, asked advice, sent drafts, and reported on the never-to-be-satisfactory financial position of the *Westminster Review*.

Chapman's personal affairs were once again complicated, not to say messy. As in the case of his relationship with Barbara Leigh Smith in 1855, a number of letters exist from Chapman to his new lover, Johanna von Heyligenstaedt, between June 1859, when he turned thirty-eight and she was eighteen, and May 1863. His diary for 1860 also survives.[60] In December 1858 Johanna became a boarder with the Chapmans in Albion Street, Hyde Park, where they had moved in March of that year.[61] She was studying to become an opera singer, and gave up some of her spare time, as Marian Evans had done nine years earlier, to teach Chapman German.

The 1860 diary reprises its 1851 predecessor in several ways. It opens in January with the same sort of self-analysis and expression of New Year resolutions as before. The entry for 5 January reads:

How difficult is self-culture – of the *whole* man! Among my many faults I desire to struggle separately with the following: 1st my unduly strong love of approbation and praise; 2nd my unduly frequent consultation of others before deciding in each case needing decision instead of quietly deciding at once for myself; 3rd my desultoriness and expansiveness in study; 4th my restless unhappiness unless basking in the smiles of Johanna, who though in respect to beauty of form and voice and certain mental qualities is a glorious & fascinating creature, is nevertheless very capricious and often both ungenerous and unjust; 5th my habit of letting all my time pass in common secular work – giving none to spiritual culture and self-elevation. How few moments of aspiration[,] how few hallowed hours I now experience![62]

Like Elisabeth Tilley, Johanna was demanding and difficult. Once again Susanna Chapman was unhappy and complaining, with the difference that she now took the children, Beatrice, aged fifteen, and Ernest, aged fourteen, into her confidence when complaining about Chapman's behaviour.[63] There is a heartfelt exclamation in Beatrice's diary at this time which reads 'the Fraulein – how I hate her!'[64] Just as there had been a silly business over music lessons and walks in the park when Susanna, Elisabeth, and Marian were the resident women at 142 Strand, so now Chapman reported Johanna's tears when Susanna removed the key to the door which connected Johanna's room to Chapman's.[65] Chapman took stock of his professional situation in July 1860, weighing up the pros and cons of various actions he might take, and he followed this with another of his emotional outbursts against his poor wife. On the question of his career options he writes:

I am greatly embarrassed to decide which of the following courses I shall adopt: 1st To go on editing the Review, living in the same house and waiting for practice as now and endeavouring to secure what subsidies for the Review I can; 2nd To try to get a government situation continuing on as in No 1 meanwhile; 3rd To continue on as in No 1 but to endeavour to cultivate a practice among insane patients; or 4th While still editing the Review to avoid writing and to qualify myself for medical practice generally so as to be able to take a country practice hereafter.[66]

Though he did not leave London to set up a practice in the country, being advised by his Bank of England friend Andrew Johnson that he was too unconventional theologically and sexually to survive such a move, he did work hard to take the membership exams of the Royal College of Surgeons, which he passed in 1861.[67] He also made some headway with the third of his listed options – cultivating a practice with insane patients.[68]

As for his domestic situation, the diary for 24 July 1860 sums it up gloomily:

The longer I live the more painful to me is residence in the same house with my wife. Whether the change is chiefly in me or equally in both of us I cannot tell: it has certainly been very gradually effected. Now the gulf is too wide ever to close again. If her personal unattractiveness were the only fact I had to deplore we might at least live together in a friendly and even affectionate relationship; but alas there are almost no elements of satisfaction: As a housekeeper she is utterly inefficient; under her rule disorder reigns everywhere, – in every room, every drawer, box, basket and cupboard . . . She can never rise early enough to secure that the breakfast shall be ready at the appointed hour; punctuality at meals is impossible; many of my most precious evening hours are lost because tea can never be made at the proper time; the domestic accounts, when she keeps them, are always in confusion; and notwithstanding all her *busi*-ness as housekeeper the cost per head of the family is either as little or is less when I am my own housekeeper as it is when she undertakes it.[69]

Chapman's final remark on the subject shows that, just as he never learned to keep clarity and transparency in his business affairs, despite being criticised and abandoned by several colleagues, so he did not improve his appreciation of his wife's unfortunate position, which was after all a direct result of his taking for himself the right to free love:

It was inevitable that my intimacy with J. v. H. should not escape the observation of the children, but the painfulness of my whole position has been greatly and needlessly increased by Mrs C's unjustifiable discussion of all matters with them.[70]

Letters to Johanna of 18 October 1860 and 5 August 1861 hint at thoughts of divorce, but to obtain it he and Johanna would have to allow Susanna to sue them for adultery, a course of action at which Johanna baulked.[71] Their relationship survived Johanna's long visits to Paris, Florence, and Milan to undertake singing engagements, and Chapman, as with Barbara, was willing to take trouble for his lover. On hearing in February 1862 that she was to sing the part of Lady Macbeth in Florence, he went to the British Museum to research eleventh-century costumes and also consulted Charles Kean, the famous actor-manager, on her behalf.[72] His ponderings the following month about leaving Susanna and settling in the country with Johanna are castles in the air, since he could not get a medical practice if he did not live a conventional life with a legal wife and the habit of going to church on Sundays. Besides, what would happen to Johanna's career?[73]

The last extant letter to Johanna, after which she seems to have disappeared from his life, was written in May 1863 from Somerset Street, Portman Square. He had moved there in January, but kept on his Albion Street house as an office and a residence for some insane patients he was now looking after.[74] From March 1863 Chapman and Susanna were no longer living together, though they visited one another and kept up friendly relations over the children.[75] Beatrice, who was helping him with the *Westminster Review* at this time, later recalled that she and Ernest had taken a hand in arranging their parents' separation, 'a bitter thing for two young people, both under twenty-one, to have to do'.[76] For his part, Chapman was preoccupied with his medical practice. He told Johanna, who was in Oporto, that he was 'trying experiments' on his poorer patients in an attempt to cure epilepsy and other ailments. He was very hopeful, he wrote. 'My discovery is a blessed reality and when it is matured and published I am confident I shall soon have many *paying* patients.'[77]

Lord Stanley was taken into Chapman's confidence about his revolutionary method of treating epilepsy, which, he divulged, was 'the use of ice externally'. Chapman had found his treatment effective in the few patients he had been able to muster; he confessed that as he was 'not a physician to any hospital', he could not get access to enough patients to test his discovery fully. Nonetheless, he was optimistic about its success, and intended, he told Stanley on 27 April 1863, to publish an account of his methods.[78] In the following letter he explained in more detail what these methods were, begging Stanley to keep the matter confidential, in case someone else claimed the discovery before Chapman could publish his findings. The treatment consisted of 'the continual application of ice along the length of the nervous column – the ice being contained in India rubber bags'.[79]

The rubber ice bag was the remedy Chapman hoped would make his fame and fortune. It was designed to keep the ice in three separate compartments to ensure that it stayed in even contact with the spine. Brass clamps were used to separate the compartments, and an elastic band went over the patient's head to keep the bag in close contact with the neck.[80] Chapman published his account of its use in cases of epilepsy and also in cases of painful or irregular menstruation, a problem which had interested him at least since 1855, when he quizzed Barbara Leigh Smith about her menstrual cycle and suggested the alternate application of heat and cold.

In December 1863 Trübner & Co. (who had taken over Chapman's own imprint from the short-lived Manwaring[81]) published his short book of seventy-four pages, *Functional Diseases of Women: Cases Illustrative of a New Method of Treating them through the Agency of the Nervous System by Means of Cold and Heat*, with an appendix 'containing cases illustrative of a new method of treating Epilepsy, Paralysis, and Diabetes'. Chapman's name appears on the title-page with all his qualifications on show – MD, Member of the Royal College of Physicians, Member of the Royal College of Surgeons – and his preface acknowledges two major London hospitals, Guy's and St Thomas's, for allowing him to practise on their patients.[82]

Treatment by heat and cold is likely to have given real pain relief to patients with a number of illnesses, as Chapman suggests in his appendix. The ice bag, which he patented in both Britain and France in 1864,[83] was a useful way of administering ice, and, along with his rubber hot-water bottle, could be seen as a forerunner of the ice packs and screw-topped hot-water bottles of the twentieth century. It was, however, recklessly sanguine of Chapman to claim that such treatment was a *cure* for all the diseases he lists. More books flowed from his pen in the next few years, each advertising the success of the application of heat and cold to the spine: *Functional Diseases of the Stomach: Sea-Sickness, its Nature and Treatment* (1864), and *Diarrhoea and Cholera: Their Origin, Proximate Cause, and Cure, through the Agency of the Nervous System, by Means of Ice* (1865), with reprints and updated editions appearing well into the 1880s. Chapman's simple view was that all the diseases he describes were caused by a malfunction of the nervous system. Even after Robert Koch discovered the cholera bacillus in 1884, Chapman was loath to give up his theory and his method, which others, too, still thought effective, as was shown when he was invited to treat patients in a Paris hospital during a cholera epidemic there in 1884.[84]

A determined self-advertiser for perfectly understandable reasons, Chapman was in the habit of quoting in each of his medical works the praise he had received from experts in the hospitals where he had connections or in the pages of the medical journals. He could claim at different times the support of well-known doctors such as John Simon, surgeon at St Thomas's (for *Functional Diseases of Women*), writers in the *Medical Times and Gazette* and *Journal of Practical Medicine and Surgery* (for *Functional Diseases of the*

Stomach), and Sir Andrew Clark, doctor to Gladstone and physician at the London Hospital (for *Diarrhoea and Cholera*).[85] Though many of these supporters were careful about how far they endorsed his claims, they certainly encouraged him and did not consider him a quack. He did not become a distinguished doctor or medical writer, but he was not far out of step with much theorising and experimentation – most of it inevitably ephemeral – in Victorian medicine.[86] This was particularly the case in the field of women's diseases, where the medical profession was hampered by questions of the propriety of men examining women's bodies. One example of this was the debate in the 1850s over the medical, social, and moral pros and cons of using a speculum for internal examination. In the 1870s respected authorities like the Harvard professor Edward Clarke and the English psychiatric pioneer Henry Maudsley opposed higher education for women on the grounds that energy put into brainwork would entail a depletion of the energy required by the female reproductive system.[87]

A surprisingly warm welcome for the ice bag came from that cold philosopher J. S. Mill. He had begun to interest himself in the *Westminster Review* again towards the end of 1859, when Chapman approached him for help in the form of articles, informing him, as encouragement, of Stanley's role as chief supporter. 'I have never ceased to consider myself as a potential contributor' to the *Westminster*, Mill replied on 5 November. He would be pleased to write an occasional article; moreover, 'so long as it cannot pay its expenses without gratuitous assistance, I should not think of accepting payment for any contributions I might furnish'. As for Lord Stanley's interest in the *Review*, Mill 'was equally surprised and pleased to hear of it'.[88] He wrote for Chapman about slavery in October 1862; in 1863 he offered two articles on Comte which appeared in the *Review* in April and July 1865 before being reprinted by Trübner later the same year as a book, *Auguste Comte and Positivism*.[89] The thawing of Mill's previously cool relations with Chapman was no doubt helped by the fact that Chapman's son Ernest and his nephew John Wallis Chapman were among Mill's political supporters; they canvassed for him in 1865, when he stood for Parliament in the Westminster constituency, winning it for the Radical party.[90] In August 1863 he even responded encouragingly to news of the ice bag, an 'important' medical discovery which he hoped would 'prove as beneficial both to the world and to yourself as there is reason to anticipate'.[91]

Mill appears to have been genuinely interested in the ice bag – in 1868 he gratefully accepted one from Chapman to treat a cold[92] – and as he also respected Chapman's long-continued efforts on behalf of radical reviewing, he was disposed to be helpful in more ways than one. In 1865 he put Chapman in touch with his young protégé Lord Amberley, son of Earl Russell and later father of Bertrand Russell, who wished to write for the *Westminster* on theological subjects, on which he held radical views. Mill spoke to Chapman and reported that Chapman felt the *Review* was 'stronger in theological contributors than in political' and would therefore prefer an article on the latter subject. Mill encouraged Amberley to comply, on the following grounds:

> The greatest utility of the Westminster Review is that it is willing to print bolder opinions on all subjects than the other periodicals: and when you feel moved to write anything that is too strong for other Reviews, you will generally be able to get it into the Westminster.[93]

Amberley's article, 'Political Economy', appeared in the *Review* in July 1865. He and Chapman were to share a platform three years later when they both spoke on the subject of overpopulation and public health at a meeting of the recently founded Dialectical Society. Like Mill, Chapman and Amberley supported birth control as a means of reducing poverty. Their speeches were reported in the *Medical Press and Circular* on 22 July, and repeated widely throughout the medical and political press during the election campaign Amberley fought in South Devon later that summer. He was defeated at the polls after being denounced in press and pulpit for advocating 'infanticide' in his Dialectical Society speech.[94]

Mill, meanwhile, encouraged Chapman in both his careers, radical editing and medical practice. Swallowing his earlier doubts about Chapman's abilities, he recognised his contribution to the promotion of advanced opinions in the *Westminster Review*, telling Chapman in December 1866 that he thought it 'eminently honourable to you that you should have been able to carry it on for so many years, and to make it as good as it has been through all that time'.[95] Mill followed this fair comment with an offer in January 1867 to take out a mortgage of £600 on the *Review* for five years. Unlike Harriet Martineau, in her similar arrangement in 1854, Mill said he would charge no interest. Chapman was saved again, and from a quarter he had ceased to consider hopeful. Mill was also fascinated by Chapman's medical efforts. In the same letter in which he offered financial relief, he wrote:

> That is glorious news about diabetes. If you can even occasionally cure such an intractable and fatal disease by your remedy, you will surely end by having a great practice. That you will leave a great name behind you as an alleviator of suffering and an improver of the medical art is now, I think, almost certain.[96]

It is strange to find Mill, no flatterer, declaring such faith in Chapman; though not a scientific expert able to judge whether Chapman really had found a cure, he saw the hard work and desire to do good which went into Chapman's efforts. Mill continued to give occasional financial support to the *Westminster Review* almost until his death in 1873. In 1869 he turned a £100 loan into a gift;[97] the following year he agreed to join an association Chapman was forming to agitate against the proposed extension of the Contagious Diseases Acts of 1866 and 1869, which were punitive towards prostitutes while doing little to stop men from using them and spreading venereal disease. Chapman wrote three campaigning articles in the *Westminster* in July 1869, January 1870, and April 1870, giving statistics about prostitutes and disease in Paris and London, and suggesting that further acts would do more harm than good.[98] He also carried an independent article on the subject by John Simon in the October 1869 number. Mill recognised, as he told a correspondent in 1869, that the *Westminster Review* under Chapman had ably continued the work begun by the original founders, Bentham and James Mill, as the only journal devoted to reform.[99] He felt it his duty to help Chapman, and he did.

In April 1860 the *Westminster Review* had carried Huxley's important review hailing Darwin's *The Origin of Species* as a masterpiece. Darwin himself, notoriously retiring and reluctant to join the hurly-burly of the London scientific and literary world, preferred to research and write in the quiet of his country house in Kent and let Huxley champion his views against vocal opposition from churchmen and others. Huxley, he wrote admiringly in his autobiography, had a mind 'as quick as a flash of lightning and as sharp as a razor'.[100] Despite his reclusiveness, however, Darwin was aware, through Huxley and his brother Erasmus Darwin, of the *Westminster Review*'s support for scientific progress, and in 1868 he joined Mill and Grote to write a circular letter for Chapman to use in the recurring task of trying to save himself and the *Review* from bankruptcy. Chapman quoted from this letter five years later, when his finances were so dire that he was on the brink of selling his household furniture 'to satisfy my creditors'. The letter ran:

> Knowing as we do the great difficulties it has had to struggle with, and the inferiority as compared with many other Reviews, of the inducements it could hold out to writers, we have been as much surprised as pleased at the high level of merit it has been able to maintain. This could only have been effected by a devotion of time and energy to the purpose on the part of the Editor, which does great honour to his public spirit, and establishes on his part a strong claim to the gratitude of the friends of advanced opinions and independent thought.[101]

The ice bag had come to Darwin's notice when Chapman published *Functional Diseases of the Stomach: Sea-Sickness* in 1864 and *Diarrhoea and Cholera* the following year. Darwin's health was wretched; since returning from the voyage of the *Beagle* he had been tortured by vomiting and diarrhoea, and had tried every form of treatment, from the Malvern water cure to looping wires round his neck and soaking his skin in vinegar, to sucking lemons every day.[102] In May 1865 a desperately weak Darwin invited Chapman to Down House, sending him an account of his symptoms:

> Age 56–57. For 25 years extreme spasmodic daily & nightly flatulence: occasional vomiting, on two occasions prolonged during months. Vomiting preceded by shivering, hysterical crying[,] dying sensations or half-faint, & copious very pallid urine. Now vomiting & every passage of flatulence preceded by ringing of ears, treading on air . . .[103]

Chapman went down to Kent to try out the spinal bag, freezing Darwin three times a day for an hour and a half each time. The treatment gave him relief, as he reported to Chapman after a few weeks, but as with every other remedy he had tried the effect of the ice bag was temporary; the sickness returned, and the experiment was abandoned.[104] As it happens, the next doctor approached by a desperate Darwin was Chapman's mentor at St George's, Henry Bence Jones, who put him on a starvation diet which was as unsuccessful as the ice bag and a lot more unpleasant.[105]

Chapman had claimed the success of his discovery in the treatment of a number of illnesses, including paralysis. For this he won praise from an unexpected quarter when his former assistant at 142 Strand, William Hale White, welcomed the treatment in an article in the *Aberdeen Herald* in August 1865. Hale White's wife Harriet had an incurable disease of the nervous system which rendered her progressively paralysed, so he was naturally interested in Chapman's therapy.[106] In his capacity as London correspondent of the *Herald* he discussed Chapman's method on 12 August 1865 in terms which suggest that he had some personal knowledge of it:

> The remedy consists in the application of ice to various parts of the body, and more particularly, to the spine. The inventor or discoverer is a Dr Chapman, and Dr Chapman, whom many persons will not know as a doctor, is no other than the Mr Chapman, formerly publisher of 142 Strand, and now Doctor of Medicine and editor of the *Westminster Review*. What may be the merits of the cure I know not, but one thing I happen to know, that Dr Chapman has, in one or two cases, literally made the paralytic lame to walk, and that he is a most painstaking student of his art, and certainly no quack.[107]

As we know from his later description of Chapman in *The Autobiography of Mark Rutherford*, Hale White was half fascinated, half repelled by Chapman, as well as by his uncompromising radicalism, particularly on religious questions. In his regular London articles for provincial newspapers (he wrote for the *Rochdale Observer* and the *Norfolk News* too), he returned from time to time to the adventures of Chapman and the *Review*. In March 1862 he noted in the *Aberdeen Herald* that the *Westminster* had changed its publisher (Trübner having just taken it out of Manwaring's hands), and launched into an account which demonstrates both his ambivalence towards his former employer and his pleasure at being able to reveal an insider's knowledge of some of the *Review*'s anonymous contributors. The change of publisher will make no difference, he says:

> It will remain as before, under the editorship of Dr John Chapman, formerly bookseller in the Strand, the gentleman who made himself so notorious, a few years ago, by breaking down the book monopoly. Since the *Westminster* has been under his care, it has greatly improved its

reputation for everything but orthodoxy, the most eminent men having occasionally contributed to it. George Eliot, *alias* Miss Evans, author of 'Adam Bede', wrote in it regularly for some years before the public discovered that she possessed any remarkable ability.[108]

Furthermore, he writes, becoming sharp on the subject of religion and religious hypocrisy,

clergymen, essayists, and reviewers, too, have written in this heretical periodical, and have used it as a convenient safety-valve, I suppose, for dangerous opinions, which might otherwise find a vent in the pulpit or drawing-room, greatly to the discomfort of their hearers or the quiet easy-going readers of the *Record*. One clergyman I know, at present having charge of a parish, has ventured upon theological criticisms in the *Westminster* which would appal both his flock and his bishop if his guilt were made public. How a man can do a thing of this sort, to a plain person like myself, believing that you cannot both prove and disprove the First Book of Euclid, is a matter of simple astonishment. Surely, the good which can be effected by sermons, supposing them to be true, or by criticism, supposing, on the other hand, that that is well founded, must be immensely outweighed by the harm done to ordinary minds when they see a minister whose conscience ought to be more delicate than that of other people, making so light of these great controversies that he can write like Strauss and preach like the Bishop of Oxford.[109]

H. B. Wilson is probably the clergyman sketched here. He was still writing the quarterly round-up of books on theology, and was one of the writers of *Essays and Reviews* who got into hot water with the ecclesiastical authorities in 1860. (Wilson and another clergyman, Rowland Williams, who wrote an article for Chapman in July 1860, were prosecuted by the Church of England Court of Arches for the 'heretical doctrines' expressed in their contributions to *Essays and Reviews*.[110]) In the 1860s Chapman could call on a number of old acquaintances for continuing contributions, and there was always a supply of newcomers ready to write for him. Science was covered by Huxley, W. B. Carpenter, and sometimes Chapman himself. Newman, Pattison, Wilson, and Call wrote about religion and philosophy, with Pattison also contributing a full-length article on education in Prussia (January 1862) and Call a piece on 'The Life and Policy of Pitt' (July 1862). Mill wrote on Comte, and his stepdaughter Helen Taylor on parliamentary elections (October 1865), while Grote reviewed a book by Mill in January 1866. Frederic Harrison became a regular contributor on history and other topics, including mountaineering (in 1864), and his fellow positivist E. S. Beesly, Professor of History at University College, discussed Kingsley's view of history in April 1861 and trades unions in October 1861. Henry Maudsley began writing for Chapman in January 1865, when he discussed *Hamlet* from a psychiatrist's point of view; from October of the same year he was the regular reviewer of medical books, a new section under the 'Contemporary Literature' heading. In January 1867 Walter Pater was recruited to write on Winckelmann, an essay which was later incorporated into his famous book, *Studies in the History of the Renaissance* (1873).[111]

Sheldon Amos, Professor of Jurisprudence at University College, contributed articles on legal subjects from 1864. He was later to put himself in Chapman's hands in an attempt to find relief from his chronic asthma. Amos tried out the ice bag and followed other instructions Chapman had given him, reporting in October 1878 that he had 'used your remedies' for a fortnight and had got some relief from applying the lumbar ice bag every night in bed.[112] Another new contributor, the young psychologist James Sully, later Professor of Mind and Logic at University College, who made his debut with an article on Mill in January 1871, recalled that at that time Chapman had made a name for himself by his 'discovery of the therapeutic value of ice-bags applied to the spine', being as famous for this as he was for editing the *Westminster Review* and for having introduced George Eliot to G. H. Lewes twenty years earlier. That Chapman had indeed achieved some repu-tation for the ice bag is further indicated by a remark in the 1871 diary of Dante Gabriel Rossetti's brother William that the poet Robert Buchanan had got relief from using it and had suggested the ailing alcoholic Swinburne should try it too.[113]

As for Chapman's continuing editorship of the *Westminster Review*, Sully, writing in 1918, remembered that Chapman was as keen as ever in the 1870s to recruit new talent, showing 'a warm concern for literature and for young writers', and that, as before at 142 Strand, he gave evening parties for his contributors.[14] These parties were held at 25 Somerset Street, where Chapman was living, no longer with Susanna, but with another 'Mrs Chapman', according to the diaries of Stanley, now Lord Derby since the death of his father in October 1869.

On 26 May 1870 Chapman wrote to Derby about the plan to appoint a Royal Commission to look into the Contagious Diseases Acts, about which he had recently published his three articles, now being reprinted as a pamphlet. He once more put his credentials before Derby, expressing his conviction that he 'could do good public service were I placed on the Commission'. Would Derby be kind enough to commend him to the Prime Minister, Gladstone, or the Home Secretary, Henry Austin Bruce? Derby noted on the letter: 'I think him well qualified, & will recommend him to the Home Sec.'[115] At last Derby's influence seemed likely to bring Chapman the prize he desired. Chapman wrote urgently to Derby on 2 November, saying he was 'anxious to have the advantage of your Lordship's advice on a point of some importance to myself'.[116] Derby agreed to see him on 9 November, and described the meeting in his diary that evening:

> Dr Chapman called: his chief business being to ask what he should do, under the following circumstances. It appears that Bruce had put his name down as a member of the commission of inquiry into the working of the Contagious Diseases Acts, and has subsequently requested him to withdraw it, at which he naturally feels aggrieved. The reason appears to be that Mrs Chapman also takes a good deal of interest in the question, and has been lecturing upon it, which Bruce, not perhaps unreasonably, thinks incompatible with the appearance of impartiality on Dr C's part. Something was also hinted at touching the marriage not being valid in law, which Dr C admits, and thinks Bruce may have heard of; but it does not seem likely that the Home Sec. would either know or care about a matter so entirely private. I told him, what I think – that the objection to his serving, founded on his wife's independent action in the matter, seemed to me a weak one; but that of that the Home Sec. was the judge, and as nothing was alleged against him personally, he had better withdraw his name and say nothing about it. This he himself seemed inclined to do.[117]

Poor Chapman. If he had still been nominally living with Susanna, who would not have been lecturing and agitating on the subject of prostitution and venereal disease, he might have realised his ambition to sit on a committee of inquiry. 'Mrs Chapman' was Hannah Macdonald, née Hughes, a young widow twelve years his junior. According to Beatrice's diary, Chapman was already living with her and calling her his wife in 1866; in that year Beatrice clashed with her father when she refused to visit Hannah, believing that 'Papa and Mrs M. have taken up a wrong position'. By 1868 Beatrice, now engaged to John Wallis Chapman, son of Chapman's cousin the engineer, had broken off relations with her father over his liaison with Hannah Macdonald.[118] It remains a mystery if or when or where Chapman could have married Hannah, since Susanna never divorced him. Perhaps they had a wedding in Paris, where Chapman mainly lived from 1874.[119] Hannah – or 'Pres', as Chapman called her – was, unlike Susanna, an active partner in his concerns, helping to edit the *Westminster Review* from Paris until his death in 1894, and carrying it on alone for several years after. His four surviving letters to her of January and February 1880, addressed to 'my own darling Wife', demonstrate that they shared their tasks and troubles (financial, as usual) without the recriminations which had characterised his relationship with Susanna.[120] If he was disappointed not to achieve the kind of public position he coveted, he at least had the loving support and active participation of his new 'wife'.

Chapman's life was a long and interesting one, full of new people and new adventures, and of an astonishing amount of hard work and expenditure of energy. Yet in some ways it was unchanging. His financial situation was never secure; nor was his sense of his own achievement or the recognition of others. A letter of 31 July 1873 to the ever-helpful Derby illustrates this. £800 was urgently needed for the *Westminster Review*; Chapman had raised subscriptions amounting to £450 and was negotiating with his creditors 'to accept a composition of 5/- in the pound'. He now turned, shamefacedly, to Derby. The old self-justifying arguments are used, but, though familiar, they strike a truthful note. In effect Chapman is saying that he has done what no one before him managed to do, namely to carry on running a radical journal – which by definition could never cover its costs – for over twenty years:

> To conduct the Westminster Review, and at the same time to have very slight extraneous sources on which to live is no easy task for anyone; and I may remark that in the course of the 22 years during which the Review has been in my hands (a period much longer than

the longest during which it had been held by any one of my predecessors) the whole of the aid which has been given to me forms a
smaller sum than has been expended on the Westminster Review in
previous periods of half the length of that during which the Review
has been in my hands.[121]

Chapman gave details: Sir William Molesworth alone had spent £9,000
on the *Westminster* in its early years. He further pointed out that several
thousands had been raised to start the rival *National Review* of Martineau,
Hodgson, and Bagehot, yet it had folded after only a few years, and that the
£10,000 put into the *Fortnightly Review* on its launch in 1865 had been used
up within eighteen months. The simple fact was that journalism, particularly radical journalism, could not pay its own way. Recognising this, Derby
sent another £100.[122]

Chapman's move to Paris the following year may have been made in order
to save money. He managed to build up a medical practice, catering mainly
for English and American residents and visitors, but his fortune was not made
here any more than it had been in London, as his letters to Derby during the
1880s show. Derby continued to help from time to time, but stopped sending
money in November 1892. He and Chapman took different sides on the
Home Rule for Ireland debate at this time, with Chapman supporting
Gladstone in the *Westminster Review* and Derby opposing the measure. Derby
noted, quite reasonably, that he intended to decline further requests, 'as the
special work which the review had to do is done, and I have very little
sympathy with the present ideas of the editor'.[123] He had helped Chapman
materially and morally for thirty-four years.

The *Westminster Review* under Chapman *had* done its work. A number
of reforms which it had advocated over the last forty years had been
achieved. There had been progress on social, medical, and educational
issues through legislation on divorce, married women's property, universal
education, higher education for women, medical education and practice,
and public health. Political progress had continued via the second Reform
Act of 1867 (though Parliament was not yet ready for Mill's amendment
calling for votes for women). Public opinion had been gradually moved,
with help from excellent articles in the *Westminster*, towards an acceptance of evolution; the names of Strauss, Comte, Mill, and Darwin no
longer struck fear and loathing into the hearts of educated readers. As if

in illustration of this, the best-selling novel of the whole nineteenth century, *Robert Elsmere*, published in 1888, was no potboiler, but a long, serious fictional account of the loss of faith of a young clergyman, written with the kind of wisdom and tolerance by now universally admired in the novels of George Eliot, if without their humour and metaphorical flair. The author was Mrs Humphry Ward, daughter of Tom Arnold and niece of Matthew, whose own childhood had been marked by her father's changes of religious belief and allegiance.[124] Robert Elsmere reads Strauss, has doubts about the Thirty-Nine Articles, and flirts with Newmanism, but ends more positively than his fictional predecessor of forty years before, Froude's Markham Sutherland in *The Nemesis of Faith*. Mary Ward's hero embraces humanism and concerns himself with organising education and practical help for London's poor.[125]

Oxford and Cambridge had by now accepted reform, not only by welcoming women, but by widening their curricula to include science, medicine, and modern languages – all subjects which the *Westminster Review* had long championed in its pages – and by dropping the requirement for graduates and fellows to sign the Thirty-Nine Articles. The new generation did not have to suffer the anxieties and loss of career that so affected Froude, Clough, Newman, Call, and many other young men in the 1840s and 1850s. The roll-call of names is a reminder that it was Chapman, as publisher and editor, who gave these displaced young men an outlet for their talent. Many of them went on to greater fame after getting their crucial start from Chapman. He furthered the careers of writers like Combe and Harriet Martineau, who had already made their names but who welcomed the *Westminster Review* and Chapman's publishing business as a way of reaching a wider public. Lewes, Spencer, and Huxley were indebted to him, the latter two for taking them on when they were unknown, untried, and, in Huxley's case, despairing. Lewes owed his introduction to Marian Evans to Chapman, and she owed him not only that same introduction, which brought happiness into her life for the first time, but also her apprenticeship as a writer.

Especially during his seven years at 142 Strand, Chapman was the pivot round which this group of talented people revolved; he brought them together at his evening parties and in his publishing office. Some moved on in later years, finding publishers who could offer them better financial returns and a higher profile through advertising. Others became disillusioned with him and broke off their friendship. After Chapman's move to Paris in 1874, he had fewer personal relationships with his authors, and the *Westminster Review*, though still a major periodical expressing reforming views, was less striking than in the 1850s, partly because it could not boast the collection of talent represented by Marian Evans, Huxley, Lewes, Spencer, Froude, and the Martineaus, partly because other liberal journals had been founded, notably the *Fortnightly Review*, whose first editor in 1865 was Lewes, and partly because, as Lord Derby noted in 1892, many of the reforms for which the *Westminster* had fought had now been achieved.

Chapman outlived most of his early authors: Combe died in 1858, Harriet Martineau in 1876, Lewes in 1878, George Eliot in 1880, Emerson in 1882, Mark Pattison in 1884, H. B. Wilson in 1888, Barbara Bodichon in 1891, Lord Derby in 1893, and Froude in October 1894, only a month before Chapman himself. He died on 25 November 1894 in Paris, aged seventy-three. By his will, proved in London on 24 December, he left his whole estate, amounting to £337.15.10, to his wife Hannah. Chapman's first, and perhaps only legal, wife Susanna had died in March 1892, aged eighty-four.[126] His son Ernest, a chemist, co-authored a book on drinking water in 1870, and died two years later at the age of twenty-six in a laboratory accident in Germany. The deaf and dumb Walter, brought up by Susanna's brother in the West Country, lived until 1922. Beatrice, the mother of three children, died in 1914. Though estranged from the father whose favourite child she had been, Beatrice showed her affinity with her father's political views when her name appeared on a petition 'for the removal of the electoral disabilities of women' presented to Parliament in June 1878.[127]

Chapman was buried on 1 December in Highgate Cemetery, near the graves of George Eliot and Lewes in the part reserved for dissenters and agnostics. Karl Marx had been buried in the same section in 1883. A newspaper cutting enclosed in the diary of George Jacob Holyoake, old acquaintance of the *Westminster* and *Leader* group, speaks of the funeral as 'of the simplest description, in accordance with the wishes of the deceased'. There was no religious service, but one of Chapman's friends and colleagues who had shared his views against the Contagious Diseases Acts and in favour of birth control, Dr Charles Robert Drysdale, 'delivered a brief address'.[128] (*The Times* gave a short account of the funeral on 3 December; on the same page it reported that Froude had left nearly £13,000 in his will.[129]) William Hale White wrote an appreciation of Chapman in the *Athenaeum* on 8 December, remembering the 1852 victory against the Booksellers' Association and recalling the important authors who had begun their careers with Chapman, particularly George Eliot.[130] The *Westminster Review* for January 1895 paid tribute to its long-serving editor's 'remarkable powers', 'indomitable energy', and 'singularly sweet qualities'. The author expressed the hope that Hannah Chapman would write a biography of her husband, but no such biography appeared. Hannah Chapman died in poverty in 1916. She apparently set fire to herself accidentally; it is likely that letters and diaries of Chapman were destroyed in the blaze.[131]

Chapman might have been a more skilful or more scrupulous businessman than he was, but equally he might not have had an eye for precocious talent, or the personal charm to attract writers and – crucially – financial supporters into his circle, or the tenacity to edit the *Westminster Review* for forty-two years through countless crises. He might have been a clearer, brighter thinker and a more succinct writer, but in that case he would probably not have been the enabler he was; rather, he himself would have needed a John Chapman to recognise his talent and give him his chance. On balance, Chapman was what was wanted, residing right at the heart of literary, journalistic, and publishing London, taking on innovative writers and offering a number of important Victorian thinkers the start they required.

Among his virtues were his energy, ambition, and openness to progressive views in every field of inquiry. He made the *Westminster Review* what it had been under Bentham and the Mills in the years leading up to the Reform Act of 1832 – a leading journal carrying strong articles by clever writers – but he added to its former importance by broadening its base. His writers were not only Utilitarians and philosophical radicals working for political reform, but also Unitarians, agnostics, evolutionists, social reformers, writers with progressive opinions in religion, philosophy, social science, medicine, education, and public health. Early feminists like Bessie Rayner Parkes and Barbara Leigh Smith were given publicity by Chapman, as were social theorists like Comte, Combe, and Spencer. Strauss and Feuerbach reached an English-speaking audience through his publication of Marian Evans's translations of their works. Emerson, too, first found a British readership through Chapman. And Marian Evans herself, so important as Chapman's helper in the early years, in turn owed him her start in a career in which she became distinguished as the novelist George Eliot. If she had never attempted fiction, however, she would still have stood out in two areas: as an important conduit of the German school of Biblical criticism and the 'religion of humanity' through her translations, and as the best literary critic of the period in her articles for the *Westminster Review*. For both of these achievements she was indebted to Chapman's enabling.

That Chapman was a philanderer and less than ideal husband is incontrovertible, though he was not a hypocrite like so many of his male contemporaries. His humble background ensured that his path was a steep and stony one; without money, family connection, or a university education, he had to struggle for every achievement, and many successes remained beyond his reach at least partly because of his social and educational disadvantages. Yet he was an individual of extraordinary enterprise and persistence, and his life is at the same time an example of what *could* be done in the Victorian period, when rapid changes were going forward and a man like Chapman was able, despite the obstacles, to make a difference. The journalist Sir William Robertson Nicoll, who had sight of Chapman's diaries, wrote in 1913 that the story of Chapman, the *Westminster Review*, and 142 Strand 'would form a romance of the most extraordinary kind'.[132] That story has now been written; while it has many elements which may be called 'romantic' in one sense or another, the strangest fact of all is that the story is true.

Biographical Register

Amberley, Viscount (1842–76), radical politician, born John Russell, eldest son of Lord John Russell and father of Bertrand Russell; friend of J. S. Mill and supporter of women's suffrage and birth control; contributed to the WR in 1865.

Amos, Sheldon (1835–86), Professor of Jurisprudence at University College London from 1869; supported women's suffrage; contributed to the WR on legal, political, and literary subjects from 1864; tried Chapman's ice-bag cure in 1878.

Arnold, Matthew (1822–88), poet, critic, and inspector of schools; son of Dr Thomas Arnold and friend at Oxford of A. H. Clough and J. A. Froude.

Arnold, Dr Thomas (1795–1842), headmaster and historian; improved educational and moral standards at Rugby School, where he had a strong influence on his pupils, including his sons Matthew and Tom and their friend A. H. Clough.

Arnold, Thomas (1823–1900), known as Tom, son of Dr Arnold and younger brother of Matthew; lived in New Zealand and Tasmania 1847–56; was converted to Roman Catholicism by J. H. Newman in 1856, reconverted to Anglicanism in 1865, and in 1876 joined the Roman Catholic church once more.

Ashwell, Samuel (1798–?), physician and lecturer in midwifery at Guy's Hospital; author of *A Practical Treatise on the Diseases peculiar to Women* (1840); Chapman consulted him about Barbara Leigh Smith's symptoms in 1855.

Atkinson, Henry George (?1815–84), mesmerist and phrenologist; friend of Harriet Martineau and co-author with her of *Letters on the Laws of Man's Nature and Development*, published by Chapman in 1851.

Bagehot, Walter (1826–77), journalist, economist, and author of *The English Constitution* (1867); studied at University College London; consorted with Henry Crabb Robinson, Richard Holt Hutton, James Martineau, and other Unitarians in Chapman's circle; joined Martineau in setting up the *National Review* in 1855 to rival the WR.

Baring, Lady Harriet, née Montagu (1805–57), daughter of the sixth Earl of Sandwich, wife of William Bingham Baring, second Lord Ashburton from 1848; society hostess and centre of a literary and social circle which included Carlyle, Tennyson, and Thackeray.

Bastard, Thomas Horlock (1796–1898), friend and correspondent of George Combe; supported Chapman's *WR* by paying for articles.

Bodichon, Barbara (see Smith, Barbara Leigh).

Brabant, Elizabeth Rebecca (1811–98), known as Rufa, friend of Marian Evans and Chapman; began the translation of Strauss's *The Life of Jesus*, published by Chapman in 1846 after Marian Evans had taken it over and completed it; married Charles Hennell (1809–50) and in 1857 W. M. W. Call.

Brabant, Robert Herbert (?1781–1866), physician and father of Rufa; subscribed to the first number of the *WR* under Chapman's management in 1852.

Bray, Caroline, née Hennell (1814–1905), known as Cara, children's writer; friend and neighbour of Marian Evans in Coventry; married to Charles Bray.

Bray, Charles (1811–84), ribbon manufacturer, freethinker, and social reformer in Coventry; friend of Marian Evans and supporter of the *WR*.

Bremer, Fredrika (1801–65), Swedish novelist; stayed at 142 Strand in 1851 during a visit to London.

Browning, Elizabeth, née Barrett (1806–61), poet; married Robert Browning in 1846; signed Barbara Leigh Smith's feminist petition to Parliament in 1856.

Browning, Robert (1812–89), poet; visited Chapman in 1851 to discuss the *WR*.

Bunsen, Christian Karl Josias von, Baron von Bunsen (1791–1860), diplomatist and scholar; Prussian ambassador to the court of St James's 1842–54; upholder of Protestantism; patron of Friedrich Max Müller and J. A. Froude.

Call, Wathen Mark Wilks (1817–90), poet and clergyman who renounced his orders in 1856 and married Rufa Hennell, née Brabant, in 1857; Chapman published his collection of poetry, *Reverberations*, in 1849.

Campbell, John, first Baron Campbell of St Andrews (1779–1861), Lord Chief Justice 1850–9; presided over the panel appointed to adjudicate on the question of free trade in books between Chapman and his supporters and the Booksellers' Association, led by Murray and Longman, in 1852.

Carlile, Richard (1790–1843), radical printer and advocate of birth control.

Carlyle, Jane Welsh (1801–66), wife of Thomas Carlyle; famous conversationalist and letter-writer and friend of European exiles.

Carlyle, Thomas (1795–1881), essayist, historian, social and political commentator; wrote the preface to Chapman's English publication of Ralph Waldo Emerson's *Essays* (1848); encouraged Chapman in his purchase of the *WR*, to which he contributed an article in 1855.

Chadwick, Edwin (1800–90), sanitary reformer and friend of W. E. Hickson, owner and editor of the *WR* before Chapman.

Chambers, Robert (1802–71), Edinburgh publisher and writer; anonymous author of

Vestiges of the Natural History of Creation (1844); friend of George Combe and subscriber to the first volume of the *WR* under Chapman.

Chapman, Edward (1804–80), bookseller and publisher, partner in the firm of Chapman & Hall; unrelated to John Chapman.

Chapman, Beatrice (1844–1914), daughter of John and Susanna Chapman.

Chapman, Ernest Theophron (1846–72), son of John and Susanna Chapman.

Chapman, Hannah, née Hughes (1833–1916), married name Macdonald, second 'wife' of John Chapman, though there is no evidence of a divorce from his first wife Susanna; lived with Chapman in Paris 1879–94; co-edited the *WR* with him.

Chapman, John (1801–54) engineer and political writer; older cousin of John Chapman; pioneer of the Great Indian Peninsular Railway; writer on India in the *WR* 1852–3; died suddenly of cholera while writing a review for the *WR* of Humboldt's *Sphere and Duties of Government*.

CHAPMAN, JOHN (1821–94), radical publisher, editor of the *WR* 1852–94; MD 1857; author of books on medicine; inventor of the ice bag.

Chapman, Susanna, née Brewitt (1807–92), married John Chapman in 1843; had three children by him, Beatrice, Ernest, and Walter; her money was used by Chapman to buy the publishing firm of John Green in 1843; took in boarders at 142 Strand to help pay the rent; separated from Chapman in 1863.

Chapman, Thomas (1816–?), older brother of John Chapman; chemist in Glasgow; briefly joined John Chapman's publishing firm, which was known as Chapman Brothers 1845–6.

Chapman, Walter John (1847–?1922), deaf and dumb son of John and Susanna Chapman; brought up in Devon by his maternal uncle Brewitt.

Clough, Arthur Hugh (1819–61), poet; friend of J. A. Froude and Matthew and Tom Arnold; associated with University College London and University Hall; visited Chapman at 142 Strand.

Cobden, Richard (1804–65), manufacturer, politician, advocate of free trade; friend of George Combe and of the Martineaus; contributed to the *WR* in 1849.

Combe, George (1788–1858), phrenologist; author of the much-reprinted *Constitution of Man* (1828); supporter of secular education and prison reform; subscribed to the first volume of the *WR* under Chapman and published articles on education and prison discipline in the *WR* in 1852 and 1854.

Congreve, Richard (1818–99), positivist and disciple of Auguste Comte; probable author of the review of Harriet Martineau's abridged translation of Comte's philosophy in the *WR* in July 1854.

Cornwallis, Caroline Frances (1786–1858), author and feminist; contributed articles on married women's legal position to the *WR* in 1856 and 1857.

Courtauld, Samuel (1793–1881), Unitarian, silk manufacturer, and philanthropist; campaigned for the abolition of church rates; subscribed to the *WR* and lent

Chapman money to help keep the *WR* in his hands during the takeover bid by James Martineau and W. B. Hodgson in 1854.

Cox, Robert (1810–72), nephew of George Combe; subscribed to the *WR* under Chapman.

Darbishire, Samuel Dukinfield (1796–1870), Unitarian solicitor in Manchester; employed J. A. Froude as tutor to his children after the publication of Froude's *The Nemesis of Faith* by Chapman in 1849.

Darwin, Charles (1809–82), naturalist, author of *The Origin of Species* (1859); joined J. S. Mill in a letter of support for Chapman and the *WR* in 1868.

Darwin, Erasmus (1804–81), brother of Charles; friend of the Carlyles and of Harriet Martineau; supported the *WR* financially in 1858.

Dickens, Charles (1812–70), novelist; took the chair at the meeting at 142 Strand, organised by Chapman, on 4 May 1852 to oppose price fixing of books by the Booksellers' Association.

Donne, William Bodham (1807–82), essayist and examiner of plays in the Lord Chamberlain's office from 1857; friend of Henry Crabb Robinson; contributed articles on English and classical literature to the *WR* 1854–62.

Druitt, Robert (1814–83), surgeon; author of *The Surgeon's Vade Mecum* (1839); medical officer of health at St George's Hospital; acted as referee for Chapman's application to become a member of the Medical Council in 1858.

Drysdale, Charles Robert (?1828/9–1907), freethinker and birth control activist; gave the address at Chapman's funeral on 1 December 1894.

Drysdale, George (1824–1904), brother of Charles; advocated contraception in his book, *Physical, Sexual, and Natural Religion*, first published in 1855 and reprinted several times under the title *The Elements of Social Science*, which sold 90,000 copies and was translated into eleven languages.

Dugdale, William (?1799/1800–68), publisher of freethinking and pornographic books in Holywell Street, opposite 142 Strand.

Eliot, George (see Evans, Marian)

Elliotson, John (1791–1868), physician and mesmerist; Professor of Medicine at University College London 1832–8, when he resigned after his controversial use of mesmerism in lectures and on the wards; treated Thackeray and was admired by Dickens.

Ellis, William (1800–81), economist and educational reformer; contributed on economics to the *WR* in its early years (1824–6); friend of George Combe; visited Chapman at 142 Strand 1851–2.

Emerson, Ralph Waldo (1803–82), Unitarian minister in Boston; resigned in 1832 and travelled to Europe, visiting Wordsworth, Coleridge, and Carlyle; Chapman published his *Poems* (1846), *Essays* (1848), and *Representative Men* (1849); stayed at 142 Strand in 1848 while on a lecture tour of Britain.

303

Engels, Friedrich (1820–95), businessman and revolutionary; lived in Manchester from 1842; collaborated with Karl Marx on *The Communist Manifesto* (1848), and supported the Marx family financially.

Evans, Marian (1819–80), novelist, known as George Eliot; her translations of David Friedrich Strauss's *The Life of Jesus* and Ludwig Feuerbach's *The Essence of Christianity* were published by Chapman in 1846 and 1854 respectively; lodged at 142 Strand 1851–3; helped Chapman to edit the WR from 1852; contributed articles to the WR until 1857, when she began publishing fiction.

Forbes, Edward (1815–54), natural historian, Professor of Botany at King's College London 1842–54; contributed three articles to the WR during 1852, the first year of Chapman's editorship.

Forster, John (1812–76), writer and literary adviser; friend and biographer of Dickens.

Forster, William Edward (1818–86), textile manufacturer and politician; married to Matthew Arnold's sister Jane; responsible for the Education Act of 1870; contributed to the WR on Quakerism and anti-slavery 1852–3.

Fox, William Johnson (1786–1864), Unitarian minister and radical politician; supported financially from 1847 by an annuity given by Samuel Courtauld; contributed an article on parliamentary reform to the first number of the WR under Chapman's editorship in January 1852.

Foxton, Frederick Joseph (?1806/7–70), lapsed Church of Wales clergyman; author of *Popular Christianity* (1840), which Chapman reprinted in 1849.

Freiligrath, Ferdinand (1810–76), German poet and businessman; fled to London in 1851 to avoid prosecution for his political poetry; met Chapman through Andrew Johnson of the Bank of England.

Froude, James Anthony (1818–94), historian and biographer of Carlyle; his novel, *The Nemesis of Faith*, published by Chapman in 1849, was publicly burnt by the Sub-Rector of Exeter College, Oxford; published a number of acclaimed articles on literature and history in the WR between 1852 and 1857.

Gaskell, Elizabeth, née Stevenson (1810–65), novelist; acquaintance of J. A. Froude and F. W. Newman in Manchester.

Gladstone, William Ewart (1809–98), politician and author, four times Prime Minister between 1868 and 1894; supported Chapman in the protest against the Booksellers' Association in 1852; contributed to the WR on Home Rule in 1887.

Greeley, Horace (1811–72), editor of the *New York Tribune*; stayed at 142 Strand in 1851.

Greg, William Rathbone (1809–81), industrialist and essayist; author of *The Creed of Christendom*, published by Chapman in 1851; contributed political articles to the WR under Chapman's editorship 1852–3; supported Martineau and Hodgson when they split from Chapman in 1854 to set up the rival *National Review*.

Griswold, Rufus Wilmot (1815–57), American journalist and editor of Poe's works; contributed short reviews of American literature to the *WR* 1852–3.

Grote, George (1794–1871), historian of Greece and radical politican; member of the Council of University College London; financial supporter of the *WR*.

Hannay, James (1827–73), journalist and author; contributor on literary and heraldic topics to the *WR* 1852–4.

Harrison, Frederic (1831–1923), positivist and author; reviewed *Essays and Reviews*, controversial essays on religious subjects, for Chapman's *WR* in 1860.

Hennell, Sara Sophia (1812–99), sister of Cara Bray and close friend of Marian Evans; lived near Chapman in Clapton in 1846, when she proofread Marian Evans's translation of Strauss's *The Life of Jesus*.

Herbert, Sidney, later Lord Herbert of Lea (1810–61), politician; chaired a committee of inquiry into the sanitary state of the army after the Crimean War; recommended the creation of a Medical Council in 1858; described the recommendations of the committee in an article in the *WR* in January 1859.

Hetherington, Henry (1792–1849), radical freethinking publisher and journalist; agitated for repeal of the taxes on paper in the 1830s; published a translation of Strauss's *The Life of Jesus* in 1846, the same year in which Chapman published Marian Evans's translation.

Heyligenstaedt, Johanna von (1840–?), German opera singer; boarded with the Chapmans at Albion Street from late 1858, becoming Chapman's mistress until 1863, when their correspondence came to an end while she was in Oporto.

Hickson, William Edward (1803–70), educational writer and owner-editor of the *WR* from 1840 to 1851, when he sold it to Chapman; wrote mainly on behalf of secular education, free trade, parliamentary reform, and sanitary reform.

Hodgson, William Ballantyne (1815–80), economist and friend of George Combe; supported the *WR* financially until 1854, when he and James Martineau called in Chapman's debts in order to take over the *WR*, which had become too radical and freethinking for their taste.

Holyoake, George Jacob (1817–1906), journalist, secularist, and founder of the co-operative movement; was imprisoned for blasphemy in 1842; edited a weekly newspaper, the *Reasoner*, in which he praised the radicalism of the *WR* under Chapman from 1852; contributed to the *Leader*, edited by G. H. Lewes and Thornton Hunt; supported European republicanism; attended parties at 142 Strand.

Howitt, Anna Mary (1824–84), painter and friend of Barbara Leigh Smith and Bessie Rayner Parkes; supported their feminist activities.

Howitt, Mary (1799–1888), writer, mother of Anna Mary Howitt and wife of William Howitt, with whom she wrote several books; a friend of the Leigh Smith family; translated works by Hans Christian Andersen and Fredrika Bremer.

Hunt, Thornton Leigh (1810–73), journalist; son of Leigh Hunt; friend of G. H. Lewes and father of four children by Lewes's wife Agnes; co-edited the *Leader* with Lewes; supported European republicanism.

Hutton, Richard Holt (1826–97), journalist and author; succeeded Clough as Principal of University Hall in 1851; edited the Unitarian *Prospective Review*, published by Chapman.

Huxley, Thomas Henry (1825–95), biologist and self-styled 'Darwin's bulldog'; reviewed scientific works for Chapman's *WR* from 1853, including *The Origin of Species* in 1860.

Ireland, Alexander (1810–94), journalist; published the *Manchester Examiner* from 1847; invited Emerson to England and arranged his lecture tour 1847–8.

Jewsbury, Geraldine (1812–80), novelist and reviewer; friend of Jane Carlyle, knew Mrs Gaskell, and met Froude in Manchester in 1849.

Johnson, Andrew (1815–80), clerk in the Bullion Office of the Bank of England from 1849; translator of F. W. J. von Schelling's *Philosophy of Art*, published by Chapman in 1845; introduced Ferdinand Freiligrath and Karl Marx to Chapman in 1851; contributed articles on monetary policy and politics to the *WR* during the 1860s.

Jones, Henry Bence (1813–73), physician at St George's Hospital, where Chapman attended his classes 1855–7; wrote a reference for Chapman's application to join the Medical Council in 1858.

Kingsley, Charles (1819–75), novelist and clergyman; supporter of sanitary reform.

Kinkel, Gottfried (1815–82), German refugee; escaped from Spandau prison in 1850; settled in London, where he taught literature, art history, and history; attended parties at 142 Strand with his wife Johanna (1810–58), a music teacher.

Lewes, George Henry (1817–78), journalist and author; edited the *Leader*, a radical newspaper, with his co-founder Thornton Hunt; his open marriage with his wife Agnes, who bore him three surviving children and Thornton Hunt four, meant that Lewes could not obtain a divorce in order to marry Marian Evans, to whom he was introduced by Chapman in 1851; contributed articles on literature and science to the *WR*; went to Germany with Marian Evans 1854–5 to research and write his *Life of Goethe*; on their return to England they lived together as man and wife.

Linton, Eliza Lynn (1822–98), journalist and novelist; born Eliza Lynn, she moved in Chapman's circle in London in the 1840s; in 1858 she married the radical printer and contributor to the *Leader*, William James Linton, but they soon separated.

Lombe, Edward (1800–52), landowner and philanthropist; lived in Florence but supported radical causes in Britain; gave financial help to Hickson for the *WR* and promised to continue supporting the *Review* under Chapman, but quarrelled with him over details and died early in 1852 before he could be persuaded to send money, except for £500 to support Harriet Martineau's translation of Comte's positive philosophy, which Chapman published in 1853.

Longman, William (1813–77), publisher and prominent member of the Booksellers' Association which prevented free trade in books until Chapman's agitation in 1852.

Maccall, William (1812–88), author and ex-Unitarian minister; lectured and wrote on philosophical subjects, including 'The Elements of Individualism', which Chapman published in 1847.

Mackay, Robert William (1803–82), philosopher; Chapman published his *Progress of the Intellect* in 1851 and *Sketch of the Rise and Progress of Christianity* in 1854.

Malleson, Elizabeth, née Whitehead (1828–1916), educationist; moved in Chapman's circle in Clapton in the 1840s; taught at Barbara Leigh Smith's experimental co-educational school 1854–5; founded the Working Women's College in 1864.

Marshall, James (dates unknown), assistant to the Grand Duke and Duchess of Weimar in the 1850s, recommended for the post by Carlyle; met Marian Evans and G. H. Lewes in Weimar in 1854.

Martineau, Harriet (1802–76), writer and journalist; political radical and religious dissenter who rejected the Unitarianism of her family; wrote an abridged translation of Comte's philosophy, published by Chapman in 1853; took out a mortgage on the *WR* in 1854 to save it from falling into the hands of her estranged brother James; broke with Chapman in 1858 when she suspected him of dishonest use of the money.

Martineau, James (1805–1900), Unitarian minister, writer, and teacher, who moved from Liverpool to London in 1857; contributed articles to the *WR* under Hickson and Chapman; supported Chapman financially until 1854, when he called in his debts, along with W. B. Hodgson, in an effort to bankrupt Chapman and take over the *WR*, which was too 'atheist' and radical for his liking; on failing in this, he and Hodgson, with W. R. Greg and Walter Bagehot, founded the *National Review* to rival the *WR*.

Marx, Karl (1818–83), revolutionary and co-author with Engels of *The Communist Manifesto* (1848); settled in London with his family in 1849; met Chapman through Andrew Johnson in 1851.

Mazzini, Giuseppe (1805–72), Italian nationalist and exile in London; friend of the Carlyles; contributed an article on the condition of Europe to the *WR* in 1852.

Mill, John Stuart (1806–73), philosopher, economist, politician, and advocate of women's rights; son of James Mill, who founded the *WR* in 1824 with Jeremy Bentham; edited the *WR* 1835–40; contributed articles to the *WR* under Chapman and supported it financially in the 1860s and 1870s.

Motley, John Lothrop (1814–77), American diplomat and historian of the Netherlands;

Chapman published *The Rise of the Dutch Republic* in three volumes in 1856; subsequent volumes were published by John Murray.

Müller, Friedrich Max (1823–1900), philologist, Professor of Modern European Languages at Oxford from 1850; friend of Bunsen and Froude.

Murray, John (1808–92), publisher; grandson of the first John Murray, founder of the publishing house, and son of the second John Murray who started the *Quarterly Review* in 1809 and published Byron, Scott, Coleridge, among other famous writers from his famous premises at 50 Albemarle Street. Murray, with Longman, was a prominent member of the Booksellers' Association.

Neuberg, Joseph (1806–67), German businessman based in Nottingham; friend of Carlyle; contributed to the *WR* on European politics 1855–6; lodged at 142 Strand when visiting London.

Newman, Francis William (1805–97), classicist, younger brother of John Henry Newman; abandoned religious orthodoxy; became Professor of Latin at University College London in 1846; Chapman published several of his books explaining his religious position 1847–54; wrote for the *WR* under Chapman, often for no pay, until 1865.

Papworth, John Buonarotti (1775–1847), architect and designer; rebuilt 142 Strand for John Wright between 1832 and 1838.

Parker, John William (1820–60), publisher with his father, also John William Parker (1792–1870) at 445 Strand; editor of *Fraser's Magazine* from 1847; friend of Froude.

Parker, Theodore (1810–60), Unitarian minister in Boston; friend of Emerson; Chapman reprinted his *Discourse of Matters pertaining to Religion* in 1852.

Parkes, Bessie Rayner, later Belloc (1829–1925), feminist and friend of Marian Evans and Barbara Leigh Smith; Chapman published her *Poems* in 1852 and her pamphlet *Remarks on the Education of Girls* in 1854.

Parkes, Joseph (1796–1865), solicitor and reformer; father of Bessie Rayner Parkes; financial subscriber to Marian Evans's translation of Strauss's *The Life of Jesus*, published by Chapman in 1846.

Pattison, Mark (1813–84), Oxford scholar; contributor to *Essays and Reviews* (1860); Rector of Lincoln College from 1861; regular contributor on philosophy and religion to the *WR* 1854–67.

Payn, James (1830–98), journalist and minor novelist; friend of Harriet Martineau; wrote articles on parody and ballads for the *WR* 1854–5.

Putnam, George Palmer (1814–72), American publisher who settled in London in 1841 and opened a shop selling American books; entered into an arrangement with Chapman in 1848 that Chapman would be his London agent and returned to New York; the arrangement broke down in 1849.

Raciborski, Adam, doctor working in Paris; author of works on female puberty (1844) and menstruation (1856).

Reid, Elisabeth Jesser, née Sturch (1789–1866), wealthy Unitarian philanthropist, friend of Henry Crabb Robinson and Harriet Martineau; founder in 1849 of the Ladies' College, Bedford Square, later known as Bedford College.

Robinson, Henry Crabb (1775–1867), Unitarian diarist and journalist; friend of Wordsworth and Coleridge; member of University College Council; benefactor of University Hall; attended parties at 142 Strand.

Ronge, Johannes (1813–87), ex-Roman Catholic priest and German exile in London from 1851; with his wife Bertha opened the first English kindergarten at his home in Hampstead.

Rossetti, Dante Gabriel (1828–82), painter, poet, member of the Pre-Raphaelite Brotherhood; friend of Barbara Leigh Smith and Bessie Rayner Parkes.

Rossetti, William Michael (1829–1919), art critic and literary editor; younger brother of Dante Gabriel Rossetti and friend of A. C. Swinburne.

Saffi, Aurelio Count (1819–90), Italian poet and nationalist living in exile in London from 1851; befriended by Jane Carlyle; contributed an article on religion in Italy to the *WR* in October 1853.

Sewell, William (1804–74), Fellow of Exeter College, Oxford; burnt Froude's *Nemesis of Faith* in the College in 1849.

Smith, Barbara Leigh, later Madame Bodichon (1827–91), artist and women's activist; friend of Marian Evans and Bessie Rayner Parkes; author of *A Brief Summary, in Plain Language, of the Most Important Laws concerning Women*, published by Chapman in 1854; corresponded with Chapman in August–September 1855 about consummating their relationship.

Smith, Benjamin (1783–1860), radical politican; father of Barbara Leigh Smith; not married to her mother; educated his sons and daughters equally and gave them financial freedom when they reached the age of twenty-one.

Smith, Julia (1799–1883), sister of Benjamin Smith and aunt of Barbara Leigh Smith; friend of Henry Crabb Robinson and Elisabeth Reid; supporter of Bedford College; lodged with the Chapmans at 43 Blandford Square in the summer of 1854.

Smith, Octavius (1796–1871), brother of Benjamin Smith and uncle of Barbara Leigh Smith; managed the family brewery; supported Chapman and the *WR* financially from 1854.

Spencer, Herbert (1820–1903), philosopher and social theorist; friend of G. H. Lewes and Marian Evans; author of *Social Statics*, published by Chapman in 1851; contributed articles on social and political subjects to the *WR*.

Stanley, Edward Henry, later fifteenth Earl of Derby (1826–93), politician; son of the fourteenth Earl of Derby; served in his father's governments in 1852, 1858–9, when he became first Secretary of State for India, and 1866–8, when he served as Foreign Secretary; though a conservative, he had liberal views on religion, education, and free trade; supported Chapman's *WR* financially 1858–92.

Sully, James (1842–1923), philosopher and psychologist, Professor of Mind and Logic at University College London from 1892; wrote articles in the WR from 1871.

Syme, Ebenezer (1826–60), ex-Unitarian minister who worked as Chapman's assistant in the publishing business in 1851; contributed to the WR until October 1852, after which he emigrated to Australia.

Tait, Robert (1816–97), portrait painter and pioneer photographer; friend of George Combe and of the Carlyles, whom he painted and photographed in the 1850s; met G. H. Lewes and Marian Evans in Weimar in 1854.

Tallis, John (1818–76), printer and publisher; published London Street Views in 1838–40 and 1847.

Tayler, John James (1797–1869), Unitarian minister and professor at Manchester New College and Principal when the College moved to London in 1853; colleague and friend of James Martineau; Chapman published his books, including Christian Aspects of Faith and Duty in 1851.

Taylor, Clementia, née Doughty (1810–1908), women's activist; wife of Peter Alfred Taylor; friend of Marian Evans; supporter of Mazzini; agitated for women's suffrage.

Taylor, Peter Alfred (1819–91), Unitarian politician and radical; nephew of Samuel Courtauld, in whose silk firm he was a partner; founded the Society of the Friends of Italy in 1847; became an MP in 1862; agitated against slavery and for the abolition of church rates and women's suffrage.

Thackeray, William Makepeace (1811–63), novelist and journalist; visited Chapman at 142 Strand; described life in London, particularly in the Strand, in his novel Pendennis (1850).

Thom, John Hamilton (1808–94), Unitarian minister and colleague of James Martineau in Liverpool; Chapman published his book St Paul's Epistle to the Corinthians in 1851; contributed to the Prospective Review, published by Chapman.

Tilley, Elisabeth (1820–?), live-in governess of the Chapman children at 142 Strand; Chapman's mistress until 1854, when she left England for Australia.

Tilt, Edward John (1815–93), physician at the Farringdon General Dispensary, where he knew Chapman; author of books on women's diseases.

Tyndall, John (1820–93), physicist and friend of T. H. Huxley; Professor of Natural Philosophy at the Royal Institution from 1853; shared with Huxley the reviewing of scientific works in the WR 1855–6.

Ward, Mary, née Arnold (1851–1920), known as Mrs Humphry Ward, novelist; daughter of Tom Arnold and author of the bestselling novel of religious doubt, Robert Elsmere, in 1888.

White, William (1807–82), bookseller and printer in Bedford, then Doorkeeper to the House of Commons; wrote a pamphlet in 1852, To Think or Not to Think, in defence of his son William Hale White, who had been expelled from theological college.

White, William Hale (1831–1913), novelist and civil servant; son of William White; rejected the Calvinism of his theological college and was expelled in 1852; became an assistant to Chapman in the publishing business and lodged at 142 Strand from 1852 to 1854, when he became a clerk in the Registrar General's office in Somerset House; recalled life at 142 Strand with Chapman and Marian Evans in several newspaper articles from the 1870s and in his most successful novel, *The Autobiography of Mark Rutherford* (1881).

Wicksteed, Charles (1810–85), Unitarian minister in Liverpool; colleague of James Martineau, J. H. Thom, and J. J. Tayler and fellow contributor to the *Prospective Review*, published by Chapman.

Williams, Rowland (1817–70), Church of England clergyman whose contribution to the controversial *Essays and Reviews* (1860) led to his being prosecuted, with another of the essayists, H. B. Wilson, for heterodoxy.

Wilson, Henry Bristow (1803–88), liberal Church of England clergyman who was prosecuted for heterodoxy with Rowland Williams after publishing a liberal essay in *Essays and Reviews* (1860); he reviewed theological books for the *WR* 1855–70.

Wilson, Thomas (1811–?), former Church of England curate and friend of Carlyle, who found him a teaching post in Weimar in 1853; there he met G. H. Lewes and Marian Evans in 1854.

Bibliography

1. Manuscript Sources

Manuscript letters to and from Chapman are scattered in a number of libraries in Britain and the United States of America. Gordon S. Haight published, or quoted from, a number of those connected with George Eliot in *The George Eliot Letters*, and printed extracts from Chapman's letters to Barbara Leigh Smith, Johanna von Heyligenstaedt, and Hannah Macdonald in *George Eliot and John Chapman, with Chapman's Diaries*. The manuscript collections I have consulted are as follows:

Beinecke Rare Book and Manuscript Library, Yale University (Chapman MSS, George Eliot/George Henry Lewes Collection).

Birmingham University Library (Harriet Martineau Papers, University of Birmingham Staff Papers: Henry Arthur Smith Papers).

Bishopsgate Library, Bishopsgate Institute and Foundation, London (Holyoake Collection).

Bodleian Library, Oxford (A. H. Clough Correspondence, Max Müller Papers, Harriet Martineau Papers, Mark Pattison Correspondence).

British Library, London (Richard Cobden Papers, W. E. Gladstone Papers, Charles Kingsley Papers, Harriet Martineau MSS).

Rare Book and Manuscript Library, Columbia University (Froude letters in Rider Haggard Papers).

Devon Record Office, Exeter (W. E. Hickson Papers).

Dr Williams's Library, London (Henry Crabb Robinson MSS).

Rare Book, Manuscript, and Special Collections Library, Duke University, Durham, North Carolina (J. A. Froude Collection, Edward Lombe Correspondence, John Chapman Correspondence).

Girton College, Cambridge (Bessie Rayner Parkes Papers).

Harris Manchester College Library, Oxford (James Martineau Papers).

Imperial College London, Library Archives and Special Collections (T. H. Huxley Papers).

Liverpool Record Office, Liverpool Libraries (Derby Papers).

National Co-operative Archive, Manchester (Holyoake Collection).

National Library of Scotland, Edinburgh (W. & R. Chambers Papers, George Combe Papers).

Natural History Museum, London (Owen Collection).

Senate House Library, University of London (J. L. Motley MSS).

University College London Library (Sheldon Amos MSS, Edwin Chadwick Papers, James Hannay Diary, College Correspondence).

2. Books and Articles

Ackroyd, Peter, *London: The Biography* (London, 2000).

Alexander, Christine, and Smith, Margaret, *The Oxford Companion to the Brontës* (Oxford, 2003).

Altick, Richard D., *The Shows of London* (London, 1978).

The Amberley Papers: The Letters and Diaries of Lord and Lady Amberley, ed. Bertrand and Patricia Russell, 2 vols. (London, 1937).

Arnold, Matthew, *The Letters of Matthew Arnold*, ed. Cyril Y. Lang, 6 vols. (London, 1996–2001).

Ashton, Rosemary, *G. H. Lewes: A Life* (Oxford, 1991, reprinted London, 2000).

—— *George Eliot: A Life* (London, 1996, reprinted 1997).

—— *The German Idea: Four English Writers and the Reception of German Thought 1800–1860* (Cambridge, 1980, reprinted London, 1994).

—— *Little Germany: Exile and Asylum in Victorian England* (Oxford, 1986, reprinted 1989).

—— 'New George Eliot Letters at the Huntington', *Huntington Library Quarterly*, LIV (Spring 1991).

—— *Thomas and Jane Carlyle: Portrait of a Marriage* (London, 2002, reprinted 2003).

Bagehot, Walter, *The Collected Works of Walter Bagehot*, ed. Norman St John-Stevas, 15 vols. (London, 1965–86).

Baker, William, and Ross, John C., *George Eliot: A Bibliographical History* (London, 2002).

Barnes, James J., *Authors, Publishers and Politicians: The Quest for an Anglo-American Copyright Agreement 1815–1854* (London, 1974).

—— *Free Trade in Books: A Study of the London Book Trade since 1800* (Oxford, 1964).

Barrett, Elizabeth, *Elizabeth Barrett to Miss Mitford*, ed. Betty Miller (London, 1954).

Bayless, Joy, *Rufus Wilmot Griswold: Poe's Literary Executor* (Nashville, Tennessee, 1943).

Bentley, Nicolas, Slater, Michael, and Burgess, Nina, *The Dickens Index* (Oxford, 1988, reprinted 1990).

Bergonzi, Bernard, *A Victorian Wanderer: The Life of Thomas Arnold the Younger* (Oxford, 2003).

Bibby, Cyril, *Scientist Extraordinary: The Life and Scientific Work of Thomas Henry Huxley 1825–1895* (London, 1972).

Bonham-Carter, Victor, *Authors by Profession*, 2 vols. (London, 1978).

Bradley, Simon and Pevsner, Nikolaus, *The Buildings of England, London 6: Westminster* (New Haven, Conn., and London, 2003).

Bray, Charles, *Phases of Opinion and Experience during a Long Life: An Autobiography* (London, 1884).

British Literary Publishing Houses, 1820–1880, ed. Patricia J. Anderson and Jonathan Rose (London, 1991).

Brontë, Charlotte, *The Letters of Charlotte Brontë*, ed. Margaret Smith, 3 vols. (Oxford, 1995–2004).

Browne, Janet, *Charles Darwin: The Power of Place* (London, 2002).

Browning, Robert, *Letters of Robert Browning*, ed. Thurman L. Hood (London, 1933).

Buchner, Wilhelm, *Ferdinand Freiligrath, ein Dichterleben in Briefen*, 2 vols. (Lahr, 1882).

Buckley, Jessie K., *Joseph Parkes of Birmingham, and the part which he played in radical reform movements from 1825 to 1845* (London, 1926).

Carlyle, Jane Welsh, *Jane Welsh Carlyle: A New Selection of her Letters*, ed. Trudy Bliss (London, 1950).

Carlyle, Thomas, *The Collected Letters of Thomas and Jane Welsh Carlyle*, Duke-Edinburgh Edition, ed. C. R. Sanders, K. J. Fielding, Clyde de L. Ryals, Ian Campbell, Aileen Christianson, et al., 33 vols. so far (Durham, North Carolina, 1970–).

——— *Reminiscences*, ed. K. J. Fielding and Ian Campbell (Oxford, 1997).

——— *Sartor Resartus*, ed. Mark Engel and Rodger L. Tarr (London, 2000).

Chambers, Robert, *Man of Letters: The Early Life and Love Letters of Robert Chambers*, ed. C. H. Layman (Edinburgh, 1990).

Chapman, John, *Brief Outlines and Review of a Work entitled 'The Principles of Nature, her Divine Revelations, and a Voice to Mankind. By and through Andrew Jackson Davis, the "Poughkeepsie Seer" and "Clairvoyant"': being the Substance of a Preface to that Work* (London, 1847).

——— *Chloroform and other Anaesthetics: Their History, and Use during Childbirth* (London, 1859).

——— *Diarrhoea and Cholera: Their Origin, Proximate Cause, and Cure, through the Agency of the Nervous System, by Means of Ice* (London, 1865).

—— *Functional Diseases of the Stomach: Sea-Sickness, its Nature and Treatment* (London, 1864).

—— *Functional Diseases of Women: Cases Illustrative of a New Method of Treating them through the Agency of the Nervous System by Means of Cold and Heat* (London, 1863).

—— *Human Nature: A Philosophical Exposition of the Divine Institution of Reward and Punishment, which obtains in the physical, intellectual, and moral constitution of Man; with an introductory essay. To which is added, a series of ethical observations, written during the perusal of the Rev. James Martineau's recent work, entitled 'Endeavours after the Christian Life'* (London, 1844).

—— *The Medical Institutions of the United Kingdom: A History exemplifying the Evils of Over-legislation* (London, 1870).

Chapman, John Wallis, 'John Chapman's Children', *George Eliot Fellowship Review*, X (1979), 11–13.

—— *Philosopher John: John Chapman of Loughborough 1801–1854, Engineer, Inventor, Political Writer* (Cartmel, 1983).

Clough, Arthur Hugh, *The Bothie of Toper-na-Fuosich: A Long-Vacation Pastoral* (Oxford and London, 1848).

—— *The Correspondence of Arthur Hugh Clough*, ed. Frederick L. Mulhauser, 2 vols. (Oxford, 1957).

—— *The Oxford Diaries of Arthur Hugh Clough*, ed. Anthony Kenny (Oxford, 1990).

Coley, N. G., 'Henry Bence-Jones', *Notes and Records of the Royal Society*, XXVIII (1973).

Combe, George, *Outlines of Phrenology*, sixth edition (Edinburgh, 1836).

Conway, Moncure Daniel, *Emerson at Home and Abroad* (London, 1883).

Cooter, Roger, *The Cultural Meaning of Popular Science: Phrenology and the Organization of Consent in Nineteenth-Century Britain* (Cambridge, 1984).

Darwin, Charles and Huxley, Thomas Henry, *Charles Darwin and Thomas Henry Huxley: Autobiographies*, ed. Gavin de Beer (London, 1974).

Desmond, Adrian, *Huxley*, 2 vols. (London, 1994 and 1997).

—— and Moore, James, *Darwin* (London, 1991).

Dickens, Charles, *The Letters of Charles Dickens*, ed. Madeleine House, Graham Storey, Kathleen Tillotson, et al., 12 vols. (Oxford, 1965–2002).

Donne, William Bodham, *William Bodham Donne and his Friends*, ed. Catharine B. Johnson (London, 1905).

Drummond, James, and Upton, C. B., *Life and Letters of James Martineau*, 2 vols. (London, 1902).

[Drysdale, George], *Physical, Sexual, and Natural Religion* (London, 1855).

Duncan, David, *The Life and Letters of Herbert Spencer* (London, 1908).

Dunn, Waldo Hilary, *James Anthony Froude: A Biography*, 2 vols. (Oxford, 1961, 1963).

[Eliot, George], *An Analytical Catalogue of Mr Chapman's Publications* (London, 1852).

Eliot, George, *Essays of George Eliot*, ed. Thomas Pinney (New York, 1963).

—— *The Essence of Christianity*, translated from the German of Ludwig Feuerbach (London, 1854, reprinted New York, 1957).

—— *The George Eliot Letters*, ed. Gordon S. Haight, 9 vols. (New Haven, Conn., 1954–5, 1978).

—— *The Life of Jesus*, translated from the German of David Friedrich Strauss (London, 1846, reprinted with an introduction by Peter C. Hodgson, 1973).

—— *Selected Critical Writings*, ed. Rosemary Ashton (Oxford, 1992).

Emerson, Ralph Waldo, *The Correspondence of Emerson and Carlyle*, ed. Joseph Slater (New York, 1964).

—— *Emerson-Clough Letters*, ed. Howard F. Lowry and Ralph Leslie Rusk (New York, 1968).

—— *The Journals and Miscellaneous Notebooks of Ralph Waldo Emerson*, ed. William H. Gilman et al., 16 vols. (Cambridge, Mass., 1960–82).

—— *The Letters of Ralph Waldo Emerson*, ed. Ralph L. Rusk and Eleanor M. Tilton, 10 vols. (New York, 1939–95).

Eve, A. S., and Creasey, C. H., *Life and Work of John Tyndall* (London, 1945).

Evelyn, John, *The Diary of John Evelyn*, ed. E. S. de Beer, 6 vols. (Oxford, 1955).

Freiligrath, Ferdinand, *Freiligraths Briefwechsel mit Marx und Engels*, ed. Manfred Häckel, 2 vols. (Berlin, 1976).

Froude, James Anthony, *The Nemesis of Faith* (London, 1849, reprinted with an introduction by Rosemary Ashton, 1988).

[——] 'Zeta', *Shadows of the Clouds* (London, 1847).

—— *Thomas Carlyle: The History of his Life in London*, 2 vols. (London, 1884).

Fryer, Peter, *The Man of Pleasure's Companion: A 19th-Century Anthology of Amorous Entertainment* (London, 1968).

Gaskell, Elizabeth, *The Letters of Mrs Gaskell*, ed. J. A. V. Chapple and Arthur Pollard (Manchester, 1966).

Gibbon, Charles, *The Life of George Combe*, 2 vols. (London, 1878).

Gibbs-Smith, C. H., *The Great Exhibition of 1851* (London, 1950, reprinted 1981).

Gladstone, Florence M., *Aubrey House Kensington 1698–1920* (London, 1922).

Gladstone, William Ewart, *The Gladstone Diaries*, ed. M. R. D. Foot and H. C. G. Matthew, 14 vols. (Oxford, 1968–94).

Gordon, Arthur Hamilton, Lord Stanmore, *Sidney Herbert, Lord Herbert of Lea: A Memoir*, 2 vols. (London, 1906).

Greeley, Horace, *Glances at Europe: in a Series of Letters from Great Britain, France, Italy, Switzerland, etc. during the summer of 1851, including Notices of the Great Exhibition, or World's Fair* (New York, 1851).

Greenspan, Ezra, *George Palmer Putnam: Representative American Publisher* (Pennsylvania, 2000).

di Gregorio, Mario A., *T. H. Huxley's Place in Natural Science* (New Haven, Conn., 1984).

Grierson, Janet, *Dr Wilson and his Malvern Hydro* (Malvern, 1998).

Haight, Gordon S., *George Eliot: A Biography* (Oxford, 1969).

―――― *George Eliot and John Chapman, with Chapman's Diaries* (London, 1940, reprinted with additions, 1969).

―――― 'The Publication of Motley's *Rise of the Dutch Republic*', *Yale University Library Gazette*, LIV (January 1980).

Hanson, Michael, *2000 Years of London: An Illustrated Survey* (London, 1967).

Harte, Negley, and North, John, *The World of UCL 1828–1990* (London, 1991).

Herstein, Sheila R., *A Mid-Victorian Feminist: Barbara Leigh Smith Bodichon* (New Haven, Conn., 1985).

Hirsch, Pam, *Barbara Leigh Smith Bodichon 1827–1891: Feminist, Artist and Rebel* (London, 1998).

Holcombe, Lee, 'Victorian Wives and Property: Reform of the Married Women's Property Law, 1857–1882', in *A Widening Sphere: Changing Roles of Victorian Women*, ed. Martha Vicinus (London, 1977).

Hollingshead, John, *My Lifetime*, 2 vols. (London, 1895).

Hollister, Paul, *The Author's Wallet* (New York, 1934).

Holmes, F. Morell, *Exeter Hall and its Associations* (London, 1881).

Holyoake, G. J., *The History of the Last Trial by Jury for Atheism in England* (London, 1850).

Howitt, Mary, *An Autobiography*, ed. Margaret Howitt, 2 vols. (London, 1889).

Huxley, Leonard, *Life and Letters of Thomas Henry Huxley*, 2 vols. (London, 1900).

Ireland, Alexander, *Ralph Waldo Emerson, his Life, Genius, and Writings: A Biographical Sketch* (London, 1882).

Jones, Henry Bence, *An Autobiography* (privately printed, London, 1929).

Lee, Amice, *Laurels & Rosemary: The Life of William and Mary Howitt* (Oxford, 1955).

Lewes, George Henry, *The Letters of George Henry Lewes*, ed. William Baker, 3 vols. (Victoria, British Columbia, 1995–9).

Lillywhite, Bryant, *London Coffee Houses: A Reference Book of Coffee Houses of the 17th, 18th, and 19th Centuries* (London, 1963).

Linton, Eliza Lynn, *The Autobiography of Christopher Kirkland*, 3 vols. (London, 1885).

―――― *My Literary Life* (London, 1899).

Lombe, Edward, 'Letters to Robert Browning', *Baylor Browning Interest Series*, VIII (September 1934).

London Scene from the Strand, ed. Gareth Cotterell (London, 1974).

London – World City 1800–1840, ed. Celina Fox (London, 1992).

Lowndes, Marie Belloc, *I, Too, Have Lived in Arcadia* (London, 1941).

McCalman, Iain, *Radical Underworld: Prophets, Revolutionaries and Pornographers in London, 1795–1840* (Oxford, 1993).

McCarthy, Justin, *Reminiscences*, 2 vols. (London, 1899).

Maclean, Catherine Macdonald, *Mark Rutherford: A Biography of William Hale White* (London, 1955).

McLaren, Angus, *Birth Control in Nineteenth-Century England* (London, 1978).

Malleson, Elizabeth, *Autobiographical Notes and Letters, with a memoir by Hope Malleson* (privately printed, 1926).

de Maré, Eric, *London 1851: The Year of the Great Exhibition* (London, 1973).

Martineau, Harriet, *Autobiography* (London, 1877, reprinted in 2 vols. with an introduction by Gaby Weiner, 1983).

———— *Harriet Martineau's Letters to Fanny Wedgwood*, ed. Elisabeth Sanders Arbuckle (Stanford, California, 1983).

———— *Harriet Martineau: Selected Letters*, ed. Valerie Sanders (Oxford, 1990).

Marx, Karl, and Engels, Friedrich, *Marx-Engels Collected Works*, 50 vols. (London, New York, Moscow, 1975–2004).

Masson, David, *Memories of London in the 'Forties* (London, 1908).

Matthew, H. C. G., *Gladstone 1809–1898* (Oxford, 1997).

Mazzini, Giuseppe, *Scritti editi ed inediti*, Edizione Nazionale, 106 vols. (Imola, 1906–90).

Mill, John Stuart, *Collected Works of John Stuart Mill*, ed. Francis E. Mineka, Dwight N. Lindley, et al., 33 vols. (London, 1963–91).

Moscucci, Ornella, *The Science of Woman: Gynaecology and Gender in England, 1800–1929* (Cambridge, 1990).

Motley, John Lothrop, *Correspondence of John Lothrop Motley, DCL*, ed. George William Curtis, 2 vols. (London, 1889).

Müller, Friedrich Max, *Chips from a German Workshop*, 4 vols. (London, 1867–75).

———— *The Life and Letters of the Right Honourable Friedrich Max Müller*, ed. his wife, 2 vols. (London, 1902).

Nead, Lynda, *Victorian Babylon: People, Streets, and Images in Nineteenth-Century London* (London, 2000).

Newman, Francis William, *Phases of Faith* (London, 1850).

———— *The Soul, her Sorrows and Aspirations* (London, 1849).

Nicoll, William Robertson, *A Bookman's Letters* (London, 1913).

[Parkes, Bessie Rayner], *Remarks on the Education of Girls, with Reference to the Social, Legal, and Industrial Position of Women in the Present Day* (London, 1854).

Pattison, Mark, *Memoirs* (London, 1885, reprinted 1969).

Payn, James, *Some Literary Recollections* (London, 1884).

Phillips, Hugh, *Mid-Georgian London: A Topographical and Social Survey of Central and Western London about 1750* (London, 1964).

318

Pichanick, Valerie Kossew, *Harriet Martineau: The Woman and her Work 1802–76* (Ann Arbor, Michigan, 1980).

Pike, E. Royston, *Human Documents of the Victorian Golden Age (1850–1875)* (London, 1967).

Poovey, Mary, *Uneven Developments: The Ideological Work of Gender in Mid-Victorian England* (Chicago, Illinois, 1988).

Pope-Hennessy, James, *Monckton Milnes: The Years of Promise 1809–1851* (London, 1949).

Porter, Bernard, *The Refugee Question in Mid-Victorian Politics* (Cambridge, 1979).

Porter, Roy, *London: A Social History* (London, 1994).

—— and Teich, Mikulas, *Sexual Knowledge, Sexual Science: The History of Attitudes to Sexuality* (Cambridge, 1994).

Poynter, F. N. L., 'John Chapman (1821–1894): Publisher, Physician, and Medical Reformer', *Journal of the History of Medicine*, V (1950).

Prickett, Stephen, *Romanticism and Religion: The Tradition of Coleridge and Wordsworth in the Victorian Church* (Cambridge, 1976).

Race, Sydney, 'John Chapman', *Notes and Queries*, CLXXXI (26 April 1941), 293.

—— 'John Chapman of Nottingham', *Nottingham Guardian* (5 July 1943), pp. 3–4.

Ray, Gordon N., *Thackeray: The Uses of Adversity (1811–1846)* (London, 1955).

—— *Thackeray: The Age of Wisdom (1847–1863)* (London, 1958).

Reid, T. Wemyss, *Life of the Right Honourable William Edward Forster*, 2 vols. (London, 1888).

Robbins, William, *The Newman Brothers: An Essay in Comparative Intellectual Biography* (London, 1966).

Robinson, Henry Crabb, *Diary, Reminiscences and Correspondence*, ed. Thomas Sadler, 3 vols. (London, 1869).

—— *Henry Crabb Robinson on Books and their Writers*, ed. E. J. Morley, 3 vols. (London, 1938).

Rogue's Progress: The Autobiography of 'Lord Chief Baron' Nicholson, ed. John L. Bradley (London, 1965).

Rosenberg, Sheila, 'The Financing of Radical Opinion: John Chapman and the *Westminster Review*', in *The Victorian Periodical Press: Samplings and Soundings*, ed. Joanne Shattock and Michael Wolff (Leicester, 1982).

—— 'The "wicked *Westminster*": John Chapman, his Contributors and Promises Fulfilled', *Victorian Periodicals Review*, LXXXVIII (Fall 2000).

Rossetti, Dante Gabriel, *Letters of Dante Gabriel Rossetti*, ed. Oswald Doughty and John Robert Wahl, 4 vols. (Oxford, 1965–7).

Rossetti, William Michael, *The Diary of W. M. Rossetti 1870–1873*, ed. Odette Bornand (Oxford, 1977).

Rudman, Harry W., *Italian Nationalists and English Letters* (London, 1940).

Sanders, C. R., *Coleridge and the Broad Church Movement* (New York, 1942, reprinted 1972).

Sarti, Roland, *Mazzini: A Life for the Religion of Politics* (London, 1997).

Secord, James A., *Victorian Sensation: The Extraordinary Publication, Reception, and Secret Authorship of* Vestiges of the Natural History of Creation (London, 2000).

Shanley, Mary Lyndon, *Feminism, Marriage and Law in Victorian England 1850–1895* (London, 1989).

Sieveking, I. Giberne, *Memoirs and Letters of Francis W. Newman* (London, 1909).

Slater, Michael, *Douglas Jerrold: A Life, 1803–1857* (London, 2001).

[Smith, Barbara Leigh], *A Brief Summary, in Plain Language, of the Most Important Laws concerning Women; together with a Few Observations thereon* (London, 1854).

Smith, Brian S., *A History of Malvern* (Leicester, 1964).

Smith, Denis Mack, *Mazzini* (London, 1994).

Spencer, Herbert, *An Autobiography*, 2 vols. (London, 1904).

Stark, Susanne, 'A "Monstrous Book" after all? James Anthony Froude and the Reception of Goethe's *Die Wahlverwandtschaften* in Nineteenth-Century Britain', *Modern Language Review*, XCVIII (January 2003).

Stephen, Barbara, *Emily Davies and Girton College* (London, 1927).

Stewart, W. A. C., and McCann, W. P., *The Educational Innovators 1750–1880*, 2 vols. (London, 1967–8).

Stone, Wilfred, *Religion and Art of William Hale White* (Stanford, California, 1954).

Sully, James, *My Life and Friends: A Psychologist's Memories* (London, 1918).

Sutherland, John, *Mrs Humphry Ward: Eminent Victorian, Pre-eminent Edwardian* (Oxford, 1990).

Tallis, John, *John Tallis's London Street Views 1838–1840, together with the revised and enlarged views of 1847*, ed. Peter Jackson (London, 1969).

Taylor, Ina, *George Eliot: Woman of Contradictions* (London, 1989).

Thackeray, William Makepeace, *The History of Pendennis*, ed. John Sutherland (Oxford, 1994).

—— *The Letters and Private Papers of William Makepeace Thackeray*, ed. Gordon N. Ray, 4 vols. (Cambridge, Mass., 1945–6).

—— *Vanity Fair*, ed. John Carey (London, 2001).

Thomson, Patricia, *George Sand and the Victorians: Her Influence and Reputation in Nineteenth-Century England* (London, 1977).

Timbs, John, *Club Life of London, with Anecdotes of the Clubs, Coffee-Houses and Taverns of the Metropolis during the 17th, 18th, and 19th Centuries*, 2 vols. (London, 1866).

Tuke, Margaret J., *A History of Bedford College for Women 1849–1937* (Oxford, 1939).

The Victorian Periodical Press: Samplings and Soundings, ed. Joanne Shattock and Michael Wolff (Leicester, 1982).

Ward, Mrs Humphry, *Robert Elsmere* (London, 1888, reprinted with an introduction by Rosemary Ashton, Oxford, 1987).

Webb, R. K., *Harriet Martineau: A Radical Victorian* (London, 1960).

The Wellesley Index to Victorian Periodicals 1824–1900, ed. Walter E. Houghton and Esther Rhoads Houghton, 5 vols. (London, 1966–90).

White, Paul, *Thomas Huxley: Making the 'Man of Science'* (Cambridge, 2003).

[White, William Hale], *The Autobiography of Mark Rutherford* (London, 1881, reprinted with an introduction by Don Cupitt, 1988).

White, William Hale, *The Early Life of Mark Rutherford (W. Hale White). By Himself* (London, 1913).

———— 'George Eliot as I Knew Her', *Bookman* (August 1902).

A Widening Sphere: Changing Roles of Victorian Women, ed. Martha Vicinus (London, 1977).

Willey, Basil, *More Nineteenth-Century Studies* (London, 1956).

Williams, Harley, *Doctors Differ: Five Studies in Contrast* (London, 1946).

Williams, Rowland, *Life and Letters*, ed. his wife, 2 vols. (London, 1874).

Winter, Alison, *Mesmerized: Powers of Mind in Victorian Britain* (London, 1998).

Worth, George J., *James Hannay: His Life and Works* (Kansas, 1964).

Youngson, A. J., *The Scientific Revolution in Victorian Medicine* (London, 1979).

Notes

Introduction

1. See *John Tallis's London Street Views 1838–1840, together with the revised and enlarged views of 1847*, ed. Peter Jackson (London, 1969), editor's introduction, pp. 9, 10, 17.
2. *The Diary of John Evelyn*, ed. E. S. de Beer, 6 vols. (Oxford, 1955), III, 246. (I have modernised the spelling in my quotation.) There are a number of excellent books on London history and topography in the nineteenth century, including Michael Hanson, *2000 Years of London: An Illustrated Survey* (London, 1967); Eric de Maré, *London 1851: The Year of the Great Exhibition* (London, 1973); *London Scene from the Strand*, ed. Gareth Cotterell (London, 1974); *London – World City 1800–1840*, ed. Celina Fox (London, 1992); Roy Porter, *London: A Social History* (London, 1994); Lynda Nead, *Victorian Babylon: People, Streets, and Images in Nineteenth-Century London* (London, 2000); Peter Ackroyd, *London: The Biography* (London, 2000).
3. 'The Story of the Strand', reprinted in *London Scene from the Strand*, p. 1.
4. See Thackeray, *Vanity Fair* (1847–8), ed. John Carey (London, 2001), p. 765. For Thackeray's life and career, see Gordon N. Ray's two-volume biography, *Thackeray: The Uses of Adversity (1811–1846)* (London, 1955) and *Thackeray: The Age of Wisdom (1847–1863)* (London, 1958).
5. See Ray, *Thackeray: The Age of Wisdom*, pp. 343ff; John Hollingshead, *My Lifetime*, 2 vols. (London, 1895), I, 154–6; *Rogue's Progress: The Autobiography of 'Lord Chief Baron' Nicholson*, ed. John L. Bradley (London, 1965). For other accounts of nineteenth-century clubs and dives, see John Timbs, *Club Life of London, with Anecdotes of the Clubs, Coffee-Houses and Taverns of the Metropolis during the 17th, 18th, and 19th Centuries*, 2 vols. (London, 1866); David Masson, *Memories of London in the 'Forties* (London, 1908); Peter Fryer, *The Man of Pleasure's Companion: A 19th-Century Anthology of Amorous Entertainment*

(London, 1968); Richard D. Altick, *The Shows of London* (London, 1978); Donald J. Gray, 'Early Victorian Scandalous Journalism: Renton Nicholson's *The Town* (1837–1842)', in *The Victorian Periodical Press: Samplings and Soundings*, ed. Joanne Shattock and Michael Wolff (Leicester, 1982), pp. 317ff. For the uses of Exeter Hall, see F. Morell Holmes, *Exeter Hall and its Associations* (London, 1881).

6. Tallis's 1847 plan lists twenty-three newspaper and periodical offices on the Strand; another half-dozen were located on streets leading off the Strand, such as Wellington Street and Catherine Street.

7. For Jerrold's life and career, see Michael Slater, *Douglas Jerrold: A Life, 1803–1857* (London, 2001).

8. See Chapman's diary, 14 June 1851, Gordon S. Haight, *George Eliot and John Chapman, with Chapman's Diaries* (London, 1940, reprinted with additions, 1969), p. 179.

9. For Lewes's life and career, see Rosemary Ashton, *G. H. Lewes: A Life* (Oxford, 1991, reprinted 2000).

10. See *London – World City*, ed. Celina Fox, p. 394.

11. Thackeray, *The History of Pendennis* (1850), ed. John Sutherland (Oxford, 1994), pp. 390–1.

12. See Nicolas Bentley, Michael Slater, and Nina Burgess, *The Dickens Index* (Oxford, 1988, reprinted 1990), p. 170.

13. See Herbert Spencer, *An Autobiography*, 2 vols. (London, 1904), I, 294, 347–9, 394; David Duncan, *The Life and Letters of Herbert Spencer* (London, 1908), p. 56.

14. *John Tallis's London Street Views* (1838 and 1847), pp. 222, 225, 288.

15. See *Athenaeum*, 12 June 1847, p. 609, for the announcement that Parker was taking over *Fraser's*. For an account of the firm, see *British Literary Publishing Houses, 1820–1880*, ed. Patricia J. Anderson and Jonathan Rose (London, 1991), pp. 233ff.

16. Justin McCarthy, *Reminiscences*, 2 vols. (London, 1899), I, 3; Rossetti to Alexander Gilchrist, 27 August 1861, *Letters of Dante Gabriel Rossetti*, ed. Oswald Doughty and John Robert Wahl, 4 vols. (Oxford, 1965–7), II, 419. The Blake poem alluded to is 'Long John Brown and Little Mary Bell'.

17. For a history of Holywell Street and an account of Dugdale's trial, see Nead, *Victorian Babylon*, pp. 161ff; for Dugdale's career, see Iain McCalman, *Radical Underworld: Prophets, Revolutionaries and Pornographers in London, 1795–1840* (Oxford, 1993).

18. See Angus McLaren, *Birth Control in Nineteenth-Century England* (London, 1978), p. 52.

19. [George Drysdale], *Physical, Sexual, and Natural Religion* (London, 1855); for

information on the book's sale, see E. Royston Pike, *Human Documents of the Victorian Golden Age (1850–1875)* (London, 1967), p. 338.

20. G. J. Holyoake, *The History of the Last Trial by Jury for Atheism in England* (London, 1850), p. 5.

21. *Westminster Review*, CXLIII (January 1895), 2.

22. See Timbs, *Club Life*, I, 313; II, 179; Giuseppe Mazzini to Giuseppe Lamberti, 13 June 1847, *Scritti editi ed inediti*, Edizione Nazionale, 106 vols. (Imola, 1906–90), XXXII, 175 and note; W. J. Linton to G. J. Holyoake, 22 April 1847, MS Holyoake Collection, National Co-operative Archive, Manchester.

23. *The Times*, 17 May 1832. For the history of the house since the seventeenth century see *John Tallis's London Street Views*, p. 222; Hugh Phillips, *Mid-Georgian London: A Topographical and Social Survey of Central and Western London about 1750* (London, 1964), pp. 170ff; Bryant Lillywhite, *London Coffee Houses: A Reference Book of Coffee Houses of the 17th, 18th, and 19th Centuries* (London, 1963), p. 616.

24. J. B. Papworth's architectural drawings for the rebuilding of 142 Strand, dated 1832, are in the RIBA British Architectural Library at the Victoria and Albert Museum, London (ref. PB 1313 PAP [125] 1–5). I am indebted to Charles Hind, Assistant Director (Special Collections) of the Library, for his help in locating and interpreting the drawings.

25. 'Stories of the Little Mother', p. 2. This is an account by Annie Chapman, Beatrice's daughter, of her mother's reminiscences, copied in typescript by the late John Wallis Chapman, Chapman's great-grandson, and used in his article 'John Chapman's Children', *George Eliot Fellowship Review*, X (1979), 11–13. Ina Taylor also quotes from the typescript in *George Eliot: A Woman of Contradictions* (London, 1989), p. 84. I am indebted to Ms Taylor for letting me have sight of the typescript.

26. See *Age*, 27 May 1838; *The Times*, 20 June, 30 July, 1 August 1838.

27. Timbs, *Club Life*, II, 95.

28. *The Times*, 4 July and 27 November 1845 and 6 January 1847. Records at the Westminster Archives Centre show the rates for 142 Strand.

29. The story of Wright's 'suicide' is in Annie Chapman, 'Stories of the Little Mother', p. 1.

30. *Athenaeum*, 24 July 1847, p. 778; *The Times*, 27 July and 11 August 1847.

31. See Horace Greeley, *Glances at Europe: in a Series of Letters from Great Britain, France, Italy, Switzerland, etc. during the summer of 1851, including Notices of the Great Exhibition, or World's Fair* (New York, 1851), p. 46; Theodore Parker to R. W. Emerson, 12 August 1844, *The Letters of Ralph Waldo Emerson*, ed. Ralph L. Rusk (vols. I-VI) and Eleanor M. Tilton (vols. VII-X), 10 vols. (New York, 1939–95), III, 287n; R. W. Griswold in *International*, 1 December 1851, see Joy

Bayless, *Rufus Wilmot Griswold: Poe's Literary Executor* (Nashville, Tennessee, 1943), p. 209.

32. Henry Crabb Robinson to his brother Thomas, 22 June 1849, MS Dr Williams's Library, London; *Critic*, 15 January 1852, p. 39; Thomas Carlyle to Robert Browning, 10 October 1851, *The Collected Letters of Thomas and Jane Welsh Carlyle*, Duke-Edinburgh Edition, ed. C. R. Sanders, K. J. Fielding, Clyde de L. Ryals, Ian Campbell, Aileen Christianson, et al., 33 vols. so far (Durham, North Carolina, 1970–), XXVI, 202.

33. Eliza Lynn Linton, *My Literary Life* (London, 1899), p. 92; see also Robert White, 'Dr John Chapman', *Athenaeum*, 15 December 1894, p. 828.

34. Carlyle to Emerson, 31 August 1847, *Collected Letters*, XXII, 49.

Chapter 1

1. See Haight, *George Eliot and John Chapman*, pp. 163, 179, 219.

2. Ibid., pp. 4–5, 260. Haight gives Susanna's date of birth as 26 August 1808; the year of her birth was 1807, according to the 1861 Census. The wedding took place in St Leodegarius Church, Basford, Nottingham, according to information in the Nottingham Register Office.

3. See Chapman's own account to George Combe of Edinburgh, July 1852, printed in *The George Eliot Letters*, ed. Gordon S. Haight, 9 vols. (New Haven, Conn., 1954–5, 1978), VIII, 56n.

4. Parker to Emerson, 12 August 1844, *Letters of Ralph Waldo Emerson*, III, 287n.

5. See *British Literary Publishing Houses*, p. 93; for information about *Prospective Review*, see *The Wellesley Index to Victorian Periodicals 1824–1900*, ed. Walter E. Houghton and Esther Rhoads Houghton, 5 vols. (London, 1966–90), III, 337–46.

6. [John Chapman], *Human Nature*, etc. (London, 1844), pp. 8, 38.

7. Robinson Diary, 7 September 1845, MS Dr Williams's Library.

8. William Maccall to Holyoake, 27 July 1853, MS Holyoake Collection, Manchester.

9. Copy of MS notes by Hale White's son J. H. Hale White, in University of Birmingham Staff Papers: Henry Arthur Smith Papers, Birmingham University Library; Carlyle to Maccall, 5 August 1848, *Collected Letters*, XXIII, 89 and n.

10. Emerson to Carlyle, 1 September 1844, *The Correspondence of Emerson and Carlyle*, ed. Joseph Slater (New York, 1964), p. 364; to Chapman, 31 August 1844; to James Munroe & Co., [31 October] 1844, *Letters of Ralph Waldo Emerson*, VII, 610–11; III, 265 and n.

11. See *Correspondence of Emerson and Carlyle*, introduction and letters *passim*.

12. Carlyle to Emerson, 29 September 1844; to Chapman, 21 March 1844, *Collected Letters*, XVIII, 225–6; XVII, 314.

13. See Rosemary Ashton, *Thomas and Jane Carlyle: Portrait of a Marriage* (London, 2002, reprinted 2003), pp. 178, 255.

14. Carlyle to John Forster, 4 October 1844, *Collected Letters*, XVIII, 228–9.

15. Carlyle to Emerson, 3 November 1844, ibid., XVIII, 258–9; see also ibid., XVIII, 229n, and Ashton, *Thomas and Jane Carlyle*, p. 198. For accounts of the copyright situation, see James J. Barnes, *Authors, Publishers and Politicians: The Quest for an Anglo-American Copyright Agreement 1815–1854* (London, 1974), pp. 153ff; Victor Bonham-Carter, *Authors by Profession*, 2 vols. (London, 1978), I, 73–4.

16. See Slater, introduction to *Correspondence of Emerson and Carlyle*, pp. 16–29.

17. Parker to Emerson, 12 August 1844, *Letters of Ralph Waldo Emerson*, III, 287n.

18. Emerson to Chapman, 26 March 1845, ibid., VIII, 17.

19. Emerson to James Munroe & Co., 13 October 1846, and to Margaret Fuller, 28 February 1847, ibid., III, 356, 378.

20. Emerson to Chapman, 31 May 1847, ibid., VIII, 118.

21. A. Andresen, *Luther Revived: or, a short account of Johannes Ronge, the bold reformer of the Catholic Church in Germany*. For Ronge in England, see Rosemary Ashton, *Little Germany: Exile and Asylum in Victorian England* (Oxford, 1986, reprinted 1989), pp. 179–81; W. A. C. Stewart and W. P. McCann, *The Educational Innovators 1750–1880*, 2 vols. (London, 1967–8), I, 298–301.

22. *Life of Jean Paul Friedrich Richter, compiled from various sources. Together with his autobiography*, translated from the German [by Eliza B. Lee]; see Carlyle to Chapman, 20 March 1844, *Collected Letters*, XVII, 313–14.

23. *Über das Verhältnis der bildenden Künste zu der Natur: The Philosophy of Art; an oration on the relation between the plastic arts and nature*, translated by A. Johnson.

24. Chapman, *Brief Outlines*, etc., pp. 5, 30. For a history of mesmerism in the nineteenth century, see Alison Winter, *Mesmerized: Powers of Mind in Victorian Britain* (London, 1998).

25. See Jane Carlyle to John Welsh, 13 December 1844, *Collected Letters*, XVIII, 283–4.

26. For the history of University College London, see Negley Harte and John North, *The World of UCL 1828–1990* (London, 1991).

27. For Elliotson's career, see Winter, *Mesmerized*; Harley Williams, *Doctors Differ: Five Studies in Contrast* (London, 1946), pp. 25–91. Further information about Elliotson's relationship with staff and students at University College London is in the UCL College Correspondence.

28. See Dickens to Emile de la Rue, 26 December 1844, and to F. M. Evans, 27 September 1849, *The Letters of Charles Dickens*, ed. Madeleine House, Graham Storey, Kathleen Tillotson, et al., 12 vols. (Oxford, 1965–2002), IV, 243 and n; V, 617 and n.

29. See Thackeray to his aunt, Mrs Ritchie, 19 November 1849, *The Letters and*

Private Papers of William Makepeace Thackeray, ed. Gordon N. Ray, 4 vols. (Cambridge, Mass., 1945–6), II, 610.

30. See Haight, *George Eliot and John Chapman*, p. 135n.

31. Copy of a letter from Chapman to his creditor Octavius Smith, 19 February 1857, MS Harriet Martineau Papers, Birmingham University Library.

32. For a discussion of Strauss and George Eliot's translation, see Rosemary Ashton, *The German Idea: Four English Writers and the Reception of German Thought 1800–1860* (Cambridge, 1980, reprinted London, 1994), pp. 147–55, and *George Eliot: A Life* (London, 1996, reprinted 1997), pp. 47ff. See also Peter C. Hodgson's introduction to the reprint of George Eliot's translation of *The Life of Jesus* (London, 1973).

33. See Gordon S. Haight, *George Eliot: A Biography* (Oxford, 1969), p. 59; William Baker and John C. Ross, *George Eliot: A Bibliographical History* (London, 2002), pp. 1–8.

34. See *The George Eliot Letters*, I, 172n, 175n. For Parkes's career, see Jessie K. Buckley, *Joseph Parkes of Birmingham, and the part which he played in radical reform movements from 1825 to 1845* (London, 1926).

35. George Eliot to Sara Hennell, 28 February 1847, and to George Combe, 27 January 1852, *The George Eliot Letters*, I, 231; VIII, 34.

36. George Eliot to Sara Hennell, 28 February 1847, ibid., I, 231.

37. See Haight, *George Eliot and John Chapman*, pp. 127n, 145, 158n.

38. Spencer, *Autobiography*, I, 347; Cara Bray to Sara Hennell, 4 November 1846, *The George Eliot Letters*, I, 225n.

39. Elizabeth Malleson, *Autobiographical Notes and Letters, with a memoir by Hope Malleson* (privately printed, 1926), pp. 101–2.

40. James Martineau, 'Strauss and Parker', *Westminster Review*, XLVII (April 1847), 137; see also James Drummond and C. B. Upton, *Life and Letters of James Martineau*, 2 vols. (London, 1902), I, 132–3.

41. George Eliot to Sara Hennell, 15 November 1846, *The George Eliot Letters*, I, 227.

42. Clough to E. Hawkins, 3 March 1849, *The Correspondence of Arthur Hugh Clough*, ed. Frederick L. Mulhauser, 2 vols. (Oxford, 1957), I, 248–9.

43. Charles Kingsley to William White, [July 1852], *The Early Life of Mark Rutherford (W. Hale White). By Himself* (London, 1913), pp. 75–6.

44. Spencer, *Autobiography*, I, 265; Robinson Diary, 5 July 1846, MS Dr Williams's Library.

45. Robinson Diary, 4 July 1846, ibid. For a good account of Newman's career, see Basil Willey, *More Nineteenth-Century Studies* (London, 1956).

46. See, for example, 'Works of Professor Newman', *Reasoner*, XV (3 August 1853), 68–9. Newman's letters to Holyoake are in the Holyoake Collection, Manchester;

Holyoake's diaries mention frequent meetings, MS Holyoake Collection, Bishopsgate Library, Bishopsgate Institute and Foundation.

47. Robinson to Thomas Robinson, 6 May 1848, MS Dr Williams's Library.

48. See Margaret J. Tuke, *A History of Bedford College for Women 1849–1937* (Oxford, 1939), pp. 22–4, 62–3, 320.

49. Robinson Diary, 21 May 1849, MS Dr Williams's Library.

50. Robinson Diary, 22 May 1849, ibid.

51. Robinson Diary, 20 June 1849; Robinson to Thomas Robinson, 22 June 1849, ibid.

52. Newman to James Martineau, 26 February and 14 September 1849, MS Martineau Papers, Harris Manchester College, Oxford.

53. Elizabeth Gaskell to Eliza Fox, 25 November 1849, *The Letters of Mrs Gaskell*, ed. J. A. V. Chapple and Arthur Pollard (Manchester, 1966), pp. 87, 88.

54. Newman, *Phases of Faith* (London, 1850), pp. 52–3; Willey, *More Nineteenth-Century Studies*, pp. 18–22.

55. For Newman's career, see I. Giberne Sieveking, *Memoirs and Letters of Francis W. Newman* (London, 1909); William Robbins, *The Newman Brothers: An Essay in Comparative Intellectual Biography* (London, 1966).

56. Willey, *More Nineteenth-Century Studies*, p. 50; Walter Bagehot to Edith Bagehot, December 1847, *The Collected Works of Walter Bagehot*, ed. Norman St John-Stevas, 15 vols. (London, 1965–86), XII, 265.

57. Tuke, *A History of Bedford College*, p. 73.

58. Robinson Diary, 19 April 1852, MS Dr Williams's Library.

59. See, for example, Diary, 4 May 1848, MS Dr Williams's Library.

60. See Drummond and Upton, *Life and Letters of James Martineau*, I, 245–6, 250–1.

61. Robinson Diary, 20 July 1848, *Diary, Reminiscences and Correspondence*, ed. Thomas Sadler, 3 vols. (London, 1869), III, 321.

62. Bagehot to W. C. Roscoe, 6 September 1848, *Collected Works*, XII, 279–80.

63. Bagehot to T. W. Bagehot, December 1848, ibid., XII, 289; see also Robinson Diary, 21 June 1852, MS Dr Williams's Library.

64. Robinson Diary, 21 June 1852, MS Dr Williams's Library.

65. George Eliot to Charles and Cara Bray, 28 June 1851; to Sara Hennell, 27 March 1874, *The George Eliot Letters*, I, 343; VI, 34.

66. See Ashton, *Thomas and Jane Carlyle*, pp. 140ff.

67. Emerson to Lidian Emerson, 27 October 1847, *Letters of Ralph Waldo Emerson*, III, 423.

68. Jane Carlyle to Lady Harriet Baring, and to W. E. Forster, 28 October 1847, *Collected Letters*, XXII, 139, 142.

69. See Emerson to Lidian Emerson, 30 October 1847, *Letters of Ralph Waldo Emerson*, III, 425–6.

70. See ibid., III, 430–1n.

71. Emerson to his mother, Ruth Haskins Emerson, 1 November 1847; to Elizabeth Hoar, 11 November 1847; and to Lidian Emerson, 13 November 1847, ibid., III, 428, 435, 438.

72. Emerson to Carlyle, 5 November 1847, *Correspondence of Emerson and Carlyle*, p. 432.

73. See *Letters of Ralph Waldo Emerson*, III, 441n; Alexander Ireland, *Ralph Waldo Emerson, his Life, Genius, and Writings: A Biographical Sketch* (London, 1882), pp. 165–6.

74. Emerson to Lidian Emerson, 2 December 1847, *Letters of Ralph Waldo Emerson*, III, 442.

75. Emerson to Margaret Fuller, 2 March 1848, ibid., IV, 26–7.

76. Emerson to Henry David Thoreau, 2 December 1847, ibid., VIII, 136.

77. Emerson to Lidian Emerson, 16 December 1847, ibid., III, 452–3.

78. See James A. Secord, *Victorian Sensation: The Extraordinary Publication, Reception, and Secret Authorship of* Vestiges of the Natural History of Creation (London, 2000), pp. 114–15, 131.

79. Robert Chambers to Alexander Ireland, April 1845, MS W. & R. Chambers Papers, National Library of Scotland.

80. Secord, *Victorian Sensation*, pp. 20–2; *Man of Letters: The Early Life and Love Letters of Robert Chambers*, ed. C. H. Layman (Edinburgh, 1990), pp. 180–1.

81. See James Payn, *Some Literary Recollections* (London, 1884), p. 142.

82. Charles Gibbon, *The Life of George Combe*, 2 vols. (London, 1878), II, 188–9; William Chilton to Holyoake, 1 February 1846, MS Holyoake Collection, Manchester; Chapman to Richard Owen, 13 January 1848, MS Owen Collection 62 (VII, 26), quoted by permission of the Board of Trustees of the Natural History Museum.

83. Emerson to Lidian Emerson, 21 or 22 February 1848, *Letters of Ralph Waldo Emerson*, IV, 19, 21.

84. Emerson to Carlyle, 2 March 1848, *Correspondence of Emerson and Carlyle*, p. 440.

85. William Hale White, 'George Eliot as I Knew her', *Bookman* (August 1902), p. 159, and 'Our London Letter', *Norfolk News*, 22 November 1873. (I am indebted to the Hale White scholar Mark Crees for these references.)

86. Susanna Chapman to George Combe, 14 July 1852, *The George Eliot Letters*, VIII, 54.

87. Chapman's advertisement is reproduced as Appendix C in Haight, *George Eliot and John Chapman*, pp. 260–1. Chapman also inserted a shorter advertisement in *The Times*, 21 March and 7 August 1850.

88. Haight, *George Eliot and John Chapman*, p. 261.

89. See Ireland, *Ralph Waldo Emerson*, p. 169.

90. See Dickens to John Forster, 29 February 1848, *Letters of Charles Dickens*, V, 256–7; Carlyle to William Bridges Adams, 7 March 1848, *Collected Letters*, XXII, 264.

91. Emerson to Lidian Emerson, 8 March 1848, *Letters of Ralph Waldo Emerson*, IV, 34; Carlyle to Emerson, 10 March 1848, *Collected Letters*, XXII, 267. For Lady Ashburton's circle and her relationship with Carlyle in particular, see Ashton, *Thomas and Jane Carlyle*, pp. 268ff.

92. Emerson to Samuel Ward, 20 March 1848, *Letters of Ralph Waldo Emerson*, VIII, 162.

93. Carlyle Journal, 14 March 1848, *Collected Letters*, XXII, 268n; Emerson to William Case, 12 March 1848, and to Lidian Emerson, 23 March 1848, *Letters of Ralph Waldo Emerson*, VIII, 159; IV, 41.

94. Carlyle to his sister, Jean Aitken, 26 March 1848, *Collected Letters*, XXII, 281.

95. 'Natural Supernaturalism' is the title of a chapter in *Sartor Resartus*; see Ashton, *Thomas and Jane Carlyle*, pp. 37–40, 144.

96. Clough to Emerson, 26 November 1847, *Correspondence of Arthur Hugh Clough*, I, 186.

97. Emerson to Lidian Emerson, 2 April 1848, *Letters of Ralph Waldo Emerson*, IV, 47–8.

98. J. A. Froude, autobiographical fragment, Waldo Hilary Dunn, *James Anthony Froude: A Biography*, 2 vols. (Oxford, 1961, 1963), I, 99.

99. Clough Diary, 8 April 1848, *The Oxford Diaries of Arthur Hugh Clough*, ed. Anthony Kenny (Oxford, 1990), p. 246.

100. Emerson to Lidian Emerson, 2 April 1848, *Letters of Ralph Waldo Emerson*, IV, 46–7.

101. Robinson to Thomas Robinson, 22 April 1848, MS Dr Williams's Library.

102. Jane Carlyle to John Sterling, 29 April 1841, *Collected Letters*, XIII, 122.

103. Robinson to Thomas Robinson, 22 April 1848, MS Dr Williams's Library; part printed in *Diary, Reminiscences and Correspondence*, III, 317.

104. Emerson Notebook, 25 April 1848, *The Journals and Miscellaneous Notebooks of Ralph Waldo Emerson*, ed. William H. Gilman et al., 16 vols. (Cambridge, Mass., 1960–82), X, 550–1.

105. Emerson to Lidian Emerson, 20 April 1848; to Froude, 6 May 1848, *Letters of Ralph Waldo Emerson*, IV, 55; VIII, 171. See also ibid., IV, 80n.

106. Emerson to James Elliot Cabot, 21 April 1848, ibid., IV, 60, 61.

107. Carlyle to Jean Aitken, 19 July 1848, *Collected Letters*, XXIII, 75; Jane Carlyle to Lady Ashburton, 14 June 1848, ibid., XXIII, 50.

108. Emerson to Elizabeth Hoar, 21 June 1848, *Letters of Ralph Waldo Emerson*, IV, 89.

109. Emerson to Lidian Emerson, 8 June 1848; to William Emerson, 23 June and 3 August 1848, ibid., IV, 80, 92, 103.

110. Emerson to Lidian Emerson, 16 and 23 June 1848, ibid., IV, 84, 87.

111. Cara Bray to Sara Hennell, 16 July 1848, Moncure Daniel Conway, *Emerson at Home and Abroad* (London, 1883), p. 274; see also *The George Eliot Letters*, I, 271n.

112. Clough to Tom Arnold, 16 July 1848, *Correspondence of Arthur Hugh Clough*, I, 215–16.

113. Emerson to Lidian Emerson, 9 February 1848, *Letters of Ralph Waldo Emerson*, IV, 14 and n.

114. Emerson to Chapman, 23 May 1849, ibid., VIII, 214. Information about editions and prices comes from Emerson's letters and also from the volumes of the *Publishers' Circular and General Record of British Literature*, published annually by Sampson Low.

115. Susanna Chapman to George Combe, 14 July 1852, *The George Eliot Letters*, VIII, 53. For the changes in copyright law between 1849 and 1851, see James J. Barnes, *Free Trade in Books: A Study of the London Book Trade since 1800* (Oxford, 1964), pp. 106–7.

116. See Barnes, *Authors, Publishers and Politicians*, pp. 155–72.

117. Emerson to Chapman, 23 May 1849, *Letters of Ralph Waldo Emerson*, VIII, 214.

118. Carlyle to Edward Chapman (of Chapman & Hall), 28 January 1846, *Collected Letters*, XX, 115; Emerson to John Chapman, 28 August 1849, *Letters of Ralph Waldo Emerson*, IV, 159 and n.

119. See Ezra Greenspan, *George Palmer Putnam: Representative American Publisher* (Pennsylvania, 2000), pp. 212, 223.

120. *Publishers' Circular*, XI (15 December 1848), 409.

121. Ibid., XII (1 September 1849), 302.

122. Emerson to Chapman, 10 October 1849, *Letters of Ralph Waldo Emerson*, VIII, 227.

123. Emerson's Account Book, 25 November 1849, ibid., VIII, 269; Emerson to Chapman, 1 October 1851, and 16 August 1852, ibid., VIII, 287–8; IV, 305.

124. Emerson to Moses Phillips, 9 August 1856; to George Bradford, 28 August 1854, ibid., V, 29; IV, 459.

125. *Publishers' Circular*, XII (1 February 1849), 40, 43.

126. Ibid., XIV (1851), XV (1852), *passim*.

127. Carlyle to his mother, Margaret Carlyle, 29 March 1850, *Collected Letters*, XXV, 57.

128. 'The Present Time', *Latter-Day Pamphlets* (1850); see Ashton, *Thomas and Jane Carlyle*, pp. 301–7.

129. Jane Carlyle to Thomas Carlyle, 6–7 September 1850, *Collected Letters*, XXV, 200.

130. James Hannay Diary, 8 March 1854, MS Add 331, University College London Library; printed with minor changes in George J. Worth, *James Hannay: His Life and Works* (Kansas, 1964), p. 171.

Chapter 2

1. For a lucid account of Froude's early career, see Willey, *More Nineteenth-Century Studies*, pp. 106ff, where the comparison with F. W. Newman is made.
2. See C. R. Sanders, *Coleridge and the Broad Church Movement* (New York, 1942, reprinted 1972), and Stephen Prickett, *Romanticism and Religion: The Tradition of Coleridge and Wordsworth in the Victorian Church* (Cambridge, 1976).
3. *Emerson-Clough Letters*, ed. Howard F. Lowry and Ralph Leslie Rusk (New York, 1968), p. vii.
4. J. A. Froude, *The Nemesis of Faith* (London, 1849, reprinted with an introduction by Rosemary Ashton, 1988), p. 35.
5. Froude, *Thomas Carlyle: The History of his Life in London*, 2 vols. (London, 1884), I, 311; *The Nemesis of Faith*, pp. 216, 221.
6. Dunn, *James Anthony Froude*, I, 17.
7. Ibid., I, 15, 17.
8. Ibid., I, 18, 21.
9. Ibid., I, 28ff; 'Zeta' [Froude], *Shadows of the Clouds* (London, 1847), p. 27.
10. Dunn, *James Anthony Froude*, I, 39.
11. Ibid., I, 72–3, 93–6.
12. Ibid., I, 126.
13. Clough, *The Bothie of Toper-na-Fuosich: A Long-Vacation Pastoral* (Oxford and London, 1848), part IX. The title was later spelt *The Bothie of Tober-na-Vuolich*.
14. For Tom Arnold see Bernard Bergonzi, *A Victorian Wanderer: The Life of Thomas Arnold the Younger* (Oxford, 2003).
15. *The Bothie*, part III.
16. Thackeray to Clough, 26 November 1848, *Letters and Private Papers*, II, 456–7.
17. Clough to Edward Hawkins, 8 October 1848, *Correspondence of Arthur Hugh Clough*, I, 219.
18. Clough to Tom Arnold, 27 November 1848, ibid., I, 224; F. W. Newman to James Martineau, 17 January 1849, MS Martineau Papers, Harris Manchester College.
19. Robinson to Thomas Robinson, 27 January 1849, MS Dr Williams's Library.
20. Clough to Philip Le Breton, 4 January 1849, *Correspondence of Arthur Hugh Clough*, I, 231.
21. Froude to Cowley Powles, autumn 1848, Dunn, *James Anthony Froude*, I, 127.
22. Froude to William Long, 29 December 1848, ibid., I, 128.

23. Froude to Clough, 31 December 1848, MS Clough Correspondence, Bodleian Library, Oxford (MS Eng lett c 190, f. 287).

24. Newman to Martineau, 17 January 1849, MS Harris Manchester College.

25. *Shadows of the Clouds*, pp. 144, 146; Robinson Diary, 3 February 1849, MS Dr Williams's Library.

26. Froude to Charles Kingsley, 1 January 1849, Dunn, *James Anthony Froude*, I, 131.

27. Froude to Clough, 29 January 1849, *Correspondence of Arthur Hugh Clough*, I, 235; Robinson Diary, 14 February 1849, MS Dr Williams's Library.

28. Froude to Clough, 25 February 1849, *Correspondence of Arthur Hugh Clough*, I, 246.

29. Quoted in Dunn, *James Anthony Froude*, I, 227–8.

30. Froude to Clough, 28 February 1849, ibid., I, 134–5.

31. Robinson Diary, 7 and 17 March 1849, MS Dr Williams's Library.

32. Robinson Diary, 13 March 1849, ibid.

33. Dunn, *James Anthony Froude*, I, 228–32; Newman to Robinson, 4 April 1849, MS Dr Williams's Library.

34. Carlyle to Jane Carlyle, 3 April 1849, *Collected Letters*, XXIV, 6–7; Arnold to Mary Arnold, 22 March 1849, *The Letters of Matthew Arnold*, ed. Cyril Y. Lang, 6 vols. (London, 1996–2001), I, 145.

35. Froude to Clough, 21 January 1849, Dunn, *James Anthony Froude*, I, 225.

36. Froude, *The Nemesis of Faith*, pp. 130–1.

37. Goethe, *Wilhelm Meisters Lehrjahre* (1795–6), Book 6; Carlyle, *Sartor Resartus* (1836), Book 1.

38. Froude to Elizabeth Long, 28 April 1851, Dunn, *James Anthony Froude*, I, 184; *Shadows of the Clouds*, p. 20.

39. *The Nemesis of Faith*, pp. 180–1.

40. Ibid., pp. 51–2.

41. Ibid., p. xiv (preface to the second edition).

42. Ibid., pp. 133, 173.

43. Froude's autobiographical account, Dunn, *James Anthony Froude*, I, 74.

44. See *Sartor Resartus*, ed. Mark Engel and Rodger L. Tarr (London, 2000), p. 145 (Book 2, Chapter 9).

45. *Novels and Tales by Goethe* (London, 1854), p. v.

46. Kingsley to Müller, 5 May 1852, MS Friedrich Max Müller Papers, Bodleian Library, Oxford (MS Eng c 2806[1], f.1). For an interesting account of Froude and *Elective Affinities* see Susanne Stark, 'A "Monstrous Book" after all? James Anthony Froude and the Reception of Goethe's *Die Wahlverwandtschaften* in Nineteenth-Century Britain', *Modern Language Review*, XCVIII (January 2003), 102–16.

47. Kingsley to Müller, 10 May 1852, MS Friedrich Max Müller Papers, Bodleian Library (MS Eng c 2806[1], f.4).

48. Carlyle to Forster, 4 April 1849, *Collected Letters*, XXIV, 13.

49. *Journals and Miscellaneous Notebooks of Ralph Waldo Emerson*, X, 520.

50. See Dunn, *James Anthony Froude*, I, 232, 233.

51. Robinson Diary, 12 March 1849, MS Dr Williams's Library.

52. See *Collected Letters*, XXIV, 13n.

53. *Reasoner*, VI (18 and 25 April 1849), 256, 266.

54. Chambers to Ireland, 4 April 1849, MS W. & R. Chambers Papers, National Library of Scotland.

55. George Eliot, review of *The Nemesis of Faith*, *Coventry Herald and Observer*, 16 March 1849, reprinted in *George Eliot: Selected Critical Writings*, ed. Rosemary Ashton (Oxford, 1992), p. 15.

56. Ibid.

57. Cara Bray to Sara Hennell, 23 March 1849, *The George Eliot Letters*, I, 279n.

58. George Eliot to Sara Hennell, 18 April 1849, ibid., I, 280.

59. *Westminster Review*, LI (April 1849), 258.

60. *Publishers' Circular*, 1 June 1849, p. 202.

61. See *The Gladstone Diaries*, ed. M. R. D. Foot and H. C. G. Matthew, 14 vols. (Oxford, 1968–94), IV, 113; Monckton Milnes to Mrs Charles MacCarthy, spring 1849, James Pope-Hennessy, *Monckton Milnes: The Years of Promise 1809–1851* (London, 1949), p. 298.

62. *The George Eliot Letters*, I, 285n, 289n; Charles Bray, *Phases of Opinion and Experience during a Long Life: An Autobiography* (London, 1884), p. 75.

63. Kingsley to his mother, [spring 1849], MS Kingsley Papers, British Library (Add 41298); part published in Dunn, *James Anthony Froude*, I, 137.

64. Froude to Elizabeth Long, 1 May 1849, Dunn, *James Anthony Froude*, I, 157; Froude's autobiographical fragment, ibid., I, 148.

65. Ibid., I, 151.

66. Ibid., I, 153–4.

67. Christian Karl Josias Bunsen to Friedrich Max Müller, 22 April 1849, Friedrich Max Müller, *Chips from a German Workshop*, 4 vols. (London, 1867–75), III, 413.

68. Ibid., III, 414–15.

69. Ibid., III, 415–16.

70. Müller to Bunsen, 9 May 1849, *The Life and Letters of the Right Honourable Friedrich Max Müller*, ed. his wife, 2 vols. (London, 1902), I, 90–1.

71. Bunsen to Müller, 22 May 1849, Müller, *Chips from a German Workshop*, III, 416.

72. Froude to Lord Houghton, 10 May [after 1863], Pope-Hennessy, *Monckton Milnes: The Years of Promise*, p. 298.

73. Froude, autobiographical fragment and letter to Elizabeth Long, 7 May 1849, Dunn, *James Anthony Froude*, I, 149, 159.

74. Froude, autobiographical fragment and letter to Elizabeth Long, 1 May 1849, ibid., I, 151, 152, 157.
75. Robinson to Thomas Robinson, 22 June 1849, MS Dr Williams's Library; part published in *Henry Crabb Robinson on Books and their Writers*, ed. E. J. Morley, 3 vols. (London, 1938), I, 690.
76. Geraldine Jewsbury to Walter Mantell, 22 January 1859, Dunn, *James Anthony Froude*, II, 596.
77. Elizabeth Gaskell to Catherine Winkworth, 21 August 1849, *The Letters of Mrs Gaskell*, pp. 83–4.
78. Gaskell to Eliza Fox, 26 April 1850, ibid., p. 113.
79. Harriet Martineau to Fanny Wedgwood, 19 January 1850, *Harriet Martineau's Letters to Fanny Wedgwood*, ed. Elisabeth Sanders Arbuckle (Stanford, California, 1983), pp. 106–7.
80. Marianne Darbishire to Louisa Darbishire, 7 August 1849, Dunn, *James Anthony Froude*, I, 154.
81. Froude to Clough, 20 September 1849, ibid., I, 162.
82. Froude to Elizabeth Long, 26 October and 16 December 1852, and to Clough, 23 May 1852, ibid., I, 192, 186.
83. Robinson Diary, 21 and 23 October 1849, MS Dr Williams's Library.
84. Froude to Müller, 25 November 1849, Dunn, *James Anthony Froude*, I, 165.
85. Clough to Tom Arnold, 29 October 1849, *Correspondence of Arthur Hugh Clough*, I, 273–4.
86. Froude, autobiographical fragment, Dunn, *James Anthony Froude*, I, 170.
87. Froude to John Prideaux Lightfoot, 15 March 1858, ibid., II, 273.
88. Ibid., II, 274, 575.
89. Froude to Chapman, 5 November 1854, ibid., II, 278–9.
90. Froude, autobiographical fragment, ibid., I, 175.
91. George Eliot to Chapman, 11 September 1851, and to Charles and Cara Bray, 24 October 1849, *The George Eliot Letters*, I, 359, 318. The scene she refers to is 'Studierzimmer' in *Faust*, Part I.

Chapter 3

1. George Eliot to Sara Hennell, 18 April 1849, and to Charles and Cara Bray, 4 December 1849, *The George Eliot Letters*, I, 280–1 and n, 321 and n.
2. George Eliot to Sara Hennell, 11 April 1850, and to Charles and Cara Bray, 30 November 1850, ibid., I, 334–5, 337.
3. George Eliot, review of *The Progress of the Intellect*, *Westminster Review* (January 1851), reprinted in *Selected Critical Writings*, p. 21.
4. Quoted in the introduction to the list of articles and contributors to *Westminster*

Review in *Wellesley Index*, III, 529. For details of the financial history of the *Westminster*, see Sheila Rosenberg, 'The Financing of Radical Opinion: John Chapman and the *Westminster Review*' in *The Victorian Periodical Press*, ed. Shattock and Wolff, pp. 167–92.

5. *Wellesley Index*, III, 531–6.

6. John Stuart Mill to Philippine Kyllmann, [after 22 January 1869], *The Later Letters of John Stuart Mill*, ed. Francis E. Mineka and Dwight N. Lindley, *Collected Works of John Stuart Mill*, 33 vols. (London, 1963–91), XVI, 1552.

7. *Wellesley Index*, III, 542.

8. W. E. Hickson to Edwin Chadwick, 5 January [1851], MS Chadwick Papers, University College London Library.

9. Hickson to Combe, 29 January 1851, MS Combe Papers, National Library of Scotland.

10. Lombe to Chapman, 10 May 1851, MS Rare Book, Manuscript, and Special Collections Library, Duke University.

11. Lombe to Chapman, 4 June 1851, ibid.

12. See Ashton, *George Eliot*, p. 19.

13. For the story of the discovery of the diaries for 1851 and 1860, see Haight, *George Eliot and John Chapman*, pp. ix-x.

14. Chapman Diary, 1 January 1851, ibid., p. 123.

15. Martineau to Hickson, 15 June 1851, MS Hickson Papers, copy in Devon Record Office.

16. Chapman Diary, 21 and 26 April, 2 and 17 May 1851, Haight, *George Eliot and John Chapman*, pp. 157–8, 159, 162, 166.

17. Chapman Diary, 27 August 1851, ibid., p. 205; see also p. 125 and n.

18. Chapman Diary, 24 May, 21 June, 13 September 1851, ibid., pp. 170, 181, 209.

19. Chapman Diary, 19 May 1851, ibid., p. 167.

20. Ibid., pp. 254, 116.

21. Robinson's MS diary at Dr Williams's Library breaks into shorthand occasionally to record some financial or sexual scandal, but never in connection with Chapman.

22. Chapman Diary, 5 and 8 January 1851, Haight, *George Eliot and John Chapman*, pp. 128, 129; George Eliot to Charles and Cara Bray, 8 January 1851, *The George Eliot Letters*, I, 341.

23. Chapman Diary, 9 January 1851, Haight, *George Eliot and John Chapman*, p. 129. Haight explains in his introduction, p. ix, that some pages have been cut out, while others have been heavily overscored, possibly by Chapman himself. Some, though not all, of these deleted passages have been recovered by modern photographic techniques.

24. Chapman Diary, 11, 12, 13, and 22 January 1851, ibid., pp. 130–5 *passim*.

25. Chapman Diary, 12 January 1851, ibid., p. 131.
26. Chapman Diary, 19 January 1851, ibid., pp. 132–3 and n; George Eliot to Charles and Cara Bray, 28 January 1851, *The George Eliot Letters*, I, 344 and n.
27. Chapman Diary, 18 February 1851, Haight, *George Eliot and John Chapman*, pp. 141–2.
28. Chapman Diary, 24 March 1851, ibid., p. 147.
29. [George Eliot], *An Analytical Catalogue of Mr Chapman's Publications* (London, 1852), pp. 21–2.
30. Chapman Diary, 30 May 1851, Haight, *George Eliot and John Chapman*, p. 172.
31. George Eliot to Chapman, 9 May 1851, *The George Eliot Letters*, I, 350.
32. Lombe to Chapman, 13 March 1851, MS Duke University Library.
33. Lombe to Chapman, 8 April 1851, ibid.
34. Chapman Diary, 16 and 18 April 1851, Haight, *George Eliot and John Chapman*, pp. 154, 155.
35. Lombe to Combe, 10 May 1851, MS Combe Papers, National Library of Scotland.
36. Lombe to Combe, 15 November 1851, ibid.
37. Lombe to Combe, 20 November 1851, ibid.
38. Ibid.
39. Lombe to Chapman, 4 June 1851, MS Duke University Library.
40. Lombe to Chapman, 10 July 1851, ibid.
41. Chapman Diary, 1 May 1851, Haight, *George Eliot and John Chapman*, pp. 161–2.
42. Chapman Diary, 7 and 8 October 1851, ibid., p. 217; George Eliot to Bray, 8 October 1851, *The George Eliot Letters*, I, 366.
43. Chapman Diary, 10 October 1851, Haight, *George Eliot and John Chapman*, p. 218; Carlyle to Browning, 10 October 1851, *Collected Letters*, XXVI, 202.
44. Browning to Carlyle, [22] October 1851, *Letters of Robert Browning*, ed. Thurman L. Hood (London, 1933), p. 36.
45. Lombe to Browning, 19 and 23 March 1851, *Baylor Browning Interest Series*, VIII (September 1934), 49. I am indebted to Scott Lewis, co-editor of the ongoing edition of *The Brownings' Correspondence*, for confirmation of the exact date of the letter from Browning to Carlyle and for drawing my attention to the two letters from Lombe to Browning.
46. Martineau to Hickson, 14 February 1851, MS Hickson Papers, Devon Record Office.
47. Chapman Diary, 27 May and 4 June 1851, Haight, *George Eliot and John Chapman*, pp. 172, 175.
48. Martineau to Hickson, 15 June 1851, MS Hickson Papers, Devon Record Office.
49. George Eliot to Chapman, 9 June 1851, *The George Eliot Letters*, VIII, 23.

50. See Ashton, *George Eliot*, pp. 6, 381–2.

51. Lombe to Chapman, 10 November 1851, MS Duke University Library.

52. Lombe to Combe, 20 November 1851, MS Combe Papers, National Library of Scotland.

53. Chapman to Combe, 13 February and 15 March 1852, ibid.

54. Chapman to Combe, 18 and 27 October and 13 November 1851, ibid.; George Eliot to Charles and Cara Bray, 5 June 1852, *The George Eliot Letters*, II, 33.

55. Chapman Diary, 6 September 1851, Haight, *George Eliot and John Chapman*, p. 207.

56. Combe to Chapman, 10 June 1851, MS Combe Papers, National Library of Scotland.

57. Combe to Lombe, 25 May 1851, ibid.

58. Ibid.

59. Combe to Chapman, 23 October 1851, Combe's note on a letter from Chapman to him dated 15 September 1851, and Combe to Lombe, 28 November 1851, ibid.

60. Combe to Lombe, 27 November 1851, ibid.

61. Gibbon, *Life of George Combe*, II, 274.

62. Ibid., I, 266–7; Combe, *Outlines of Phrenology*, sixth edition (Edinburgh, 1836), frontispiece.

63. Gibbon, *Life of George Combe*, II, 261–2.

64. Ibid., II, 309, 20.

65. Ibid., I, 305.

66. Combe to Lombe, 30 May 1851, MS Combe Papers, National Library of Scotland; Bray, *Phases of Opinion*, p. 22. For information about Combe, Deville, and the history of phrenology, see Roger Cooter, *The Cultural Meaning of Popular Science: Phrenology and the Organization of Consent in Nineteenth-Century Britain* (Cambridge, 1984).

67. Combe to Richard Cobden, 5 July 1850, and Cobden to Combe, 19 November 1850, MSS Cobden Papers, British Library (Add MS 43660).

68. Gibbon, *Life of George Combe*, II, 215, 298; Combe Journal, 10 October 1850 and 25 May 1851, MS Combe Papers, National Library of Scotland.

69. Combe Journal, 29 May 1852, MS Combe Papers, National Library of Scotland.

70. Combe Journal, 21 June 1851, ibid.

71. Combe Journal, 5 September 1851, ibid.

72. Combe Journal, 29 August 1851, quoted in *The George Eliot Letters*, VIII, 27–8.

73. Combe to Chapman, 7 December 1851, quoted ibid., VIII, 33.

74. Chapman Diary, 21 September 1851, Haight, *George Eliot and John Chapman*, p. 213.

75. Mill to Hickson, 29 April 1851, *Later Letters, Collected Works*, XIV, 63.

76. Mill to Hickson, 6 May 1851, ibid., XIV, 65.

77. Mill to Chapman, 23 May 1851, ibid., XIV, 67.

78. Mill to Chapman, 9 June 1851, ibid., XIV, 67–8.

79. Ibid., XIV, 69.

80. George Eliot to Chapman, 12 June 1851, *The George Eliot Letters*, VIII, 24.

81. George Eliot to Chapman, 15 June 1851, ibid., I, 351–2.

82. Mill to Chapman, 20 June 1851, *Later Letters, Collected Works*, XIV, 72.

83. Chapman Diary, 9 and 21 June 1851, Haight, *George Eliot and John Chapman*, pp. 176, 182.

84. Mill to Chapman, 17 October 1851, *Later Letters, Collected Works*, XIV, 79.

85. Mill to Chapman, 13 January 1867, ibid., XVI, 1228.

86. Mill to Hickson, 9 June and 15 October 1851, ibid., XIV, 69, 77–8.

87. Carlyle to John Carlyle, 27 November 1835, *Collected Letters* , VIII, 263.

88. Prospectus for *Westminster Review*, published in *Athenaeum*, 27 December 1851, p. 1386.

89. Ibid.

90. Robinson Diary, 28 October 1851, MS Dr Williams's Library.

91. See Ashton, *G. H. Lewes*, pp. 56–7.

92. Ibid., p. 86.

93. Ibid., p. 91; G. H. Lewes to Thornton Hunt, 28 November or 5 December, and 1 or 8 December 1849, *The Letters of George Henry Lewes*, ed. William Baker, 3 vols. (Victoria, British Columbia, 1995–9), I, 179–82.

94. Froude to Kingsley, 10 November 1849, Dunn, *James Anthony Froude*, I, 164.

95. Ibid.

96. *Leader*, I (30 March, 6 and 20 April, 22 and 29 June, 6, 13, and 20 July 1850), 18, 42, 91, 307, 332, 356, 381, 405.

97. J. A. Froude, 'The Laws of Marriage', *Leader*, I (6 July 1850), 350.

98. Carlyle to John Carlyle, 23 November 1850, *Collected Letters*, XXV, 293.

99. Froude to Lewes, 7 February 1851, Ashton, *G. H. Lewes*, p. 105.

100. Bunsen to Müller, 15 May 1850, Müller, *Chips from a German Workshop*, III, 418; Müller to Bunsen, 17 May 1850, Müller, *Life and Letters*, I, 110–11.

101. Chapman Diary, 1 August 1851, Haight, *George Eliot and John Chapman*, p. 197.

102. George Eliot to Chapman, 15 June 1851, *The George Eliot Letters*, I, 352–3 and n.

103. See Ashton, *G. H. Lewes*, pp. 108–9.

104 . Chapman Diary, 27 August, 12 and 14 June 1851, Haight, *George Eliot and John Chapman*, pp. 203, 177, 178–9.

105. George Eliot to Chapman, 20 June 1851, *The George Eliot Letters*, I, 355.

106. Chapman Diary, 21 June 1851, Haight, *George Eliot and John Chapman*, p. 182; George Eliot to Chapman, 1 August 1851, *The George Eliot Letters*, I, 357.

107. Chapman Diary, 27 August 1851, Haight, *George Eliot and John Chapman*, p. 203.

108. Chapman Diary, 23 September 1851, ibid., p. 213.

109. Chapman Diary, 6 October 1851, ibid., p. 217.

110. George Eliot to Bray, 8 October 1851, *The George Eliot Letters*, I, 367.

111. *Leader*, II (22 February 1851), 178.

112. Spencer, *Autobiography*, I, 356–7.

113. Ibid., I, 357.

114. Ibid., I, 372, 388.

115. See George Eliot to Cara Bray, 27 November 1851, *The George Eliot Letters*, I, 377.

116. Spencer, *Autobiography*, I, 365. Spencer gives no date for this letter, which was probably written at the end of 1851.

117. Ibid., I, 369.

118. R. K. Webb, *Harriet Martineau: A Radical Victorian* (London, 1960), p.1; Harriet Martineau to Edward Moxon, 6 November 1850, Valerie Kossew Pichanick, *Harriet Martineau: The Woman and her Work 1802–76* (Ann Arbor, Michigan, 1980), p. 187.

119. Harriet Martineau to H. G. Atkinson, 30 January [1846?], MS Harriet Martineau Papers, Birmingham University Library.

120. Chapman, *Chloroform and other Anaesthetics: Their History, and Use during Childbirth* (London, 1859), p. 9 (reprinted from the *Westminster Review*, January 1859).

121. George Eliot to Charles and Cara Bray, 15 February 1851, *The George Eliot Letters*, I, 346.

122. George Eliot to Sara Hennell, 21 January 1852, ibid., II, 4–5.

123. Gaskell to Mary Carpenter, 25 October 1852, *The Letters of Mrs Gaskell*, p. 206 and n.

124. Robinson to Thomas Robinson, 8 March 1851, and Diary, 4 March 1851, MSS Dr Williams's Library; Diary, 8 February 1851, *Henry Crabb Robinson On Books*, II, 707.

125. *Leader*, II (1 and 8 March 1851), 201–3, 227–8.

126. Lewes's literary receipts, published in *The George Eliot Letters*, VII, 369, 371.

127. Bray to Combe, 20 July 1852, MS Combe Papers, National Library of Scotland; Combe Journal, 5 June 1852, quoted in *The George Eliot Letters*, VIII, 47n.

Chapter 4

1. Chapman Diary, 29 September, 4 and 5 October 1851, Haight, *George Eliot and John Chapman*, pp. 215–16.

2. For an account of William Ellis's career, see Stewart and McCann, *The Educational Innovators*, I, 326–41.

3. George Eliot to Charles Bray, 6 October, and to Sara Hennell, 9 October 1851, *The George Eliot Letters*, I, 365, 368.

4. Chapman Diary, 8 October 1851, Haight, *George Eliot and John Chapman*, pp. 217–18.

5. George Eliot to Charles Bray, 8 October 1851, *The George Eliot Letters*, I, 366.

6. George Eliot to Sara Hennell, 9 October 1851, ibid., I, 367.

7. George Eliot to Cara Bray, 3 October 1851, ibid., I, 363.

8. George Eliot to Cara Bray, 8 November 1843, ibid., I, 164.

9. Chapman Diary, 27 June 1851, Haight, *George Eliot and John Chapman*, pp. 185–6.

10. Eliza Lynn Linton, *The Autobiography of Christopher Kirkland*, 3 vols. (London, 1885), I, 288–9. See Ashton, *George Eliot*, pp. 48–9.

11. George Eliot to Sara Hennell, 13 October 1851, *The George Eliot Letters*, I, 369.

12. George Eliot to Bray, 4 October, and to Sara Hennell, 13 October 1851, ibid., I, 364, 368.

13. For a brief but detailed account, see C. H. Gibbs-Smith, *The Great Exhibition of 1851* (London, 1950, reprinted 1981).

14. See, for example, Chapman Diary, 12 and 13 May, 22 July, 15 and 16 August 1851, Haight, *George Eliot and John Chapman*, pp. 165, 194, 201, 202.

15. Chapman Diary, 8 May and 28 July 1851, ibid., pp. 164, 195. For the slump in the book trade during the Great Exhibition, see Barnes, *Free Trade in Books*, p. 115.

16. Greeley, *Glances at Europe: in a Series of Letters*, p. 46.

17. Chapman Diary, 8 September 1851, Haight, *George Eliot and John Chapman*, p. 207.

18. Chapman Diary, 9 October, ibid., p. 218 and n.

19. Chapman, circular for the *Westminster Review*, 10 October 1851, published in *The George Eliot Letters*, VIII, 29–30.

20. Combe to Chapman, 28 November 1851, ibid., VIII, 32.

21. Chapman to Combe, 26 November 1851, ibid., VIII, 31.

22. See George Eliot to Sara Hennell, 13 October, and to the Brays, 22 October 1851, ibid., I, 369, 370.

23. George Eliot to Cara Bray, [October 1851], ibid., I, 371.

24. George Eliot to Charles and Cara Bray, 23 December 1851, ibid., I, 378.

25. Under the pseudonym 'F. B.', Rogers caricatured Newman in *The Eclipse of Faith, or, a Visit to a Religious Sceptic* (London, 1852).

26. *Edinburgh Review*, XCV (January 1852), 276.

27. *Quarterly Review*, XC (December 1851), 163–205.

28. *Westminster Review*, new series I (January 1852), 33, 41.
29. Ibid., I, 62, 64.
30. Ibid., I, 119, 131.
31. Froude to Clough, 16 May 1852, Dunn, *Life of Froude*, I, 185.
32. *Westminster Review*, new series I (January 1852), 163.
33. George Eliot, draft letter to James Martineau, 29 August 1851, *The George Eliot Letters*, VIII, 25–6.
34. Ibid., VIII, 26, 27.
35. Chapman Diary, 9 September 1851, Haight, *George Eliot and John Chapman*, p. 208.
36. George Eliot to Chapman, 24 July 1852, *The George Eliot Letters*, II, 47.
37. *Westminster Review*, new series I (January 1852), 187–8.
38. Ibid., I, 227–8.
39. Ibid., I, 249, reprinted in *Essays of George Eliot*, ed. Thomas Pinney (New York, 1963), p. 49.
40. Ibid., I, 281.
41. Ibid.
42. *Leader*, III (10 January 1852), 37.
43. *Reasoner*, XII (January 1852), 35.
44. Combe to Chapman, 16 January 1852, MS Combe Papers, National Library of Scotland.
45. Robinson Diary, 6 and 11 January 1852, and letter to Thomas Robinson, 10 January 1852, MSS Dr Williams's Library.
46. Robinson Diary, 19 January 1852, ibid.
47. George Eliot to Sara Hennell, 21 January 1852, *The George Eliot Letters*, II, 4.
48. George Eliot to Combe, 27 January 1852, ibid., VIII, 35.
49. George Eliot to Chapman, 25 July 1852, ibid., II, 49.
50. Combe Journal, 5 June and 6 July 1852, quoted in *The George Eliot Letters*, VIII, 46–7n, 56n.
51. Combe Journal, 10 September 1852, MS Combe Papers, National Library of Scotland.
52. Harriet Martineau, *Autobiography* (1877, reprinted in 2 vols. with an introduction by Gaby Weiner, 1983), II, 371.
53. Chapman Diary, 19 April 1851, Haight, *George Eliot and John Chapman*, p. 156.
54. Lombe to Chapman, 10 May 1851, MS Duke University Library.
55. Chapman Diary, 9 August 1851, Haight, *George Eliot and John Chapman*, pp. 199–200; Lombe to Chapman, 19 May 1851, MS Duke University Library.
56. Lombe to Chapman, 18 August 1851, MS Duke University Library.
57. Chapman Diary, 23 and 27 August 1851, Haight, *George Eliot and John Chapman*, pp. 204–5, 205.

58. Chapman Diary, 28 August 1851, ibid., p. 206.

59. Harriet Martineau, 'Account of money received from Mr Lombe', MS Harriet Martineau Papers, Birmingham University Library.

60. Harriet Martineau, *Autobiography*, II, 384.

61. See Haight, *George Eliot and John Chapman*, p. 209n.

62. Chapman Diary, 13 September 1851, ibid., pp. 209–10.

63. Chapman Diary, 16 September 1851, ibid., p. 211.

64. George Eliot to Chapman, 18 September 1851, *The George Eliot Letters*, I, 360–1.

65. Chapman Diary, 24 September 1851, Haight, *George Eliot and John Chapman*, p. 214.

66. Chapman to Harriet Martineau, 8 October 1851, MS Harriet Martineau Papers, Birmingham University Library.

67. Combe to Lombe, 5 October 1851, Combe Letterbook 1851–5, MS Combe Papers, National Library of Scotland.

68. Lombe to Combe, 15 October and 4 November 1851, MS Combe Papers, ibid.

69. See Lombe to Combe, 4, 15, and 20 November 1851, ibid.

70. Lombe to Harriet Martineau, 27 November 1851, MS Harriet Martineau Papers, Birmingham University Library.

71. Copy of Chapman to Lombe, 3 December 1851, in MS Combe Papers, National Library of Scotland.

72. Combe to Lombe, 8 December 1851, Combe Letterbook 1851–5, ibid.

73. Harriet Martineau, *Autobiography*, II, 384. See also George Eliot to Cara Bray, 30 March 1852, *The George Eliot Letters*, II, 17.

74. Harriet Martineau, *Autobiography*, II, 411.

75. *Leader*, IV (3 December 1853), 1171–2.

76. Mill to Harriet Mill, 9 January 1854, *Later Letters, Collected Works*, XIV, 126.

77. George Eliot to Sara Hennell, 18 November 1853, *The George Eliot Letters*, II, 126. The article in the *Westminster Review* is tentatively attributed to Congreve in *Wellesley Index*, III, 621–2.

78. See Chapman's statement in *Westminster Review*, CXXV (March 1891), 326 7; *Life and Letters of James Martineau*, I, 220–1; Webb, *Harriet Martineau*, pp. 299–301.

79. Harriet Martineau to Chapman, 19 March [1853], MS Bodleian Library (Eng lett d 2, f. 175).

80. Harriet Martineau to Holyoake, 9 April [1853], Harriet Martineau MSS, British Library (Add 42726); Spencer, *Autobiography*, I, 492–3.

81. George Eliot to Sara Hennell, 31 January 1852, *The George Eliot Letters*, II, 8.

82. Chapman, 'The Commerce of Literature', *Westminster Review*, new series I (April 1852), 544–5.

83. Ibid., pp. 514–15, 519, 530.

84. Chapman to Combe, 5 April 1852, published in *The George Eliot Letters*, VIII, 39.

85. John Murray to the editor of *The Times*, 2 April 1852, p. 5.
86. Chapman to W. E. Gladstone, 8 April 1852, MS Gladstone Papers, British Library (Add 44372).
87. See Barnes, *Free Trade in Books*, pp. 75–80, and H. C. G. Matthew, *Gladstone 1809–1898* (Oxford, 1997), p. 658.
88. See George Eliot to Cara Bray, 13 May 1852, *The George Eliot Letters*, II, 25.
89. William Longman to Gladstone, 22 May 1852, MS Gladstone Papers, British Library (Add 44372).
90. Chapman to Combe, 15 March 1852, MS Combe Papers, National Library of Scotland.
91. See Barnes, *Free Trade in Books*, pp. 27, 188–9.
92. George Eliot to Bray, 17 April 1852, and to Combe, 22 April 1852, *The George Eliot Letters*, II, 17–18, VIII, 44.
93. *Athenaeum*, 3 April 1852, p. 381.
94. George Eliot to Charles and Cara Bray, 5 May 1852, *The George Eliot Letters*, II, 23.
95. Chapman's statement was published in full in his *Report* of the proceedings; it was reprinted, with all the other speeches, in Paul Hollister, *The Author's Wallet* (New York, 1934), pp. 46–64.
96. George Eliot to Charles and Cara Bray, 5 May 1852, *The George Eliot Letters*, II, 24.
97. Chapman to Gladstone, 12 July 1852, MS Gladstone Papers, British Library (Add 44372). For an account of the Booksellers' Association meeting on 28 May 1852, see *Publishers' Circular*, XV (1 June 1852), 193.
98. Carlyle to Joseph Neuberg, 31 May 1852, *Collected Letters*, XXVII, 131–2.
99. See George Eliot to Charles and Cara Bray, 22 November 1852, *The George Eliot Letters*, II, 68–9.
100. Chapman to Combe, 4 August 1852, and Combe Journal, 6 July 1852, MSS Combe Papers, National Library of Scotland (quoted in part in *The George Eliot Letters*, VIII, 56n).
101. *Leader*, III (22 May 1852), 493.
102. George Eliot to Cara Bray, 27 May 1852, *The George Eliot Letters*, II, 29.
103. Chapman to Gladstone, 10 May 1887, MS Gladstone Papers, British Library (Add 44372).
104. Chapman to Gladstone, 11 December 1887, ibid.

Chapter 5

1. Susanna Chapman to Combe, 14 July 1852, published in *The George Eliot Letters*, VIII, 52–4.

2. Ibid., VIII, 52.

3. George Eliot to Herbert Spencer, [16?] July 1852, ibid., VIII, 57. See also Ashton, *George Eliot*, pp. 98–100.

4. George Eliot to Combe, 16 July 1852, *The George Eliot Letters*, VIII, 56.

5. George Eliot to Charles Bray, 14 July 1852, ibid., II, 43–4.

6. George Eliot to Cara Bray, 19 August 1852, ibid., II, 51.

7. Combe, draft letter to Bray, 18 July 1852, MS Combe Papers, National Library of Scotland.

8. Bray to Combe, 20 July 1852, *The George Eliot Letters*, VIII, 58.

9. Combe, draft reply to Bray, 24 July 1852, ibid., VIII, 59–60.

10. George Eliot to Charles and Cara Bray, 4 December 1852, ibid., II, 70.

11. Sheila Rosenberg, 'The Financing of Radical Opinion', p. 177.

12. George Eliot to Chapman, 24–25 July 1852, *The George Eliot Letters*, II, 47.

13. Ibid., II, 48–9.

14. George Eliot to Charles and Cara Bray, 7 and 12 October 1852, ibid., II, 59, 60.

15. Combe Journal, 20 October 1852, MS Combe Papers, National Library of Scotland.

16. George Eliot to Sara Hennell, 25 September 1852, *The George Eliot Letters*, II, 57.

17. See John Wallis Chapman, *Philosopher John: John Chapman of Loughborough 1801–1854, Engineer, Inventor, Political Writer* (Cartmel, 1983), pp. 13, 28, 40, 45. *The Times* of 25 March 1943 commemorates the centenary of the collaboration on an aeroplane in 1843 by Chapman and William Henson.

18. George Eliot to Sara Hennell, 2 September 1852, *The George Eliot Letters*, II, 54.

19. *Leader*, III (2 October 1852), 949.

20. See Elizabeth Malleson, *Autobiographical Notes*, pp. 40–1. See also Haight, *George Eliot and John Chapman*, pp. 64–5.

21. See Florence M. Gladstone, *Aubrey House Kensington 1698–1920* (London, 1922), p. 47.

22. *Leader*, I (16 November 1850), 813. For Kinkel and other German exiles, see Ashton, *Little Germany*; for Mazzini, see Harry W. Rudman, *Italian Nationalists and English Letters* (London, 1940), Denis Mack Smith, *Mazzini* (London, 1994), and Roland Sarti, *Mazzini: A Life for the Religion of Politics* (London, 1997); for a general study of exiles in Britain, see Bernard Porter, *The Refugee Question in Mid-Victorian Politics* (Cambridge, 1979).

23. George Eliot to Sara Hennell, 21 January 1852, *The George Eliot Letters*, II, 5.

24. George Eliot to Clementia Taylor, 27 March 1852, ibid., II, 15 and n.

25. See Ashton, *Thomas and Jane Carlyle*, pp. 210–11.

26. Carlyle to the editor of *The Times*, 18 June 1844, *Collected Letters*, XVIII, 74.

27. Carlyle to Lady Ashburton, 16 February 1852, ibid., XXVII, 45.

28. Jane Carlyle to Thomas Carlyle, 12 July 1865, *Jane Welsh Carlyle: A New Selection of her Letters*, ed. Trudy Bliss (London, 1950), p. 323.

29. Thomas Carlyle, *Reminiscences*, ed. K. J. Fielding and Ian Campbell (Oxford, 1997), p. 94; see also Ashton, *Thomas and Jane Carlyle*, pp. 210ff.

30. George Eliot to Charles Bray, 17 April 1852, *The George Eliot Letters*, II, 18.

31. See Mazzini to his mother, 24 April 1852, *Scritti editi ed inediti*, XLVII, 244. Mazzini's letters, as well as his essays, expound his vague romantic ideas about politics, particularly Italian politics.

32. See George Eliot to William Findlay Watson, 14 December 1852, *The George Eliot Letters*, II, 72 and n.

33. Jane Carlyle to Carlyle, 25 August, Carlyle to Chapman, 26 August, and Jane Carlyle to Carlyle, 12 September 1852, *Collected Letters*, XXVII, 252, 253–4, 281. Saffi's article appeared in the *Westminster Review* in October 1853.

34. Chapman Diary, 27 July 1851, Haight, *George Eliot and John Chapman*, p. 195.

35. See Wilhelm Buchner, *Ferdinand Freiligrath, ein Dichterleben in Briefen*, 2 vols. (Lahr, 1882), II, 241–2; Ashton, *Little Germany*, p. 87.

36. *Leader*, II (15 February 1851), 144; see also Ashton, *Little Germany*, pp. 81–7; *Freiligraths Briefwechsel mit Marx und Engels*, ed. Manfred Häckel, 2 vols. (Berlin, 1976), I, lxxiv.

37. Chapman Diary, 8 February 1851, Haight, *George Eliot and John Chapman*, p. 139.

38. Friedrich Wilhelm Joseph von Schelling, *Über das Verhältnis der bildenden Künste zu der Natur*; *The Philosophy of Art: An Oration between the Plastic Arts and Nature*, translated by A. Johnson (London, 1845).

39. Sarah Millard, archivist at the Bank of England, gave me the following information about Johnson's career: joined aged seventeen in February 1832; appointed to the Bullion Office in January 1849; promoted to Deputy Principal Bullion Clerk in February 1856; became Principal Bullion Clerk in March 1866; retired in February 1873.

40. See Chapman Diary, 10 January, 10 February, 25 April, and 25 May 1851, Haight, *George Eliot and John Chapman*, pp. 130, 140, 159, 170.

41. Chapman Diary, 27 August 1851, ibid., p. 205.

42. Chapman Diary, 11 June 1851, ibid., p. 177.

43. Chapman Diary, 25 June 1851, ibid., p. 184.

44. See *Wellesley Index*, III, 632, 635, 640–1.

45. See Chapman Diary, 3 and 10 February and 19 March 1851, and Chapman to Johanna von Heyligenstaedt, 6 March 1862, Haight, *George Eliot and John Chapman*, pp. 138, 140, 146, 113.

46. Ferdinand Freiligrath to Karl Marx, 28 May 1851, *Freiligraths Briefwechsel mit Marx und Engels*, I, 20 (my translation).

47. Marx to Engels, 28 October 1852, *Marx-Engels Collected Works*, 50 vols. (London, New York, Moscow, 1975–2004), XXXIX, 227.

48. See Ashton, *Little Germany*, pp. 20, 62.

49. See Marx to Engels, 20 January 1852, *Marx-Engels Collected Works*, XXXIX, 9; Freiligrath to Marx, 17 February 1852, *Briefwechsel*, I, 41.

50. Marx to Engels, 18 and 23 February 1852, *Marx-Engels Collected Works*, XXXIX, 37, 43.

51. Marx to Engels, 5 August 1852, ibid., XXXIX, 146; Freiligrath to Marx, 5 August 1852, *Briefwechsel*, I, 45.

52. Marx to Engels, 8 and 9 September 1852, *Marx-Engels Collected Works*, XXXIX, 181, 183.

53. Marx to Engels, 2 September 1852, ibid., XXXIX, 175.

54. See Ashton, *Little Germany*, pp. 103–4.

55. See William Hale White, *The Early Life of Mark Rutherford*, pp. 37–8, 46–7, 56–63.

56. [William Hale White], *The Autobiography of Mark Rutherford* (1881), ed. Don Cupitt (London, 1988), pp. 19–20.

57. Ibid., p. 23.

58. William Hale White, *Early Life*, pp. 66–77.

59. Ibid., pp. 79–81.

60. Ibid., pp. 82–3; a more elaborate version of the meeting is given in [William Hale White], *The Autobiography of Mark Rutherford*, pp. 104–5.

61. William Hale White, 'George Eliot as I Knew Her', *Bookman*, August 1902, p. 159.

62. [William Hale White], *The Autobiography of Mark Rutherford*, p. 107.

63. William Hale White, *Early Life*, p. 83.

64. [William Hale White], *The Autobiography of Mark Rutherford*, pp. 112–14.

65. William Hale White, 'George Eliot as I Knew Her', p. 159.

66. William Hale White to William White, 3 May 1853, quoted in Wilfred Stone, *Religion and Art of William Hale White* (Stanford, California, 1954), p. 52.

67. William Hale White, *Early Life*, pp. 83, 88.

68. George Eliot to Bessie Rayner Parkes, 12 July 1853, *The George Eliot Letters*, II, 109.

69. George Eliot to Combe, 13 November 1852, ibid., VIII, 66.

70. George Eliot to Bray, 24 January 1853, ibid., II, 83.

71. George Eliot to Charles and Cara Bray, 22 November 1852, ibid., II, 68.

72. For accounts of the early months of the relationship between Lewes and Marian Evans, see Ashton, *G. H. Lewes*, pp. 132–40, and *George Eliot*, pp. 101–7.

73. George Eliot to Charles and Cara Bray, 11 and 16 April 1853, *The George Eliot Letters*, II, 97, 98.

74. George Eliot to Bray, 18 March 1853, ibid., II, 93.

75. George Eliot to Combe, 18 February 1853, ibid., VIII, 72.

76. William Hale White, 'George Eliot as I Knew Her', p. 159.

77. Chapman to Combe, 10 January 1853, MS Combe Papers, National Library of Scotland; part published in *The George Eliot Letters*, VIII, 70–1n.

78. Combe to Chapman, 11 and 15 January, and Chapman to Combe, 13 January 1853, MSS Combe Papers, National Library of Scotland.

79. Chapman to Combe, 22 January 1853, ibid.

80. George Eliot to Combe, 22 January, and to Bray, 8 January 1853, *The George Eliot Letters*, VIII, 70, II, 80.

81. George Eliot to Cara Bray, 16 April 1853, ibid., II, 97–8.

82. George Eliot to Bray, 25 January 1853, ibid., II, 83.

83. Bray to Combe, 17 January 1853, MS Combe Papers, National Library of Scotland.

84. George Eliot to Combe, 18 February 1853, *The George Eliot Letters*, VIII, 71–2.

85. Notebook, quoted in Stone, *Religion and Art of William Hale White*, p. 51n.

86. George Eliot to Charles and Cara Bray, 12 March 1853, *The George Eliot Letters*, II, 92.

87. Clough to Emerson, 9 October 1853, *Correspondence of Arthur Hugh Clough*, II, 463.

88. Clough to C. E. Norton, 29 November 1853, ibid., II, 468.

89. Froude to Elizabeth Long, 20 September 1853, Dunn, *James Anthony Froude*, I, 197.

90. See George Eliot to Sara Hennell, 21 July 1855, *The George Eliot Letters*, II, 211.

91. George Eliot to Chapman, 24 October 1852, ibid., VIII, 63. Forster's articles appeared in January and April 1853.

92. Matthew Arnold to Jane Forster, 14 April 1853, *Letters of Matthew Arnold*, I, 261.

93. Arnold to Clough, 9 April 1852, ibid., I, 236.

94. Arnold to Jane Forster, 4 December 1853, ibid., I, 283.

95. Forster to Chapman, early 1852, T. Wemyss Reid, *Life of the Right Honourable William Edward Forster*, 2 vols. (London, 1888), I, 286–8.

96. *Westminster Review*, LVII (April 1852), 57.

97. Arnold to Clough, 25 August 1853, *Letters*, I, 271.

98. Charlotte Brontë to William Smith Williams, 6 November 1847, and to Lewes, 6 November 1847, *The Letters of Charlotte Brontë*, ed. Margaret Smith, 3 vols. (Oxford, 1995–2004), I, 557, 559–60.   For the relationship between

Lewes and Charlotte Brontë see Ashton, *G. H. Lewes*, pp. 66–8, 101–2, 104, 139–41.

99. Charlotte Brontë to Ellen Nussey, 12 June 1850, *Letters of Charlotte Brontë*, II, 414.

100. Lewes, 'The Lady Novelists', *Westminster Review*, LVIII (July 1852), 138, '*Ruth and Villette*', *Westminster Review*, LIX (April 1853), 485.

101. See Christine Alexander and Margaret Smith, *The Oxford Companion to the Brontës* (Oxford, 2003), pp. 134–40.

102. Spencer, *Autobiography*, I, 347.

103. George Eliot to Sara Hennell, 16 July 1852, *The George Eliot Letters*, II, 45. For Barbara Leigh Smith, later Bodichon, see Sheila R. Herstein, *A Mid-Victorian Feminist: Barbara Leigh Smith Bodichon* (New Haven, Conn., 1985), and Pam Hirsch, *Barbara Leigh Smith Bodichon 1827–1891: Feminist, Artist and Rebel* (London, 1998).

104. Spencer, *Autobiography*, I, 348.

105. Robinson Diary, 8 March 1852, MS Dr Williams's Library.

106. George Eliot to Charles and Cara Bray, 14 June 1852, *The George Eliot Letters*, II, 35.

107. Spencer, *Autobiography*, I, 397, 398–9.

108. Ibid., I, 348; Spencer to John Cross, 13 January 1884, quoted in Haight, *George Eliot*, p. 128 and n.

109. Spencer, 'A Theory of Population', *Westminster Review*, LVII (April 1852), 475–6, 501.

110. Spencer, *Autobiography*, I, 402.

111. George Eliot to Bessie Rayner Parkes, 24 February, and to Charles and Cara Bray, 26 February 1853, *The George Eliot Letters*, II, 89.

112. George Eliot to Combe, 25 November 1853, ibid., VIII, 89.

113. *Westminster Review*, LXI (January 1854), 233.

114. For Huxley's life and career, see Leonard Huxley, *Life and Letters of Thomas Henry Huxley*, 2 vols. (London, 1900), Cyril Bibby, *Scientist Extraordinary: The Life and Scientific Work of Thomas Henry Huxley 1825–1895* (London, 1972), Mario A. di Gregorio, *T. H. Huxley's Place in Natural Science* (New Haven, Conn., 1984), Adrian Desmond, *Huxley*, 2 vols. (London, 1994 and 1997), and Paul White, *Thomas Huxley: Making the 'Man of Science'* (Cambridge, 2003).

115. Huxley, autobiography (written 1889), in *Life and Letters*, I, 23–4.

116. Huxley to various correspondents 1851–3, *Life and Letters*, I, 74–9, 107. For an account of the career difficulties facing Huxley and other scientists, see White, *Thomas Huxley*, pp. 35–8.

117. Huxley to Henrietta Heathorn, 1 January 1854, MS Huxley Papers, Library Archives and Special Collections, Imperial College London (Correspondence

with Henrietta Heathorn, f. 259). White, *Thomas Huxley*, gives the most thorough account of the courtship.

118. Chapman to Huxley, 12 August 1853, MS Huxley Papers, Imperial College London (Vol. 12, f. 168).

119. Huxley, 'Science at Sea', *Westminster Review*, LXI (January 1854), 101, 104.

120. Ibid., LXI, 112, 117, 119, 100, 107.

121. Chapman to Huxley, 23 October 1853, with Huxley's draft reply written on the back, MS Huxley Papers, Imperial College London (Vol. 12, f. 169).

122. Chapman to Huxley, 26 October 1853, ibid. (Vol. 12, f. 170).

123. George Eliot to Combe, 28 November 1853, *The George Eliot Letters*, VIII, 90.

124. Huxley, 'Contemporary Literature: Science', *Westminster Review*, LXI (January 1854), 255.

125. Lewes, 'Goethe as a Man of Science', ibid., LVIII (October 1852), 479.

126. *Leader*, V (14 January 1854), 40.

127. George Eliot to Chapman, probably 17 December 1853, *The George Eliot Letters*, II, 132.

128. George Eliot to Chapman, probably 19 December 1853, Rosemary Ashton, 'New George Eliot Letters at the Huntington', *Huntington Library Quarterly*, LIV (Spring 1991), 119–20.

129. George Eliot to Chapman, 19 December 1853, *The George Eliot Letters*, II, 133.

130. Huxley, 'Contemporary Literature: Science', *Westminster Review*, LXI (January 1854), 255.

131. Huxley to Tyndall, 17 October 1854, MS Huxley Papers, Imperial College London (Vol. 8, f. 16).

132. See Tyndall Journal, 25 April 1854, A. S. Eve and C. H. Creasey, *Life and Work of John Tyndall* (London, 1945), p. 53.

133. Tyndall to Huxley, 18 October 1854, MS Huxley Papers, Imperial College London (Vol. 8, f. 17).

134. Huxley to Tyndall, 22 October 1854, published in Huxley, *Life and Letters*, I, 121.

135. See *Westminster Review*, LXII (October 1854), 473.

136. Huxley to Tyndall, 22 October, Tyndall to Huxley, 27 October, and Huxley to Tyndall, 29 October 1854, MSS Huxley Papers, Imperial College London (Vol. 8, ff. 18, 19, 20). Huxley's letters of 22 and 29 October are part published in *Life and Letters*, I, 120–1.

137. Huxley to Tyndall, 29 October 1854, ibid.

138. See Sheila Rosenberg, 'The "wicked *Westminster*": John Chapman, his Contributors and Promises Fulfilled', *Victorian Periodicals Review*, LXXXVIII (Fall 2000), 237.

139. See Huxley to Darwin, 23 November 1859, *Life and Letters*, I, 176. Huxley's

review of *The Origin of Species* appeared in the *Westminster Review* in April 1860.

140. Huxley to Tyndall, 17 October 1854, MS Huxley Papers, Imperial College London (Vol. 8, f. 16).

Chapter 6

1. George Eliot to Sara Hennell, 1 October 1853, *The George Eliot Letters*, II, 118; Chapman to Combe, 3 October 1853, ibid., VIII, 79.
2. George Eliot to Bray, 3 November 1853, ibid., II, 122 and n.; *Leader*, IV (12 November 1853), 1087.
3. George Eliot to Combe, 7 June 1853, *The George Eliot Letters*, VIII, 75.
4. Combe to George Eliot, 17 November 1853, ibid., VIII, 86.
5. See Gibbon, *Life of George Combe*, II, 327–9.
6. George Eliot to Combe, 20 November 1853, *The George Eliot Letters*, VIII, 87.
7. Combe to Chapman, 2 March 1854, ibid., VIII, 100. See also Chapman to Combe, 1 March 1854, ibid., VIII, 99.
8. George Eliot to Combe, 3 March 1854, ibid., VIII, 104.
9. Chapman to Combe, 13 April 1854, ibid., VIII, 110.
10. See George Eliot to Charles and Cara Bray, 26 February 1853, ibid., II, 90 and n.; *Leader*, IV (18 June 1853), 600.
11. George Eliot to Chapman, 2 December 1853, *The George Eliot Letters*, II, 130–1.
12. George Eliot to Sara Hennell, 18 January 1854, ibid., II, 137.
13. Ludwig Feuerbach, *The Essence of Christianity*, translated by Marian Evans (London, 1854, reprinted New York, 1957), 159, xxxvi, 140, 153.
14. See George Eliot to Sara Hennell, 18 April 1849, and to Charles and Cara Bray, 4 December 1849, *The George Eliot Letters*, I, 280–1, 321; Ashton, *George Eliot*, pp. 130–1, 153–4. For a discussion of the translations of Strauss, Feuerbach, and Spinoza, see Ashton, *The German Idea*, pp. 147–66.
15. George Eliot to Sara Hennell, 29 April 1854, *The George Eliot Letters*, II, 153.
16. George Eliot to Sara Hennell, 6 February 1854, ibid., II, 141.
17. George Eliot to Cara Bray, 14 April 1854, and to Sara Hennell, 3 June 1854, ibid., II, 149, 159.
18. George Eliot to Cara Bray, 18 April 1854, ibid., II, 151.
19. George Eliot to Cara Bray, 19 May 1854, ibid., II, 157.
20. George Eliot to Bray, 27 May 1854, ibid., II, 158.
21. George Eliot to Sara Hennell, 3 June 1854, ibid., II, 159, and to Chapman, 15 October 1854, ibid., VIII, 125.
22. Elisabeth Tilley to George Eliot, 16 December 1878, Haight, *George Eliot*, pp. 94–5.

23. George Eliot to Sara Hennell, 3 and 10 July 1854, *The George Eliot Letters*, II, 164, 165.

24. George Eliot to Charles and Cara Bray and Sara Hennell, 19 July 1854, ibid., II, 166.

25. Froude to Chapman, 2 August 1854, MS Rider Haggard Papers, Rare Book and Manuscript Library, Columbia University.

26. See Haight, *George Eliot and John Chapman*, p. 76.

27. See introductory essay on *Prospective Review* in *Wellesley Index*, III, 337, 340n, 342–3, 345.

28. George Eliot to Sara Hennell, 18 August 1853, *The George Eliot Letters*, II, 114–15.

29. Martineau to Hutton, 3 July 1854, Drummond, *Life and Letters of James Martineau*, I, 264.

30. Combe to Lombe, 25 May 1851, MS Combe Papers, National Library of Scotland.

31. See *Wellesley Index*, III, 621.

32. Martineau, 'Biographical Memoranda' (1877), *Life and Letters*, I, 264.

33. The subscribers are listed in Robinson Diary, 19 December 1854, MS Dr Williams's Library.

34. Martineau, 'Biographical Memoranda', *Life and Letters*, I, 265.

35. W. B. Hodgson, 'The School Claims of Languages, Ancient and Modern', *Westminster Review*, LX (October 1853), 450–98.

36. Robinson Diary, 11 and 16 October 1853, MS Dr Williams's Library.

37. T. H. Bastard to Combe, 14 February 1854, MS Combe Papers, National Library of Scotland.

38. Combe Journal, 13 September 1854, ibid.

39. Robert Cox to Combe, 13 September 1854, ibid.

40. Combe Journal, 15 September 1854, ibid.; published in *The George Eliot Letters*, VIII, 118.

41. Chapman to Combe, 22 September 1854, and Combe's draft reply, 2 October 1854, MSS Combe Papers, National Library of Scotland.

42. Hodgson to Combe, 15 September 1854, ibid.

43. Martineau, 'Biographical Memoranda', *Life and Letters*, I, 265; see also *Harriet Martineau's Letters to Fanny Wedgwood*, p. 151.

44. Samuel Courtauld to Chapman, 13 November 1854, enclosing a copy of his note to Martineau, 12 November 1854, MSS Harriet Martineau Papers, Birmingham University Library.

45. Robinson Diary, 3 and 9 November 1854, MSS Dr Williams's Library.

46. *Westminster Review*, LXII (October 1854), 559.

47. Chapman to Robert Chambers, 16 October 1854, and Sara Hennell to George Eliot, 15 November 1854, *The George Eliot Letters*, VIII, 125, II, 187.

48. Sara Hennell to George Eliot, 15 November, and George Eliot to Sara Hennell, 22 November 1854, ibid., II, 187, 189.
49. Robinson Diary, 27 November 1854, MS Dr Williams's Library.
50. See *Harriet Martineau's Letters to Fanny Wedgwood*, p. 129.
51. Harriet Martineau, *Autobiography*, II, 425–6.
52. Ibid., II, 427.
53. Harriet Martineau to Wedgwood, 17 September 1854, *Letters to Fanny Wedgwood*, pp. 127–8.
54. Spencer, *Autobiography*, I, 375.
55. Harriet Martineau to Wedgwood, 17 September 1854, *Letters to Fanny Wedgwood*, p. 128.
56. Harriet Martineau's statement, written in June 1858 for George Grote, MS Harriet Martineau Papers, Birmingham University Library.
57. See Hodgson to Combe, 14 December 1854, MS Combe Papers, National Library of Scotland.
58. George Eliot to Chapman, 4 October 1854, *The George Eliot Letters*, II, 175.
59. Bray to Combe, 23 September 1854, MS Combe Papers, National Library of Scotland.
60. See Spencer, *Autobiography*, I, 457–61, II, 33.
61. See Duncan, *Life and Letters of Herbert Spencer*, pp. 77–8, 547.
62. Gladstone Diary, 19 July 1852, *The Gladstone Diaries*, IV, 444; Mark Pattison Diary, 28 September 1852, *Memoirs* (London, 1885, reprinted 1969), p. 297.
63. George Eliot to Combe, 14 December 1852, *The George Eliot Letters*, VIII, 67.
64. George Eliot to Combe, 29 October 1852, ibid., VIII, 64.
65. Harriet Martineau to Chapman, 1 November 1854, MS Bodleian Library (Eng lett d 2, f. 177).
66. Mill to Hickson, 15 October 1851, *Later Letters*, *Collected Works of John Stuart Mill*, XIV, 78; Bagehot to Robinson, 14 January 1855, *Collected Works of Walter Bagehot*, XIII, 354 (where the letter is wrongly dated 1854).
67. Robinson Diary, 19 November 1854, MS Dr Williams's Library.
68. Harriet Martineau to Chapman, 1 November 1854, MS Bodleian Library (Eng lett d 2, f. 177).
69. Newman to Holyoake, 23 August 1854, MS Holyoake Collection, Manchester.
70. Newman to Martineau, 27 November 1854, MS Martineau Papers, Harris Manchester College.
71. Newman to Martineau, 14 June 1855, ibid.
72. Harriet Martineau to Chapman, 1 November 1854, MS Bodleian Library (Eng lett d 2, f. 177).
73. George Eliot to Chapman, 15 October 1854, *The George Eliot Letters*, VIII, 125.

74. Combe Journal, 21 December 1854, MS Combe Papers, National Library of Scotland.

75. Froude to Chapman, 5 November 1854, Dunn, *Life of Froude*, II, 278.

76. See Robinson Diary, 16 and 19 November and 25 December 1854, MSS Dr Williams's Library; introductory essay on the *National Review* in *Wellesley Index*, III, 135–46; Bagehot, *Collected Works*, XIII, 353–4n.

77. See Robinson Diary, 3 and 7 February 1855, MSS Dr Williams's Library, part quoted in Bagehot, *Collected Works*, XIII, 356n.

78. Bagehot to Robinson, 8 February 1855, *Collected Works*, XIII, 357.

79. Martineau to Charles Wicksteed, 18 February 1855, *Life and Letters of James Martineau*, I, 269.

80. See *Wellesley Index*, III, 141, 145.

81. Bagehot to Hutton, 4 March 1855, and to Robinson, 5 April 1855, *Collected Works*, XIII, 361, 369.

82. Bagehot to Robinson, 14 January 1855, ibid., XIII, 354.

83. Bagehot to Martineau, 18 March 1855, ibid., XIII, 365.

84. Bagehot to Hutton, 19 April 1855, ibid., XIII, 372.

85. Froude to Chapman, 20 May 1855, MS J. A. Froude Collection, Rare Book, Manuscript, and Special Collections Library, Duke University.

86. Chapman to Pattison, 30 October 1854, MS Mark Pattison Correspondence, Bodleian Library (MS Pattison 50, f. 402). For Pattison's and Wilson's division of the philosophy and theology section of *Westminster Review*, see *Wellesley Index*, III, 622–3.

87. Bagehot to Hutton, 1 February 1856, *Collected Works*, XIII, 381–2.

88. See Ashton, *George Eliot*, pp. 114–18.

89. George Eliot Journal, 5 August 1854, *The Journals of George Eliot*, ed. Margaret Harris and Judith Johnston (Cambridge, 1998), p. 19.

90. George Eliot to Chapman, 6 August 1854, *The George Eliot Letters*, VIII, 115.

91. Ibid., VIII, 116.

92. George Eliot to Bray, 16 August 1854, ibid., II, 170, 171. For Bray's mistress and children, see Ashton, *George Eliot*, pp. 55–6.

93. George Eliot to Chapman, 30 August 1854, *The George Eliot Letters*, II, 173.

94. See ibid., I, 345 and n; Carlyle to Lady Stanley, 31 May 1854, *Collected Letters*, XXIX, 107.

95. Carlyle to Margaret Carlyle, 17 March 1853, *Collected Letters*, XXVIII, 83.

96. Carlyle to James Marshall, 14 July 1854, ibid., XXIX, 128–9.

97. Harriet Martineau to Fanny Wedgwood, 17 September 1854, *Harriet Martineau's Letters to Fanny Wedgwood*, p. 129.

98. See Webb, *Harriet Martineau*, pp. 14, 99.

99. Tait to Combe, 28 August 1854, MS Combe Papers, National Library of Scotland.

100. Tait to Combe, 14 September 1854, ibid.

101. Tait to Combe, 10 October 1854, ibid.

102. Ibid.

103. Ibid.

104. Ibid.

105. Cara Bray to Cecilia Combe, 23 September 1854, *The George Eliot Letters*, VIII, 119.

106. Chapman to Combe, 4 October 1854, ibid., VIII, 122.

107. Bray to Combe, 8 October 1854, ibid., VIII, 123.

108. Combe to Bray, 15 November 1854, ibid., VIII, 129.

109. Combe Journal, 18 September 1851, quoted in Ashton, *George Eliot*, pp. 55–6.

110. Carlyle to John Carlyle, 2 November 1854, *Collected Letters*, XXIX, 184–5.

111. See ibid., XXIX, 184 and n; Ashton, *Thomas and Jane Carlyle*, pp. 355–6 (Tait's portrait of Carlyle and some of his photographs are reproduced between pp. 372 and 373).

112. Tait to Combe, 15 October 1854, MS Combe Papers, National Library of Scotland.

113. See Ashton, *G. H. Lewes*, p. 162.

114. Chapman to Chambers, 16 October 1854, *The George Eliot Letters*, VIII, 126.

115. Parkes to Bessie Rayner Parkes, 1 October 1854, MS Bessie Rayner Parkes Collection, quoted by permission of the Mistress and Fellows of Girton College, Cambridge.

116. Parkes to Bessie Rayner Parkes, 14 October 1854, ibid.

117. Parkes to Bessie Rayner Parkes, 10 October 1854, ibid.

118. Combe to Bray, 15 November 1854, *The George Eliot Letters*, VIII, 129.

119. Bray to Combe, 19 November 1854, ibid., VIII, 130–1.

120. Tait to Combe, 22 October 1854, MS Combe Papers, National Library of Scotland.

121. Parkes to Bessie Rayner Parkes, 1 October 1854, MS Bessie Rayner Parkes Collection, Girton College, Cambridge. For Parkes's unfaithfulness to his wife – at an unspecified period – see the account by his granddaughter Marie Belloc Lowndes in *I, Too, Have Lived in Arcadia* (London, 1941), p. 39.

122. George Eliot Journal, 11 October 1854, *Journals of George Eliot*, p. 26.

123. George Eliot Journal, 20 October 1854, ibid., p. 28.

124. Lewes to Carlyle, 19 October 1854, *The George Eliot Letters*, II, 176.

125. Ibid., II, 177n.

126. George Eliot to Bray, 1 or 2 November 1854, ibid., II, 183.

127. See Carlyle to John Carlyle, 6 July 1855, *Collected Letters*, XXX, 5.

128. *Westminster Review*, LXIII (January 1855), 89.

129. Bray to Combe, 7 January 1855, MS Combe Papers, National Library of Scotland.

Chapter 7

1. George Eliot to Sara Hennell, 22 November 1854, *The George Eliot Letters*, II, 188.

2. See George Eliot to Chapman, 9 December 1854, ibid., VIII, 131.

3. Sara Hennell to George Eliot, 15 November 1854, ibid., II, 187.

4. Robinson Diary, 14 October 1854, MS Dr Williams's Library.

5. 'Woman in France: Madame de Sablé', *Westminster Review* (October 1854), reprinted in *George Eliot: Selected Critical Writings*, pp. 68, 41–2.

6. 'Belles lettres', *Westminster Review* (July 1855), ibid., pp. 111–12.

7. Ibid., p. 113.

8. George Eliot Journal, 9 April 1855, *Journals of George Eliot*, p. 56.

9. See George Eliot to Bessie Rayner Parkes, 16 March 1855, *The George Eliot Letters*, II, 196.

10. See George Eliot to Bray, 1 May 1855, ibid., II, 199.

11. George Eliot to Cara Bray, 4 September 1855, ibid., II, 214.

12. George Eliot to Bray, 16 July 1855, ibid., II, 210.

13. George Eliot to Bessie Rayner Parkes, 1 May 1855, ibid., II, 200.

14. George Eliot to Cara Bray, 4 September 1855, ibid., II, 214.

15. Chapman, 'The Position of Woman in Barbarism and among the Ancients', *Westminster Review*, LXII (October 1855), 408.

16. Ibid., LXII, 436.

17. Chapman, 'The English Law of Divorce', *Westminster Review*, LXV (April 1856), 338–55. *Wellesley Index* does not attribute this article, but Chapman's authorship is established in a letter to Harriet Martineau of 22 October 1855, MS Harriet Martineau Papers, Birmingham University Library. For the history of the reform of legislation in respect of women, see Lee Holcombe, 'Victorian Wives and Property: Reform of the Married Women's Property Law, 1857–1882', in *A Widening Sphere: Changing Roles of Victorian Women*, ed. Martha Vicinus (London, 1977), pp. 3–28; Mary Poovey, *Uneven Developments: The Ideological Work of Gender in Mid-Victorian England* (Chicago, Illinois, 1988); Mary Lyndon Shanley, *Feminism, Marriage and Law in Victorian England 1850–1895* (London, 1989).

18. George Eliot to Chapman, 25 June 1855, *The George Eliot Letters*, II, 205–6.

19. Ibid., II, 206.

20. Ibid., II, 207.

21. George Eliot to Chapman, 27 June 1855, ibid., II, 208.

22. 'Evangelical Teaching: Dr Cumming', *Westminster Review* (October 1855), in *George Eliot: Selected Critical Writings*, pp. 138–9.

23. Ibid., pp. 149–50.

24. Ibid., pp. 167–8.
25. Bray to George Eliot, 13 October 1855, MS George Eliot Collection, Beinecke Rare Book and Manuscript Library, Yale University.
26. George Eliot to Bray, 15 October 1855, *The George Eliot Letters*, II, 218.
27. See 'George Eliot's Literary Earnings', ibid., VII, 358.
28. 'The Natural History of German Life', *Westminster Review* (July 1856), in *George Eliot: Selected Critical Writings*, pp. 263–4.
29. George Eliot to Chapman, 5 July 1856, *The George Eliot Letters*, II, 258.
30. 'Belles lettres', *Westminster Review* (July 1855), in *George Eliot: Selected Critical Writings*, p. 120.
31. George Eliot to Chapman, 20 July 1856, *The George Eliot Letters*, II, 258.
32. 'Silly Novels by Lady Novelists', *Westminster Review* (October 1856), *George Eliot: Selected Critical Writings*, p. 296.
33. Ibid., p. 299.
34. Ibid., p. 305.
35. Ibid., p. 313.
36. Ibid., p. 315.
37. Ibid., pp. 320–1.
38. George Eliot Journal, 23 September 1856, *Journals of George Eliot*, p. 63.
39. Chapman to George Eliot, 15 January 1857, *The George Eliot Letters*, VIII, 163.
40. See Lewes to John Blackwood, 6 November 1856, ibid., II, 269; George Eliot Journal, 25 December 1856, *Journals of George Eliot*, p. 64.
41. George Eliot to Chapman, 15 January 1857, Ashton, 'New George Eliot Letters at the Huntington', *Huntington Library Quarterly*, LIV, 122.
42. George Eliot to Chapman, 27 September 1857 and 26 January 1858, *The George Eliot Letters*, II, 385, 427.
43. George Eliot Journal, 5 November 1858, *Journals of George Eliot*, p. 74.
44. See George Eliot Journal, 12 October 1856, ibid., p. 64; Spencer, *Autobiography*, I, 492; George Eliot to Chapman, 5 November 1858, *The George Eliot Letters*, II, 494.
45. George Eliot Journal, 30 November 1858, *Journals of George Eliot*, p. 75.
46. George Eliot to Chapman, 27 May 1857, *The George Eliot Letters*, VIII, 171.
47. Ibid.
48. Spencer, *Autobiography*, II, 38; Chapman, 'Adam Bede', *Westminster Review*, LXXI (April 1859), 510.
49. Lewes Journal, 12 February 1859, and Lewes to Chapman, 12 February 1859, *The George Eliot Letters*, III, 12–13 and n.
50. 'Adam Bede', *Westminster Review*, LXXI, 488, 502.
51. Review of *Adam Bede* and *Scenes of Clerical Life*, *Edinburgh Review*, CX (July

1859), 223–46. *Wellesley Index*, vol. I, identifies the reviewer as Caroline Norton.

52. 'Eliot's Novels', *Quarterly Review*, CVIII (October 1860), 469–99. *Wellesley Index*, vol. I, identifies the reviewer as James Craigie Robertson.

53. Chapman to George Eliot, 16 January 1860, *The George Eliot Letters*, VIII, 257.

54. G. H. Lewes Journal, 18 January 1860, ibid., VIII, 257n.

55. T. P. O'Connor, article of December 1899, quoted in Haight, *George Eliot and John Chapman*, pp. 261–2.

56. [Bessie Rayner Parkes], *Remarks on the Education of Girls, with Reference to the Social, Legal, and Industrial Position of Women in the Present Day* (London, 1854), pp. 8, 10.

57. Dante Gabriel Rossetti to Barbara Leigh Smith, 19 April, 2 and 9 May 1854, *Letters*, ed. Oswald Doughty and John Robert Wahl, 4 vols. (Oxford, 1965–7), I, 185, 188, 192–3; Hirsch, *Barbara Leigh Smith Bodichon*, p. 50.

58. [Bessie Rayner Parkes], *Remarks*, pp. 13, 14.

59. Elizabeth Barrett to Mary Mitford, *Elizabeth Barrett to Miss Mitford*, ed. Betty Miller (London, 1954), pp. 144–5; Charlotte Brontë to G. H. Lewes, 12 January 1848, *Letters of Charlotte Brontë*, II, 10; Jane Carlyle to Jeannie Welsh, 18 or 19 January 1843, *Collected Letters*, XVI, 20. For the reception of George Sand in Britain, see Patricia Thomson, *George Sand and the Victorians: Her Influence and Reputation in Nineteenth-Century England* (London, 1977).

60. [Bessie Rayner Parkes], *Remarks*, p. 20.

61. George Eliot to Sara Hennell, 6 October 1858, *The George Eliot Letters*, II, 486.

62. W. C. Roscoe, 'Woman', *National Review*, VII (October 1858), 349, 353.

63. Hirsch, *Barbara Leigh Smith Bodichon*, pp. 37, 44.

64. Preface to the second edition of *Remarks* (London, 1856), p. iii; Bessie Rayner Parkes to Bella Leigh Smith, August 1854, Hirsch, *Barbara Leigh Smith Bodichon*, pp. 99–100.

65. Dante Gabriel Rossetti to Christina Rossetti, 8 November 1853, *Letters*, I, 163.

66. Hirsch, *Barbara Leigh Smith Bodichon*, pp. 8–9.

67. Mary Howitt, *An Autobiography*, ed. Margaret Howitt, 2 vols. (London, 1889), II, 34–5.

68. Hirsch, *Barbara Leigh Smith Bodichon*, p. 45.

69. Ibid., pp. 71–2, 74–6, 78.

70. George Eliot to Bray, 14 July 1854, *The George Eliot Letters*, II, 165.

71. Hirsch, *Barbara Leigh Smith Bodichon*, pp. 85–6.

72. *A Brief Summary, in Plain Language, of the Most Important Laws concerning Women; together with a Few Observations thereon* (London, 1854), pp. 3, 13.

73. Hirsch, *Barbara Leigh Smith Bodichon*, pp. 91–4. For the text of Barbara's petition, see *Westminster Review*, LXVI (October 1856), 336–8n.

74. George Eliot Journal, 16 January 1856, *Journals of George Eliot*, p. 58; Barbara

Leigh Smith to George Eliot, 14 January 1856, MS George Eliot Collection, Yale University.

75. Caroline Frances Cornwallis, 'The Property of Married Women', *Westminster Review*, LXVI (October 1856), 336–8n.

76. See Holcombe, 'Victorian Wives and Property', A *Widening Sphere*, pp. 8–12; Amice Lee, *Laurels & Rosemary: The Life of William and Mary Howitt* (Oxford, 1955), p. 215.

77. *Westminster Review*, XCII (July 1869), 253–5.

78. For the founding of Girton College and Barbara Bodichon's part in it, see Barbara Stephen, *Emily Davies and Girton College* (London, 1927).

79. George Eliot to Bray, 4 April, and to Cara Bray, probably October 1855, *The George Eliot Letters*, II, 197, 217.

80. Hirsch, *Barbara Leigh Smith Bodichon*, pp. 32, 101–2.

81. Ibid., p. 103; George Eliot to Chapman, 9 December 1854, *The George Eliot Letters*, VIII, 132 and n.

82. See, for example, Hirsch's discussion of the letters, *Barbara Leigh Smith Bodichon*, pp. 105–13, and, more circumspectly, Haight in *George Eliot and John Chapman*, p. 90. As Haight points out, ibid., p. 88n, the letters survive not in manuscript, but in a typescript prepared by Clement Shorter around 1915 and kept in the Beinecke Rare Book and Manuscript Library at Yale University.

83. Mary Howitt, *Autobiography*, II, 111.

84. Chapman to Barbara Leigh Smith, 8 and 9 August 1855, TS Yale.

85. George Eliot to Sara Hennell, 19 February 1856, *The George Eliot Letters*, II, 228.

86. Chapman to Barbara Leigh Smith, 15 August 1855, TS Yale.

87. Chapman to Barbara Leigh Smith, 25 August 1855, ibid.

88. Chapman to Harriet Martineau, 22 October 1855, MS Harriet Martineau Papers, Birmingham University Library.

89. Ibid.

90. Chapman to Barbara Leigh Smith, 13, 14, and 17 August 1855, TS Yale.

91. Chapman to Barbara Leigh Smith, 20 and 22 August 1855, ibid.

92. Chapman to Barbara Leigh Smith, 27 August 1855, ibid. For the Malvern water cure see Brian S. Smith, *A History of Malvern* (Leicester, 1964), and Janet Grierson, *Dr Wilson and his Malvern Hydro* (Malvern, 1998).

93. Chapman to Barbara Leigh Smith, 28 August 1855, TS Yale.

94. For medicine in the nineteenth century, particularly with reference to sexuality and women, see E. Royston Pike, *Human Documents of the Victorian Golden Age*, chapter 8, 'Sex and the Victorians'; Ornella Moscucci, *The Science of Woman: Gynaecology and Gender in England, 1800–1929* (Cambridge, 1990);

Roy Porter and Mikulas Teich, *Sexual Knowledge, Sexual Science: The History of Attitudes to Sexuality* (Cambridge, 1994).

95. Chapman to Barbara Leigh Smith, 29 August 1855, TS Yale.

96. Chapman to Barbara Leigh Smith, 4 and 12 September 1855, ibid.

97. Chapman to Barbara Leigh Smith, 17 September 1855, ibid.

98. See McLaren, *Birth Control in Nineteenth-Century England*, pp. 124–6. Raciborski published *De la puberté et de l'age critique chez la femme* (Paris, 1844) and *Du rôle de la menstruation dans la pathologie et la thérapeutique* (Paris, 1856).

99. Chapman to Barbara Leigh Smith, 29 August 1855, TS Yale.

100. Chapman to Barbara Leigh Smith, 7 September 1855, ibid.

101. See Chapman to Barbara Leigh Smith, 14 September 1855, ibid.

102. Chapman to Barbara Leigh Smith, 22 September 1855, ibid.

103. Chapman to Harriet Martineau, 13 September 1855, MS Harriet Martineau Papers, Birmingham University Library.

104. Chapman to Harriet Martineau, 27 September 1855, ibid.

105. Harriet Martineau to Chapman, 16 September 1855, *Harriet Martineau: Selected Letters*, ed. Valerie Sanders (Oxford, 1990), p. 131.

106. Ibid., p. 132.

107. Anna Mary Howitt to Chapman, 1 October 1855, Hirsch, *Barbara Leigh Smith Bodichon*, p. 113.

108. See John Wallis Chapman, 'John Chapman's Children', p. 12.

Chapter 8

1. Harriet Martineau, *Autobiography*, II, 431.

2. Harriet Martineau to Chapman, 16 September 1855, *Harriet Martineau: Selected Letters*, p. 130.

3. Chapman to Harriet Martineau, 19 November 1855, MS Harriet Martineau Papers, Birmingham University Library.

4. Chapman to Harriet Martineau, 6 January 1856, ibid.

5. 'Medical Despotism', *Westminster Review*, LXV (April 1856), 530–62, and 'Medical Reform', *Westminster Review*, LXIX (April 1858), 478–530.

6. See Henry Bence Jones, *An Autobiography* (privately printed, London, 1929), and N. G. Coley, 'Henry Bence-Jones', *Notes and Records of the Royal Society*, XXVIII (1973), 31–56.

7. 'Medical Education', *Westminster Review*, LXX (July 1858), 126–7. For Elliotson, see Williams, *Doctors Differ*, pp. 27–8.

8. Chapman to Harriet Martineau, 6 January 1856, MS Harriet Martineau Papers, Birmingham University Library.

9. See Haight, *George Eliot and John Chapman*, pp. 4–5.

10. Haight is scathing about Chapman's medical study and the practice of selling degrees at St Andrews, ibid., pp. 93–5, 268–71; F. N. L. Poynter defends both Chapman and St Andrews in 'John Chapman (1821–1894): Publisher, Physician, and Medical Reformer', *Journal of the History of Medicine*, V (1950), 1–22.

11. Chapman to Harriet Martineau, 27 April 1857, MS Harriet Martineau Papers, Birmingham University Library.

12. Chapman to Harriet Martineau, 9 May 1857, ibid.

13. Chapman to Harriet Martineau, 14 May 1857, ibid.

14. See the entry for Chapman in *Medical Register* for 1860, p. 61.

15. Harriet Martineau to Chapman, 22 July 1857, *Harriet Martineau: Selected Letters*, p. 146.

16. 'Medical Reform', *Westminster Review*, LXIX (April 1858), 478–9, 486, 496, 519, 520, 528.

17. Chapman, *The Medical Institutions of the United Kingdom: A History exemplifying the Evils of Over-legislation* (London, 1870), p. 1.

18. Chapman to Edward Henry Stanley, 29 March 1858, Derby Papers, Liverpool Record Office.

19. Chapman to Stanley, 30 March 1858, ibid.

20. Ibid.; an undated note from Harriet Martineau to Chapman, enclosed with Chapman's letter to Stanley, lists the subscribers.

21. See Haight, *George Eliot and John Chapman*, p. 223n; Harriet Martineau to Fanny Wedgwood, 10 January 1858, *Harriet Martineau's Letters to Fanny Wedgwood*, pp. 157, 159.

22. Lord Stanley's endorsement on the back of Chapman's letter to him of 30 March 1858, Derby Papers, Liverpool Record Office.

23. Chapman to Stanley, 21 July 1858, ibid.

24. Ibid.

25. Stanley's note on Chapman's letter to him of 11 July 1858, ibid.

26. Chapman to Stanley, 11 September 1858, ibid.

27. Chapman to Stanley, 6 December 1858, ibid.

28. Chapman to Stanley, 11 September 1858, ibid.

29. Chapman, 'Medical Education', *Westminster Review*, LXX (July 1858), 108.

30. See Arthur Hamilton Gordon, Lord Stanmore, *Sidney Herbert, Lord Herbert of Lea: A Memoir*, 2 vols. (London, 1906), II, 119, 125, 130, 137.

31. Sidney Herbert to Chapman, 23 April 1858, MS Rare Book, Manuscript, and Special Collections Library, Duke University.

32. Lord Stanmore, *Sidney Herbert*, II, 162, 199.

33. Harriet Martineau to Erasmus Darwin, 10 January 1858, published in *Harriet Martineau's Letters to Fanny Wedgwood*, p. 157.

34. Chapman's letters to Harriet Martineau, with copies of some of her replies, are in the Harriet Martineau Papers, Birmingham University Library.

35. Harriet Martineau to Chapman (copy), 16 July 1858, ibid.; part quoted in Haight, *George Eliot and John Chapman*, p. 272.

36. Chapman to Harriet Martineau, 29 July 1858, and to Maria Martineau, 2 August 1858, MSS Harriet Martineau Papers, Birmingham University Library.

37. Harriet Martineau to Chapman (copy), 6 August 1858, ibid.

38. See Harriet Martineau's memos of the Courtauld-Chapman correspondence, ibid.

39. George Grote to Harriet Martineau, 4, 11, and 22 June 1858, ibid.

40. George Eliot to Bray, 13 October 1858, *The George Eliot Letters*, II, 490.

41. James Payn, *Some Literary Recollections*, pp. 111–12.

42. George Eliot to Sara Hennell, 11 October 1858, *The George Eliot Letters*, II, 489.

43. See Harriet Martineau to Henry Reeve, editor of *Edinburgh Review*, 24 June 1858, *Harriet Martineau: Selected Letters*, p. 155.

44. 'Neo-Christianity', *Westminster Review*, LXXIV (October 1860), 293–332.

45. See Stanley to Chapman (copy), 13 January 1860, MS Liverpool Record Office.

46. Chapman to Stanley, 30 March 1860, ibid.

47. See Chapman Diary, 2 and 4 April 1860, Haight, *George Eliot and John Chapman*, p. 241; for an account of the complicated dealings with Manwaring, see ibid., pp. 104–5.

48. John Motley to Chapman, 28 August and 25 October 1854, MSS Senate House Library, University of London (MS [S.L.] V 20). Three separate letters are printed by Gordon S. Haight, 'The Publication of Motley's *Rise of the Dutch Republic*', *Yale University Library Gazette*, LIV (January 1980), 135–40.

49. Froude to Chapman, 18 September 1855, in Haight, 'Publication of Motley's *Rise of the Dutch Republic*', p. 138; Motley to Chapman, 18 November 1855, MS Senate House Library, University of London (MS [S.L.] V 20).

50. Motley to his mother, 1 April 1856, *Correspondence of John Lothrop Motley, DCL*, ed. George William Curtis, 2 vols. (London, 1889), I, 190.

51. Motley to his mother, 13 February 1860, ibid., I, 334.

52. Chapman, *Chloroform and other Anaesthetics*, pp. 7, 9, 21, 39–40.

53. See Chapman to Stanley, 20 May, 17 and 20 June 1859, with Stanley's comments, MSS Liverpool Record Office.

54. Chapman to Stanley, 17 June 1859, ibid.

55. Chapman to Stanley, 31 January 1861, ibid.

56. Stanley's MS diaries are in the Liverpool Record Office. John Vincent edited three volumes of selections from the diaries between 1978 and 2003, but none of the many entries which make reference to Chapman and *Westminster Review* is included.

57. Chapman to Stanley, 6, 13, and 15 December 1859, MS Liverpool Record Office.

58. See Porter, *London: A Social History*, p. 298.

59. Chapman to Stanley, 20 December 1859, MS Liverpool Record Office.

60. The MS letters to Johanna are in the George Eliot Collection at the Beinecke Rare Book and Manuscript Library, Yale University; Haight prints the 1860 diary in *George Eliot and John Chapman*.

61. See Haight, *George Eliot and John Chapman*, pp. 98, 106ff.

62. Chapman Diary, 5 January 1860, ibid., p. 224.

63. Chapman Diary, 8 February and 24 June 1860, ibid., pp. 234, 243.

64. See John Wallis Chapman, 'John Chapman's Children', p. 12.

65. Chapman Diary, 19 and 20 February 1860, Haight, *George Eliot and John Chapman*, p. 237.

66. Chapman Diary, 24 July 1860, ibid., p. 245.

67. Chapman to Johanna von Heyligenstaedt, 18 October 1860 and 6 March 1862, MS George Eliot Collection, Yale; Haight, *George Eliot and John Chapman*, pp. 112–13.

68. See Haight, *George Eliot and John Chapman*, p. 113 and n.

69. Chapman Diary, 24 July 1860, ibid., pp. 245–6.

70. Ibid.

71. Chapman to Johanna von Heyligenstaedt, 18 October 1860 and 5 August 1861, MSS George Eliot Collection, Yale.

72. Chapman to Johanna von Heyligenstaedt, 20 February 1862, ibid.

73. Chapman to Johanna von Heyligenstaedt, 6 March 1862, ibid.; part quoted in Haight, *George Eliot and John Chapman*, p. 113.

74. See Haight, *George Eliot and John Chapman*, p. 113 and n.

75. Chapman Diary, 9 March 1863, Haight, *George Eliot and John Chapman*, p. 254. Haight gives an account of this diary, which was quoted by Sydney Race in the *Nottingham Guardian* in 1915, but was subsequently lost.

76. Annie Chapman, 'Stories of the Little Mother', p. 48.

77. Chapman to Johanna von Heyligenstacdt, 1 May 1863, MS George Eliot Collection, Yale.

78. Chapman to Stanley, 27 April 1863, MS Liverpool Record Office.

79. Chapman to Stanley, 30 April 1863, ibid.

80. Chapman describes the ice bag in *Functional Diseases of the Stomach: Sea-Sickness* (London, 1864), pp. 37–9.

81. See Haight, *George Eliot and John Chapman*, p. 111.

82. Chapman, *Functional Diseases of Women* (London, 1863), p. xv.

83. See Chapman, *Functional Diseases of the Stomach: Sea-Sickness*, p. 39n; Chapman to Stanley, 3 August 1864, MS Liverpool Record Office; Poynter, 'John Chapman', p. 17.

84. Poynter, 'John Chapman', pp. 17–18.

85. *Functional Diseases of Women*, p. xv; *Functional Diseases of the Stomach: Sea-Sickness*, advertisements on the back page; Sir Andrew Clark in the *Medical Times and Gazette*, 3 November 1866.

86. See Poynter, 'John Chapman', pp. 16–17.

87. See Moscucci, *The Science of Woman*, pp. 104, 112–18.

88. Mill to Chapman, 5 November 1859, *Later Letters*, *Collected Works*, XV, 644.

89. Mill to Chapman, 16 March 1863, ibid., XV, 849.

90. Annie Chapman, 'Stories of the Little Mother', p. 45.

91. Mill to Chapman, 1 August 1863, *Later Letters*, *Collected Works*, XV, 876.

92. Mill to Chapman, 19 November 1868, ibid., XVI, 1488.

93. Mill to Chapman, 28 February and 10 March 1865, and to Lord Amberley, 8 March 1865, ibid., XVI, 1000, 1008, 1007.

94. For the whole story of the Dialectical Society meeting and the South Devon election, see *The Amberley Papers: The Letters and Diaries of Lord and Lady Amberley*, ed. Bertrand and Patricia Russell, 2 vols. (London, 1937), II, 167–249.

95. Mill to Chapman, 2 December 1866, *Later Letters*, *Collected Works*, XVI, 1219.

96. Mill to Chapman, 13 January 1867, ibid., XVI, 1228.

97. Mill to Chapman, 12 June 1869, ibid., XVII, 1614.

98. Chapman, 'Prostitution in Relation to the National Health', *Westminster Review*, XCII (July 1869), 179–234; 'Prostitution: Governmental Experiments in controlling it', ibid., XCIII (January 1870), 119–79; 'Prostitution; how to deal with it: The Contagious Diseases Acts, 1866 and 1869', ibid., XCIII (April 1870), 477–535. For a discussion of the Contagious Diseases Acts and the agitation against them, see Moscucci, *The Science of Woman*, pp. 123–5.

99. Mill to Philippina Kyllmann, *c.* 22 January 1869, *Later Letters*, *Collected Works*, XVII, 1551.

100. Charles Darwin, autobiography, published in *Charles Darwin and Thomas Henry Huxley: Autobiographies*, ed. Gavin de Beer (London, 1974), p. 62.

101. Chapman to Stanley, 31 July 1873, MS Liverpool Record Office.

102. See Adrian Desmond and James Moore, *Darwin* (London, 1991), pp. 363–7, 405–6.

103. Darwin to Chapman, 16 May 1865, ibid., pp. 530–1. See also Janet Browne, *Charles Darwin: The Power of Place* (London, 2002), p. 263.

104. Desmond and Moore, *Darwin*, pp. 531–2.

105. Browne, *Charles Darwin*, p. 263.

106. See Catherine Macdonald Maclean, *Mark Rutherford: A Biography of William Hale White* (London, 1955), p. 206.

107. *Aberdeen Herald*, 12 August 1865. I am indebted to Mark Crees for the reference.

108. *Aberdeen Herald*, 8 March 1862.

109. Ibid.

110. See Rowland Williams, *Life and Letters*, ed. his wife, 2 vols. (London, 1874), II, 17–19, 55–60; Basil Willey, *More Nineteenth-Century Studies*, pp. 137–85.

111. See *Wellesley Index*, II, 631–9.

112. Sheldon Amos to Chapman, 18 October 1878, MS University College London (MS Misc 3A-3B).

113. Entry for 13 April 1871, *The Diary of W. M. Rossetti 1870–1873*, ed. Odette Bornand (Oxford, 1977), pp. 55–6.

114. James Sully, *My Life and Friends: A Psychologist's Memories* (London, 1918), p. 136.

115. Chapman to Stanley (now Lord Derby), 26 May 1870, MS Liverpool Record Office.

116. Chapman to Derby, 2 November 1870, ibid.

117. Derby Diary, 9 November 1870, ibid.

118. See John Wallis Chapman, 'John Chapman's Children', p. 13.

119. See Haight, *George Eliot and John Chapman*, p. 116.

120. Chapman to Hannah Macdonald Chapman, January and February 1880, MSS George Eliot Collection, Yale University; part quoted in Haight, *George Eliot and John Chapman*, pp. 116–19.

121. Chapman to Derby, 31 July 1873, MS Liverpool Record Office.

122. Derby, endorsement on Chapman's letter of 31 July 1873, ibid.

123. Chapman to Derby, 7 October 1890 and 27 October 1892, with endorsements by Derby, ibid.

124. For Mary Ward, see John Sutherland, *Mrs Humphry Ward: Eminent Victorian, Pre-eminent Edwardian* (Oxford, 1990).

125. Mrs Humphry Ward, *Robert Elsmere* (London, 1888, reprinted with an introduction by Rosemary Ashton, Oxford, 1987).

126. Information about the deaths and wills of Chapman and Susanna are in the Family Records Centre and Probate Search Room in London.

127. Information about Beatrice, Ernest, and Walter comes from Haight, *George Eliot and John Chapman*, p. 158; Sydney Race, 'John Chapman', *Notes and Queries*, CLXXXI (26 April 1941), 293; John Wallis Chapman, 'John Chapman's Children', p. 11; and a family tree drawn by John Wallis Chapman for Ina Taylor, who kindly let me have sight of it. The petition to Parliament, with Beatrice's name on it, appeared in *The Times*, 7 June 1878.

128. Cutting from an unnamed newspaper of December 1894 enclosed in Holyoake Diary for 1894, MS Holyoake Collection, Bishopsgate Library, Bishopsgate Institute and Foundation, London (Holyoake/2/43).

129. *The Times*, 3 December 1894.
130. W[illiam] H[ale] W[hite], 'Dr John Chapman', *Athenaeum*, 8 December 1894, p. 790.
131. *Westminster Review*, CXLIII (January 1895), 3; Haight, *George Eliot and John Chapman*, pp. 118–19, 255, 274.
132. Sir William Robertson Nicoll, *A Bookman's Letters* (London, 1913), p. 372.

Index

Index

Index